CAMBRIDGE GREEK AND LATIN CLASSICS

PLATO

REPUBLIC

BOOK I

EDITED BY

DAVID SANSONE
University of Illinois, Urbana-Champaign

Shaftesbury Road, Cambridge CB2 8EA, United Kingdom

One Liberty Plaza, 20th Floor, New York, NY 10006, USA

477 Williamstown Road, Port Melbourne, VIC 3207, Australia

314–321, 3rd Floor, Plot 3, Splendor Forum, Jasola District Centre,
New Delhi – 110025, India

103 Penang Road, #05–06/07, Visioncrest Commercial, Singapore 238467

Cambridge University Press is part of Cambridge University Press & Assessment,
a department of the University of Cambridge.

We share the University's mission to contribute to society through the pursuit of education, learning and research at the highest international levels of excellence.

www.cambridge.org
Information on this title: www.cambridge.org/9781108833455

DOI: 10.1017/9781108980784

First published 2023

A catalogue record for this publication is available from the British Library

A Cataloging-in-Publication data record for this book is available from the Library of Congress

ISBN 978-1-108-83345-5 Hardback
ISBN 978-1-108-97047-1 Paperback

CONTENTS

List of Abbreviations vii

Introduction 1
1 Plato's *Republic*, or What Is Justice? 1
2 Book One, or What Justice Is Not 8
3 Setting 12
4 Dramatis Personae 15
(a) Socrates 15
(b) Cephalus 17
(c) Polemarchus 20
(d) Thrasymachus 22
(e) Adeimantus and Glaucon 31
5 The Transmission of Plato's Text 32

ΠΛΑΤΩΝΟΣ ΠΟΛΙΤΕΙΑΣ Α 37

Commentary 73

Works Cited 192
Indexes 200
General Index 200
Index of Greek Words 201

ABBREVIATIONS

The names of ancient Greek authors and titles of their works are abbreviated according to the conventions of LSJ, sometimes expanded for clarity. In the commentary, the names of Plato, Socrates and Thrasymachus are abbreviated P., S. and T.

Beekes	R. Beekes, *Etymological dictionary of Greek*, Leiden, 2009
CGCG	E. van Emde Boas et al., *The Cambridge grammar of Classical Greek*, Cambridge, 2019
CGL	J. Diggle et al., *The Cambridge Greek lexicon*, Cambridge, 2021
CPG	E. L. von Leutsch and F. W. Schneidewin (eds.), *Corpus paroemiographorum Graecorum*, Göttingen, 1839–51
DK	H. Diels and W. Kranz (eds.), *Die Fragmente der Vorsokratiker*[6], Berlin, 1952
FGrHist	F. Jacoby (ed.), *Die Fragmente der griechischen Historiker*, Leiden, 1923–58
Gildersleeve	B. L. Gildersleeve, *Syntax of Classical Greek from Homer to Demosthenes*, New York, 1900–11
GP	J. D. Denniston, *The Greek particles*[2], Oxford, 1954
IG	*Inscriptiones Graecae*, Berlin, 1877–
KG	R. Kühner and B. Gerth, *Ausführliche Grammatik der griechischen Sprache: Satzlehre*[4], Hannover, 1955
Laks–Most	A. Laks and G. W. Most (eds.), *Early Greek philosophy*, vol. 8: *Sophists*, part 1, Cambridge, MA, 2016
LSJ	H. G. Liddell, R. Scott and H. Stuart Jones, *A Greek–English lexicon*[9], Oxford, 1940 (with *Revised supplement*, Oxford, 1996)
PCG	R. Kassel and C. Austin (eds.), *Poetae comici Graeci*, Berlin, 1983–
SMT	W. W. Goodwin, *Syntax of the moods and tenses of the Greek verb*, rev. ed., London, 1889
Smyth	H. W. Smyth, *Greek grammar*, rev. ed., Cambridge, MA, 1956
SSR	G. Giannantoni (ed.), *Socratis et Socraticorum reliquiae*, Naples, 1990
TrGF	B. Snell et al. (eds.), *Tragicorum Graecorum fragmenta*, Göttingen, 1971–2004

INTRODUCTION

1 PLATO'S *REPUBLIC*, OR WHAT IS JUSTICE?

The primary manuscripts that preserve Plato's text give to the dialogue that is now his most widely read the title and subtitle Πολιτεία ἢ περὶ δικαίου.[1] The title is attested as early as the time of Aristotle, who refers to his teacher's work by that name on a number of occasions.[2] The subtitle, like that for each of Plato's works, appears also in the catalogue of his dialogues arranged in tetralogies by Thrasyllus in the first century (D.L. 3.57–61), although the practice of affixing subtitles is likely to have originated with booksellers already in the fourth century.[3] The standard translation of Πολιτεία in English and other modern languages has been influenced by the title of Cicero's *De re publica*, written in emulation of its Greek predecessor. But "Republic" is not an entirely satisfactory rendering of the title of Plato's dialogue. The word πολιτεία designates that arrangement, whatever form it might take, that a people chooses to adopt in order to live together in a community (which, for a Greek, is a polis). That is the sense the word has when Plato puts it into the mouth of Socrates at the beginning of *Timaeus*, written some years after *Republic*. There Socrates refers to a summary of the presentation that he gave to his companions the previous day as "concerned with the political system (περὶ πολιτείας) and its citizenry that seemed to me would be the best."[4] The material covered in the summary includes several of the distinctive ideas for which *Republic* is most famous: the division of society into classes according to natural ability; the philosophically rigorous program of education for the Guardians, who are to repudiate the possession of private property; the equality of men and women with regard to their capacity to contribute to the state; the abolition of the "nuclear family," so that spouses, siblings, parents and children are to be considered as common to all those of the appropriate age; eugenic management by the state of mating among the citizens and the production of children; official monitoring of children to determine who is worthy of elevation to, or demotion from, the ranks

[1] *Republic* was not necessarily Plato's most widely read dialogue in antiquity; see Baltzly et al. 2018: 1–9.

[2] *Pol.* 2.1261a6, a9, 1264b28, 4.1291a11, 5.1316a1, 8.1342a33, *Rhet.* 3.1406 b32.

[3] Rijksbaron 2007: 15–23. The sequence of the dialogues according to Thrasyllus' arrangement is the basis for the order in which they appear in medieval manuscripts and in the Oxford Classical Texts edition.

[4] *Tim.* 17c1–3. The summary occupies 17c–19b.

of potential Guardians. This represents a mere fraction of the contents of *Republic* as we have it, drawing material only from Books Two, Three and Five.[5] It is not, however, intended as a synopsis of the entire work, only of those portions that are concerned with what Socrates in *Timaeus* considers the optimal arrangements for society.[6] Nor does the subtitle do justice to the range of topics treated in *Republic*. For, while the framework around which the dialogue is constructed is the search for a definition of justice – which is not found until Book Four – *Republic* presents Plato's thinking at the time of composition, not only in the areas of political philosophy and ethics, but psychology, aesthetics, epistemology and metaphysics as well.

The question of when that time of composition was has been subject to disagreement among scholars for more than two centuries.[7] The matter is complicated by the fact that *Republic*, being a substantial and wide-ranging work, is likely to have occupied Plato over a period of time, as well as by a conviction on the part of some scholars that Book One was written much earlier than the remaining books and was originally intended as a stand-alone work that ended, like some of Plato's other early dialogues, in aporia, that is, without arriving at a satisfactory answer to the question that the dialogue hoped to address. The view taken here accords with that for the most part held today, that *Republic* was conceived and written as a unified whole at some time in the middle period of Plato's creative output, most likely when he was in his fifties.[8] That is, its composition

[5] Thrasyllus' catalogue refers to *Republic* as consisting of ten books, but that division is almost certainly not original with Plato. There seem also to have been ancient texts of the work in six books, which would give an average book length of less than 15,000 words, still shorter than *Timaeus* (24,000 words) or Gorgias (27,000). Sedley (2013: 70–3) argues that this was the earlier arrangement, perhaps even going back to the author. He suggests that in those texts the first book ended at 369a; compare Tucker (1900) and Emlyn-Jones (2007), who treat as a unit everything up to 369b6 and 368c4, respectively. These figures are the "Stephanus numbers" by which the text of Plato is regularly cited, referring to the pages and page divisions in the three-volume edition of Plato published by Henri Estienne under his Latinized name in 1578 (Boter 1989: 247–51); *Republic* appears in his second volume.

[6] In any event, Plato signals to the reader that the conversation that Socrates had "yesterday" with his companions in *Timaeus* is distinct from the conversation recorded in *Republic*. The latter is narrated, to an unidentified audience, by Socrates the day after the festival in honor of Bendis on 19 Thargelion (see 327a1n.), whereas *Timaeus* is set at the time of the Panathenaea (*Tim.* 21a2, 26c–e), not necessarily in the same year, on 28 Hecatombaion.

[7] For the contentious history of attempts to date Plato's dialogues, see Thesleff 1982, with a comprehensive listing of the proposed chronologies at 8–17 (= Thesleff 2009: 154–63); Ledger 1989; Brandwood 1990, summarized in Brandwood 1992.

[8] The length of *Republic* is comparable to that of the large-scale histories of Herodotus and Thucydides, the latter unfinished, which occupied their authors

seems to belong in the 370s BC, after the group of early dialogues that includes *Euthyphro, Apology* and *Crito* but before those works that we have good reason to believe were written in the last two decades of Plato's life, which ended in 348/7 BC. Those late works include *Laws, Philebus, Sophist, Statesman, Timaeus* and the incomplete *Critias*. The assignment of these dialogues to the last period of Plato's career is based on a number of factors, namely perceived developments in Plato's thinking and a cluster of stylistic features that distinguishes them from earlier works. Among those late features are an avoidance of certain kinds of hiatus, increasing preference for "rhythmical" clausulae, the distribution of reply formulae such as τί μήν; and μάλιστα and abandonment of the narrative mode found in *Republic* in preference for an exclusively "dramatic" form of dialogue.[9] In the introduction to *Theaetetus*, itself in dramatic form, Eucleides tells Terpsion that he made a written record of the conversation between Theaetetus and Socrates in dramatic form in order to eliminate the distraction of repeated "he said" and "I said" (143b–c). This may be taken as an indication that Plato was no longer interested in using the narrative form and that, therefore, *Theaetetus* belongs with those dialogues that can be dated after *Republic*.[10] As we have just seen, *Timaeus* refers to material found in *Republic* and, since the latter is not generally characterized by those features that mark the latest works, it is reasonable to conclude that composition of *Republic* preceded that of all those works that are stylistically related to *Timaeus*.

We can be confident, then, that *Republic* was written at a time before Plato composed the last group of his dialogues. That still leaves a fairly long period, perhaps as much as a quarter-century, in which he might have written and revised or even completely overhauled his dialogue on justice. As it happens, a number of scholars have been attracted by the theory that our Book One was originally a self-contained dialogue that was later revised and reused to serve as the introduction to the monumental *Republic* that we now have. The theory originated with Karl Friedrich

over a period of many years. Unlike Plato, however, those historians wrote nothing else. In addition to his many other works, Plato composed the even longer *Laws*, which Aristotle tells us explicitly (*Pol.* 2.1264b26–7) was written after *Republic*, so it is not necessary to assume, as some have, that composition of *Republic* extended over decades.

[9] See Brandwood 1990: 153–66 (hiatus), 167–206 (clausulae), 55–86 and 96–109 (reply formulae), summarizing the work of earlier scholars.

[10] Finkelberg 2019: 5–9. The dramatic form is found as well in a few early dialogues, such as *Crito, Euthyphro* and *Ion*, so the statement in *Theaetetus* can only be used to exclude from the latest group those dialogues narrated either by Socrates, such as *Republic, Charmides* and *Lysis*, or by someone else, such as *Phaedo* and *Symposium*.

Hermann in 1839, and the supposed original, for which there is no independent evidence, was later given the title *Thrasymachus*, on the analogy of other Platonic dialogues.[11] Support for the theory seemed to be provided in the late nineteenth century by statistical studies that were interpreted as showing a change in Plato's practice between Book One and the other nine books.[12] More recently, a few influential scholars have argued in favor of the theory on the basis of considerations that go beyond verbal style and relate rather to the content of Book One.[13] A difficulty, however, is posed by the appearance of what many scholars regard as references to *Republic* in Aristophanes' *Ecclesiazusae*, produced in 391 or 392 BC. For the references are not to anything that appears in Book One, but to the extraordinary proposals in Books Four and Five for the collective possession of property and the community of wives and children.[14] As we have seen, those same proposals are mentioned in the summary that Socrates gives in *Timaeus*, along with material from Books Two and Three relating to the division of classes and the training of the Guardians, but nothing from elsewhere in *Republic*. The content referred to by Aristophanes and Socrates, combined, amounts to approximately sixty-five pages in the Stephanus text of *Republic*, the equivalent of two ancient "books." As it happens, Aulus Gellius says that Plato initially published his *Republic* in "roughly two books."[15] This has led to the view, argued for in detail by

[11] For details, see Kahn 1993: 131. In the nineteenth century, under the influence of developments in biblical criticism, scholars not only made an effort to discover layers of composition in *Republic* and other works, they also called into question the authenticity of some of the dialogues that have traditionally been ascribed to Plato.

[12] See Brandwood 1990: 73–8, 106–8 and 215–20, reporting the findings of Constantin Ritter and Hans von Arnim. Difference in time of composition, however, is not the only possible explanation for the perceived stylistic variation; see below.

[13] Friedländer 1964: 50–66, treating Book One as a separate dialogue and saving discussion of *Republic* for the third volume of his *Plato*; Thesleff 1982: 107–10 = 2009: 256–9; Vlastos 1991: 248–51. Kraut (1992: 5) takes for granted the earlier composition of Book One as an independent dialogue.

[14] For detailed discussion, see Adam's appendix to Book Five (1902: I 345–55). Morosi (2020) finds allusions to Books Four and Five also in Aristophanes' *Wealth* (388 BC).

[15] 14.3.3 *duobus fere libris qui primi in uolgus exierant*; cf. A. Diès *apud* Chambry 1932: xxxix–xliii. But *fere* is suspicious; if Gellius or his source is not sure if the work was in two or three books, how much confidence can we have in the rest of the information given? Gellius goes on to say that this is the version of *Republic* that Xenophon read, inspiring him to write his *Cyropaedia* (in eight books) in response, detailing his own view of the proper form of government, to which Plato in turn responded dismissively in *Laws* (3.694c). He does not cite an authority for this account, but the context makes clear that it comes from a tradition that sought to portray Plato and Xenophon as bitter rivals; cf. Athenaeus 11.504e–505a. In

Holger Thesleff and Debra Nails, that the *Republic* that has come down to us was "cobbled together" from an early aporetic dialogue on justice and an approximately two-book ur-*Republic* dating to the 390s, to which were added the remaining contents of the surviving work in a final revision several years later.[16]

There are, then, two claims, that Book One was originally intended as a self-contained aporetic dialogue and that an ur-*Republic* independent of that dialogue was published before the completion of our *Republic*, and two types of evidence, stylistic and external. The two types of evidence have been used selectively in arguing for one or the other of the two claims. When taken together, however, each has the effect of undermining the other. The stylistic features that are used to show a statistical correlation between the *Republic* that we have and the dialogues of Plato's middle period, roughly the 370s and 360s, are also used to demonstrate the incompatibility of Book One with the rest of the dialogue. The same statistics, however, do not demonstrate a significant difference between the books that make up the hypothetical ur-*Republic* and the later books.[17] And yet the external evidence is alleged to date the ur-*Republic* to the 390s, the same decade in which the hypothetical *Thrasymachus* is presumed to have been written. That is, the chronological distance that separates Book One from the ur-*Republic* is much less than that separating the latter from Books Six through Ten, which have not been shown to differ from it stylistically to any significant degree. References to "final editing" or "late revision" only serve to call attention to the fragility of this line of argument.[18] For if Plato was conscious of the need to integrate the ur-*Republic* stylistically into the completed product, he would surely have done the same with Book One, given the exceptional care he took with the construction of the opening of his dialogues.[19]

any event, Gellius' "roughly two books" would not have included the material in Books Four and Five that Aristophanes supposedly parodied, nor would it have corresponded to the first two of the six-book *Republic* (above, n. 5), since nothing in the current Book One is relevant.

[16] Thesleff 1997; Nails 1995: 116–25 and 1998 (cf. Nails 2002: 324–6), from whom the quotation is taken (1998: 385). Nails also mentions (393) the argument of Gerald Else that much of Book Ten was a still later addition.

[17] See Brandwood 1990: 67–72 and 79–82. Ledger, who adopts different criteria from those used by nineteenth-century scholars and who does not provide separate statistics for the individual books, dates *Republic* as a whole to the 370s, with *Euthydemus, Symposium* and *Cratylus* (1989: 212–17).

[18] Thesleff 1997: 150 = 2009: 520; Nails 1995: 123–6 and 1998: 394 (cf. 395 "revised late into an almost seamless whole").

[19] For the importance Plato attached to the opening of his dialogues, see Kaklamanou's Introduction (1–9) to Kaklamanou et al. 2021 and the papers in that volume; also 327a1n.

The alternative to accepting the view of *Republic* as an assemblage of *disiecta membra* requires an explanation of why Book One seems to differ stylistically from the remaining books and how Aristophanes in the 390s could seemingly refer to a work dating to the 370s. The latter difficulty only arises, however, if we convince ourselves that the comic poet must have been inspired by a work *in written form.* But philosophical inquiry in Classical Greece, especially of the sort engaged in by Socrates and his followers, was carried out primarily by means of face-to-face discussion, so that, for example, the general Nicias can be represented as saying to Socrates, "I have often heard you say that everyone is good in respect of that in which he is wise" (*Lach.* 194d1–2). And Plato's Socrates himself acknowledges that it was his practice of personally confronting politicians, poets and craftsmen (*Apol.* 21b–23a) that contributed to the hostility toward him among the Athenians and influenced the verdict at his trial. Similarly, we may assume that the ideas that were eventually enshrined in Plato's written works were repeatedly aired in conversation with his associates and others, and that the more outrageous of them, particularly those relating to the status of women and personal property, are likely to have been reported in the form of gossip outside Plato's immediate circle.[20] Even among his writings, we find ideas mentioned in passing or expressed in a tentative way that were expounded more systematically in a later dialogue.[21]

As far as the stylistic differences between Book One and the rest of *Republic* – and it is worth stressing, again, that "the rest of *Republic*" has generally been found to be stylistically uniform – time of composition is not the only possible explanation. Statistical studies, whether carried out using pen and paper or software designed for computational analysis, have traditionally treated each of Plato's works, or occasionally each book

[20] Some of the doctrines regarding women that we think of as Platonic may in fact have originated with Socrates (Blair 2012: 39–55), which reminds us that the Aristophanes who produced *Clouds* had no need to consult a written text for his portrayal of Socrates, who wrote nothing. Plato's reference to *Clouds* in his *Apology* (19c–d) – no such reference is found in Xenophon's version of Socrates' speech – and his insistence on correcting its misrepresentations suggest that Plato was indeed attentive to developments on the contemporary comic stage and that in *Republic* he may have sought to clarify what had been presented, without naming Plato, as comic fantasy in *Ecclesiazusae.* For the relationship between Plato and contemporary comedy, which occasionally refers to him and the Academy, see Brock 1990.

[21] Kahn 1996. See also the list of correspondences between elements systematically laid out in *Timaeus* and doctrines found here and there in earlier dialogues, including several from *Republic*, compiled by Sedley (2017: 106–7, with discussion at 94–6).

within the longer work, as a unit for the purpose of determining either date of composition or authenticity. But anyone who has read the speeches in *Symposium* or that of Lysias in *Phaedrus* recognizes Plato's ability to vary his style according to speaker.[22] In the case of *Republic*, Plato has made the deliberate choice to compose the work in such a way that Socrates is seen to converse with three non-Athenians in Book One and with two Athenians who happen to be Plato's brothers in Books Two through Ten. Further, the dominant interlocutor in Book One, Thrasymachus, is one of the most memorably characterized individuals in Plato's works. Not only is he openly belligerent toward Socrates, he is given to using vocabulary that Plato does not put into the mouth of other speakers.[23] His truculence shows up *inter alia* in the types of responses he gives to Socrates' questions and, because of their frequency, reply formulae have been at the heart of a number of stylistic studies.[24] Thus, it is to be expected that, because of the nature of the discussion reported in Book One, it will exhibit a different stylistic character from that seen in the remaining books, in which Socrates' interlocutors are the entirely congenial Glaucon and Adeimantus, with whose conversational mannerisms Plato was intimately familiar.[25] There is, then, need of studies that compare the language of Glaucon with that of Thrasymachus or the language of Socrates in Book One with that in, say, Book Seven. Until such investigations have been carried out, there is no good reason to suppose that existing stylistic studies can reliably tell us that Book One dates to a different period in Plato's career than the other books of *Republic*. In the absence of more compelling evidence and more convincing arguments it is reasonable to proceed on the assumption that *Republic* was conceived as a whole and was written at one time, likely in the 370s BC. The commentary below will call attention to a number of points at which Plato seems to be anticipating in Book One what is to come in later books.[26]

[22] Whether that extends to those aspects of "style" that are not under the author's conscious control, the sorts of things that computer-assisted analysis is particularly good at uncovering, can only be known when the words spoken by Socrates and those spoken by each of his interlocutors are analyzed as separate "texts."

[23] See 336c2, 337a3, 338d3, 343a6nn. Plato marks the uniqueness of Thrasymachus also by having Socrates describe his behavior using words not occurring elsewhere in the dialogues; see 336b5–6, b6, 337a3nn. For Thrasymachus, see further below, 4(d).

[24] Brandwood 1990: 48–91, 96–114, 208–20.

[25] So Kahn 1993: 134.

[26] See in general Kahn 1993.

2 BOOK ONE, OR WHAT JUSTICE IS NOT

In a series of earlier Platonic dialogues, Socrates is shown attempting, with the help of a variety of interlocutors, to define different virtues: piety in *Euthyphro*, courage in *Laches*, sophrosyne in *Charmides* and, in *Meno*, virtue itself, of which these others are sometimes said to be a "part."[27] On each occasion the attempt is unsuccessful, ending in aporia.[28] The same is true of Book One of *Republic*, in which Socrates and his acquaintances fail to arrive at a successful definition of justice. As we have seen, some scholars have been encouraged by this outcome to conclude that Book One was originally a self-contained, aporetic dialogue. But there is an element of the discussion in Book One that makes it different from that in the earlier dialogues (and in the later *Theaetetus*). Elsewhere, Socrates and his interlocutors attempt to define qualities that they regard as unambiguously good and deserving of universal admiration. They are, after all, seeking to define what are customarily regarded as virtues.[29] So it never occurs to them to ask what these qualities are good *for* or why we should admire them. In the first book of *Republic* not only is the question raised what advantage justice provides, we are introduced to a character in the person of Thrasymachus who is convinced that, so far from being advantageous, acting justly is a hindrance to an individual's success and happiness. This will entail for Socrates the need for a better understanding of function (ἔργον) – that is, what such things as eyes, pruning hooks and souls are good for – and will prompt Glaucon, in Book Two, to propose a novel typology of goods (ἀγαθά).[30] The remainder of *Republic* constitutes Socrates' response to the plea of Glaucon and Adeimantus that he supply not only a definition of justice, but an explanation of what justice is good for and how it benefits its possessor (2.367d).

[27] E.g. *Lach.* 199e (courage), *Prot.* 330a (wisdom), 329c–d and *Meno* 78d–e (justice, sophrosyne and piety); at *Euthphr.* 12d it is agreed that piety is a part of justice. In a sense these dialogues, like Book One, are preludes to a more comprehensive inquiry into the nature of, and relationships among, the virtues; cf. the opening sentence of Book Two, in which Socrates acknowledges that the preceding conversation turned out to be no more than a προοίμιον.

[28] *Chrm.* 175b, *Euthphr.* 15c, *Lach.* 200e, *Meno* 100b. The subject of *Theaetetus* is the search for a definition of knowledge (ἐπιστήμη, identified with σοφία at 145e); it too ends in disappointment.

[29] For ἀρετή and ἀγαθός as "the most powerful words of commendation used of a man both in Homer and in later Greek," see Adkins 1960: 30–4. In case it needs to be made explicit, Socrates and Meno agree that ἀρετή is an ἀγαθόν (*Meno* 87d2–4).

[30] For ἔργον and its relation to ἀρετή, see 352e2–3n.; for the division of goods into those desirable for themselves, those only for the benefits they provide and those both for themselves and for their consequences, see 2.357b–d, with 330c5n.

There is another respect in which the opening book of *Republic* stands apart from Plato's other dialogues that seek to define a specific virtue. In each of those earlier works, Socrates' interlocutor ought to be expected to be able to define the specific virtue about which he is being asked. For, in each case, the interlocutor is an acknowledged representative of the virtue in question: Euthyphro, being a prophet, is regularly consulted by others on matters relating to the gods, Laches and Nicias were each elected general by their fellow Athenians on more than one occasion, and Charmides is introduced as someone who is recognized as being "far and away the most self-controlled of his generation."[31] There are, as is often the case in Plato, multiple levels of irony involved. Apart from the fact that Charmides, who is presented as a charmingly demure teenager at the time of the dialogue named after him, would end up fighting and dying in support of the ruthless regime of the Thirty Tyrants, Plato portrays Socrates himself as surpassing all his interlocutors, indeed all mortals, in each of the virtues that his interlocutors supposedly embody. In *Symposium*, Alcibiades praises Socrates' unparalleled courage and sophrosyne, and Phaedo ends his account of Socrates' death by recording his pious last words and characterizing him as "the most virtuous, most wise and most just man of his time."[32] If this man does not know what courage is, or justice – as is implied by his constant inquiring of others – how is it possible for the rest of us to come to an understanding of those things that it is most important for us to know?

One implication of Plato's *Apology* is that it is not possible, since Socrates owes his designation as unsurpassed for wisdom to nothing more than his acknowledgment of the extent of his ignorance (23a–b). Another implication is that it is imperative that we all persist in our search for understanding, since "for a human being, the unexamined life is not worth living" (38a5–6). And so we find Socrates, in Book One of *Republic*, pressing his acquaintances for a definition of justice. The discussion does not begin, however, with justice, or virtue, or advantage. Rather, Socrates opens the conversation by asking the elderly Cephalus, a notably wealthy metic (a non-Athenian permanently residing in Athens), about old age

[31] *Chrm.* 157d6–7 πάνυ πολὺ δοκεῖ σωφρονέστατος εἶναι τῶν νυνί. Similarly, the young Theaetetus is lauded by Theodorus for possessing all the virtues, especially intelligence (*Tht.* 144a–b).

[32] Courage: *Symp.* 220d–221c (also *Lach.* 181a–b); sophrosyne: 216d; last words ("We owe a cock to Asclepius, Crito; do not neglect to repay the debt") and concluding judgment (ἀρίστου καὶ ἄλλως φρονιμωτάτου καὶ δικαιοτάτου): *Phd.* 118a. Additionally, we have the word of the god at Delphi that no one is wiser than Socrates: μηδένα σοφώτερον εἶναι, *Apol.* 21a7.

and whether he finds it burdensome.[33] Cephalus admits that many of his contemporaries complain about the advancing years, but he himself has come to terms with being old, attributing his serenity to his character (τρόπος, 329d4) which, we are to assume, he regards as even-tempered and good-natured. Socrates wonders if Cephalus' great wealth may have gone some way toward easing the burden for him, which Cephalus does not deny. All of this is by way of introduction to Socrates' question, "What do you think is the greatest advantage (ἀγαθόν, 330d2) you have enjoyed from acquiring a great fortune?" Cephalus acknowledges that his answer will come as a surprise to some, namely that the possession of great wealth enables a person who has lived life righteously and piously (δικαίως καὶ ὁσίως, 331a3–4) to ensure that all debts to men and gods have been paid before taking leave of this life. The consequence of this is peace of mind and the avoidance of torments in the afterlife, should the stories of such torments turn out to be accurate. When Socrates objects that there are circumstances in which a person is not considered just (δίκαιος, 331c6) in giving back what is owed, offering as an example the need to resist and to dissemble when a friend who has gone mad asks for the return of a weapon that has been lent, Cephalus excuses himself and goes off to fulfill his religious obligation to perform a sacrifice. He will not be seen or heard from again.

Thus unobtrusively does Plato introduce, while simultaneously seeming to dismiss, a number of themes that will recur not only in Book One, but throughout *Republic*. These include the importance of one's character, in contrast to external factors, in determining one's happiness; the association of justice and piety; the advantages to the individual of possessing both these virtues; the potential risks of acting impiously or unjustly; and, in general, framing these issues in transactional terms of gains and losses, rewards and punishments. Character, in the form of the disposition of the personal soul, will be the focus of discussion throughout the dialogue, and will involve the question of education, which Socrates defines as turning the soul from darkness toward the light (7.518b–d, 521c). The nominal subject of *Republic* is, as we have seen, justice rather than piety, yet the two virtues are introduced together, with the latter seeming to disappear with the departure of Cephalus.[34] Similarly, the religious celebration in honor of the goddess Bendis that serves as the occasion for Socrates' visit

[33] 328e. For Cephalus, see below, 4(b).

[34] In *Euthyphro*, which is concerned with the search for the meaning of piety, the discussion begins with the prophet explaining that his decision to prosecute his father was just. Socrates claims to be impressed with the wisdom (4b1) of this man who is so confident of his understanding of both justice and piety.

to the house of Cephalus is mentioned again briefly at the end of Book One (354a10) but is subsequently ignored. While piety is sometimes said to rank as one of the "cardinal virtues," and is of obvious importance to Cephalus, it is not included in Socrates' treatment in Book Four.[35] There, the city that Socrates and Plato's brothers construct will be designed so as to be σοφή τε ... καὶ ἀνδρεία καὶ σώφρων καὶ δικαία (427e9–10), and Socrates regards this list as exhaustive, so that the fourth virtue, justice, can be confidently identified once the other three have been discovered.[36] In *Republic*, piety is treated as a branch of justice, namely that which concerns proper relations with the gods.[37] It will reappear in Book Ten, when the rewards in the afterlife for those who have shown themselves to have been righteous and pious (δίκαιοι καὶ ὅσιοι, 615b6) recall the aspirations of Cephalus in Book One. This association of piety with justice, as well as the association of both with rewards and payments, illustrates what these two have in common and what distinguishes them from wisdom, courage and sophrosyne. Unlike these latter virtues, which can be exercised in private, justice and piety are manifested only in one's interactions with others, whether human or divine. Further, contraventions of the norms of justice and piety, unlike failure to adhere to the other virtues, are subject not only to disapproval but to punishment, either in a court of law or by action of the gods. This means that, while wisdom, courage and sophrosyne can be investigated in isolation from society at large, the investigation of justice in the individual requires an investigation of social practice as well. By the end of Book One, that investigation is only in its preliminary stages.[38]

[35] See Dover 1974: 66–7 for the traditional inclusion of piety, in the form of εὐσέβεια, which goes back at least as far as Aeschylus' *Seven against Thebes*, where Amphiaraus, earlier described as ἄνδρα σωφρονέστατον (568), is praised as σώφρων δίκαιος ἀγαθὸς εὐσεβὴς ἀνήρ (610). Amphiaraus is a prophet, as is the title character of *Euthyphro*, Plato's earlier investigation of piety, so the emphasis on that virtue in these instances is understandable.

[36] 4.428a. The absence of piety is ironically highlighted by prefacing the enumeration of virtues with Glaucon's reminder that Socrates had said that it was impious (οὐχ ὅσιον, 427e1; cf. 2.368c1) not to do everything in his power to come to the defense of justice.

[37] Annas 1981: 110; cf. the pseudo-Platonic *Definitiones* 412e14 εὐσέβεια· δικαιοσύνη περὶ θεούς and *Rep.* 4.443a, where temple-robbery and neglect of the gods are among the behaviors that one would least expect the just person to exhibit. In the earlier *Euthyphro* the possibility had been raised that piety is a species of knowledge (4e–5a, 14d), in the same way it is suggested in *Protagoras* (360d) and *Laches* (194d, 196c–d) that courage also is a form of knowledge, namely of what is and what is not to be feared.

[38] For discussion of why Plato chose to dramatize these preliminary stages largely in the form of a dialogue between Socrates and Thrasymachus, see 4(d) below.

3 SETTING

As is the case with some of Plato's other dialogues, *Republic* is set at a specific time in a specific place.[39] The place is the house of Cephalus and Polemarchus in the Piraeus, and the time is the Bendid(e)ia, celebrated on 19 Thargelion.[40] Plato specifies in the first sentence that Socrates' attendance was prompted by the novelty of the event. Based on inscriptional evidence, two years have found favor with scholars as the time of the festival to which Plato is referring, 429 and 413, with the latter being more generally preferred.[41] The earlier date, however, has been forcefully advocated by Christopher Planeaux.[42] This has the effect of associating Socrates' interest in the Thracian deity with his military service in northern Greece, where he took part in the prolonged siege of Potidaea and where, according to Alcibiades' memorable account, he once spent twenty-four hours standing still in silent self-absorption.[43] His return to Athens from combat duty there serves as the setting of *Charmides*, which is imagined as having taken place only a week or two before 19 Thargelion 429.[44] This date for Socrates' excursion to the Piraeus seems incompatible

[39] For example, *Crito* is set in Socrates' prison cell two days before his execution in 399 BC, and the conversation recorded in *Symposium* takes place in the home of the playwright Agathon in 416, the day after he celebrated his first victory in the dramatic competition. In contrast to *Republic*, which opens with Socrates going down to the Piraeus (327a1n.), the frame narrative of *Symposium* refers to Apollodorus going up to the city (εἰς ἄστυ οἴκοθεν ἀνιών, 172a2); later in that dialogue Diotima will initiate Socrates into the mysteries of the ascent to the Forms (210a–212a) from contemplation of which the philosopher's descent into the Cave is described in *Republic* (7.516c–517a); see Rowe (1998) on *Symp.* 172a3.

[40] For this festival (the spelling of the name varies in our sources) held annually in honor of the Thracian goddess Bendis, see Garland 1987: 118–22, 231–3 and 1992: 111–14; Planeaux 2000; Pache 2001; Wijma 2014: 126–55. The sanctuary of the goddess was located in the Piraeus close to that of Artemis, with whom she was identified.

[41] See Arnaoutoglou 2015: 30–8, concluding that *IG* I[3] 383 (429/8 BC) reflects the incorporation of Bendis into the pantheon of gods recognized by the Athenian state, while *IG* I[3] 136 (413/12 BC) documents certain "modifications to the celebrations" (38), which occasioned Socrates' visit to the Piraeus. But Socrates was attracted not by modifications to an existing festival. He went to the Piraeus "to see in what way they were going to conduct the festivities, since this was the first time (ἅτε νῦν πρῶτον ἄγοντες)," and he has to be told by Adeimantus and Polemarchus (328a) what some of the features of the celebration are.

[42] Planeaux 2000; also Graham 2007: 69–70.

[43] *Symp.* 220c–d. Such behavior was associated with Thracian shamans; see Dodds 1951: 142–4 with nn. 46 and 60–1, comparing the extended disappearance of Zalmoxis (for whom, see 354a10n. below).

[44] For the dramatic date of *Charmides* (May 429), see Nails 2002: 311–12, also the commentary below on 336a4 (Περδίκκου) and 354a10 (ἐν τοῖς Βενδιδίοις). Composition of *Charmides* appears to date to a time not long before that of *Republic* (Ledger 1989: 223–4).

with some of the details we know, or think we know, about the men with whom Socrates interacts in Plato's dialogue, and this has been partially responsible for the preference for a dramatic date in 413. For example, the usual understanding of the age of Plato's brothers makes them too young to participate in the conversation at the earlier date.[45] But there is no time at which *Republic* can be imagined as having taken place that does not involve serious chronological incompatibilities, hence the wide range in the dates that have been proposed by scholars.[46] We should not be surprised. Plato had no interest in creating narratives that satisfy modern philologists' standards of strict consistency when dramatizing conversations that are supposed to have taken place in his childhood some forty or fifty years before he wrote them down in, probably, the 370s. Other works that date from the same general period of Plato's output exhibit blatant anachronisms and, what is more, anachronisms involving much more recent events, such that they would have been obvious to his earliest readers, for example the references to the partition of Mantinea in or after 385 by the Spartans in *Symposium* and to the bribing of Ismenias the Theban in *Meno*, both of which occurred after the death of Socrates.[47] As it happens, Ismenias is mentioned by Socrates also in Book One, likely on account of the same act of corruption that made him notorious.[48]

The pressing question, then, is not the one that has exercised critics in the past, how this or that inconvenient detail can be explained, or explained away, so as to accommodate a single, coherent dramatic date. Rather, the question is a literary-critical one, namely why Plato has chosen to set his most ambitious work in the Piraeus at the time of a newly established festival in honor of a non-Greek divinity, a setting to which our attention is called at the very beginning and at the end of (what we

[45] Nails (2002: 2 and 154) gives the birth dates of Adeimantus as "±432" and Glaucon as "≤429." If these dates are approximately correct, the two were just barely old enough for the role they play in the conversation even if it took place in 413; further, Socrates' praise of them in Book Two (368a) for distinguishing themselves in combat at Megara is problematic, whether the reference is to an engagement in 424 (Thuc. 4.72), when they were minors, or 409 (D.S. 13.65.1–2), which had not yet occurred.

[46] Nails, who herself considers Book One to have been written earlier as a separate dialogue (above, n. 16), gives "a smattering from the modern bibliography" (2002: 325–6) in which various dramatic dates for *Republic* are advocated, ranging from 431 to 407.

[47] *Symp.* 193a, *Meno* 90a; Graham 2007: 67. For a similarly cavalier attitude toward chronological consistency in the Socratic dialogues of Aeschines and Xenophon, see Kahn 1996: 28–34, noting also the egregious anachronism in Plato's *Menexenus*, in which Socrates listens to a speech referring to an event that occurred in 386, not long before the dialogue's presumable time of composition.

[48] See 336a4–5n. and, for another apparent chronological incongruity, 329b7n.

have come to know as) Book One. The references to Bendis in the opening sentence and at 354a serve as bookends, so to speak, marking off Socrates' conversation with three non-Athenians as a προοίμιον (2.357a2) to the work as a whole. The two features of the festival that Socrates mentions specifically at the very start are its novelty and its ecumenical character, consisting as it does of processions by both local worshippers and Thracians. It is difficult to avoid the conclusion that the unaccustomed location and the unfamiliarity of the celebration are Plato's way of announcing that we are entering novel territory for both Plato and Socrates. Cephalus' first words to Socrates (328c5–6) are a reproach over the infrequency of his visits to the Piraeus, and elsewhere as well Plato draws our attention to the fact that Socrates rarely ventures outside the urban confines of the city of Athens (*Phdr.* 230c–d). It has been noted that Socrates' "descent" into the cosmopolitan commercial port of Athens foreshadows the requirement in Book Seven that the philosopher go back into the figurative Cave from which his studies have liberated him and to which he must temporarily return for the purpose of overseeing his less enlightened compatriots.[49] It is not only the locale, however, that is unaccustomed. The scale of *Republic* is far more imposing than anything its author had attempted previously, and the character of Socrates, who in earlier dialogues denied that he was capable of teaching anything because he disavowed knowledge of everything except the extent of his own ignorance, now expounds the nature of the individual soul, the place of justice and of all of virtue within the soul, the structure of human society and much else along the way; he is even prepared to give a lecture, accompanied by a diagram (6.509d–511e), explaining the very nature and object of knowledge. Whether this transformation reflects a shift from a Plato who was more or less faithfully transmitting Socratic doctrines to one who only now gives voice to his own distinctive thinking is the subject of scholarly controversy that will not be pursued here.[50] What is beyond dispute is that *Republic* represents a departure from Plato's previous compositional habits. The unfamiliarity of the setting and the novelty of the ritual attended by Socrates alert the reader to expect something new and different. And so we will be presented with a blueprint for a society in which the ruling class has renounced the nuclear family and which is governed by philosophers.[51] What begins with an inquiry into justice, which

[49] Burnyeat 1997: 6; Vegetti 1998: 103–4; see also above, n. 39. The "justice" of the requirement is emphasized by Socrates (οὐδὲ ἀδικήσομεν … ἀλλὰ δίκαια, 520a6–7) and affirmed by Glaucon (δίκαια … ἐπιτάξομεν, e1).

[50] Representative of this view is Vlastos, who separates Book One from the rest of *Republic* (above, n. 13); for an opposing view, see Kahn 1996.

[51] 5.473c–d, virtually quoted in the Seventh Letter (326a–b), in the context of

is initially discussed in terms of the behavior of one person in relation to another, will become by degrees an investigation into the character of human society as a whole and ends up with the Myth of Er, an account set on a cosmic scale.

4 DRAMATIS PERSONAE

(a) Socrates

All of Plato's dialogues previous to *Republic* had featured Socrates as the primary character, and he was to continue in that capacity until late in Plato's career, when other, sometimes anonymous, figures assume that role.[52] These works belong to a literary genre to which Plato was not the only contributor, nor did it originate with him.[53] The central figure of Socrates bears some elusive resemblance to the historical individual who was known personally, in varying degrees, to most or all of those who wrote Socratic dialogues. The Socrates we meet in Book One is familiar from other Platonic works. His piety is attested, as it is elsewhere, in the opening sentence, which explains that he has walked more than two hours to pay his respects to the goddess whose worship has recently been introduced in Athens.[54] And his accustomed profession of ignorance is very much in evidence in Book One. For example, he claims not to know what Simonides means when he says that it is just to render to each person what is owed (331e6–7) and, more pertinently, he denies that he knows what justice is (337e5, 354b–c). This trait is so well known that the visiting Thrasymachus characterizes an instance of the behavior as "that customary Socratic affectation" (ἐκείνη ἡ εἰωθυῖα εἰρωνεία Σωκράτους, 337a4) and he complains that Socrates is now, as usual, refusing to reveal what he thinks. As it happens, Socrates skillfully outmaneuvers Thrasymachus

Plato's decision to draw back from participation in Athenian politics and to travel for the first time to Italy and Sicily.

[52] For example, the visitor from Elea in *Statesman*, the Athenian in *Laws* and Timaeus of Locri in the dialogue named for him.

[53] For a survey of these Σωκρατικοὶ λόγοι, see Kahn 1996: 1–35. They include the surviving *Apology*, *Memorabilia*, *Oeconomicus* and *Symposium* of Xenophon and a number of dialogues from the fourth century that have not survived, composed by Aeschines of Sphettus, Antisthenes and other followers of Socrates. The fragments and testimonia are collected in *SSR*.

[54] Plato and Xenophon often stress Socrates' observance of religious obligations, defending their friend posthumously against the charge of impiety that cost him his life (e.g. *Phd.* 61b, 118a, *Phdr.* 242b–243d, *Symp.* 220d; Xen. *Anab.* 3.1.5, *Mem.* 1.1.2). At his trial Socrates was accused (among other things) of καινὰ δαιμόνια εἰσφέρων (Xen. *Mem.* 1.1.1) but, as Denyer (2019: 17) points out, "Athenian law had no general objection to the introduction of new divinities," naming Bendis, Pan, Asclepius and others.

by getting him to give his own definition of justice, which he proceeds to subject to a series of questions.

Socrates (that is, Plato) thus makes it very difficult for us to know whether his questions arise out of simple curiosity – his first question to Cephalus, for instance, is in effect, "What is it like to be very old?" – or, as Thrasymachus suggests, constitute a devious strategy for avoiding difficult questions himself.[55] For his questions often take the form of "Don't you think that X?" or "Wouldn't you say that X?," leaving Socrates uncommitted as to whether he thinks X is the case or not. So, for example, the argument that leads to the unexpected conclusion that the just person is equally proficient at safeguarding and stealing money (334a) begins with the question, "Isn't the skilled boxer equally adept at delivering and fending off blows?" And the doctrine that the crafts are distinguished from one another by each having its own capability (δύναμις) and conferring its own benefit (ὠφελία) is not stated outright but is introduced with "Don't we regularly say that ...?" (346a). Even the uncontroversial claim that we ought to take seriously how we live our lives is presented as a question directed at Thrasymachus (344e), "Do you think it is a trivial matter ...?" Only rarely in Book One does Socrates state his own position. Even then it may be expressed ambiguously, as when he affirms that he agrees with Thrasymachus that justice is συμφέρον τι (339b4–5), without saying for whom he thinks it is advantageous. Thrasymachus' frustration is thus understandable.

There are, however, a few places in Book One where Socrates declares unequivocally his position on a matter of philosophical importance. At 335e he affirms confidently that the foregoing discussion with Polemarchus has shown that under no circumstances is it right to cause harm to anyone, even in retaliation, and he offers – ironically, one assumes – to take up arms in defense of the proposition.[56] This is the point at which Thrasymachus intrudes into the conversation, so that no defense is immediately required. But the doctrine is revisited in Book

[55] Ancient Greek seems not to have had a word for simple curiosity. The closest Greek comes is θαῦμα, which both Plato (*Tht.* 155d) and Aristotle (*Met.* 982b12–13) identify as the source of philosophical inquiry, but neither it nor πολυπραγμοσύνη (for which, see Leigh 2013) is quite the right word to describe what motivates such questions as, "Why do we find in Plato's manuscripts sometimes ἄν, sometimes ἤν and sometimes ἐάν?" φιλομαθία (6.499e2–3) was perhaps coined by Plato, as a less elevated synonym for φιλοσοφία, to fill the gap; cf. φιλομαθής (2.376b–c), likely also a Platonic coinage.

[56] 335e5–6 οὐδαμοῦ γὰρ δίκαιον οὐδένα ἡμῖν ἐφάνη ὂν βλάπτειν; cf. *Cri.* 49b7 οὐδαμῶς ἄρα δεῖ ἀδικεῖν. Characteristically, the line of argument had begun with a question (b2–3): Ἔστιν ἄρα ... δικαίου ἀνδρὸς βλάπτειν καὶ ὁντινοῦν ἀνθρώπων;

Two, where it underlies Socrates' argument that the gods cannot be the cause of harm, since the gods are good and nothing good can be the cause of harm.[57] Only in the argument that extends from 346e to 347e does Socrates briefly abandon the question-and-answer format, when he explains in expository mode the reasoning behind his total disagreement with Thrasymachus' definition of the just as the advantage of the superior. Having demonstrated that no τέχνη and no position of leadership exists to serve its own advantage, Socrates makes the provocative statement that, for this reason, everyone who undertakes a position of leadership must either be compensated or subjected to a penalty. At this point Glaucon speaks up, asking what penalty Socrates has in mind. This prompts Socrates' explanation that those who are not motivated by greed or ambition face the dire prospect of being ruled by their inferiors, namely those who are so motivated. Socrates does not wait to see if Glaucon, or Thrasymachus, is convinced by his argument, and he immediately moves on to another question, resuming his interrogation of Thrasymachus, which continues until the end of the book. They, and we, have to wait until Book Seven, by which time the theoretical groundwork will have been laid justifying the claim that the philosopher, that is, the genuine ruler, will consent to return to the metaphorical Cave and rule his inferiors, thereby ensuring that the polis in which he lives will not be overwhelmed by violent factionalism (520c–d). Thus, with this brief interlude, Plato gives us a preview not only of some of the contents of the later books but also of the roles that Socrates and Glaucon, along with Glaucon's brother, will play later on. For the Socrates who professes ignorance and spends his time interrogating others in Book One, as generally in the earlier dialogues, will give way in the rest of *Republic* to the confident man who knows that a life spent acting justly is preferable to the unjust life admired by Thrasymachus, and who is prepared to explain at length why that is the case.

(b) Cephalus

The conversation recorded in *Republic* takes place in the home of the elderly Cephalus, although Socrates refers to it as the home of Polemarchus (328b4), Cephalus' eldest son, who has now assumed management of the estate. The situation is similar to that in the *Odyssey* and in Euripides' *Alcestis*, where the authority has been handed over by the still-living patriarch to his mature son. Whether this reflects the actual case in the

[57] 379b3 οὐδέν γε τῶν ἀγαθῶν βλαβερόν. What the gods do is right and good (δίκαιά τε καὶ ἀγαθά, 380b1).

household of the historical Cephalus we are in no position to know.[58] What we do know about the metic Cephalus we learn mostly from the opening pages of Lysias 12, *Against Eratosthenes*: that he was persuaded by Pericles to move from Syracuse to Athens, where he lived for thirty years, owning a factory for the manufacture of arms that employed over one hundred enslaved workers. On his death, at some unknown date before the end of the Peloponnesian War, his estate passed into the hands of his three sons, all of whom are present at the conversation between Cephalus and Socrates (328b4–5). The entire estate, including the assets of the factory, the slaves and three houses, in one of which *Republic* is set, were appropriated by the Thirty in 404 BC. The oligarchs justified on political grounds their confiscation of the property of metics like Cephalus but, as Lysias bluntly puts it, in reality it was simply a means of raising funds for a regime that was in financial need.[59]

What distinguishes Cephalus among Socrates' interlocutors is his wealth. Nicias and Alcibiades, among others, were quite wealthy, but they were also notable for other reasons. In the case of Cephalus it is only for his money-making ability, along with his advanced age, that he is introduced into the dialogue. In the later books of *Republic* money-making will be drastically devalued and relegated to an activity to be pursued only by the lowest class of citizens. Money-making is characteristic of the iron and bronze offspring who drag the aristocracy into the debased form of government that Socrates calls "timocracy" (8.547b). In the still more debased oligarchy, respect for money-making increases in proportion as respect for virtue declines (550e). The money-maker will claim that the pleasure of making a profit exceeds that of gaining respect or learning (9.581d), in contrast to the man whose soul is in harmony with itself, who will recognize that amassing a fortune is not the means to happiness (591d). Socrates at one point even criticizes Homer for representing Achilles as swayed by bribes and being φιλοχρήματος (3.390e9). Given this attitude, one might expect Socrates to have little time for someone like Cephalus.[60] Instead, Socrates treats Cephalus with the utmost courtesy

[58] For Cephalus, see S. Campese *apud* Vegetti 1998: 133–57; Beversluis 2000: 185–202; Gifford 2001: 52–8; Blondell 2002: 165–75; Nails 2002: 84–5; Todd 2007: 5–12.

[59] τῶι δὲ ἔργωι χρηματίζεσθαι, 12.6. The democratic sympathies of the family, which Lysias understandably emphasizes in speaking before the post-restoration jury, were likely sincere, given the connection to Pericles.

[60] Compare the contempt and even pity that Apollodorus, Socrates' most fanatical follower, expresses for his unnamed companions' interest in talking only about wealth and money-making (*Symp.* 173c–d).

and respect, based on the latter's age and the longstanding friendship that is suggested by what Cephalus says at 328c–d.

Critics have arrived at remarkably divergent assessments of Cephalus' character. He has been seen, according to one, as an unscrupulous arms manufacturer whose profits from supplying armaments to the imperialist project of fifth-century Athens are indicative of a disregard of basic morality and, according to another, as someone whose character is in no need of improvement, for which reason Plato dismisses him early on from the edifying conversation.[61] Most scholars recognize that Cephalus is neither the moral equal of Socrates nor a lineal ancestor of Albert Speer, Hitler's Minister of Armaments and War Production. Considering what is to follow in the remainder of *Republic*, it is difficult in any event to imagine why Plato would have wished to portray Cephalus as either of these extremes. Far more likely – and more in line with the majority view of Cephalus' character – is that Plato intends us to see Cephalus as a basically decent individual who behaves in accord with conventional moral standards, without being prepared to define or defend the intellectual foundation of those standards.[62] He values truth-telling and rendering to men and gods what is owed to them, and he respects authority, as evidenced by his approval of what has been said by revered figures from the past, such as Sophocles, Themistocles and Pindar. Further, Cephalus recognizes the decisive influence a person's character (τρόπος, 329d4) has on one's actions. This brings him closer in attitude to Socrates than to his son Polemarchus or to Thrasymachus, both of whom define justice in terms of actions taken (341a3n.). In short, he would seem to be the model for members of the productive class in Socrates' Callipolis, the ideal community that will be constructed later in the dialogue.[63] His wealth shows that he has excelled in, and is well suited to, his chosen profession, a profession that supports the class above his own by supplying the military with arms. At the same time, he has no ambition to join that class, or the class above that. He respects and appreciates the value of philosophical discussion, but he recognizes his own limitations and is happy to leave it to others more gifted than himself. He is content with his life and with

[61] Respectively Gifford (2001: 67–81) and Reeve (1988: 9), according to whom his "character is already as good as Socrates'."

[62] Lycos 1987: 26–31; Beversluis 2000: 185–202; Blondell 2002: 168–73; Emlyn-Jones 2007: 13–15.

[63] What characterizes the productive class is the preponderance of the appetitive (ἐπιθυμητικόν) element in the souls of its members (4.440e–441a). The story Cephalus tells about the aged Sophocles (329b–d) to illustrate his current frame of mind suggests that he too was dominated by his own appetites, as if by "a raving, violent master," until they were tempered by old age.

his status as someone who can be useful to the state without demanding to rule.[64] All of this is conveyed to us on the narrative level by his physical incapacity to ascend to the heights of the polis and by his status as a metic.

(c) *Polemarchus*

In his conversation with Socrates, Cephalus talks about the vicissitudes of his family's financial fortunes. His grandfather inherited an estate about equal in value to what Cephalus now possesses and increased its size many-fold, but his father squandered much of its value and Cephalus industriously restored it to its former standing. Plato has thus prepared us for the possibility that Cephalus' son, whose role as heir to his father's part in the conversation as well as to his property is emphasized (331d), may have a character different from his father's.[65] While Polemarchus does share some of his father's traits – a propensity to think in economic terms, respect for the authority of poets, professed interest in philosophical discussion – his engagement with Socrates is quite unlike that of his father.[66] It has been noted that the situation here resembles that in *Gorgias*, when Polus, who is like Polemarchus and Cephalus in that he comes from Sicily, breaks into the discussion and takes over from the older Sicilian Gorgias as Socrates' conversational partner.[67] The discussion with Polus concerns rhetoric, not justice, but it is relevant – and perhaps preparatory – to that between Socrates and Polemarchus. Just before Callicles' interruption puts an end to the interrogation of Polus, Socrates claims that his questioning has

[64] Compare the (admittedly self-serving) description by Lysias of his father's family under the democracy, living a life that avoided giving offense to, and occasioned no unjust treatment at the hands of, other Athenians: οὕτως ᾠκοῦμεν δημοκρατούμενοι ὥστε μήτε εἰς τοὺς ἄλλους ἐξαμαρτάνειν μήτε ὑπὸ τῶν ἄλλων ἀδικεῖσθαι, 12.4. Lysias goes on to affirm that his family had paid numerous taxes and performed all the other obligations expected of them, demonstrating that they were compliant and well-behaved (κόσμιοι, 20; cf. 329d4) members of society.

[65] Plato was keenly aware of intergenerational discontinuities, singling out the sons of Themistocles, Aristeides, Pericles, Thucydides (not the historian) and Polycleitus as not having matched the accomplishments of their distinguished fathers (*Meno* 93b–94e, *Prot.* 319e–320a, 328c) and using this discontinuity as the premise from which the discussion in *Laches* takes its departure. Even in the selectively bred population of Callipolis it will occasionally happen that "golden" parents will have "silver" offspring or vice versa (3.415a–c).

[66] For Polemarchus, see S. Gastaldi *apud* Vegetti 1998: 171–91; Beversluis 2000: 203–20; Gifford 2001: 83–97; Nails 2002: 251; Blondell 2002: 174–80, especially 175–6.

[67] Beversluis 2000: 315; as Dodds (1959: 11) notes, Polus is "young enough to be Socrates' or Gorgias' son (461cd)." Also, like Polus, Polemarchus will be succeeded by an unusually aggressive interlocutor.

shown that rhetoric is not at all useful, unless there is need to cause harm to one's enemy, in which case, paradoxically, it is useful in helping one's enemy to escape punishment, ensuring that the enemy's depraved character not be corrected (*Gorg.* 480e–481b). Similarly paradoxical is the outcome of Socrates' argument ending at 333e, in which he claims to have shown that justice, as Polemarchus understands it, is a thing of no value. Polemarchus' failure to challenge this conclusion, merely responding at 333d12 with Κινδυνεύει, is indicative of his character. On the one hand, he welcomes the opportunity to engage in discourse on serious matters; it is he, after all, who threatens to use force to ensure that Socrates stay in the Piraeus for the conversation at his house and, in *Phaedrus*, Socrates expresses the hope that the young Lysias will turn his attention to philosophy, "just like his brother Polemarchus" (257b). On the other hand, Polemarchus is too easily swayed by authority, whether that of Socrates or of poets like Simonides, whom he quotes for the definition of justice that serves as his entry into the discussion.

Polemarchus, then, is a work in progress. He is receptive to instruction in philosophy, and he has inherited the conventional view that justice is a good thing, although he has not yet developed the intellectual skills that might allow him to mount a successful defense of that view. We see the beginnings of that progress already in Book One. Early in the conversation Socrates, treating Polemarchus like the victim of an eristic display, claims that the discussion has shown that the truth of the matter is "the exact opposite" (334e3) of what Polemarchus had put forth as a definition of justice, namely helping friends and harming enemies. The argument had hinged on Polemarchus' agreement that people can be mistaken about who is truly worthy of their friendship, leading to the conclusion that it could therefore be just to harm one's friend. Later, Polemarchus triumphantly interrupts the conversation between Socrates and Thrasymachus (340a1), saying that it is perfectly obvious that the former had shown that the truth of the matter was the opposite of Thrasymachus' definition of justice as the interest of the superior. His demonstration had involved getting Thrasymachus to agree that rulers sometimes mistake what is in their best interests, resulting in their ordering their subjects to do what is, according to Thrasymachus' definition, contrary to the interests of the ruler. This interruption shows Polemarchus' continuing acquiescence in the authority of Socrates, but at the same time it reveals that he has learned from the earlier demonstration, as is clear from the way he argues in what follows against Clitophon's defense of Thrasymachus. His intervention helps motivate a significant clarification of Thrasymachus' definition, which now includes an explanation of what is meant by "the superior." Later still, in Book Five, Polemarchus intrudes once more, but this time much more discreetly. Seemingly chastened by a recognition that others in the party have a more secure grasp of the issues, instead of impetuously disrupting the conversation as he had done in Book One, he asks Adeimantus in a whisper if they are going to let Socrates get away with what he has just said without demanding from him an explanation (449b). His reaction is to Socrates' provocative statement about the need for the Guardians in Callipolis to hold spouses and children in common. Polemarchus' question is overheard by Socrates, and this leads to what is, in effect, a digression lasting for three books, introducing some of the best-known elements of the work: the essential intellectual equality of women and men, the need for philosophers to be the rulers in the ideal society, the requisite training of the philosophers and the analogies of the Sun, the Divided Line and the Cave.

While Polemarchus is not on the intellectual level of Glaucon and Adeimantus, he is portrayed as someone who has the curiosity and the capacity at least to surpass his father in the pursuit of philosophical investigation. In his lifetime, however, he seems not to have fulfilled what potential he might have had. He was murdered by the Thirty in 404 BC, being obliged, like Socrates, to drink hemlock (Lysias 12.17). This parallel with Socrates, who was executed not, however, by the rebellious oligarchical faction but by the recently restored democratic government, may have suggested to Plato that the home of Polemarchus was an appropriate location for a dialogue that explores, among other things, political pathology and that suggests a cure for societal ills.

(d) Thrasymachus

Like the other characters in *Republic*, Thrasymachus is a historical individual.[68] He was a teacher of rhetoric and a citizen of Chalcedon, located on the Asiatic side of what is today the city of Istanbul. We are not told the occasion of his visit to Athens, but we are probably intended to assume a professional motive on his part; at one point in Book One he makes it clear that he expects payment from Socrates for expressing his views regarding the nature of justice (337d6), and on another occasion Socrates singles out Thrasymachus as the representative of those who teach the art of public speaking to "whoever is willing to make tribute payments to them as if to kings" (*Phdr.* 266c). In the second half of the fifth century, democratic Athens was the intellectual center of the

[68] For Thrasymachus, see Quincey 1981; White 1995; Vegetti 1998: 233–56; Nails 2002: 288–90; Barney 2006 and 2017; Narcy 2016; Wedgwood 2017.

Greek world, and it attracted visiting writers, artists and teachers from all over. Some were invited by prosperous residents of Athens as a way of enhancing their prestige as cultural leaders, much as tyrants in other poleis had drawn poets like Pindar and Aeschylus to their court, and many of these visitors can be found in the pages of Plato's dialogues. In *Protagoras*, Callias, the wealthiest man in Athens, hosts the sophists Protagoras, Prodicus and Hippias, who are in the city to recruit students who can afford their high-priced tuition.[69] There is no indication in that dialogue of the time of year at which the conversation is supposed to have taken place, but clearly visitors were more likely to come to Athens at the time of one of the many festivals that regularly attracted foreigners.[70] So, for example, in *Parmenides* the philosophers Zeno and Parmenides have come from Elea at the time of the Panathenaic festival; they are staying with Pythodorus in the Ceramicus, where the young Socrates has the opportunity to converse with them.[71] The Panathenaea is also the occasion for the visit of the statesman Hermocrates of Syracuse and the philosopher and scientist Timaeus of Locri, who are lodged in the home of Plato's relative Critias.[72]

The festival that coincides with Thrasymachus' visit, however, is a recent import into Athens, as is Thrasymachus' host, further indications, perhaps, that Plato wishes to mark *Republic* as a departure from his other dialogues.[73] The metic Cephalus resembles the Athenians who serve as hosts to distinguished visitors in other Platonic dialogues in that he is wealthy and has some intellectual pretentions. More importantly, he has sons who are appropriate candidates for Thrasymachus' tuition. In addition

[69] *Prot.* 311a, 315b–d. One of Callias' houses was in the Piraeus; Xenophon's *Symposium* is set in it. Socrates claims that Callias "paid more money to sophists than everyone else combined," presumably for the education of his two sons (*Apol.* 20a).

[70] Similarly, the Olympic and other Panhellenic Games were a popular venue for sophists and others to display their skills in the hopes of attracting students and clients from the wider Greek world; see *Hp.Mi.* 363c–364a, 368b–d, Dio Chrys. 8.9–12, Luc. *Herod.* 1, *Peregr.* 3. In Athens such festivals included the dramatic competitions at the Great Dionysia, held at a time when, during the existence of the Delian League, representatives of the allied cities brought their monetary contributions to Athens. By contrast, Agathon's first victory, celebrated in *Symposium* (above, n. 39), was at the Lenaea, which took place before the sailing season began, so that, unlike in *Republic*, which is set in the summertime, all the guests are Athenians.

[71] *Parm.* 127a–c. Elsewhere (*Alc.I* 119a4–6) we are told that Pythodorus attained intellectual respectability by paying 100 minas to Zeno; for a sense of the value of this figure, see 337d6n.

[72] *Tim.* 20c–d, 26e; for the date, see n. 6.

[73] See above, section 3.

to Polemarchus, whom we have met, Cephalus had two younger sons, Euthydemus and Lysias, who are present, along with Thrasymachus, when Socrates and Glaucon arrive at Cephalus' house (328b), although neither of them speaks in the course of *Republic.* About Euthydemus almost nothing is known; he is in any event to be distinguished from the sophist from Chios who gives his name to another of Plato's dialogues. Lysias is the famous rhetorician, several of whose speeches survive; a caricature of his style can be found in *Phaedrus.*[74] His silence in *Republic* seems to be intended by Plato as an indication of his youth at the time at which the conversation is supposed to have taken place. While the date of Lysias' birth is not known, it is likely to have been in the mid-440s BC, which would make him a teenager in 429.[75]

Equally uncertain is the date of Thrasymachus' birth. His notoriety in Athens as early as 427 would be confirmed if we could be confident that the Thrasymachus named in Aristophanes' lost *Banqueters,* produced in that year, was the rhetorician from Chalcedon. In a fragment of that play (205 *PCG*) a father abuses his dissolute son for the outlandish vocabulary he is accused of having learned from orators and advocates, ῥήτορες and ξυνήγοροι, addressing him in line 8 as "Thrasymachus." It is generally assumed that this is the father's way of branding his son as a devotee of the latest linguistic fads, calling him by the name of a prominent representative.[76] At any rate, Aristotle, in discussing the development of rhetorical theory, locates Thrasymachus after Tisias and before Theodorus of Byzantium.[77] He would thus seem to be ten to fifteen years older than Lysias and a suitable age to serve as tutor in rhetoric to the aspiring

[74] *Phdr.* 230e–234c. See Nails 2002: 151 for Euthydemus and 190–4 for Lysias.

[75] See Todd 2007: 5–17 for a full discussion of the evidence. As we have seen, a dramatic date of 429 creates difficulties of its own. Regardless, what Plato presents in the setting of his dialogue is a connection between Lysias, whose reticence is attributable to his age, and Thrasymachus, who, as the only non-resident present at the gathering, has the status of a visiting celebrity.

[76] Storey (1988), however, raises serious questions about this interpretation, arguing that Thrasymachus is actually the name Aristophanes has given to the feisty son, coined as an appropriate designation, in the manner of "Dicaeopolis" and "Strepsiades." If he is right, we must reckon with the remarkable coincidence that a notably feisty orator named Thrasymachus – the name is not common – in fact attained prominence around the time of the production of *Banqueters.*

[77] Arist. *SE* 183b32–3 = DK 85 A2 = 35 D7 Laks–Most. Cicero, quoting Aristotle (*Brutus* 12.46 = Arist. fr. 137 Rose), puts the activity of Tisias in the aftermath of the Sicilian tyrannies, that is, in the middle of the fifth century. Little is known about Theodorus (Nails 2002: 281), but given the proximity of Byzantium to Chalcedon one wonders if he was not a pupil of Thrasymachus; Plato ridicules him for inventing outlandish technical terminology (*Phdr.* 266d–e).

orator.[78] There is no evidence that Lysias was in fact Thrasymachus' pupil, but it serves Plato's purpose to associate them, as he does in *Phaedrus* when he refers to the methodological approach to the art adopted by the two of them.[79] As far as we can tell, the technique of Lysias does not resemble that of Thrasymachus, of whose writings we have only a little over 300 words, almost all of which come from a single fragment. Dionysius regards the two men as representatives of different styles, Lysias of the "plain and simple," Thrasymachus of the "mixed" (*Dem.* 2–3). But it is all the same to Plato, for whom all rhetoric as it has been practiced up to his day is fraudulent, since it makes no pretense of aiming at the truth.[80]

We are thus encouraged to assume that Thrasymachus' presence in Athens is occasioned by an interest on the part of Cephalus and his sons in having the distinguished rhetorician share his wisdom, for a price, with one or more of those sons. But why has Plato chosen to introduce his large-scale investigation into the nature of justice with a lengthy conversation between Socrates and a specialist in rhetorical theory? As we have seen, Socrates is usually seen interrogating people who are recognized experts in the topic under discussion.[81] In the case of Euthyphro, Laches and Nicias their knowledge concerning piety and courage is presupposed by their professional experience, and the acknowledgment of Charmides' sophrosyne is the very occasion for the discussion of that virtue. But until Thrasymachus' abrupt intervention his presence has been completely ignored, apart from the initial mention of him as one of the guests in Cephalus' house. To a certain degree this is a literary device serving to enhance the impact of Thrasymachus' dramatic entry into the conversation. But it also prompts the question of what exactly is Thrasymachus' area of expertise. Plato supplies no reason for us to believe that he had, or was thought to have, some special insight into the nature of justice. Rather, he was a teacher of rhetorical technique and author of technical

[78] Dionysius of Halicarnassus, writing in the time of Augustus, considers Lysias to be older than Thrasymachus (*Lys.* 6), but his dating of Lysias' birth is based on inference from faulty assumptions (Todd 2007: 7).

[79] ἧι [*sc.* μεθόδωι] Λυσίας τε καὶ Θρασύμαχος πορεύεται, *Phdr.* 269d7. By the time of the (uncertain) dramatic date of *Phaedrus*, Lysias has established himself as a leading orator.

[80] See *Gorg.* 454d–455a, 471e–472b, *Phdr.* 267a, 272d, 273b. For Plato's Socrates, the ἀρετή of the orator is to tell the truth (*Apol.* 18a5–6). That he loses his case points to the contrast between Socrates' practice and that of his prosecutors, experienced public speakers who succeed in persuading the jurors to convict on baseless grounds.

[81] This departure from the pattern seen in *Charmides, Euthyphro* and *Laches* perhaps supplies another argument against the theory that Book One was originally a self-contained aporetic dialogue.

treatises. In *Phaedrus* Socrates claims that he characterized himself as "expert in provoking crowds to anger and then, once their ire has been aroused, enchanting them with spells" and as "unsurpassed at both producing and invalidating defamations regardless of their source."[82] The titles of some of his writings seem to confirm this description: his Ἔλεοι must have dealt with verbal strategies for arousing pity, and his Ὑπερβάλλοντες [*sc.* λόγοι] with methods of counteracting opponents' arguments.[83] It may be, then, that his appearance in *Republic* is owed to his skill as a controversialist rather than to his political or moral outlook, if indeed he had coherent and well-defined views on these matters.

When Thrasymachus erupts at 336b, Plato ensures that we know that he has been impatiently awaiting an opportunity to join the conversation, frustrated by the unwillingness of Socrates to provide his own definition of justice. Unless Socrates expresses a point of view, there is nothing for Thrasymachus to counteract, and he is deprived of a potent means of displaying his skill in argumentation in order to impress potential clients. That being the case, he resorts to goading Socrates into begging him to define justice himself, and the definition he gives is guaranteed to provoke a spirited reaction from Socrates: "I declare that the just is nothing other than what is advantageous to the superior."[84] Whether this view of justice bears any resemblance to the thinking of the historical Thrasymachus we have no way of knowing, for the few surviving fragments of his work tell us almost nothing about what he himself thought.[85] Even when a source explicitly quotes his words we cannot necessarily tell whether he is expressing his own feelings or those of a client (see 352a10n.) or, indeed, whether the sentiment appeared in a generic model speech created for the purpose of advertising his rhetorical expertise.[86] After all, when Aristotle (*Rhet.* 3.1415a20–1) quotes Sophocles as saying, "My father was Polybus," he understands, and expects his readers to understand, that the poet is not making a statement about himself but is writing words for a character in one of his plays to deliver. Similarly,

[82] *Phdr.* 267c9–d2, ὀργίσαι τε αὖ πολλοὺς ἅμα δεινὸς ... καὶ πάλιν ὠργισμένοις ἐπάιδων κηλεῖν, ... διαβάλλειν τε καὶ ἀπολύσασθαι διαβολὰς ὁθενδὴ κράτιστος. In Book Two Glaucon will observe that this master of casting spells appears himself to have been enchanted (κηληθῆναι, 358b3) by Socrates.

[83] See 336c2, 336e9–337a2nn. for possible allusions to both these works.

[84] 338c2–3. For the extensive bibliography on this definition, which is subjected to scrutiny by Socrates in the ensuing discussion, see Boter 1986 and Barney 2017.

[85] The ancient testimonia and the fragments of his writings are collected in DK, Untersteiner 1954: 2–37 and, most recently, Laks–Most 475–513.

[86] Yunis (1997) argues that the one long excerpt we have (DK 85 B1 = 35 D16 Laks–Most) may in fact have come from one of the model prooemia, Ἀφορμαὶ ῥητορικαί, he is said to have written: *Suda* θ 462 = DK 85 A1 = 35 D2 Laks–Most.

when Lysias writes, "I was accused of uprooting an olive tree" (7.2), we know that he is not speaking *in propria persona.* The same, of course, is true of Plato, who is constantly quoted, by Aristotle and others, as saying X or Y, when in fact it was Crito who said Y and Socrates who said X. We are fortunate to have, apparently, everything Plato wrote, but unless one or two of the Letters are genuine, everything in his works is spoken by someone other than the author. We also have a much fuller set of testimonia for Plato than for Thrasymachus, which, combined with the dialogues, has provided critics with ample material on which an outline of Plato's thought can be based.

We cannot then identify any specific doctrines espoused by Thrasymachus of Chalcedon. Surely we can discover what the fictional Thrasymachus believes or, rather, what Plato wishes to represent him as believing? His discussion with Socrates occupies two thirds of Book One, and he is given every opportunity to defend or amend his original definition. It is true that there has been vigorous debate among scholars regarding whether Thrasymachus maintains a coherent position throughout the discussion (n. 84). But regardless of the question of Thrasymachus' consistency, it emerges from a remarkable passage that whether Thrasymachus actually believes what he says makes no difference to Socrates or, presumably, to Plato. At 349a Socrates expresses amazement that Thrasymachus appears to be serious about his claim that injustice is an admirable and powerful thing (καλὸν καὶ ἰσχυρόν), and that he even goes so far as to put it in the same class as excellence and intelligence (ἐν ἀρετῆι καὶ σοφίαι). When Thrasymachus responds by asking what difference it makes to Socrates whether he really believes this or not, Socrates says, "None." This conflicts with what Plato's Socrates says on some other occasions, that his interlocutor is expected to express his sincerely held beliefs (see 346a3–4n.). And it conflicts with what Nicias says about Socrates' regular practice. Nicias, whose son Niceratus accompanies Polemarchus at the start of *Republic,* is obviously familiar with the manner of Socrates' interrogations, and he explains to Lysimachus (*Lach.* 187d–188a) that everyone who enters into conversation with Socrates on any subject is eventually compelled to give an accounting of how he has spent his life and what kind of life he is presently living. The implication is that the ultimate object of Socrates' investigations is the moral convictions of his interlocutors and the degree to which they have been faithful to those convictions, so that truthful answers to Socrates' questions are essential. This is the Socrates familiar from *Apology* (29d–30a, 37e–38a).

The abandonment here of this fundamental principle of the Socratic elenchus, called by Gregory Vlastos "the 'say what you believe' requirement," marks yet another significant shift in Plato's compositional practice.[87] And Plato goes out of his way to draw our attention to his abandonment of the principle by having Socrates say to Thrasymachus, immediately before he summarily dismisses the say-what-you-believe requirement, "I must not shy away from engaging with and scrutinizing your argument, *as long as I am correct in assuming that you are saying just what you think.*"[88] When one interacts with real people in the palaestra or the agora with the aim of effecting a change in their moral outlook, as Socrates was in the habit of doing, it is essential that they respond by expressing their sincere beliefs. Plato had been experimenting during the early part of his career with trying to represent that kind of interaction in his writing. In *Apology* he has Socrates describe the hostility he aroused among experts in various fields when he subjected them to his unremitting interrogation, exposing their intellectual and moral failings. *Ion* and *Euthyphro* dramatize such encounters, but whether the rhapsode or the prophet has changed his outlook or behavior we do not know, since each of them leaves the stage before they can tell us or show us. In two works belonging to a somewhat later stage of his career Plato does attempt to give us some insight into the effect of being interrogated by Socrates by providing (fictionalized) first-person accounts by men who, like Nicias, claim to be acquainted with the experience. The title character of *Meno*, an admirer of Gorgias who says that he has given many lectures on the subject of ἀρετή himself, reveals under questioning by Socrates that he is now unable even to say what ἀρετή is, and he compares the helplessness he feels to the paralysis brought on by the sting of an electric ray, "for in truth both my mind and my tongue are numb."[89] Meno's statement is prompted by the feeling of aporia induced by Socrates' fifteen-minute elenchus, although he says that he was expecting some such experience, having heard stories from others before he had even met Socrates. What he heard must have been similar to what Alcibiades tells his fellow symposiasts, based on his intimate acquaintance with Socrates' practice (*Symp.* 215d–216c): he is overwhelmed and transfixed, captivated as if by the Sirens, yet he wishes to run away and never see the man again because

[87] Vlastos 1994: 7. For criticism of Vlastos' treatment of the requirement, or "constraint," see Beversluis 2000: 37–58, preferring to refer to the "sincere assent requirement," with discussion of *Rep.* 349a at 236–7.

[88] ἕως ἂν σε ὑπολαμβάνω λέγειν ἅπερ διανοῆι, 349a5.

[89] *Meno* 80a–b. For the historical Meno, see Nails 2002: 204–5, quoting Xenophon's firsthand assessment of his character – Meno was, like Xenophon, an officer in the mercenary army recruited by Cyrus the Younger – which makes him sound like an embodiment of the very qualities that are so warmly admired by Plato's Thrasymachus (Xen. *Anab.* 2.6.21–6).

Socrates makes him feel shame at his failure to subject his own behavior to moral scrutiny.

The aim of the Socratic elenchus is to compel the interlocutor to justify himself as a moral agent. In a series of dialogues Plato first shows us the elenchus in action and then has two of its participants, Alcibiades and Meno, describe how they were affected by being subjected to Socrates' questioning. By the time he wrote *Republic* Plato must have come to realize that doing philosophy by trying to replicate in writing the give and take of the Socratic elenchus had major limitations. In particular, the disorienting effect the in-person elenchus seems to have had by revealing its victim's firmly held beliefs to be invalid could not be expected to carry over in the case of the reader of a written dialogue, who may not have held those same beliefs, or may not have held them as firmly as Euthyphro or Meno. Indeed, Plato would disparage the very medium of writing as a vehicle for serious philosophical inquiry at the conclusion of his *Phaedrus* and in his Seventh Letter.[90] The Letter certainly and *Phaedrus* most likely postdate *Republic*.[91] Still, Plato would not abandon the written word, nor would he forsake the dialogue form.

With *Republic* the character of Plato's writing, and with it the persona of Socrates, enters a more straightforwardly didactic phase, while still maintaining the conversational mode for which he was noted.[92] This phase is introduced in Book One with an encounter between Socrates and Thrasymachus that is presented by Plato as embodying everything that can frustrate the successful progress of philosophical inquiry when carried out by means of in-person conversation. At least Socrates and Euthyphro were in agreement that, in attempting to define piety, they were searching for a definition of the same thing, and they could attribute their lack of success to ineptitude on their part. Thrasymachus, however, is unlike other victims of Socratic elenchus. He and Socrates are not talking about the same thing when they talk about justice, nor can he be brought to a point of admitting that he may be mistaken about its nature. On the

[90] 341b–344d. Whether the Seventh Letter is genuine or not continues to be subject to vigorous disagreement among scholars.

[91] The Seventh Letter was written after 354, since it refers to the death of Dion in that year. Stylistic considerations place *Phaedrus* shortly after *Republic* (Ledger 1989: 209–10), and Plato seems in fact to allude playfully to *Republic* in his denigration of writing as a serious occupation when Phaedrus exclaims (276e1–3) what a fine pastime (παιδιά) it is when one has the opportunity to amuse oneself in words (ἐν λόγοις ... παίζειν) by talking about justice and other such things; cf. *Rep.* 7.536c1 ἐπαίζομεν, referring to the imaginative project of *Republic*.

[92] See especially Blondell 2002: 190–228. For Plato's temporary return, after *Republic*, to the aporetic dialogue with *Theaetetus* and the various attempts to account for it, see Giannopoulou 2013; Brown 2018.

contrary, he repeatedly and confidently insists on the extent of his knowledge.[93] This makes him incapable of learning and, consequently, poses an obstacle to his, and the reader's, progress toward an understanding of the nature of justice. The reader, presumably, shares the position of Socrates and Glaucon that justice is to be prized and is preferable to injustice.[94] But Thrasymachus claims not to accept, or pretends that he does not accept, the view held by most people that justice is a virtue. He resists Socrates' suggestion that he must therefore regard it as a vice (348c10–d1). Rather, for Thrasymachus, the person who behaves in a manner that is universally considered just is simply benighted, forgoing all the supposed benefits of acting unjustly, namely wealth and power and being the object of others' envy. This attitude on the part of Thrasymachus, as Socrates himself points out (348e), means that it is especially difficult for Socrates to bring to light an inconsistency in Thrasymachus' thinking, and he must resort to a questionable argument from analogy (see 349b1–350e10n.). The difference between the two is not that they cannot agree on which acts are to be regarded as just and which unjust. Both men would acknowledge that it is just to obey the laws and to tell the truth. Where they differ is in their fundamental assessment of the value to the agent of obeying laws and speaking truthfully. Nor is it even clear that Thrasymachus' assessment represents his sincerely held belief. This being the case, no further progress can be made, and the conversation between Socrates and Thrasymachus, who is impervious to the effects of the elenchus, of necessity runs into a dead end.

According to a particularly poetic passage in the Seventh Letter (344a–b), progress can be made only through face-to-face interaction between individuals who have a natural affinity with things that are just and with things that are otherwise admirable. Only such interaction, carried out over a long period of time and involving the assessment and testing of ideas by means of a series of well-meaning cross-examinations (ἐν εὐμενέσιν ἐλέγχοις) engaged in by those who pose questions and deliver answers with no sense of rivalry (ἄνευ φθόνων ἐρωτήσεσιν καὶ ἀποκρίσεσιν χρωμένων), can result in the spark of enlightenment catching on and bursting into flame (ἐξέλαμψε φρόνησις). Depending on whether the Letter is genuine or not, this ideal of in-person philosophical dialogue must be modeled on

[93] 337a5, 341a8, 345e4, 350e1. Contrast Polemarchus' admission of ignorance (οὐκέτι οἶδα ἔγωγε ὅτι ἔλεγον, 334b6) and Socrates' own confession in the last sentence of Book One that he does not know what justice is. Given the proper circumstances, however, namely the congenial fellowship of Glaucon and Adeimantus, Socrates will succeed in defining justice in Book Four.

[94] 336e7 (more valuable than gold), 345a2–4, 347e7, 352d1–5.

testimony about, or direct recollection of, the interaction between Plato himself and Socrates, which in turn surely served as the inspiration for the way in which Plato engaged with his pupils and associates. Plato's continuing commitment to the written word, however, along with his lifelong reluctance to represent himself as speaking any of the words that appear in his published writings, encouraged him to cast aside such interlocutors as Thrasymachus and Callicles (in *Gorgias*) in preference for more sympathetic characters, like Theaetetus and his own brothers, for whose sincerity he could vouch.

(e) Adeimantus and Glaucon

Apart from the fleeting appearance of Glaucon in the opening frame narrative of *Symposium*, neither of Plato's brothers plays a role in a dialogue earlier than *Republic*.[95] Their role in Book One is limited, but they will take over as Socrates' interlocutors for the remainder of *Republic*, becoming the cofounders, along with Socrates, of Callipolis.[96] Of all the characters in Plato's dialogues, they are the ones with whom the author was most intimately familiar, and it is reasonable to assume that his characterization of them is true to life; they are not idealized as is Socrates, nor are they caricatured like Prodicus in *Protagoras*. Adeimantus was the older of the two and the less intensely committed to philosophical inquiry. Consequently, his contribution to the discussion in Books Two through Ten, though substantial, is on a smaller scale than that of his brother. This disparity is anticipated in Book One, in which Adeimantus utters only a single sentence of little consequence (328a1–2). By contrast, Glaucon speaks up (337d8–9) in response to Thrasymachus' demand for a fee, and his intervention at 347a6 provides Socrates with an opportunity to explain what he means by the penalty for refusing to rule. This leads in turn to a brief exchange between Socrates and Glaucon regarding how they should go about persuading Thrasymachus that justice is superior to injustice. Glaucon's preference – for proceeding through a series of mutually agreed-upon stages rather than by means of a confrontation between set speeches aimed at influencing the feelings of an external audience – is of course the Socratic

95 For Adeimantus and Glaucon, see Nails 2002: 2–3 and 154–6. The Glaucon who is named at *Symp.* 172c3 without identification of his father or deme is generally assumed to be Plato's brother; see Rowe (1998) on 172a3. Adeimantus is mentioned, along with Plato, as being present at Socrates' trial (*Apol.* 34a1–2). Both of Plato's brothers, as well as his half-brother Antiphon, appear briefly in the opening narrative of (the later) *Parmenides*.

96 Blondell 2002: 206. Blondell's entire treatment of the two brothers (190–228) is especially sensitive and valuable.

method that Plato has been transposing into the written mode. This is not Thrasymachus' preference, and he complains that Socrates will not let him discourse at length (350d7–e4). The attempt at persuasion is therefore inconclusive, and a different, and more productive, method needs to be adopted. At the beginning of Book Two, after no satisfactory definition of justice has been reached, Adeimantus and Glaucon will emerge as the saviors of the inquiry, by resuscitating Thrasymachus' argument, while making it clear that they are not expressing their sincerely held beliefs, in the hopes that Socrates can demonstrate conclusively the superiority of justice to injustice, in the manner recommended in the Seventh Letter, by means of a series of well-meaning discussions devoid of any sense of rivalry. The brothers are the ideal participants in such a discussion, since they lack Thrasymachus' antagonistic spirit. At the same time, they are not so compliant as Polemarchus, who had put up no serious resistance to Socrates' questioning. On the contrary, the uncompromising thoroughness with which they reformulate Thrasymachus' argument causes Socrates to praise the martial spirit of "the sons of Ariston" (2.368a4). It is, therefore, for good reason that Plato, another son of Ariston, has chosen Adeimantus and Glaucon to serve as Socrates' interlocutors for the remainder of this, his most daring and far-reaching effort to convey his philosophical thinking in written form.

5 THE TRANSMISSION OF PLATO'S TEXT

Given that more than two millennia separate us from the time when Plato composed *Republic*, and given that the oldest manuscript that preserves the full text of the work was written over a dozen centuries after the death of the author, it is perhaps surprising that there are few substantive differences between one modern edition of his text and another.[97] This is in striking contrast to the vigorous disagreements over how to interpret what the generally accepted text of Plato says.[98] It also contrasts with the variation among editions of, say, Aeschylus, whose poetic language is quite remote from that spoken by the scribes who struggled to preserve his text.

[97] See Slings' verdict (1998: 93) in his review of the first volume of the new Oxford Classical Text: "The text is not all that different from Burnet's." Major disagreements among editors have for the most part been concerned with the assessment of the value of a given manuscript for the constitution of the text; see Boter (1989: 3–22) on the *status quaestionis.*

[98] See, for example, the controversy aroused by Karl Popper's (1945) reading of *Republic* as, essentially, a training manual for modern dictatorship: Levinson 1953; Bambrough 1967.

We are fortunate in having more than fifty manuscripts that preserve the Greek text of all or parts of Plato's *Republic*.[99] But that number is deceptive, since several of the manuscripts that we now have can be shown to be descended, either directly or through intermediaries, from three of the surviving manuscripts, which are therefore considered primary, that is, as independent witnesses to what Plato wrote:

A = Parisinus gr. 1807. Date: ninth century. Contents: Tetralogies VIII–IX, the *Definitiones* and the *Spuria*.[100] See Boter 1989: 45–8, 80–91; Jonkers 2017: 65–8, 93–6, 149–62.

D = Venice, Marcianus gr. 185. Date: twelfth century. Contents: Tetralogies I–IV plus *Clitophon* and *Republic*. See Boter 1989: 57–8, 91–9.

F = Vindobonensis suppl. gr. 39. Date: thirteenth or fourteenth century. Contents: from the middle of Tetralogy VI (*Gorgias* and *Meno*) to the beginning of IX (*Minos*). See Dodds 1959: 41–7; Bluck 1961: 135–40; Boter 1989: 62–4, 99–110; Jonkers 2017: 89, 97–100, 165–75.

Agreement among these three does not necessarily represent exactly what Plato wrote, since they may all preserve an ancient error. Nor should we regard the evidence of the secondary manuscripts as worthless, since the manuscript tradition of Plato has been subject to a great deal of "contamination," that is, the adoption by a scribe of one or more readings that result from comparison with a source other than the scribe's principal or sole exemplar, a source that may no longer be available. The term, given its shared etymology with "contagion" and its association with defilement and disease, is unfortunate. Textual critics use the term in connection with a manuscript tradition that resists their efforts to determine pure lines of descent. In fact, a correct reading – that is, a reading that reflects what Plato actually wrote – can appear in a manuscript for reasons other than the scribe's accurate transcription of the text of the scribe's primary source. It can arise from contamination (which may include consultation not only of manuscripts of Plato but also of manuscripts of authors who quote the Platonic text), from conjecture or even from inadvertence, since the same factors that can cause a scribe to write ἡμῶν for an original ὑμῶν may lead to the accidental correction of a corrupt ἡμῶν. Each

[99] Boter 1989: xx. Boter provides a comprehensive treatment of the manuscript tradition. To date eleven papyri of *Republic* have been published, of which only one, *POxy*. 3509, relates to Book One (1989: 253); it appears to anticipate a correction made by Richards (see the apparatus at 330a6).

[100] For Thrasyllus' tetralogic arrangement of the dialogues, see above, n. 3. Tetralogy VIII consists of *Clitophon*, *Republic*, *Timaeus* and *Critias*.

variant reading, therefore, regardless of its source, needs to be evaluated on its merits, taking into consideration meaning, Platonic usage and likely causes of corruption.[101]

The reason for the contamination of the Platonic manuscript tradition is in fact the same as the reason for the general reliability of the text that it preserves. For the works of Plato were fundamental to the study and the teaching that took place in the school that carried on the tradition of Platonic philosophy and which continued in existence, although not necessarily in the same location or even always in Athens, for several centuries. While there is no explicit evidence that the Academy housed a library or anything like an "official" text of the works of Plato, those works were very well known to Plato's pupils and followers, scholars like Aristotle and Plato's nephew Speusippus, and it is surely likely that they had access, if not to the Master's autographs, at least to first- or second-generation copies, probably in the Academy itself.[102] These philosophers and their successors will have wanted, and will have known how to procure, reliable texts of Plato's dialogues. They would therefore be expected to compare the text to which they had access with others for the purposes of correcting their copy or supplementing it by writing variants in the margin or between the lines.[103] This should not be thought of as wanton miscegenation but as an attempt to accomplish just what modern editors hope to do, namely to come as close as possible to recreating the original text. Scholars or scribes might introduce variants not only from other manuscripts of *Republic* but from manuscripts of works that quote or comment on Plato's text. Because *Republic* was widely studied and discussed, both in the Academy and outside it, the text was frequently referred to and quoted. The authors represented in the copious testimonia range in date from Aristotle to Eustathius, the twelfth-century Archbishop of Thessalonica.[104]

[101] See the apparatus at 353d6 (with n.) and 354b4 for instances of secondary manuscripts (*recentiores*) seeming to have a correct reading not found in **ADF**.

[102] Lygouri-Tolia (2020) has recently argued that the large (40 × 40 m) peristyle dating to the third century BC, the foundations of which were excavated near the intersection of Monastiriou and Eukleidou streets, was in fact the site of the library of the Academy.

[103] For an example of this in Book One, see the apparatus to 345c3. This can lead to corruption as well as to improvement, as when a gloss intrudes into the text, as at 335a8, or is mistaken for a variant reading and replaces the true reading; see 349b5n.

[104] For the value of the indirect tradition of *Republic*, see Boter 1989: 285–9, with a full listing of the testimonia to Book One at 290–7; a selection is given in Slings' Oxford Classical Text (2003: 411–12). These include not only direct quotations but also references and allusions, from which the reading in the text used by the author can sometimes be inferred. When Cicero quotes from *Republic* (see 329b4, c2, 331c5nn.), he does so in his own elegant Latin translations.

And, given that the work is notable not only for its philosophical importance but also for its literary merit, the authors quoting it include, in addition to the expected Academic and Neoplatonic commentators, the critics known as "Demetrius" and "Longinus" as well as the anthologist Stobaeus, the satirist Lucian and a number of Christian authors for whom Plato was an eloquent pagan precursor.[105] As can be seen, however, from the abbreviated apparatus given below, which is generally representative of the state of transmission of the text, the indirect tradition is for the most part limited to supporting one reading or another that was already known from the direct tradition, and rarely preserves a unique reading that deserves our consideration.[106] We should note that these quoting authors have their own manuscript traditions that are at least as open to corruption as that of Plato, and some of those authors (e.g. Eustathius) are themselves later than the earliest witness in the direct tradition.

The text of Book One below relies gratefully upon the tireless efforts of those who have collated Plato's manuscripts and have searched the texts of those later authors who quote from *Republic.* In particular, Gerard Boter's monograph provides a detailed study of the manuscripts and their relations, as well as a compilation of the testimonia, and Simon Slings' Oxford Classical Text, which has benefited greatly from Boter's researches, is the source on which the reporting of manuscript readings in this edition depends. The apparatus given has been severely reduced, and the reader is referred to Slings' text for a fuller account of the manuscript evidence. The choice of readings differs from Slings' in only a handful of places, usually with some justification given in the commentary.[107] There is, however, one way in which the presentation of this text differs in a noticeable way from the Oxford Classical Text and from previous printed editions, namely in using *scriptio plena* throughout.[108] The treatment of elision and crasis in papyri, medieval manuscripts and, consequently, in printed texts is inconsistent and incoherent and cannot be held to provide evidence for Plato's practice.

[105] See now Tarrant et al. 2018 for the reception of Plato in antiquity down to the sixth century.

[106] The same, unfortunately, is true of the scholia, now expertly edited by Cufalo (2011), which are of little value for the constitution of the text of *Republic.*

[107] See 330a6, b1, e4, 331e3, 349b5, 352b1, 353d6nn.

[108] For a single exception, where *scriptio plena* would make no sense, see 339a1n. In addition, an attempt has been made to be consistent in printing nu-*ephelkystikon* only before vowels or marks of punctuation, regardless of the practice of manuscripts and earlier editions.

ΠΛΑΤΩΝΟΣ ΠΟΛΙΤΕΙΑΣ Α

ΠΛΑΤΩΝΟΣ ΠΟΛΙΤΕΙΑΣ Α

Κατέβην χθὲς εἰς Πειραιᾶ μετὰ Γλαύκωνος τοῦ Ἀρίστωνος 327
προσευξόμενός τε τῆι θεῶι καὶ ἅμα τὴν ἑορτὴν βουλόμενος θεάσασθαι τίνα τρόπον ποιήσουσιν ἅτε νῦν πρῶτον ἄγοντες. καλὴ
μὲν οὖν μοι καὶ ἡ τῶν ἐπιχωρίων πομπὴ ἔδοξεν εἶναι, οὐ μέντοι
ἧττον ἐφαίνετο πρέπειν ἣν οἱ Θρᾶικες ἔπεμπον. προσευξάμενοι
δὲ καὶ θεωρήσαντες ἀπῆιμεν πρὸς τὸ ἄστυ. κατιδὼν οὖν πόρρω- b
θεν ἡμᾶς οἴκαδε ὡρμημένους Πολέμαρχος ὁ Κεφάλου ἐκέλευσε
δραμόντα τὸν παῖδα περιμεῖναί ἑ κελεῦσαι. καί μου ὄπισθεν ὁ παῖς
λαβόμενος τοῦ ἱματίου, Κελεύει ὑμᾶς, ἔφη, Πολέμαρχος περιμεῖναι.
καὶ ἐγὼ μετεστράφην τε καὶ ἠρόμην ὅπου αὐτὸς εἴη. Οὗτος, ἔφη,
ὄπισθεν προσέρχεται· ἀλλὰ περιμένετε. Ἀλλὰ περιμενοῦμεν, ἦ δὲ
ὃς ὁ Γλαύκων.

Καὶ ὀλίγωι ὕστερον ὅ τε Πολέμαρχος ἧκε καὶ Ἀδείμαντος ὁ τοῦ c
Γλαύκωνος ἀδελφὸς καὶ Νικήρατος ὁ Νικίου καὶ ἄλλοι τινὲς ὡς
ἀπὸ τῆς πομπῆς.

Ὁ οὖν Πολέμαρχος ἔφη· Ὦ Σώκρατες, δοκεῖτέ μοι πρὸς ἄστυ ὡρμῆσθαι ὡς ἀπιόντες.

Οὐ γὰρ κακῶς δοξάζεις, ἦν δὲ ἐγώ.

Ὁρᾶις οὖν ἡμᾶς, ἔφη, ὅσοι ἐσμέν;

Πῶς γὰρ οὔ;

Ἢ τοίνυν τούτων, ἔφη, κρείττους γένεσθε ἢ μένετε αὐτοῦ.

Οὐκοῦν, ἦν δὲ ἐγώ, ἔτι ἐλλείπεται τὸ ἢν πείσωμεν ὑμᾶς ὡς χρὴ ἡμᾶς ἀφεῖναι;

Ἦ καὶ δύναισθε ἄν, ἦ δὲ ὅς, πεῖσαι μὴ ἀκούοντας;

Οὐδαμῶς, ἔφη ὁ Γλαύκων.

Ὡς τοίνυν μὴ ἀκουσομένων, οὕτω διανοεῖσθε.

Καὶ ὁ Ἀδείμαντος, Ἆρά γε, ἦ δὲ ὅς, οὐδὲ ἴστε ὅτι λαμπὰς ἔσται 328
πρὸς ἑσπέραν ἀφ' ἵππων τῆι θεῶι;

Ἀφ' ἵππων; ἦν δὲ ἐγώ· καινόν γε τοῦτο. λαμπάδια ἔχοντες διαδώσουσιν ἀλλήλοις ἁμιλλώμενοι τοῖς ἵπποις; ἢ πῶς λέγεις;

Οὕτως, ἔφη ὁ Πολέμαρχος. καὶ πρός γε παννυχίδα ποιήσουσιν, ἣν ἄξιον θεάσασθαι· ἐξαναστησόμεθα γὰρ μετὰ τὸ δεῖπνον
καὶ τὴν παννυχίδα θεασόμεθα. καὶ συνεσόμεθά τε πολλοῖς τῶν
νέων αὐτόθι καὶ διαλεξόμεθα. ἀλλὰ μένετε καὶ μὴ ἄλλως ποιεῖτε. b

Καὶ ὁ Γλαύκων, Ἔοικεν, ἔφη, μενετέον εἶναι.

Ἀλλ᾽ εἰ δοκεῖ, ἦν δ᾽ ἐγώ, οὕτω χρὴ ποιεῖν.

Ἦιμεν οὖν οἴκαδε εἰς τοῦ Πολεμάρχου, καὶ Λυσίαν τε αὐτόθι
κατελάβομεν καὶ Εὐθύδημον, τοὺς τοῦ Πολεμάρχου ἀδελφούς,
καὶ δὴ καὶ Θρασύμαχον τὸν Καλχηδόνιον καὶ Χαρμαντίδην τὸν
Παιανιᾶ καὶ Κλειτοφῶντα τὸν Ἀριστωνύμου· ἦν δ᾽ ἔνδον καὶ ὁ
πατὴρ ὁ τοῦ Πολεμάρχου Κέφαλος. καὶ μάλα πρεσβύτης μοι
c ἔδοξεν εἶναι· διὰ χρόνου γὰρ καὶ ἑωράκη αὐτόν. καθῆστο δὲ
ἐστεφανωμένος ἐπί τινος προσκεφαλαίου τε καὶ δίφρου· τεθυκὼς
γὰρ ἐτύγχανεν ἐν τῆι αὐλῆι. ἐκαθεζόμεθα οὖν παρ᾽ αὐτόν· ἔκειντο
γὰρ δίφροι τινὲς αὐτόθι κύκλωι.

Εὐθὺς οὖν με ἰδὼν ὁ Κέφαλος ἠσπάζετό τε καὶ εἶπεν· Ὦ Σώκρατες, οὐδὲ θαμίζεις ἡμῖν καταβαίνων εἰς τὸν Πειραιᾶ. χρῆν
μέντοι. εἰ μὲν γὰρ ἐγὼ ἔτι ἐν δυνάμει ἦ τοῦ ῥαιδίως πορεύεσθαι
d πρὸς τὸ ἄστυ, οὐδὲν ἂν σὲ ἔδει δεῦρο ἰέναι, ἀλλ᾽ ἡμεῖς ἂν παρὰ
σὲ ἦιμεν· νῦν δέ σε χρὴ πυκνότερον δεῦρο ἰέναι. ὡς εὖ ἴσθι ὅτι
ἔμοιγε ὅσον αἱ ἄλλαι αἱ κατὰ τὸ σῶμα ἡδοναὶ ἀπομαραίνονται,
τοσοῦτον αὔξονται αἱ περὶ τοὺς λόγους ἐπιθυμίαι τε καὶ ἡδοναί.
μὴ οὖν ἄλλως ποίει, ἀλλὰ τοῖσδέ τε τοῖς νεανίαις σύνισθι καὶ
δεῦρο παρ᾽ ἡμᾶς φοίτα ὡς παρὰ φίλους τε καὶ πάνυ οἰκείους.

Καὶ μήν, ἦν δ᾽ ἐγώ, ὦ Κέφαλε, χαίρω γε διαλεγόμενος τοῖς
e σφόδρα πρεσβύταις· δοκεῖ γάρ μοι χρῆναι παρ᾽ αὐτῶν πυνθάνε-
σθαι, ὥσπερ τινὰ ὁδὸν προεληλυθότων ἣν καὶ ἡμᾶς ἴσως δεήσει
πορεύεσθαι, ποία τίς ἐστιν, τραχεῖα καὶ χαλεπὴ ἢ ῥαιδία καὶ εὔπορος. καὶ δὴ καὶ σοῦ ἡδέως ἂν πυθοίμην ὅτι σοι φαίνεται τοῦτο,
ἐπειδὴ ἐνταῦθα ἤδη εἶ τῆς ἡλικίας, ὃ δὴ "ἐπὶ γήραος οὐδῶι" φασιν
εἶναι οἱ ποιηταί, πότερον χαλεπὸν τοῦ βίου, ἢ πῶς σὺ αὐτὸ
ἐξαγγέλλεις.

329 Ἐγώ σοι, ἔφη, νὴ τὸν Δία ἐρῶ, ὦ Σώκρατες, οἷόν γέ μοι φαίνεται. πολλάκις γὰρ συνερχόμεθά τινες εἰς τὸ αὐτὸ παραπλησίαν
ἡλικίαν ἔχοντες, διασώιζοντες τὴν παλαιὰν παροιμίαν· οἱ οὖν
πλεῖστοι ἡμῶν ὀλοφύρονται συνιόντες, τὰς ἐν τῆι νεότητι ἡδονὰς
ποθοῦντες καὶ ἀναμιμνῃσκόμενοι περί τε τἀφροδίσια καὶ περὶ
πότους τε καὶ εὐωχίας καὶ ἄλλ᾽ ἄττα ἃ τῶν τοιούτων ἔχεται,
καὶ ἀγανακτοῦσιν ὡς μεγάλων τινῶν ἀπεστερημένοι καὶ τότε
b μὲν εὖ ζῶντες, νῦν δὲ οὐδὲ ζῶντες. ἔνιοι δὲ καὶ τὰς τῶν οἰκείων

328c6 οὐδὲ **ADF**: οὔτι Ast   d5 νεανίαις **A** Thom. Mag.: νεανίσκοις **DF** Stob.

προπηλακίσεις τοῦ γήρως ὀδύρονται, καὶ ἐπὶ τούτωι δὴ τὸ γῆρας ὑμνοῦσιν ὅσων κακῶν σφίσιν αἴτιον. ἐμοὶ δὲ δοκοῦσιν, ὦ Σώκρατες, οὗτοι οὐ τὸ αἴτιον αἰτιᾶσθαι· εἰ γὰρ ἦν τοῦτο αἴτιον, καὶ ἂν ἐγὼ τὰ αὐτὰ ταῦτα ἐπεπόνθη, ἕνεκά γε γήρως, καὶ οἱ ἄλλοι πάντες ὅσοι ἐνταῦθα ἦλθον ἡλικίας. νῦν δὲ ἔγωγε ἤδη ἐντετύχηκα οὐχ οὕτως ἔχουσι καὶ ἄλλοις, καὶ δὴ καὶ Σοφοκλεῖ ποτε τῶι ποιητῆι παρεγε-
νόμην ἐρωτωμένωι ὑπό τινος· Πῶς, ἔφη, ὦ Σοφόκλεις, ἔχεις πρὸς c
τὰ ἀφροδίσια; ἔτι οἷός τε εἶ γυναικὶ συγγίγνεσθαι; καὶ ὅς, Εὐφήμει, ἔφη, ὦ ἄνθρωπε· ἁσμενέστατα μέντοι αὐτὸ ἀπέφυγον, ὥσπερ λυττῶντά τινα καὶ ἄγριον δεσπότην ἀποφυγών. εὖ οὖν μοι καὶ τότε ἔδοξεν ἐκεῖνος εἰπεῖν, καὶ νῦν οὐχ ἧττον. παντάπασι γὰρ τῶν γε τοιούτων ἐν τῶι γήραι πολλὴ εἰρήνη γίγνεται καὶ ἐλευθερία· ἐπειδὰν αἱ ἐπιθυμίαι παύσωνται κατατείνουσαι καὶ χαλάσωσιν,
παντάπασι τὸ τοῦ Σοφοκλέους γίγνεται, δεσποτῶν πάνυ πολλῶν d
[ἐστι] καὶ μαινομένων ἀπηλλάχθαι. ἀλλὰ καὶ τούτων πέρι καὶ τῶν γε πρὸς τοὺς οἰκείους μία τις αἰτία ἐστίν, οὐ τὸ γῆρας, ὦ Σώκρατες, ἀλλ᾽ ὁ τρόπος τῶν ἀνθρώπων. ἂν μὲν γὰρ κόσμιοι καὶ εὔκολοι ὦσιν, καὶ τὸ γῆρας μετρίως ἐστὶν ἐπίπονον· εἰ δὲ μή, καὶ γῆρας, ὦ Σώκρατες, καὶ νεότης χαλεπὴ τῶι τοιούτωι συμβαίνει.

Καὶ ἐγὼ ἀγασθεὶς αὐτοῦ εἰπόντος ταῦτα, βουλόμενος ἔτι λέγειν
αὐτὸν ἐκίνουν καὶ εἶπον· Ὦ Κέφαλε, οἶμαί σου τοὺς πολλούς, ὅταν e
ταῦτα λέγηις, οὐκ ἀποδέχεσθαι ἀλλὰ ἡγεῖσθαί σε ῥαιδίως τὸ γῆρας φέρειν οὐ διὰ τὸν τρόπον ἀλλὰ διὰ τὸ πολλὴν οὐσίαν κεκτῆσθαι· τοῖς γὰρ πλουσίοις πολλὰ παραμύθιά φασιν εἶναι.

Ἀληθῆ, ἔφη, λέγεις· οὐ γὰρ ἀποδέχονται. καὶ λέγουσι μέν τι, οὐ μέντοι γε ὅσον οἴονται· ἀλλὰ τὸ τοῦ Θεμιστοκλέους εὖ ἔχει, ὃς τῶι
Σεριφίωι λοιδορουμένωι καὶ λέγοντι ὅτι οὐ δι᾽ αὐτὸν ἀλλὰ διὰ 330
τὴν πόλιν εὐδοκιμοῖ, ἀπεκρίνατο ὅτι οὔτ᾽ ἂν αὐτὸς Σερίφιος ὢν ὀνομαστὸς ἐγένετο οὔτ᾽ ἐκεῖνος Ἀθηναῖος. καὶ τοῖς δὴ μὴ πλουσίοις, χαλεπῶς δὲ τὸ γῆρας φέρουσιν, εὖ ἔχει ὁ αὐτὸς λόγος, ὅτι οὔτ᾽ ἂν ὁ ἐπιεικὴς πάνυ τι ῥαιδίως γῆρας μετὰ πενίας ἐνέγκοι οὔθ᾽ ὁ μὴ ἐπιεικὴς πλουτήσας εὔκολός ποτ᾽ ἂν ἐν αὐτῶι γένοιτο.

Πότερον δέ, ἦν δ᾽ ἐγώ, ὦ Κέφαλε, ὧν κέκτησαι τὰ πλείω παρέλαβες ἢ ἐπεκτήσω;

329d2 ἐστι del. Stallbaum 330a6 ἐν αὐτῶι Richards, *POxy.* 3509 ut vid.: ἑαυτῶι **ADF**

b Ὁποῖα ἐπεκτησάμην, ἔφη, ὦ Σώκρατες, μέσος τις γέγονα χρηματιστὴς τοῦ τε πάππου καὶ τοῦ πατρός. ὁ μὲν γὰρ πάππος τε καὶ ὁμώνυμος ἐμοὶ σχεδόν τι ὅσην ἐγὼ νῦν οὐσίαν κέκτημαι παραλαβὼν πολλάκις τοσαύτην ἐποίησεν, Λυσανίας δὲ ὁ πατὴρ ἔτι ἐλάττω αὐτὴν ἐποίησε τῆς νῦν οὔσης· ἐγὼ δὲ ἀγαπῶ ἐὰν μὴ ἐλάττω καταλίπω τούτοισιν, ἀλλὰ βραχεῖ γέ τινι πλείω ἢ παρέλαβον.

Οὗ τοι ἕνεκα ἠρόμην, ἦν δὲ ἐγώ, ὅτι μοι ἔδοξας οὐ σφόδρα ἀγα-
c πᾶν τὰ χρήματα, τοῦτο δὲ ποιοῦσιν ὡς τὸ πολὺ οἳ ἂν μὴ αὐτοὶ κτήσωνται· οἱ δὲ κτησάμενοι διπλῆι ἢ οἱ ἄλλοι ἀσπάζονται αὐτά. ὥσπερ γὰρ οἱ ποιηταὶ τὰ αὑτῶν ποιήματα καὶ οἱ πατέρες τοὺς παῖδας ἀγαπῶσιν, ταύτηι τε δὴ καὶ οἱ χρηματισάμενοι τὰ χρήματα σπουδάζουσιν ὡς ἔργον ἑαυτῶν, καὶ κατὰ τὴν χρείαν ἧιπερ οἱ ἄλλοι. χαλεποὶ οὖν καὶ συγγενέσθαι εἰσίν, οὐδὲν ἐθέλοντες ἐπαινεῖν ἀλλὰ ἢ τὸν πλοῦτον.

Ἀληθῆ, ἔφη, λέγεις.

d Πάνυ μὲν οὖν, ἦν δὲ ἐγώ. ἀλλά μοι ἔτι τοσόνδε εἰπέ· τί μέγιστον οἴει ἀγαθὸν ἀπολελαυκέναι τοῦ πολλὴν οὐσίαν κεκτῆσθαι;

Ὅ, ἦ δὲ ὅς, ἴσως οὐκ ἂν πολλοὺς πείσαιμι λέγων. εὖ γὰρ ἴσθι, ἔφη, ὦ Σώκρατες, ὅτι, ἐπειδάν τις ἐγγὺς ἦι τοῦ οἴεσθαι τελευτήσειν, εἰσέρχεται αὐτῶι δέος καὶ φροντὶς περὶ ὧν ἔμπροσθεν οὐκ εἰσήιει. οἵ τε γὰρ λεγόμενοι μῦθοι περὶ τῶν ἐν Ἅιδου, ὡς τὸν ἐνθάδε ἀδικήσαντα δεῖ ἐκεῖ διδόναι δίκην, καταγελώμενοι τέως, τότε δὴ στρέ-
e φουσιν αὐτοῦ τὴν ψυχὴν μὴ ἀληθεῖς ὦσιν, καὶ αὐτός, ἤτοι ὑπὸ τῆς τοῦ γήρως ἀσθενείας ἢ καὶ ὥσπερ ἤδη ἐγγυτέρω ὢν τῶν ἐκεῖ, μᾶλλόν τι καθορᾶι αὐτά· ὑποψίας δὲ οὖν καὶ δείματος μεστὸς γίγνεται καὶ ἀναλογίζεται ἤδη καὶ σκοπεῖ εἴ τινά τι ἠδίκησεν. ὁ μὲν οὖν εὑρίσκων ἑαυτοῦ ἐν τῶι βίωι πολλὰ ἀδικήματα καὶ ἐκ τῶν ὕπνων, ὥσπερ οἱ παῖδες, θαμὰ ἐγειρόμενος δειμαίνει καὶ ζῆι μετὰ
331 κακῆς ἐλπίδος· τῶι δὲ μηδὲν ἑαυτῶι ἄδικον συνειδότι ἡδεῖα ἐλπὶς ἀεὶ πάρεστι καὶ ἀγαθὴ γηροτρόφος, ὡς καὶ Πίνδαρος λέγει. χαριέντως γάρ τοι, ὦ Σώκρατες, τοῦτο ἐκεῖνος εἶπεν, ὅτι ὃς ἂν δικαίως καὶ ὁσίως τὸν βίον διαγάγηι,

γλυκεῖά οἱ καρδίαν
ἀτάλλοισα γηροτρόφος συναορεῖ

330b1 ὁποῖ' Tucker: ποῖ' **ADF** c4 τὰ **F** Stob.: περὶ τὰ **AD** e4 ἠδίκησεν **A**[sl]**D** Iustin.: ἠδίκηκεν **AF** Stob.

Ἐλπίς, ἃ μάλιστα θνατῶν πολύστροφον γνώμαν κυβερνᾶι.

εὖ οὖν λέγει θαυμαστῶς ὡς σφόδρα. πρὸς δὴ τοῦτο ἔγωγε τίθημι τὴν τῶν χρημάτων κτῆσιν πλείστου ἀξίαν εἶναι, οὔ τι παντὶ ἀνδρὶ b ἀλλὰ τῶι ἐπιεικεῖ. τὸ γὰρ μηδὲ ἄκοντά τινα ἐξαπατῆσαι ἢ ψεύσασθαι, μηδὲ αὖ ὀφείλοντα ἢ θεῶι θυσίας τινὰς ἢ ἀνθρώπωι χρήματα ἔπειτα ἐκεῖσε ἀπιέναι δεδιότα, μέγα μέρος εἰς τοῦτο ἡ τῶν χρημάτων κτῆσις συμβάλλεται. ἔχει δὲ καὶ ἄλλας χρείας πολλάς, ἀλλά γε ἓν ἀντὶ ἑνὸς οὐκ ἐλάχιστον ἔγωγε θείην ἂν εἰς τοῦτο ἀνδρὶ νοῦν ἔχοντι, ὦ Σώκρατες, πλοῦτον χρησιμώτατον εἶναι.

Παγκάλως, ἦν δὲ ἐγώ, λέγεις, ὦ Κέφαλε. τοῦτο δὲ αὐτό, τὴν c δικαιοσύνην, πότερα τὴν ἀλήθειαν αὐτὸ φήσομεν εἶναι ἁπλῶς οὕτως καὶ τὸ ἀποδιδόναι ἄν τίς τι παρά του λάβηι, ἢ καὶ αὐτὰ ταῦτα ἔστιν ἐνίοτε μὲν δικαίως, ἐνίοτε δὲ ἀδίκως ποιεῖν; οἷον τοιόνδε λέγω· πᾶς ἄν που εἴποι, εἴ τις λάβοι παρὰ φίλου ἀνδρὸς σωφρονοῦντος ὅπλα, εἰ μανεὶς ἀπαιτοῖ, ὅτι οὔτε χρὴ τὰ τοιαῦτα ἀποδιδόναι, οὔτε δίκαιος ἂν εἴη ὁ ἀποδιδοὺς οὐδὲ αὖ πρὸς τὸν οὕτως ἔχοντα πάντα ἐθέλων τὰ ἀληθῆ λέγειν.

Ὀρθῶς, ἔφη, λέγεις. d

Οὐκ ἄρα οὗτος ὅρος ἐστὶ δικαιοσύνης, ἀληθῆ τε λέγειν καὶ ἃ ἂν λάβηι τις ἀποδιδόναι.

Πάνυ μὲν οὖν, ἔφη, ὦ Σώκρατες, ὑπολαβὼν ὁ Πολέμαρχος, εἴπερ γέ τι χρὴ Σιμωνίδηι πείθεσθαι.

Καὶ μέντοι, ἔφη ὁ Κέφαλος, καὶ παραδίδωμι ὑμῖν τὸν λόγον· δεῖ γάρ με ἤδη τῶν ἱερῶν ἐπιμεληθῆναι.

Οὐκοῦν, ἔφη, ἐγώ, ὁ Πολέμαρχος, τῶν γε σῶν κληρονόμος;

Πάνυ γε, ἦ δὲ ὃς γελάσας, καὶ ἅμα ἤιει πρὸς τὰ ἱερά.

Λέγε δή, εἶπον ἐγώ, σὺ ὁ τοῦ λόγου κληρονόμος· τί φῂς τὸν e Σιμωνίδην λέγοντα ὀρθῶς λέγειν περὶ δικαιοσύνης;

Ὅτι; ἦ δὲ ὅς· τὸ τὰ ὀφειλόμενα ἑκάστωι ἀποδιδόναι δίκαιόν ἐστιν· τοῦτο λέγων δοκεῖ ἔμοιγε καλῶς λέγειν.

Ἀλλὰ μέντοι, ἦν δὲ ἐγώ, Σιμωνίδηι γε οὐ ῥάιδιον ἀπιστεῖν· σοφὸς γὰρ καὶ θεῖος ὁ ἀνήρ. τοῦτο μέντοι ὅτι ποτὲ λέγει, σὺ μέν, ὦ Πολέμαρχε, ἴσως γιγνώσκεις, ἐγὼ δὲ ἀγνοῶ· δῆλον γὰρ ὅτι οὐ

331d8 ἔφη ἐγώ **AD**: ἔφην ἐγώ Venet. 184: ἐγὼ ἔφη **F**   e6 ὁ ἀνήρ **DF**^{pc}: ἀνήρ **AF**

τοῦτο λέγει, ὅπερ ἄρτι ἐλέγομεν, τό τινος παρακαταθεμένου τι
332 ὁτῳοῦν μὴ σωφρόνως ἀπαιτοῦντι ἀποδιδόναι. καίτοι γε ὀφειλόμενόν πού ἐστι τοῦτο ὃ παρακατέθετο· ἦ γάρ;

Ναί.

Ἀποδοτέον δέ γε οὐδὲ ὁπωστιοῦν τότε ὁπότε τις μὴ σωφρόνως ἀπαιτοῖ;

Ἀληθῆ, ἦ δὲ ὅς.

Ἄλλο δή τι ἢ τὸ τοιοῦτον, ὡς ἔοικεν, λέγει Σιμωνίδης τὸ τὰ ὀφειλόμενα δίκαιον εἶναι ἀποδιδόναι.

Ἄλλο μέντοι νὴ Δία, ἔφη· τοῖς γὰρ φίλοις οἴεται ὀφείλειν τοὺς φίλους ἀγαθὸν μέν τι δρᾶν, κακὸν δὲ μηδέν.

Μανθάνω, ἦν δὲ ἐγώ, ὅτι οὐ τὰ ὀφειλόμενα ἀποδίδωσιν ὃς ἄν
b τωι χρυσίον ἀποδῶι παρακαταθεμένωι, ἐάνπερ ἡ ἀπόδοσις καὶ ἡ λῆψις βλαβερὰ γίγνηται, φίλοι δὲ ὦσιν ὅ τε ἀπολαμβάνων καὶ ὁ ἀποδιδούς· οὐχ οὕτω λέγειν φῂς τὸν Σιμωνίδην;

Πάνυ μὲν οὖν.

Τί δέ; τοῖς ἐχθροῖς ἀποδοτέον ὅτι ἂν τύχηι ὀφειλόμενον;

Παντάπασι μὲν οὖν, ἔφη, ὅ γε ὀφείλεται αὐτοῖς· ὀφείλεται δέ γε, οἶμαι, παρά γε τοῦ ἐχθροῦ τῶι ἐχθρῶι ὅπερ καὶ προσήκει, κακόν τι.

Ἠινίξατο ἄρα, ἦν δὲ ἐγώ, ὡς ἔοικεν, ὁ Σιμωνίδης ποιητικῶς τὸ
c δίκαιον ὃ εἴη. διενοεῖτο μὲν γάρ, ὡς φαίνεται, ὅτι τοῦτο εἴη δίκαιον, τὸ προσῆκον ἑκάστωι ἀποδιδόναι, τοῦτο δὲ ὠνόμασεν ὀφειλόμενον.

Ἀλλὰ τί οἴει; ἔφη.

Πρὸς Διός, ἦν δὲ ἐγώ, εἰ οὖν τις αὐτὸν ἤρετο· Ὦ Σιμωνίδη, ἡ τίσιν οὖν τί ἀποδιδοῦσα ὀφειλόμενον καὶ προσῆκον τέχνη ἰατρικὴ καλεῖται; τί ἂν οἴει ἡμῖν αὐτὸν ἀποκρίνασθαι;

Δῆλον ὅτι, ἔφη, ἡ σώμασι φάρμακά τε καὶ σιτία καὶ ποτά.

Ἡ δὲ τίσι τί ἀποδιδοῦσα ὀφειλόμενον καὶ προσῆκον τέχνη μαγειρικὴ καλεῖται;

d Ἡ τοῖς ὄψοις τὰ ἡδύσματα.

Εἶέν· ἡ οὖν δὴ τίσι τί ἀποδιδοῦσα τέχνη δικαιοσύνη ἂν καλοῖτο;

Εἰ μέν τι, ἔφη, δεῖ ἀκολουθεῖν, ὦ Σώκρατες, τοῖς ἔμπροσθεν εἰρημένοις, ἡ τοῖς φίλοις τε καὶ ἐχθροῖς ὠφελίας τε καὶ βλάβας ἀποδιδοῦσα.

Τὸ τοὺς φίλους ἄρα εὖ ποιεῖν καὶ τοὺς ἐχθροὺς κακῶς δικαιοσύνην λέγει;

Δοκεῖ μοι.

Τίς οὖν δυνατώτατος κάμνοντας φίλους εὖ ποιεῖν καὶ ἐχθροὺς κακῶς πρὸς νόσον καὶ ὑγίειαν;

Ἰατρός.

Τίς δὲ πλέοντας πρὸς τὸν τῆς θαλάττης κίνδυνον; e

Κυβερνήτης.

Τί δὲ ὁ δίκαιος; ἐν τίνι πράξει καὶ πρὸς τί ἔργον δυνατώτατος φίλους ὠφελεῖν καὶ ἐχθροὺς βλάπτειν;

Ἐν τῶι προσπολεμεῖν καὶ ἐν τῶι συμμαχεῖν, ἔμοιγε δοκεῖ.

Εἶέν· μὴ κάμνουσί γε μήν, ὦ φίλε Πολέμαρχε, ἰατρὸς ἄχρηστος.

Ἀληθῆ.

Καὶ μὴ πλέουσι δὴ κυβερνήτης.

Ναί.

Ἆρα καὶ τοῖς μὴ πολεμοῦσιν ὁ δίκαιος ἄχρηστος;

Οὐ πάνυ μοι δοκεῖ τοῦτο.

Χρήσιμον ἄρα καὶ ἐν εἰρήνηι δικαιοσύνη; **333**

Χρήσιμον.

Καὶ γὰρ γεωργία· ἢ οὔ;

Ναί.

Πρός γε καρποῦ κτῆσιν;

Ναί.

Καὶ μὴν καὶ σκυτοτομική;

Ναί.

Πρός γε ὑποδημάτων ἄν, οἶμαι, φαίης κτῆσιν;

Πάνυ γε.

Τί δὲ δή; τὴν δικαιοσύνην πρὸς τίνος χρείαν ἢ κτῆσιν ἐν εἰρήνηι φαίης ἂν χρήσιμον εἶναι;

Πρὸς τὰ συμβόλαια, ὦ Σώκρατες.

Συμβόλαια δὲ λέγεις κοινωνήματα ἤ τι ἄλλο;

Κοινωνήματα δῆτα.

Ἆρ' οὖν ὁ δίκαιος ἀγαθὸς καὶ χρήσιμος κοινωνὸς εἰς πεττῶν θέσιν, ἢ ὁ πεττευτικός; **b**

Ὁ πεττευτικός.

Ἀλλ' εἰς πλίνθων καὶ λίθων θέσιν ὁ δίκαιος χρησιμώτερός τε καὶ ἀμείνων κοινωνὸς τοῦ οἰκοδομικοῦ;

Οὐδαμῶς.

Ἀλλ' εἰς τίνος δὴ κοινωνίαν ὁ δίκαιος ἀμείνων κοινωνὸς τοῦ κιθαριστικοῦ, ὥσπερ ὁ κιθαριστικὸς τοῦ δικαίου εἰς κρουμάτων;

333b7 τίνος Richards: τίνα **ADF**

Εἰς ἀργυρίου, ἔμοιγε δοκεῖ.

Πλήν γε ἴσως, ὦ Πολέμαρχε, πρὸς τὸ χρῆσθαι ἀργυρίωι, ὅταν
c δέηι ἀργυρίου κοινῆι πρίασθαι ἢ ἀποδόσθαι ἵππον· τότε δέ, ὡς ἐγὼ οἶμαι, ὁ ἱππικός. ἦ γάρ;

Φαίνεται.

Καὶ μὴν ὅταν γε πλοῖον, ὁ ναυπηγὸς ἢ ὁ κυβερνήτης;

Ἔοικεν.

Ὅταν οὖν τί δέηι ἀργυρίωι ἢ χρυσίωι κοινῆι χρῆσθαι, ὁ δίκαιος χρησιμώτερος τῶν ἄλλων;

Ὅταν παρακαταθέσθαι καὶ σῶν εἶναι, ὦ Σώκρατες.

Οὐκοῦν λέγεις ὅταν μηδὲν δέηι αὐτῶι χρῆσθαι ἀλλὰ κεῖσθαι;

Πάνυ γε.

Ὅταν ἄρα ἄχρηστον ἦι ἀργύριον, τότε χρήσιμος ἐπὶ αὐτῶι ἡ
d δικαιοσύνη;

Κινδυνεύει.

Καὶ ὅταν δὴ δρέπανον δέηι φυλάττειν, ἡ δικαιοσύνη χρήσιμος καὶ κοινῆι καὶ ἰδίαι· ὅταν δὲ χρῆσθαι, ἡ ἀμπελουργική;

Φαίνεται.

Φήσεις δὲ καὶ ἀσπίδα καὶ λύραν ὅταν δέηι φυλάττειν καὶ μηδὲν χρῆσθαι, χρήσιμον εἶναι τὴν δικαιοσύνην, ὅταν δὲ χρῆσθαι, τὴν ὁπλιτικὴν καὶ τὴν μουσικήν;

Ἀνάγκη.

Καὶ περὶ τὰ ἄλλα δὴ πάντα ἡ δικαιοσύνη ἑκάστου ἐν μὲν χρήσει ἄχρηστος, ἐν δὲ ἀχρηστίαι χρήσιμος;

Κινδυνεύει.

e Οὐκ ἂν οὖν, ὦ φίλε, πάνυ γέ τι σπουδαῖον εἴη ἡ δικαιοσύνη, εἰ πρὸς τὰ ἄχρηστα χρήσιμον ὂν τυγχάνει. τόδε δὲ σκεψώμεθα· ἆρα οὐχ ὁ πατάξαι δεινότατος ἐν μάχηι εἴτε πυκτικῆι εἴτε τινὶ καὶ ἄλληι, οὗτος καὶ φυλάξασθαι;

Πάνυ γε.

Ἆρα οὖν καὶ νόσον ὅστις δεινὸς φυλάξασθαι, καὶ λαθεῖν οὗτος δεινότατος ἐμποιήσας;

Ἔμοιγε δοκεῖ.

334 Ἀλλὰ μὴν στρατοπέδου γε ὁ αὐτὸς φύλαξ ἀγαθὸς ὅσπερ καὶ τὰ τῶν πολεμίων κλέψαι καὶ βουλεύματα καὶ τὰς ἄλλας πράξεις;

Πάνυ γε.

333e7 ἐμποιήσας Schneider: ἐμποιῆσαι **ADF**

Ὅτου τις ἄρα δεινὸς φύλαξ, τούτου καὶ φὼρ δεινός.

Ἔοικεν.

Εἰ ἄρα ὁ δίκαιος ἀργύριον δεινὸς φυλάττειν, καὶ κλέπτειν δεινός.

Ὡς γοῦν ὁ λόγος, ἔφη, σημαίνει.

Κλέπτης ἄρα τις ὁ δίκαιος, ὡς ἔοικεν, ἀναπέφανται, καὶ κινδυνεύεις παρὰ Ὁμήρου μεμαθηκέναι αὐτό· καὶ γὰρ ἐκεῖνος τὸν τοῦ Ὀδυσσέως πρὸς μητρὸς πάππον Αὐτόλυκον ἀγαπᾶι τε καί φησιν b
αὐτὸν πάντας "ἀνθρώπους κεκάσθαι κλεπτοσύνηι θ' ὅρκωι τε." ἔοικεν οὖν ἡ δικαιοσύνη καὶ κατὰ σὲ καὶ κατὰ Ὅμηρον καὶ κατὰ Σιμωνίδην κλεπτική τις εἶναι, ἐπὶ ὠφελίαι μέντοι τῶν φίλων καὶ ἐπὶ βλάβηι τῶν ἐχθρῶν. οὐχ οὕτως ἔλεγες;

Οὐ μὰ τὸν Δία, ἔφη, ἀλλὰ οὐκέτι οἶδα ἔγωγε ὅτι ἔλεγον· τοῦτο μέντοι ἔμοιγε δοκεῖ ἔτι, ὠφελεῖν μὲν τοὺς φίλους ἡ δικαιοσύνη, βλάπτειν δὲ τοὺς ἐχθρούς.

Φίλους δὲ λέγεις εἶναι πότερον τοὺς δοκοῦντας ἑκάστωι c
χρηστοὺς εἶναι, ἢ τοὺς ὄντας, καὶ ἂν μὴ δοκῶσι, καὶ ἐχθροὺς ὡσαύτως;

Εἰκὸς μέν, ἔφη, οὓς ἄν τις ἡγῆται χρηστοὺς φιλεῖν, οὓς δὲ ἂν πονηροὺς μισεῖν.

Ἆρα οὖν οὐχ ἁμαρτάνουσιν οἱ ἄνθρωποι περὶ τοῦτο, ὥστε δοκεῖν αὐτοῖς πολλοὺς μὲν χρηστοὺς εἶναι μὴ ὄντας, πολλοὺς δὲ τὸ ἐναντίον;

Ἁμαρτάνουσιν.

Τούτοις ἄρα οἱ μὲν ἀγαθοὶ ἐχθροί, οἱ δὲ κακοὶ φίλοι;

Πάνυ γε.

Ἀλλὰ ὅμως δίκαιον τότε τούτοις τοὺς μὲν πονηροὺς ὠφελεῖν, τοὺς δὲ ἀγαθοὺς βλάπτειν; d

Φαίνεται.

Ἀλλὰ μὴν οἵ γε ἀγαθοὶ δίκαιοί τε καὶ οἷοι μὴ ἀδικεῖν;

Ἀληθῆ.

Κατὰ δὴ τὸν σὸν λόγον τοὺς μηδὲν ἀδικοῦντας δίκαιον κακῶς ποιεῖν.

Μηδαμῶς, ἔφη, ὦ Σώκρατες· πονηρὸς γὰρ ἔοικεν εἶναι ὁ λόγος.

Τοὺς ἀδίκους ἄρα, ἦν δὲ ἐγώ, δίκαιον βλάπτειν, τοὺς δὲ δικαίους ὠφελεῖν;

Οὗτος ἐκείνου καλλίων φαίνεται.

Πολλοῖς ἄρα, ὦ Πολέμαρχε, συμβήσεται, ὅσοι διημαρτήκασιν τῶν ἀνθρώπων, δίκαιον εἶναι τοὺς μὲν φίλους βλάπτειν, e
πονηροὶ γὰρ αὐτοῖς εἰσιν, τοὺς δὲ ἐχθροὺς ὠφελεῖν, ἀγαθοὶ γάρ·

καὶ οὕτως ἐροῦμεν αὐτὸ τὸ ἐναντίον ἢ τὸν Σιμωνίδην ἔφαμεν λέγειν.

Καὶ μάλα, ἔφη, οὕτω συμβαίνει. ἀλλὰ μεταθώμεθα· κινδυνεύομεν γὰρ οὐκ ὀρθῶς τὸν φίλον καὶ ἐχθρὸν θέσθαι.

Πῶς θέμενοι, ὦ Πολέμαρχε;

Τὸν δοκοῦντα χρηστόν, τοῦτον φίλον εἶναι.

Νῦν δὲ πῶς, ἦν δὲ ἐγώ, μεταθώμεθα;

Τὸν δοκοῦντά τε, ἦ δὲ ὅς, καὶ [τὸν] ὄντα χρηστὸν φίλον· τὸν
335 δὲ δοκοῦντα μέν, ὄντα δὲ μή, δοκεῖν ἀλλὰ μὴ εἶναι φίλον. καὶ περὶ
τοῦ ἐχθροῦ δὲ ἡ αὐτὴ θέσις.

Φίλος μὲν δή, ὡς ἔοικε, τούτωι τῶι λόγωι ὁ ἀγαθὸς ἔσται, ἐχθρὸς δὲ ὁ πονηρός.

Ναί.

Κελεύεις δὴ ἡμᾶς προσθεῖναι τῶι δικαίωι ἢ ὡς τὸ πρῶτον ἐλέγομεν, λέγοντες δίκαιον εἶναι τὸν μὲν φίλον εὖ ποιεῖν, τὸν δὲ ἐχθρὸν κακῶς, νῦν πρὸς τούτωι ὧδε λέγειν, τὸν μὲν φίλον ἀγαθὸν ὄντα εὖ ποιεῖν, τὸν δὲ ἐχθρὸν κακὸν ὄντα βλάπτειν;

b Πάνυ μὲν οὖν, ἔφη, οὕτως ἄν μοι δοκεῖ καλῶς λέγεσθαι.

Ἔστιν ἄρα, ἦν δὲ ἐγώ, δικαίου ἀνδρὸς βλάπτειν καὶ ὁντινοῦν ἀνθρώπων;

Καὶ πάνυ γε, ἔφη· τούς γε πονηρούς τε καὶ ἐχθροὺς δεῖ βλάπτειν.

Βλαπτόμενοι δὲ ἵπποι βελτίους ἢ χείρους γίγνονται;

Χείρους.

Ἆρα εἰς τὴν τῶν κυνῶν ἀρετήν, ἢ εἰς τὴν τῶν ἵππων;

Εἰς τὴν τῶν ἵππων.

Ἆρα οὖν καὶ κύνες βλαπτόμενοι χείρους γίγνονται εἰς τὴν τῶν κυνῶν ἀλλὰ οὐκ εἰς τὴν τῶν ἵππων ἀρετήν;

Ἀνάγκη.

c Ἀνθρώπους δέ, ὦ ἑταῖρε, μὴ οὕτω φῶμεν βλαπτομένους εἰς τὴν ἀνθρωπείαν ἀρετὴν χείρους γίγνεσθαι;

Πάνυ μὲν οὖν.

Ἀλλὰ ἡ δικαιοσύνη οὐκ ἀνθρωπεία ἀρετή;

Καὶ τοῦτο ἀνάγκη.

Καὶ τοὺς βλαπτομένους ἄρα, ὦ φίλε, τῶν ἀνθρώπων ἀνάγκη ἀδικωτέρους γίγνεσθαι.

334e10 τὸν del. Bremi   335a8 λέγειν **F**: λέγειν ὅτι ἔστιν δίκαιον **AD**

Ἔοικεν.

Ἆρα οὖν τῆι μουσικῆι οἱ μουσικοὶ ἀμούσους δύνανται ποιεῖν;

Ἀδύνατον.

Ἀλλὰ τῆι ἱππικῆι οἱ ἱππικοὶ ἀφίππους;

Οὐκ ἔστιν.

Ἀλλὰ τῆι δικαιοσύνηι δὴ οἱ δίκαιοι ἀδίκους; ἢ καὶ συλλήβδην
ἀρετῆι οἱ ἀγαθοὶ κακούς; d

Ἀλλὰ ἀδύνατον.

Οὐ γὰρ θερμότητος, οἶμαι, ἔργον ψύχειν ἀλλὰ τοῦ ἐναντίου.

Ναί.

Οὐδὲ ξηρότητος ὑγραίνειν ἀλλὰ τοῦ ἐναντίου.

Πάνυ γε.

Οὐδὲ δὴ τοῦ ἀγαθοῦ βλάπτειν ἀλλὰ τοῦ ἐναντίου.

Φαίνεται.

Ὁ δέ γε δίκαιος ἀγαθός;

Πάνυ γε.

Οὐκ ἄρα τοῦ δικαίου βλάπτειν ἔργον, ὦ Πολέμαρχε, οὔτε φίλον οὔτε ἄλλον οὐδένα, ἀλλὰ τοῦ ἐναντίου, τοῦ ἀδίκου.

Παντάπασί μοι δοκεῖς ἀληθῆ λέγειν, ἔφη, ὦ Σώκρατες. e

Εἰ ἄρα τὰ ὀφειλόμενα ἑκάστωι ἀποδιδόναι φησί τις δίκαιον εἶναι, τοῦτο δὲ δὴ νοεῖ αὐτῶι τοῖς μὲν ἐχθροῖς βλάβην ὀφείλεσθαι παρὰ τοῦ δικαίου ἀνδρός, τοῖς δὲ φίλοις ὠφελίαν, οὐκ ἦν σοφὸς ὁ ταῦτα εἰπών· οὐ γὰρ ἀληθῆ ἔλεγεν. οὐδαμοῦ γὰρ δίκαιον οὐδένα ἡμῖν ἐφάνη ὂν βλάπτειν.

Συγχωρῶ, ἦ δὲ ὅς.

Μαχούμεθα ἄρα, ἦν δὲ ἐγώ, κοινῆι ἐγώ τε καὶ σύ, ἐάν τις αὐτὸ φῆι ἢ Σιμωνίδην ἢ Βίαντα ἢ Πιττακὸν εἰρηκέναι ἤ τινα ἄλλον τῶν σοφῶν τε καὶ μακαρίων ἀνδρῶν.

Ἐγὼ γοῦν, ἔφη, ἕτοιμός εἰμι κοινωνεῖν τῆς μάχης.

Ἀλλὰ οἶσθα, ἦν δὲ ἐγώ, οὗ μοι δοκεῖ εἶναι τὸ ῥῆμα, τὸ φάναι 336
δίκαιον εἶναι τοὺς μὲν φίλους ὠφελεῖν, τοὺς δὲ ἐχθροὺς βλάπτειν;

Τίνος; ἔφη.

Οἶμαι αὐτὸ Περιάνδρου εἶναι ἢ Περδίκκου ἢ Ξέρξου ἢ Ἰσμηνίου τοῦ Θηβαίου ἤ τινος ἄλλου μέγα οἰομένου δύνασθαι πλουσίου ἀνδρός.

Ἀληθέστατα, ἔφη, λέγεις.

Εἶεν, ἦν δὲ ἐγώ· ἐπειδὴ δὲ οὐδὲ τοῦτο ἐφάνη ἡ δικαιοσύνη ὂν οὐδὲ τὸ δίκαιον, τί ἂν ἄλλο τις αὐτὸ φαίη εἶναι;

b Καὶ ὁ Θρασύμαχος πολλάκις μὲν καὶ διαλεγομένων ἡμῶν μεταξὺ ὥρμα ἀντιλαμβάνεσθαι τοῦ λόγου, ἔπειτα ὑπὸ τῶν παρακαθημένων διεκωλύετο βουλομένων διακοῦσαι τὸν λόγον· ὡς δὲ διεπαυσάμεθα καὶ ἐγὼ ταῦτα εἶπον, οὐκέτι ἡσυχίαν ἦγεν, ἀλλὰ συστρέψας ἑαυτὸν ὥσπερ θηρίον ἧκεν ἐπὶ ἡμᾶς ὡς διαρπασόμενος. καὶ ἐγώ τε καὶ ὁ Πολέμαρχος δείσαντες διεπτοήθημεν· ὁ δὲ **c** εἰς τὸ μέσον φθεγξάμενος, Τίς, ἔφη, ὑμᾶς πάλαι φλυαρία ἔχει, ὦ Σώκρατες; καὶ τί εὐηθίζεσθε πρὸς ἀλλήλους ὑποκατακλινόμενοι ὑμῖν αὐτοῖς; ἀλλὰ εἴπερ ὡς ἀληθῶς βούλει εἰδέναι τὸ δίκαιον ὅτι ἐστίν, μὴ μόνον ἐρώτα μηδὲ φιλοτιμοῦ ἐλέγχων ἐπειδάν τίς τι ἀποκρίνηται, ἐγνωκὼς τοῦτο, ὅτι ῥᾶιον ἐρωτᾶν ἢ ἀποκρίνεσθαι, ἀλλὰ καὶ αὐτὸς ἀπόκριναι καὶ εἰπὲ τί φῄς εἶναι τὸ δίκαιον. καὶ ὅπως μοι **d** μὴ ἐρεῖς ὅτι τὸ δέον ἐστὶ μηδὲ ὅτι τὸ ὠφέλιμον μηδὲ ὅτι τὸ λυσιτελοῦν μηδὲ ὅτι τὸ κερδαλέον μηδὲ ὅτι τὸ συμφέρον, ἀλλὰ σαφῶς μοι καὶ ἀκριβῶς λέγε ὅτι ἂν λέγηις· ὡς ἐγὼ οὐκ ἀποδέξομαι ἐὰν ὕθλους τοιούτους λέγηις.

Καὶ ἐγὼ ἀκούσας ἐξεπλάγην καὶ προσβλέπων αὐτὸν ἐφοβούμην, καί μοι δοκῶ, εἰ μὴ πρότερος ἑωράκη αὐτὸν ἢ ἐκεῖνος ἐμέ, ἄφωνος ἂν γενέσθαι. νῦν δὲ ἡνίκα ὑπὸ τοῦ λόγου ἤρχετο ἐξαγριαίνεσθαι, **e** προσέβλεψα αὐτὸν πρότερος, ὥστε αὐτῶι οἷός τε ἐγενόμην ἀποκρίνασθαι, καὶ εἶπον ὑποτρέμων· Ὦ Θρασύμαχε, μὴ χαλεπὸς ἡμῖν ἴσθι· εἰ γάρ τι ἐξαμαρτάνομεν ἐν τῆι τῶν λόγων σκέψει ἐγώ τε καὶ ὅδε, εὖ ἴσθι ὅτι ἄκοντες ἁμαρτάνομεν. μὴ γὰρ δὴ οἴου, εἰ μὲν χρυσίον ἐζητοῦμεν, οὐκ ἄν ποτε ἡμᾶς ἑκόντας εἶναι ὑποκατακλίνεσθαι ἀλλήλοις ἐν τῆι ζητήσει καὶ διαφθείρειν τὴν εὕρεσιν αὐτοῦ, δικαιοσύνην δὲ ζητοῦντας, πρᾶγμα πολλῶν χρυσίων τιμιώτερον, ἔπειτα οὕτως ἀνοήτως ὑπείκειν ἀλλήλοις καὶ οὐ σπουδάζειν ὅτι μάλιστα φανῆναι αὐτό. οἴου γε σύ, ὦ φίλε. ἀλλὰ οἶμαι οὐ δυνάμεθα· ἐλεεῖσθαι οὖν **337** ἡμᾶς πολὺ μᾶλλον εἰκός ἐστί που ὑπὸ ὑμῶν τῶν δεινῶν ἢ χαλεπαίνεσθαι.

Καὶ ὃς ἀκούσας ἀνεκάκχασέ τε μάλα σαρδάνιον καὶ εἶπεν· Ὦ Ἡράκλεις, ἔφη, αὕτη ἐκείνη ἡ εἰωθυῖα εἰρωνεία Σωκράτους, καὶ ταῦτα ἐγὼ ἤιδη τε καὶ τούτοις προύλεγον, ὅτι σὺ ἀποκρίνασθαι μὲν οὐκ ἐθελήσοις, εἰρωνεύσοιο δὲ καὶ πάντα μᾶλλον ποιήσοις ἢ ἀποκρινοῖο, εἴ τίς τί σε ἐρωτᾶι.

336e3 γάρ τι **DF**: γὰρ **A** e9 οἴου γε Bekker: οἴου τε **ADF**

Σοφὸς γὰρ εἶ, ἦν δ' ἐγώ, ὦ Θρασύμαχε· εὖ οὖν ᾔδησθα ὅτι εἴ
τινα ἔροιο ὁπόσα ἐστὶ τὰ δώδεκα, καὶ ἐρόμενος προείποις αὐτῶι· b
Ὅπως μοι, ὦ ἄνθρωπε, μὴ ἐρεῖς ὅτι ἐστὶ τὰ δώδεκα δὶς ἓξ μηδὲ
ὅτι τρὶς τέτταρα μηδὲ ὅτι ἑξάκις δύο μηδὲ ὅτι τετράκις τρία· ὡς
οὐκ ἀποδέξομαί σου ἐὰν τοιαῦτα φλυαρῇς, δῆλον, οἶμαι, σοι ἦν
ὅτι οὐδεὶς ἀποκρινοῖτο οὕτως πυνθανομένωι. ἀλλ' εἴ σοι εἶπεν·
Ὦ Θρασύμαχε, πῶς λέγεις; μὴ ἀποκρίνωμαι ὧν προεῖπες μηδέν;
πότερον, ὦ θαυμάσιε, μηδ' εἰ τούτων τι τυγχάνει ὄν, ἀλλ' ἕτερον
εἴπω τι τοῦ ἀληθοῦς; ἢ πῶς λέγεις; τί ἂν αὐτῶι εἶπες πρὸς ταῦτα; c

Εἶέν, ἔφη· ὡς δὴ ὅμοιον τοῦτο ἐκείνωι.

Οὐδέν γε κωλύει, ἦν δ' ἐγώ· εἰ δ' οὖν καὶ μὴ ἔστιν ὅμοιον, φαίνεται δὲ τῶι ἐρωτηθέντι τοιοῦτον, ἧττόν τι αὐτὸν οἴει ἀποκρινεῖσθαι
τὸ φαινόμενον ἑαυτῶι, ἐάντε ἡμεῖς ἀπαγορεύωμεν ἐάντε μή;

Ἄλλο τι οὖν, ἔφη, καὶ σὺ οὕτω ποιήσεις; ὧν ἐγὼ ἀπεῖπον, τούτων τι ἀποκρινῇ;

Οὐκ ἂν θαυμάσαιμι, ἦν δ' ἐγώ, εἴ μοι σκεψαμένωι οὕτω δόξειεν.

Τί οὖν, ἔφη, ἂν ἐγὼ δείξω ἑτέραν ἀπόκρισιν παρὰ πάσας ταύτας d
περὶ δικαιοσύνης, βελτίω τούτων; τί ἀξιοῖς παθεῖν;

Τί ἄλλο, ἦν δ' ἐγώ, ἢ ὅπερ προσήκει πάσχειν τῶι μὴ εἰδότι;
προσήκει δέ που μαθεῖν παρὰ τοῦ εἰδότος· καὶ ἐγὼ οὖν τοῦτο
ἀξιῶ παθεῖν.

Ἡδὺς γὰρ εἶ, ἔφη· ἀλλὰ πρὸς τῶι μαθεῖν καὶ ἀπότεισον ἀργύριον.

Οὐκοῦν ἐπειδάν μοι γένηται, εἶπον.

Ἀλλ' ἔστιν, ἔφη ὁ Γλαύκων. ἀλλ' ἕνεκα ἀργυρίου, ὦ Θρασύμαχε, λέγε· πάντες γὰρ ἡμεῖς Σωκράτει εἰσοίσομεν.

Πάνυ γε οἶμαι, ἦ δ' ὅς, ἵνα Σωκράτης τὸ εἰωθὸς διαπράξηται, e
αὐτὸς μὲν μὴ ἀποκρίνηται, ἄλλου δ' ἀποκρινομένου λαμβάνηι
λόγον καὶ ἐλέγχηι.

Πῶς γὰρ ἄν, ἔφην ἐγώ, ὦ βέλτιστε, τις ἀποκρίναιτο πρῶτον
μὲν μὴ εἰδὼς μηδὲ φάσκων εἰδέναι, ἔπειτα, εἴ τι καὶ οἴεται περὶ
τούτων, ἀπειρημένον αὐτῶι εἴη ὅπως μηδὲν ἐρεῖ ὧν ἡγεῖται ὑπ'
ἀνδρὸς οὐ φαύλου; ἀλλὰ σὲ δὴ μᾶλλον εἰκὸς λέγειν· σὺ γὰρ δὴ φῂς 338
εἰδέναι καὶ ἔχειν εἰπεῖν. μὴ οὖν ἄλλως ποίει, ἀλλ' ἐμοί τε χαρίζου
ἀποκρινόμενος καὶ μὴ φθονήσηις καὶ Γλαύκωνα τόνδε διδάξαι καὶ
τοὺς ἄλλους.

Εἰπόντος δέ μου ταῦτα ὅ τε Γλαύκων καὶ οἱ ἄλλοι ἐδέοντο αὐτοῦ μὴ ἄλλως ποιεῖν. καὶ ὁ Θρασύμαχος φανερὸς μὲν ἦν ἐπιθυμῶν
εἰπεῖν ἵνα εὐδοκιμήσειεν, ἡγούμενος ἔχειν ἀπόκρισιν παγκάλην·

προσεποιεῖτο δὲ φιλονικεῖν πρὸς τὸ ἐμὲ εἶναι τὸν ἀποκρινόμενον.
b τελευτῶν δὲ συνεχώρησεν, καὶ ἔπειτα, Αὕτη δή, ἔφη, ἡ Σωκράτους
σοφία, αὐτὸν μὲν μὴ ἐθέλειν διδάσκειν, παρὰ δὲ τῶν ἄλλων περι-
ιόντα μανθάνειν καὶ τούτων μηδὲ χάριν ἀποδιδόναι.

Ὅτι μέν, ἦν δὲ ἐγώ, μανθάνω παρὰ τῶν ἄλλων, ἀληθῆ εἶπες, ὦ
Θρασύμαχε, ὅτι δὲ οὔ με φῂς χάριν ἐκτίνειν, ψεύδηι· ἐκτίνω γὰρ
ὅσην δύναμαι. δύναμαι δὲ ἐπαινεῖν μόνον· χρήματα γὰρ οὐκ ἔχω.
ὡς δὲ προθύμως τοῦτο δρῶ, ἐάν τίς μοι δοκῆι εὖ λέγειν, εὖ εἴσηι
c αὐτίκα δὴ μάλα, ἐπειδὰν ἀποκρίνηι· οἶμαι γάρ σε εὖ ἐρεῖν.

Ἄκουε δή, ἦ δὲ ὅς. φημὶ γὰρ ἐγὼ εἶναι τὸ δίκαιον οὐκ ἄλλο τι ἢ
τὸ τοῦ κρείττονος συμφέρον. ἀλλὰ τί οὐκ ἐπαινεῖς; ἀλλ᾽ οὐκ
ἐθελήσεις.

Ἐὰν μάθω γε πρῶτον, ἔφην, τί λέγεις· νῦν γὰρ οὔπω οἶδα. τὸ
τοῦ κρείττονος φῂς συμφέρον δίκαιον εἶναι. καὶ τοῦτο, ὦ Θρασύμαχε, τί ποτε λέγεις; οὐ γάρ που τό γε τοιόνδε φῄς· εἰ Πουλυδάμας
ἡμῶν κρείττων ὁ παγκρατιαστὴς καὶ αὐτῶι συμφέρει τὰ βόεια κρέα
d πρὸς τὸ σῶμα, τοῦτο τὸ σιτίον εἶναι καὶ ἡμῖν τοῖς ἥττοσιν ἐκείνου
συμφέρον ἅμα καὶ δίκαιον.

Βδελυρὸς γὰρ εἶ, ἔφη, ὦ Σώκρατες, καὶ ταύτηι ὑπολαμβάνεις ἧι
ἂν κακουργήσαις μάλιστα τὸν λόγον.

Οὐδαμῶς, ὦ ἄριστε, ἦν δὲ ἐγώ· ἀλλὰ σαφέστερον εἰπὲ τί λέγεις.

Εἶτα οὐκ οἶσθα, ἔφη, ὅτι τῶν πόλεων αἱ μὲν τυραννοῦνται, αἱ δὲ
δημοκρατοῦνται, αἱ δὲ ἀριστοκρατοῦνται;

Πῶς γὰρ οὔ;

Οὐκοῦν τοῦτο κρατεῖ ἐν ἑκάστηι πόλει, τὸ ἄρχον;

Πάνυ γε.

e Τίθεται δέ γε τοὺς νόμους ἑκάστη ἡ ἀρχὴ πρὸς τὸ αὑτῆι συμφέρον, δημοκρατία μὲν δημοκρατικούς, τυραννὶς δὲ τυραννικούς,
καὶ αἱ ἄλλαι οὕτως· θέμεναι δὲ ἀπέφηναν τοῦτο δίκαιον τοῖς ἀρχομένοις εἶναι, τὸ σφίσι συμφέρον, καὶ τὸν τούτου ἐκβαίνοντα κολά-
ζουσιν ὡς παρανομοῦντά τε καὶ ἀδικοῦντα. τοῦτο οὖν ἐστιν, ὦ
339 βέλτιστε, ὃ λέγω ἐν ἁπάσαις ταῖς πόλεσιν ταὐτὸν εἶναι δίκαιον, τὸ
τῆς καθεστηκυίας ἀρχῆς συμφέρον· αὕτη δέ που κρατεῖ, ὥστε συμβαίνει τῶι ὀρθῶς λογιζομένωι πανταχοῦ εἶναι τὸ αὐτὸ δίκαιον, τὸ
τοῦ κρείττονος συμφέρον.

Νῦν, ἦν δὲ ἐγώ, ἔμαθον ὃ λέγεις· εἰ δὲ ἀληθὲς ἢ μή, πειράσομαι
μαθεῖν. τὸ συμφέρον μὲν οὖν, ὦ Θρασύμαχε, καὶ σὺ ἀπεκρίνω
δίκαιον εἶναι, καίτοι ἔμοιγε ἀπηγόρευες ὅπως μὴ τοῦτο ἀποκρινοίμην·

πρόσεστι δὲ δὴ αὐτόθι τὸ τοῦ κρείττονος. b

Σμικρά γε ἴσως, ἔφη, προσθήκη.

Οὔπω δῆλον οὐδὲ εἰ μεγάλη· ἀλλ' ὅτι μὲν τοῦτο σκεπτέον εἰ ἀληθῆ λέγεις, δῆλον. ἐπειδὴ γὰρ συμφέρον γέ τι εἶναι καὶ ἐγὼ ὁμολογῶ τὸ δίκαιον, σὺ δὲ προστίθης καὶ αὐτὸ φῂς εἶναι τὸ τοῦ κρείττονος, ἐγὼ δὲ ἀγνοῶ, σκεπτέον δή.

Σκόπει, ἔφη.

Ταῦτα ἔσται, ἦν δ' ἐγώ. καί μοι εἰπέ· οὐ καὶ πείθεσθαι μέντοι τοῖς ἄρχουσιν δίκαιον φῂς εἶναι;

Ἔγωγε.

Πότερον δὲ ἀναμάρτητοί εἰσιν οἱ ἄρχοντες ἐν ταῖς πόλεσιν ἑκά- c
σταις ἢ οἷοί τι καὶ ἁμαρτεῖν;

Πάντως που, ἔφη, οἷοί τι καὶ ἁμαρτεῖν.

Οὐκοῦν ἐπιχειροῦντες νόμους τιθέναι τοὺς μὲν ὀρθῶς τιθέασιν, τοὺς δέ τινας οὐκ ὀρθῶς;

Οἶμαι ἔγωγε.

Τὸ δὲ ὀρθῶς ἆρα τὸ τὰ συμφέροντά ἐστι τίθεσθαι ἑαυτοῖς, τὸ δὲ μὴ ὀρθῶς ἀσύμφορα; ἢ πῶς λέγεις;

Οὕτως.

Ἃ δ' ἂν θῶνται ποιητέον τοῖς ἀρχομένοις, καὶ τοῦτό ἐστι τὸ δίκαιον;

Πῶς γὰρ οὔ;

Οὐ μόνον ἄρα δίκαιόν ἐστι κατὰ τὸν σὸν λόγον τὸ τοῦ κρείτ- d
τονος συμφέρον ποιεῖν ἀλλὰ καὶ τὸ ἐναντίον, τὸ μὴ συμφέρον.

Τί λέγεις σύ; ἔφη.

Ἃ σὺ λέγεις, ἔμοιγε δοκῶ. σκοπῶμεν δὴ βέλτιον· οὐχ ὡμολόγηται τοὺς ἄρχοντας τοῖς ἀρχομένοις προστάττοντας ποιεῖν ἄττα ἐνίοτε διαμαρτάνειν τοῦ ἑαυτοῖς βελτίστου, ἃ δ' ἂν προστάττωσιν οἱ ἄρχοντες δίκαιον εἶναι τοῖς ἀρχομένοις ποιεῖν; ταῦτα οὐχ ὡμολόγηται;

Οἶμαι ἔγωγε, ἔφη.

Οἴου τοίνυν, ἦν δ' ἐγώ, καὶ τὸ ἀσύμφορα ποιεῖν τοῖς ἄρχουσί e
τε καὶ κρείττοσι δίκαιον εἶναι ὡμολογῆσθαί σοι, ὅταν οἱ μὲν ἄρχοντες ἄκοντες κακὰ αὑτοῖς προστάττωσιν, τοῖς δὲ δίκαιον εἶναι φῂς ταῦτα ποιεῖν ἃ ἐκεῖνοι προσέταξαν· ἆρα τότε, ὦ σοφώτατε

339d4 δὴ **AD**: δὲ **F**

Θρασύμαχε, οὐκ ἀναγκαῖον συμβαίνειν αὐτὸ ούτωσί, δίκαιον εἶναι ποιεῖν τὸ ἐναντίον ἢ ὃ σὺ λέγεις; τὸ γὰρ τοῦ κρείττονος ἀσύμφορον
δήπου προστάττεται τοῖς ἥττοσιν ποιεῖν.
340 Ναὶ μὰ Δία, ἔφη, ὦ Σώκρατες, ὁ Πολέμαρχος, σαφέστατά γε.
Ἐάν σύ γε, ἔφη, αὐτῶι μαρτυρήσηις, ὁ Κλειτοφῶν ὑπολαβών.
Καὶ τί, ἔφη, δεῖται μάρτυρος; αὐτὸς γὰρ Θρασύμαχος ὁμολογεῖ
τοὺς μὲν ἄρχοντας ἐνίοτε ἑαυτοῖς κακὰ προστάττειν, τοῖς δὲ δίκαιον
εἶναι ταῦτα ποιεῖν.
Τὸ γὰρ τὰ κελευόμενα ποιεῖν, ὦ Πολέμαρχε, ὑπὸ τῶν ἀρχόντων
δίκαιον εἶναι ἔθετο Θρασύμαχος.
Καὶ γὰρ τὸ τοῦ κρείττονος, ὦ Κλειτοφῶν, συμφέρον δίκαιον εἶναι
b ἔθετο. ταῦτα δὲ ἀμφότερα θέμενος ὡμολόγησεν αὖ ἐνίοτε τοὺς
κρείττους τὰ αὑτοῖς ἀσύμφορα κελεύειν τοὺς ἥττους τε καὶ ἀρχομένους ποιεῖν. ἐκ δὲ τούτων τῶν ὁμολογιῶν οὐδὲν μᾶλλον τὸ τοῦ
κρείττονος συμφέρον δίκαιον ἂν εἴη ἢ τὸ μὴ συμφέρον.
Ἀλλά, ἔφη ὁ Κλειτοφῶν, τὸ τοῦ κρείττονος συμφέρον ἔλεγεν ὃ
ἡγοῖτο ὁ κρείττων αὑτῶι συμφέρειν· τοῦτο ποιητέον εἶναι τῶι
ἥττονι, καὶ τὸ δίκαιον τοῦτο ἐτίθετο.
Ἀλλ' οὐχ οὕτως, ἦ δὲ ὃς ὁ Πολέμαρχος, ἐλέγετο.
c Οὐδέν, ἦν δὲ ἐγώ, ὦ Πολέμαρχε, διαφέρει, ἀλλ' εἰ νῦν οὕτω
λέγει Θρασύμαχος, οὕτως αὐτοῦ ἀποδεχώμεθα. καί μοι εἰπέ, ὦ
Θρασύμαχε· τοῦτο ἦν ὃ ἐβούλου λέγειν τὸ δίκαιον, τὸ τοῦ κρείττονος συμφέρον δοκοῦν εἶναι τῶι κρείττονι, ἐάντε συμφέρηι ἐάντε μή;
οὕτω σε φῶμεν λέγειν;
Ἥκιστά γε, ἔφη· ἀλλὰ κρείττω με οἴει καλεῖν τὸν ἐξαμαρτάνοντα ὅταν ἐξαμαρτάνηι;
Ἔγωγε, εἶπον, ὤιμην σε τοῦτο λέγειν ὅτε τοὺς ἄρχοντας ὡμο-
d λόγεις οὐκ ἀναμαρτήτους εἶναι ἀλλά τι καὶ ἐξαμαρτάνειν.
Συκοφάντης γὰρ εἶ, ἔφη, ὦ Σώκρατες, ἐν τοῖς λόγοις· ἐπεὶ αὐτίκα ἰατρὸν καλεῖς σὺ τὸν ἐξαμαρτάνοντα περὶ τοὺς κάμνοντας
κατ' αὐτὸ τοῦτο ὃ ἐξαμαρτάνει; ἢ λογιστικόν, ὃς ἂν ἐν λογισμῶι
ἁμαρτάνηι, τότε ὅταν ἁμαρτάνηι, κατὰ ταύτην τὴν ἁμαρτίαν;
ἀλλ' οἶμαι λέγομεν τῶι ῥήματι οὕτως, ὅτι ὁ ἰατρὸς ἐξήμαρτεν
καὶ ὁ λογιστὴς ἐξήμαρτεν καὶ ὁ γραμματιστής· τὸ δ' οἶμαι ἕκαστος
e τούτων, καθ' ὅσον τοῦτ' ἔστιν ὃ προσαγορεύομεν αὐτόν, οὐδέποτε ἁμαρτάνει· ὥστε κατὰ τὸν ἀκριβῆ λόγον, ἐπειδὴ καὶ σὺ ἀκριβολογῆι, οὐδεὶς τῶν δημιουργῶν ἁμαρτάνει. ἐπιλιπούσης γὰρ
ἐπιστήμης ὁ ἁμαρτάνων ἁμαρτάνει, ἐν ὧι οὐκ ἔστι δημιουργός·

ὥστε δημιουργὸς ἢ σοφὸς ἢ ἄρχων οὐδεὶς ἁμαρτάνει τότε ὅταν ἄρχων ἦι, ἀλλὰ πᾶς γε ἂν εἴποι ὅτι ὁ ἰατρὸς ἥμαρτεν καὶ ὁ ἄρχων ἥμαρτεν. τοιοῦτον οὖν δή σοι καὶ ἐμὲ ὑπόλαβε νυνδὴ ἀποκρίνεσθαι, τὸ δὲ ἀκριβέστατον ἐκεῖνο τυγχάνει ὄν, τὸν ἄρχοντα, κατὰ ὅσον ἄρχων ἐστί, μὴ ἁμαρτάνειν, μὴ ἁμαρτάνοντα δὲ τὸ αὑτῶι βέλτιστον **341**
τίθεσθαι, τοῦτο δὲ τῶι ἀρχομένωι ποιητέον. ὥστε, ὅπερ ἐξ ἀρχῆς ἔλεγον, δίκαιον λέγω τὸ τοῦ κρείττονος ποιεῖν συμφέρον.

Εἶέν, ἦν δὲ ἐγώ, ὦ Θρασύμαχε· δοκῶ σοι συκοφαντεῖν;

Πάνυ μὲν οὖν, ἔφη.

Οἴει γάρ με ἐξ ἐπιβουλῆς ἐν τοῖς λόγοις κακουργοῦντά σε ἐρέσθαι ὡς ἠρόμην;

Εὖ μὲν οὖν οἶδα, ἔφη. καὶ οὐδέν γέ σοι πλέον ἔσται· οὔτε γὰρ ἄν με λάθοις κακουργῶν, οὔτε μὴ λαθὼν βιάσασθαι τῶι λόγωι δύναιο. **b**

Οὐδέ γε ἂν ἐπιχειρήσαιμι, ἦν δὲ ἐγώ, ὦ μακάριε. ἀλλ' ἵνα μὴ αὖθις ἡμῖν τοιοῦτον ἐγγένηται, διόρισαι ποτέρως λέγεις τὸν ἄρχοντά τε καὶ τὸν κρείττονα, τὸν ὡς ἔπος εἰπεῖν ἢ τὸν ἀκριβεῖ λόγωι, ὃ νυνδὴ ἔλεγες, οὗ τὸ συμφέρον κρείττονος ὄντος δίκαιον ἔσται τῶι ἥττονι ποιεῖν.

Τὸν τῶι ἀκριβεστάτωι, ἔφη, λόγωι ἄρχοντα ὄντα. πρὸς ταῦτα κακούργει καὶ συκοφάντει, εἴ τι δύνασαι· οὐδέν σου παρίεμαι. ἀλλ' οὐ μὴ οἷός τε ἦις. **c**

Οἴει γὰρ ἄν με, εἶπον, οὕτω μανῆναι ὥστε ξυρεῖν ἐπιχειρεῖν λέοντα καὶ συκοφαντεῖν Θρασύμαχον;

Νῦν γοῦν, ἔφη, ἐπεχείρησας, οὐδὲν ὢν καὶ ταῦτα.

Ἅδην, ἦν δὲ ἐγώ, τῶν τοιούτων. ἀλλ' εἰπέ μοι· ὁ τῶι ἀκριβεῖ λόγωι ἰατρός, ὃν ἄρτι ἔλεγες, πότερον χρηματιστής ἐστιν ἢ τῶν καμνόντων θεραπευτής; καὶ λέγε τὸν τῶι ὄντι ἰατρὸν ὄντα.

Τῶν καμνόντων, ἔφη, θεραπευτής.

Τί δὲ κυβερνήτης; ὁ ὀρθῶς κυβερνήτης ναυτῶν ἄρχων ἐστὶν ἢ ναύτης;

Ναυτῶν ἄρχων. **d**

Οὐδὲν οἶμαι τοῦτο ὑπολογιστέον, ὅτι πλεῖ ἐν τῆι νηί, οὐδέ ἐστι κλητέος ναύτης· οὐ γὰρ κατὰ τὸ πλεῖν κυβερνήτης καλεῖται, ἀλλὰ κατὰ τὴν τέχνην καὶ τὴν τῶν ναυτῶν ἀρχήν.

Ἀληθῆ, ἔφη.

Οὐκοῦν ἑκάστωι τούτων ἔστι τι συμφέρον;

Πάνυ γε.

Οὐ καὶ ἡ τέχνη, ἦν δὲ ἐγώ, ἐπὶ τούτωι πέφυκεν, ἐπὶ τῶι τὸ συμφέρον ἑκάστωι ζητεῖν τε καὶ ἐκπορίζειν;

Ἐπὶ τούτωι, ἔφη.

Ἆρα οὖν καὶ ἑκάστηι τῶν τεχνῶν ἔστι τι συμφέρον ἄλλο ἢ ὅτι μάλιστα τελέαν εἶναι;

e Πῶς τοῦτο ἐρωτᾶις;

Ὥσπερ, ἔφην ἐγώ, εἴ με ἔροιο εἰ ἐξαρκεῖ σώματι εἶναι σώματι ἢ προσδεῖταί τινος, εἴποιμι ἂν ὅτι Παντάπασι μὲν οὖν προσδεῖται· διὰ ταῦτα καὶ ἡ τέχνη ἐστὶν ἡ ἰατρικὴ νῦν ηὑρημένη, ὅτι σῶμά ἐστι πονηρὸν καὶ οὐκ ἐξαρκεῖ αὐτῶι τοιούτωι εἶναι. τούτωι οὖν ὅπως ἐκπορίζηι τὰ συμφέροντα, ἐπὶ τοῦτο παρεσκευάσθη ἡ τέχνη. ἦ ὀρθῶς σοι δοκῶ, ἔφην, ἂν εἰπεῖν οὕτω λέγων, ἢ οὔ;

342a Ὀρθῶς, ἔφη.

Τί δὲ δή; αὐτὴ ἡ ἰατρική ἐστι πονηρά, ἢ ἄλλη τις τέχνη ἔστιν ὅτι προσδεῖταί τινος ἀρετῆς (ὥσπερ ὀφθαλμοὶ ὄψεως καὶ ὦτα ἀκοῆς, καὶ διὰ ταῦτα ἐπὶ αὐτοῖς δεῖ τινος τέχνης τῆς τὸ συμφέρον εἰς ταῦτα σκεψομένης τε καὶ ἐκποριούσης), ἆρα καὶ ἐν αὐτῆι τῆι τέχνηι ἔνι τις πονηρία, καὶ δεῖ ἑκάστηι τέχνηι ἄλλης τέχνης ἥτις αὐτῆι τὸ συμφέρον σκέψεται, καὶ τῆι σκοπουμένηι ἑτέρας αὖ τοιαύτης, καὶ τοῦτό ἐστιν
b ἀπέραντον, ἢ αὐτὴ αὑτῆι τὸ συμφέρον σκέψεται; ἢ οὔτε αὑτῆς οὔτε ἄλλης προσδεῖται ἐπὶ τὴν αὑτῆς πονηρίαν τὸ συμφέρον σκοπεῖν (οὔτε γὰρ πονηρία οὔτε ἁμαρτία οὐδεμία οὐδεμιᾶι τέχνηι πάρεστιν), οὐδὲ προσήκει τέχνηι ἄλλωι τὸ συμφέρον ζητεῖν ἢ ἐκείνωι οὗ τέχνη ἐστίν, αὐτὴ δὲ ἀβλαβὴς καὶ ἀκέραιός ἐστιν ὀρθὴ οὖσα, ἕωσπερ ἂν ἦι ἑκάστη ἀκριβὴς ὅλη ἥπερ ἐστίν; καὶ σκόπει ἐκείνωι τῶι ἀκριβεῖ λόγωι· οὕτως ἢ ἄλλως ἔχει;

Οὕτως, ἔφη, φαίνεται.

c Οὐκ ἄρα, ἦν δὲ ἐγώ, ἰατρικὴ ἰατρικῆι τὸ συμφέρον σκοπεῖ ἀλλὰ σώματι.

Ναί, ἔφη.

Οὐδὲ ἱππικὴ ἱππικῆι ἀλλὰ ἵπποις, οὐδὲ ἄλλη τέχνη οὐδεμία ἑαυτῆι (οὐδὲ γὰρ προσδεῖται), ἀλλὰ ἐκείνωι οὗ τέχνη ἐστίν.

Φαίνεται, ἔφη, οὕτως.

Ἀλλὰ μήν, ὦ Θρασύμαχε, ἄρχουσί γε αἱ τέχναι καὶ κρατοῦσιν ἐκείνου οὗπέρ εἰσι τέχναι.

Συνεχώρησεν ἐνταῦθα καὶ μάλα μόγις.

341e6 τοῦτο **F**: τούτωι **AD**

Οὐκ ἄρα ἐπιστήμη γε οὐδεμία τὸ τοῦ κρείττονος συμφέρον σκοπεῖ οὐδὲ ἐπιτάττει, ἀλλὰ τὸ τοῦ ἥττονός τε καὶ ἀρχομένου ὑπὸ ἑαυτῆς. d

Συνωμολόγησε μὲν καὶ ταῦτα τελευτῶν, ἐπεχείρει δὲ περὶ αὐτὰ μάχεσθαι· ἐπειδὴ δὲ ὡμολόγησεν, Ἄλλο τι οὖν, ἦν δὲ ἐγώ, οὐδὲ ἰατρὸς οὐδείς, κατὰ ὅσον ἰατρός, τὸ τῶι ἰατρῶι συμφέρον σκοπεῖ οὐδὲ ἐπιτάττει, ἀλλὰ τὸ τῶι κάμνοντι; ὡμολόγηται γὰρ ὁ ἀκριβὴς ἰατρὸς σωμάτων εἶναι ἄρχων ἀλλὰ οὐ χρηματιστής. ἢ οὐχ ὡμολόγηται;

Συνέφη.

Οὐκοῦν καὶ ὁ κυβερνήτης ὁ ἀκριβὴς ναυτῶν εἶναι ἄρχων ἀλλὰ οὐ ναύτης; e

Ὡμολόγηται.

Οὐκ ἄρα ὅ γε τοιοῦτος κυβερνήτης τε καὶ ἄρχων τὸ τῶι κυβερνήτηι συμφέρον σκέψεταί τε καὶ προστάξει, ἀλλὰ τὸ τῶι ναύτηι τε καὶ ἀρχομένωι.

Συνέφησε μόγις.

Οὐκοῦν, ἦν δὲ ἐγώ, ὦ Θρασύμαχε, οὐδὲ ἄλλος οὐδεὶς ἐν οὐδεμιᾶι ἀρχῆι, κατὰ ὅσον ἄρχων ἐστίν, τὸ αὑτῶι συμφέρον σκοπεῖ οὐδὲ ἐπιτάττει, ἀλλὰ τὸ τῶι ἀρχομένωι καὶ ὧι ἂν αὐτὸς δημιουργῆι, καὶ πρὸς ἐκεῖνο βλέπων καὶ τὸ ἐκείνωι συμφέρον καὶ πρέπον, καὶ λέγει ἃ λέγει καὶ ποιεῖ ἃ ποιεῖ ἅπαντα;

Ἐπειδὴ οὖν ἐνταῦθα ἦμεν τοῦ λόγου καὶ πᾶσι καταφανὲς ἦν ὅτι 343 ὁ τοῦ δικαίου λόγος εἰς τὸ ἐναντίον περιειστήκει, ὁ Θρασύμαχος ἀντὶ τοῦ ἀποκρίνεσθαι, Εἰπέ μοι, ἔφη, ὦ Σώκρατες, τίτθη σοι ἔστιν;

Τί δέ; ἦν δὲ ἐγώ· οὐκ ἀποκρίνεσθαι χρῆν μᾶλλον ἢ τοιαῦτα ἐρωτᾶν;

Ὅτι τοί σε, ἔφη, κορυζῶντα περιορᾶι καὶ οὐκ ἀπομύττει δεόμενον, ὅς γε αὐτῆι οὐδὲ πρόβατα οὐδὲ ποιμένα γιγνώσκεις.

Ὅτι δὴ τί μάλιστα; ἦν δὲ ἐγώ.

Ὅτι οἴει τοὺς ποιμένας ἢ τοὺς βουκόλους τὸ τῶν προβάτων ἢ τὸ b τῶν βοῶν ἀγαθὸν σκοπεῖν, καὶ παχύνειν αὐτοὺς καὶ θεραπεύειν πρὸς ἄλλο τι βλέποντας ἢ τὸ τῶν δεσποτῶν ἀγαθὸν καὶ τὸ αὑτῶν, καὶ δὴ καὶ τοὺς ἐν ταῖς πόλεσιν ἄρχοντας, οἳ ὡς ἀληθῶς ἄρχουσιν, ἄλλως πως ἡγῆι διανοεῖσθαι πρὸς τοὺς ἀρχομένους ἢ ὥσπερ ἄν τις πρὸς πρόβατα διατεθείη, καὶ ἄλλο τι σκοπεῖν αὐτοὺς διὰ νυκτὸς καὶ ἡμέρας ἢ τοῦτο ὅθεν αὐτοὶ ὠφελήσονται. καὶ οὕτω πόρρω εἶ περί c τε τοῦ δικαίου καὶ δικαιοσύνης καὶ ἀδίκου τε καὶ ἀδικίας, ὥστε ἀγνοεῖς ὅτι ἡ μὲν δικαιοσύνη καὶ τὸ δίκαιον ἀλλότριον ἀγαθὸν τῶι

ὄντι, τοῦ κρείττονός τε καὶ ἄρχοντος συμφέρον, οἰκεία δὲ τοῦ πειθομένου τε καὶ ὑπηρετοῦντος βλάβη, ἡ δὲ ἀδικία τὸ ἐναντίον, καὶ ἄρχει τῶν ὡς ἀληθῶς εὐηθικῶν τε καὶ δικαίων, οἱ δὲ ἀρχόμενοι ποιοῦσιν τὸ ἐκείνου συμφέρον κρείττονος ὄντος, καὶ εὐδαίμονα ἐκεῖνον
d ποιοῦσιν ὑπηρετοῦντες αὐτῶι, ἑαυτοὺς δὲ οὐδὲ ὁπωστιοῦν. σκοπεῖσθαι δέ, ὦ εὐηθέστατε Σώκρατες, οὑτωσὶ χρή, ὅτι δίκαιος ἀνὴρ ἀδίκου πανταχοῦ ἔλαττον ἔχει· πρῶτον μὲν ἐν τοῖς πρὸς ἀλλήλους συμβολαίοις, ὅπου ἂν ὁ τοιοῦτος τῶι τοιούτωι κοινωνήσηι, οὐδαμοῦ ἂν εὕροις ἐν τῆι διαλύσει τῆς κοινωνίας πλέον ἔχοντα τὸν δίκαιον τοῦ ἀδίκου ἀλλὰ ἔλαττον· ἔπειτα ἐν τοῖς πρὸς τὴν πόλιν, ὅταν τέ τινες εἰσφοραὶ ὦσιν, ὁ μὲν δίκαιος ἀπὸ τῶν ἴσων πλέον εἰσφέρει, ὁ
e δὲ ἔλαττον, ὅταν τε λήψεις, ὁ μὲν οὐδέν, ὁ δὲ πολλὰ κερδαίνει. καὶ γὰρ ὅταν ἀρχήν τινα ἄρχηι ἑκάτερος, τῶι μὲν δικαίωι ὑπάρχει, καὶ εἰ μηδεμία ἄλλη ζημία, τά γε οἰκεῖα διὰ ἀμέλειαν μοχθηροτέρως ἔχειν, ἐκ δὲ τοῦ δημοσίου μηδὲν ὠφελεῖσθαι διὰ τὸ δίκαιον εἶναι, πρὸς δὲ τούτοις ἀπεχθέσθαι τοῖς τε οἰκείοις καὶ τοῖς γνωρίμοις, ὅταν μηδὲν ἐθέληι αὐτοῖς ὑπηρετεῖν παρὰ τὸ δίκαιον· τῶι δὲ ἀδίκωι πάντα τούτων τὰ ἐναντία ὑπάρχει. λέγω γὰρ ὅνπερ νυνδὴ ἔλεγον,
344 τὸν μεγάλα δυνάμενον πλεονεκτεῖν· τοῦτον οὖν σκόπει, εἴπερ βούλει κρίνειν ὅσωι μᾶλλον συμφέρει ἰδίαι αὐτῶι ἄδικον εἶναι ἢ τὸ δίκαιον.

Πάντων δὲ ῥᾶιστα μαθήσηι, ἐὰν ἐπὶ τὴν τελεωτάτην ἀδικίαν ἔλθηις, ἣ τὸν μὲν ἀδικήσαντα εὐδαιμονέστατον ποιεῖ, τοὺς δὲ ἀδικηθέντας καὶ ἀδικῆσαι οὐκ ἂν ἐθέλοντας ἀθλιωτάτους. ἔστι δὲ τοῦτο τυραννίς, ἣ οὐ κατὰ σμικρὸν τὰ ἀλλότρια καὶ λάθραι καὶ βίαι ἀφαιρεῖται,
b καὶ ἱερὰ καὶ ὅσια καὶ ἴδια καὶ δημόσια, ἀλλὰ συλλήβδην· ὧν ἐπὶ ἑκάστωι μέρει ὅταν τις ἀδικήσας μὴ λάθηι, ζημιοῦταί τε καὶ ὀνείδη ἔχει τὰ μέγιστα· καὶ γὰρ ἱερόσυλοι καὶ ἀνδραποδισταὶ καὶ τοιχωρύχοι καὶ ἀποστερηταὶ καὶ κλέπται οἱ κατὰ μέρη ἀδικοῦντες τῶν τοιούτων κακουργημάτων καλοῦνται. ἐπειδὰν δέ τις πρὸς τοῖς τῶν πολιτῶν χρήμασιν καὶ αὐτοὺς ἀνδραποδισάμενος δουλώσηται, ἀντὶ τούτων τῶν αἰσχρῶν ὀνομάτων εὐδαίμονες καὶ μακάριοι κέκληνται, οὐ μόνον
c ὑπὸ τῶν πολιτῶν ἀλλὰ καὶ ὑπὸ τῶν ἄλλων ὅσοι ἂν πύθωνται αὐτὸν τὴν ὅλην ἀδικίαν ἠδικηκότα· οὐ γὰρ τὸ ποιεῖν τὰ ἄδικα ἀλλὰ τὸ πάσχειν φοβούμενοι ὀνειδίζουσιν οἱ ὀνειδίζοντες τὴν ἀδικίαν. οὕτως, ὦ Σώκρατες, καὶ ἰσχυρότερον καὶ ἐλευθεριώτερον καὶ δεσποτικώτερον ἀδικία δικαιοσύνης ἐστὶν ἱκανῶς γιγνομένη, καὶ ὅπερ ἐξ ἀρχῆς ἔλεγον, τὸ μὲν τοῦ κρείττονος συμφέρον τὸ δίκαιον τυγχάνει ὄν, τὸ δὲ ἄδικον ἑαυτῶι λυσιτελοῦν τε καὶ συμφέρον.

Ταῦτα εἰπὼν ὁ Θρασύμαχος ἐν νῶι εἶχεν ἀπιέναι, ὥσπερ βαλα- d
νεὺς ἡμῶν καταντλήσας κατὰ τῶν ὤτων ἁθρόον καὶ πολὺν τὸν
λόγον· οὐ μὴν εἴασάν γε αὐτὸν οἱ παρόντες, ἀλλὰ ἠνάγκασαν ὑπο-
μεῖναί τε καὶ παρασχεῖν τῶν εἰρημένων λόγον. καὶ δὴ ἔγωγε καὶ
αὐτὸς πάνυ ἐδεόμην τε καὶ εἶπον· Ὦ δαιμόνιε Θρασύμαχε, οἷον
ἐμβαλὼν λόγον ἐν νῶι ἔχεις ἀπιέναι πρὶν διδάξαι ἱκανῶς ἢ μαθεῖν
εἴτε οὕτως εἴτε ἄλλως ἔχει. ἢ σμικρὸν οἴει ἐπιχειρεῖν πρᾶγμα διορί- e
ζεσθαι, ἀλλὰ οὐ βίου διαγωγήν, ἧι ἂν διαγόμενος ἕκαστος ἡμῶν
λυσιτελεστάτην ζωὴν ζώιη;

Ἐγὼ γὰρ οἶμαι, ἔφη ὁ Θρασύμαχος, τουτὶ ἄλλως ἔχειν;

Ἔοικας, ἦν δὲ ἐγώ, ἤτοι ἡμῶν γε οὐδὲν κήδεσθαι, οὐδέ τι φροντί-
ζειν εἴτε χεῖρον εἴτε βέλτιον βιωσόμεθα ἀγνοοῦντες ὃ σὺ φῂς εἰδέναι.
ἀλλά, ὦ ἀγαθέ, προθυμοῦ καὶ ἡμῖν ἐνδείξασθαι· οὔ τοι κακῶς σοι **345**
κείσεται ὅτι ἂν ἡμᾶς τοσούσδε ὄντας εὐεργετήσηις. ἐγὼ γὰρ δή σοι
λέγω τό γε ἐμόν, ὅτι οὐ πείθομαι οὐδὲ οἶμαι ἀδικίαν δικαιοσύνης
κερδαλεώτερον εἶναι, οὐδὲ ἐὰν ἐᾶι τις αὐτὴν καὶ μὴ διακωλύηι πράττειν ἃ βούλεται. ἀλλά, ὦ ἀγαθέ, ἔστω μὲν ἄδικος, δυνάσθω δὲ ἀδικεῖν ἢ τῶι λανθάνειν ἢ τῶι διαμάχεσθαι, ὅμως ἐμέ γε οὐ πείθεις ὡς ἔστι
τῆς δικαιοσύνης κερδαλεώτερον. ταῦτα οὖν καὶ ἕτερος ἴσως τις ἡμῶν b
πέπονθεν, οὐ μόνος ἐγώ· πεῖσον οὖν, ὦ μακάριε, ἱκανῶς ἡμᾶς ὅτι οὐκ
ὀρθῶς βουλευόμεθα δικαιοσύνην ἀδικίας περὶ πλείονος ποιούμενοι.

Καὶ πῶς, ἔφη, σε πείσω; εἰ γὰρ οἷς νυνδὴ ἔλεγον μὴ πέπεισαι, τί σοι
ἔτι ποιήσω; ἢ εἰς τὴν ψυχὴν φέρων ἐνθῶ τὸν λόγον;

Μὰ Δία, ἦν δὲ ἐγώ, μὴ σύ γε· ἀλλὰ πρῶτον μέν, ἃ ἂν εἴπηις, ἔμμε-
νε τούτοις, ἢ ἐὰν μετατιθῆι, φανερῶς μετατίθεσο καὶ ἡμᾶς μὴ ἐξαπάτα.
νῦν δὲ ὁρᾶις, ὦ Θρασύμαχε (ἔτι γὰρ τὰ ἔμπροσθεν ἐπισκεψώμεθα), c
ὅτι τὸν ὡς ἀληθῶς ἰατρὸν τὸ πρῶτον ὁριζόμενος τὸν ὡς ἀληθῶς
ποιμένα οὐκέτι ὤιου δεῖν ὕστερον ἀκριβῶς φυλάξαι, ἀλλὰ πιαίνειν
οἴει αὐτὸν τὰ πρόβατα, κατὰ ὅσον ποιμήν ἐστιν, οὐ πρὸς τὸ τῶν
προβάτων βέλτιστον βλέποντα ἀλλά, ὥσπερ δαιτυμόνα τινὰ καὶ
μέλλοντα ἑστιάσεσθαι, πρὸς τὴν εὐωχίαν, ἢ αὖ πρὸς τὸ ἀποδόσθαι,
ὥσπερ χρηματιστὴν ἀλλὰ οὐ ποιμένα. τῆι δὲ ποιμενικῆι οὐ δήπου d
ἄλλου του μέλει ἢ ἐπὶ ὧι τέτακται, ὅπως τούτωι τὸ βέλτιστον
ἐκποριεῖ· ἐπεὶ τά γε αὑτῆς ὥστε εἶναι βελτίστη ἱκανῶς δήπου ἐκπεπόρισται, ἕως γε ἂν μηδὲν ἐνδέηι τοῦ ποιμενικὴ εἶναι. οὕτω δὴ

345a6 πείθεις Vindobon. phil. gr. 89, Ficino (*suades*): πείθει **ADF**   c3 πιαίνειν **A** Euseb. Galen.: ποιμαίνειν $\mathbf{A}^{mg}$**D**: παχύνει **F**

ὤιμην ἔγωγε νυνδὴ ἀναγκαῖον εἶναι ἡμῖν ὁμολογεῖν πᾶσαν ἀρχήν, κατὰ ὅσον ἀρχή, μηδενὶ ἄλλωι τὸ βέλτιστον σκοπεῖσθαι ἢ ἐκείνωι, e τῶι ἀρχομένωι τε καὶ θεραπευομένωι, ἔν τε πολιτικῆι καὶ ἰδιωτικῆι ἀρχῆι. σὺ δὲ τοὺς ἄρχοντας ἐν ταῖς πόλεσιν, τοὺς ὡς ἀληθῶς ἄρχοντας, ἑκόντας οἴει ἄρχειν;

Μὰ Δία οὔκ, ἔφη· ἀλλ᾽ εὖ οἶδα.

Τί δέ, ἦν δὲ ἐγώ, ὦ Θρασύμαχε; τὰς ἄλλας ἀρχὰς οὐκ ἐννοεῖς ὅτι οὐδεὶς ἐθέλει ἄρχειν ἑκών, ἀλλὰ μισθὸν αἰτοῦσιν, ὡς οὐχὶ αὐτοῖσιν 346 ὠφελίαν ἐσομένην ἐκ τοῦ ἄρχειν ἀλλὰ τοῖς ἀρχομένοις; ἐπεὶ τοσόνδε εἰπέ· οὐχὶ ἑκάστην μέντοι φαμὲν ἑκάστοτε τῶν τεχνῶν τούτωι ἑτέραν εἶναι, τῶι ἑτέραν τὴν δύναμιν ἔχειν; καί, ὦ μακάριε, μὴ παρὰ δόξαν ἀποκρίνου, ἵνα τι καὶ περαίνωμεν.

Ἀλλὰ τούτωι, ἔφη, ἑτέρα.

Οὐκοῦν καὶ ὠφελίαν ἑκάστη ἰδίαν τινὰ ἡμῖν παρέχεται ἀλλ᾽ οὐ κοινήν, οἷον ἰατρικὴ μὲν ὑγίειαν, κυβερνητικὴ δὲ σωτηρίαν ἐν τῶι πλεῖν, καὶ αἱ ἄλλαι οὕτω;

Πάνυ γε.

b Οὐκοῦν καὶ μισθωτικὴ μισθόν; αὕτη γὰρ αὐτῆς ἡ δύναμις· ἢ τὴν ἰατρικὴν σὺ καὶ τὴν κυβερνητικὴν τὴν αὐτὴν καλεῖς; ἢ ἐάνπερ βούληι ἀκριβῶς διορίζειν, ὥσπερ ὑπέθου, οὐδέν τι μᾶλλον, ἐάν τις κυβερνῶν ὑγιὴς γίγνηται διὰ τὸ συμφέρειν αὐτῶι πλεῖν ἐν τῆι θαλάττηι, ἕνεκα τούτου καλεῖς μᾶλλον αὐτὴν ἰατρικήν;

Οὐ δῆτα, ἔφη.

Οὐδέ γε, οἶμαι, τὴν μισθωτικήν, ἐὰν ὑγιαίνηι τις μισθαρνῶν.

Οὐ δῆτα.

Τί δέ; τὴν ἰατρικὴν μισθαρνητικήν, ἐὰν ἰώμενός τις μισθαρνῆι;

c Οὔκ, ἔφη.

Οὐκοῦν τήν γε ὠφελίαν ἑκάστης τῆς τέχνης ἰδίαν ὡμολογήσαμεν εἶναι;

Ἔστω, ἔφη.

Ἥντινα ἄρα ὠφελίαν κοινῆι ὠφελοῦνται πάντες οἱ δημιουργοί, δῆλον ὅτι κοινῆι τινι τῶι αὐτῶι προσχρώμενοι ἀπὸ ἐκείνου ὠφελοῦνται.

Ἔοικεν, ἔφη.

Φαμὲν δέ γε τὸ μισθὸν ἀρνυμένους ὠφελεῖσθαι τοὺς δημιουργοὺς ἀπὸ τοῦ προσχρῆσθαι τῆι μισθωτικῆι τέχνηι γίγνεσθαι αὐτοῖς.

346b4 ξυμφέρειν **F**: ξυμφέρον **AD**

Συνέφη μόγις.

Οὐκ ἄρα ἀπὸ τῆς αὑτοῦ τέχνης ἑκάστωι αὕτη ἡ ὠφελία ἐστίν, ἡ d
τοῦ μισθοῦ λῆψις, ἀλλά, εἰ δεῖ ἀκριβῶς σκοπεῖσθαι, ἡ μὲν ἰατρικὴ
ὑγίειαν ποιεῖ, ἡ δὲ μισθαρνητικὴ μισθόν, καὶ ἡ μὲν οἰκοδομικὴ οἰκίαν,
ἡ δὲ μισθαρνητικὴ αὐτῆι ἑπομένη μισθόν, καὶ αἱ ἄλλαι πᾶσαι οὕτως
τὸ αὑτῆς ἑκάστη ἔργον ἐργάζεται καὶ ὠφελεῖ ἐκεῖνο ἐπὶ ὧι τέτακται.
ἐὰν δὲ μὴ μισθὸς αὐτῆι προσγίγνηται, ἔστιν ὅτι ὠφελεῖται ὁ δημιουργὸς ἀπὸ τῆς τέχνης;

Οὐ φαίνεται, ἔφη.

Ἆρα οὖν οὐδὲ ὠφελεῖ τότε, ὅταν προῖκα ἐργάζηται; e

Οἶμαι ἔγωγε.

Οὐκοῦν, ὦ Θρασύμαχε, τοῦτο ἤδη δῆλον, ὅτι οὐδεμία τέχνη οὐδὲ
ἀρχὴ τὸ αὑτῆι ὠφέλιμον παρασκευάζει, ἀλλ', ὅπερ πάλαι ἐλέγομεν,
τὸ τῶι ἀρχομένωι καὶ παρασκευάζει καὶ ἐπιτάττει, τὸ ἐκείνου συμφέρον ἥττονος ὄντος σκοποῦσα, ἀλλ' οὐ τὸ τοῦ κρείττονος; διὰ δὴ
ταῦτα ἔγωγε, ὦ φίλε Θρασύμαχε, καὶ ἄρτι ἔλεγον μηδένα ἐθέλειν
ἑκόντα ἄρχειν καὶ τὰ ἀλλότρια κακὰ μεταχειρίζεσθαι ἀνορθοῦντα,
ἀλλὰ μισθὸν αἰτεῖν, ὅτι ὁ μέλλων καλῶς τῆι τέχνηι πράξειν οὐδέ- 347
ποτε αὑτῶι τὸ βέλτιστον πράττει οὐδὲ ἐπιτάττει κατὰ τὴν τέχνην
ἐπιτάττων, ἀλλὰ τῶι ἀρχομένωι· ὧν δὴ ἕνεκα, ὡς ἔοικε, μισθὸν δεῖν
ὑπάρχειν τοῖς μέλλουσιν ἐθελήσειν ἄρχειν, ἢ ἀργύριον ἢ τιμήν, ἢ
ζημίαν ἐὰν μὴ ἄρχηι.

Πῶς τοῦτο λέγεις, ὦ Σώκρατες; ἔφη ὁ Γλαύκων. τοὺς μὲν γὰρ
δύο μισθοὺς γιγνώσκω, τὴν δὲ ζημίαν ἥντινα λέγεις καὶ ὡς ἐν μισθοῦ
μέρει εἴρηκας, οὐ συνῆκα.

Τὸν τῶν βελτίστων ἄρα μισθόν, ἔφην, οὐ συνίης, δι' ὃν ἄρχουσιν b
οἱ ἐπιεικέστατοι, ὅταν ἐθέλωσιν ἄρχειν. ἢ οὐκ οἶσθα ὅτι τὸ φιλότιμόν
τε καὶ φιλάργυρον εἶναι ὄνειδος λέγεταί τε καὶ ἔστιν;

Ἔγωγε, ἔφη.

Διὰ ταῦτα τοίνυν, ἦν δ' ἐγώ, οὔτε χρημάτων ἕνεκα ἐθέλουσιν
ἄρχειν οἱ ἀγαθοὶ οὔτε τιμῆς· οὔτε γὰρ φανερῶς πραττόμενοι τῆς
ἀρχῆς ἕνεκα μισθὸν μισθωτοὶ βούλονται κεκλῆσθαι, οὔτε λάθραι
αὐτοὶ ἐκ τῆς ἀρχῆς λαμβάνοντες κλέπται· οὐδ' αὖ τιμῆς ἕνεκα· οὐ
γάρ εἰσι φιλότιμοι. δεῖ δὴ αὐτοῖς ἀνάγκην προσεῖναι καὶ ζημίαν, εἰ c
μέλλουσιν ἐθέλειν ἄρχειν· ὅθεν κινδυνεύει τὸ ἑκόντα ἐπὶ τὸ ἄρχειν
ἰέναι ἀλλὰ μὴ ἀνάγκην περιμένειν αἰσχρὸν νενομίσθαι. τῆς δὲ ζημίας
μεγίστη τὸ ὑπὸ πονηροτέρου ἄρχεσθαι, ἐὰν μὴ αὐτὸς ἐθέληι ἄρχειν·
ἣν δείσαντές μοι φαίνονται ἄρχειν, ὅταν ἄρχωσιν, οἱ ἐπιεικεῖς, καὶ
τότε ἔρχονται ἐπὶ τὸ ἄρχειν, οὐχ ὡς ἐπ' ἀγαθόν τι ἰόντες οὐδ' ὡς

εὐπαθήσοντες ἐν αὐτῶι, ἀλλὰ ὡς ἐπὶ ἀναγκαῖον, καὶ οὐκ ἔχοντες
d ἑαυτῶν βελτίοσιν ἐπιτρέψαι οὐδὲ ὁμοίοις. ἐπεὶ κινδυνεύει πόλις ἀνδρῶν ἀγαθῶν εἰ γένοιτο, περιμάχητον ἂν εἶναι τὸ μὴ ἄρχειν ὥσπερ νυνὶ τὸ ἄρχειν, καὶ ἐνταῦθα ἂν καταφανὲς γενέσθαι ὅτι τῶι ὄντι ἀληθινὸς ἄρχων οὐ πέφυκε τὸ αὑτῶι συμφέρον σκοπεῖσθαι ἀλλὰ τὸ τῶι ἀρχομένωι· ὥστε πᾶς ἂν ὁ γιγνώσκων τὸ ὠφελεῖσθαι μᾶλλον ἕλοιτο ὑπὸ ἄλλου ἢ ἄλλον ὠφελῶν πράγματα ἔχειν. τοῦτο μὲν οὖν
e ἔγωγε οὐδαμῆι συγχωρῶ Θρασυμάχωι, ὡς τὸ δίκαιόν ἐστι τὸ τοῦ κρείττονος συμφέρον. ἀλλὰ τοῦτο μὲν δὴ καὶ εἰς αὖθις σκεψόμεθα· πολὺ δέ μοι δοκεῖ μεῖζον εἶναι ὃ νῦν λέγει Θρασύμαχος, τὸν τοῦ ἀδίκου βίον φάσκων εἶναι κρείττω ἢ τὸν τοῦ δικαίου. σὺ οὖν ποτέρως, ἦν δὲ ἐγώ, ὦ Γλαύκων, αἱρῆι; καὶ πότερον ἀληθεστέρως δοκεῖ σοι λέγεσθαι;

Τὸν τοῦ δικαίου ἔγωγε λυσιτελέστερον βίον εἶναι.

348a Ἤκουσας, ἦν δὲ ἐγώ, ὅσα ἄρτι Θρασύμαχος ἀγαθὰ διῆλθε τῶι τοῦ ἀδίκου;

Ἤκουσα, ἔφη, ἀλλὰ οὐ πείθομαι.

Βούλει οὖν αὐτὸν πείθωμεν, ἂν δυνώμεθά πηι ἐξευρεῖν, ὡς οὐκ ἀληθῆ λέγει;

Πῶς γὰρ οὐ βούλομαι; ἦ δὲ ὅς.

Ἂν μὲν τοίνυν, ἦν δὲ ἐγώ, ἀντικατατείναντες λέγωμεν αὐτῶι λόγον παρὰ λόγον, ὅσα αὖ ἀγαθὰ ἔχει τὸ δίκαιον εἶναι, καὶ αὖθις οὗτος, καὶ ἄλλον ἡμεῖς, ἀριθμεῖν δεήσει τὰ ἀγαθὰ καὶ μετρεῖν ὅσα
b ἑκάτεροι ἐν ἑκατέρωι λέγομεν, καὶ ἤδη δικαστῶν τινων τῶν διακρινούντων δεησόμεθα· ἂν δὲ ὥσπερ ἄρτι ἀνομολογούμενοι πρὸς ἀλλήλους σκοπῶμεν, ἅμα αὐτοί τε δικασταὶ καὶ ῥήτορες ἐσόμεθα.

Πάνυ μὲν οὖν, ἔφη.

Ποτέρως οὖν σοι, ἦν δὲ ἐγώ, ἀρέσκει.

Οὕτως, ἔφη.

Ἴθι δή, ἦν δὲ ἐγώ, ὦ Θρασύμαχε, ἀπόκριναι ἡμῖν ἐξ ἀρχῆς. τὴν τελέαν ἀδικίαν τελέας οὔσης δικαιοσύνης λυσιτελεστέραν φὴις εἶναι;

c Πάνυ μὲν οὖν καί φημι, ἔφη, καὶ διὰ ἅ, εἴρηκα.

Φέρε δή, τὸ τοιόνδε περὶ αὐτῶν πῶς λέγεις; τὸ μέν που ἀρετὴν αὐτοῖν καλεῖς, τὸ δὲ κακίαν;

Πῶς γὰρ οὔ;

348a1 ἤκουσας **A**: ἤκουσας οὖν **F**: ἤκουσας οὖς **D**

Οὐκοῦν τὴν μὲν δικαιοσύνην ἀρετήν, τὴν δὲ ἀδικίαν κακίαν;

Εἰκός γε, ἔφη, ὦ ἥδιστε, ἐπειδή γε καὶ λέγω ἀδικίαν μὲν λυσιτελεῖν, δικαιοσύνην δὲ οὔ.

Ἀλλὰ τί μήν;

Τὸ ἐναντίον, ἦ δὲ ὅς.

Ἦ τὴν δικαιοσύνην κακίαν;

Οὔκ, ἀλλὰ πάνυ γενναίαν εὐήθειαν. d

Τὴν ἀδικίαν ἄρα κακοήθειαν καλεῖς;

Οὔκ, ἀλλὰ εὐβουλίαν, ἔφη.

Ἦ καὶ φρόνιμοί σοι, ὦ Θρασύμαχε, δοκοῦσιν εἶναι καὶ ἀγαθοὶ οἱ ἄδικοι;

Οἵ γε τελέως, ἔφη, οἷοί τε ἀδικεῖν, πόλεις τε καὶ ἔθνη δυνάμενοι ἀνθρώπων ὑπὸ ἑαυτοὺς ποιεῖσθαι· σὺ δὲ οἴει με ἴσως τοὺς τὰ βαλλάντια ἀποτέμνοντας λέγειν. λυσιτελεῖ μὲν οὖν, ἦ δὲ ὅς, καὶ τὰ τοιαῦτα, ἐάνπερ λανθάνηι· ἔστι δὲ οὐκ ἄξια λόγου, ἀλλὰ ἃ νυνδὴ ἔλεγον.

Τοῦτο μέν, ἔφην, οὐκ ἀγνοῶ ὃ βούλει λέγειν, ἀλλὰ τόδε ἐθαύ- e
μασα, εἰ ἐν ἀρετῆς καὶ σοφίας τίθης μέρει τὴν ἀδικίαν, τὴν δὲ δικαιοσύνην ἐν τοῖς ἐναντίοις.

Ἀλλὰ πάνυ οὕτω τίθημι.

Τοῦτο, ἦν δὲ ἐγώ, ἤδη στερεώτερον, ὦ ἑταῖρε, καὶ οὐκέτι ῥάιδιον ἔχειν ὅτι τις εἴπηι. εἰ γὰρ λυσιτελεῖν μὲν τὴν ἀδικίαν ἐτίθεσο, κακίαν μέντοι ἢ αἰσχρὸν αὐτὸ ὡμολόγεις εἶναι ὥσπερ ἄλλοι τινές, εἴχομεν ἄν τι λέγειν κατὰ τὰ νομιζόμενα λέγοντες· νῦν δὲ δῆλος εἶ ὅτι φήσεις αὐτὸ καὶ καλὸν καὶ ἰσχυρὸν εἶναι καὶ τὰ ἄλλα αὐτῶι πάντα προσθήσεις ἃ ἡμεῖς τῶι δικαίωι προσετίθεμεν, ἐπειδή γε καὶ ἐν ἀρετῆι αὐτὸ **349**
καὶ σοφίαι ἐτόλμησας θεῖναι.

Ἀληθέστατα, ἔφη, μαντεύηι.

Ἀλλὰ οὐ μέντοι, ἦν δὲ ἐγώ, ἀποκνητέον γε τῶι λόγωι ἐπεξελθεῖν σκοπούμενον, ἕως ἄν σε ὑπολαμβάνω λέγειν ἅπερ διανοῆι. ἐμοὶ γὰρ δοκεῖς σύ, ὦ Θρασύμαχε, ἀτεχνῶς νῦν οὐ σκώπτειν, ἀλλὰ τὰ δοκοῦντα περὶ τῆς ἀληθείας λέγειν.

Τί δέ σοι, ἔφη, τοῦτο διαφέρει, εἴτε μοι δοκεῖ εἴτε μή, ἀλλὰ οὐ τὸν λόγον ἐλέγχεις;

Οὐδέν, ἦν δὲ ἐγώ. ἀλλὰ τόδε μοι πειρῶ ἔτι πρὸς τούτοις ἀποκρί- b
νασθαι· ὁ δίκαιος τοῦ δικαίου δοκεῖ τί σοι ἂν ἐθέλειν πλέον ἔχειν;

Οὐδαμῶς, ἔφη· οὐ γὰρ ἂν ἦν ἀστεῖος, ὥσπερ νῦν, καὶ εὐήθης.

Τί δέ; τῆς δικαίας πράξεως;

Οὐδὲ τῆς πράξεως, ἔφη.

Τοῦ δὲ ἀδίκου πότερον ἀξιοῖ ἂν πλεονεκτεῖν καὶ ἡγοῖτο δίκαιον εἶναι, ἢ οὐκ ἂν ἡγοῖτο;

Ἡγοῖτο ἄν, ἦ δὲ ὅς, καὶ ἀξιοῖ, ἀλλὰ οὐκ ἂν δύναιτο.

c Ἀλλὰ οὐ τοῦτο, ἦν δὲ ἐγώ, ἐρωτῶ, ἀλλὰ εἰ τοῦ μὲν δικαίου μὴ ἀξιοῖ πλέον ἔχειν μηδὲ βούλεται ὁ δίκαιος, τοῦ δὲ ἀδίκου;

Ἀλλὰ οὕτως, ἔφη, ἔχει.

Τί δὲ δὴ ὁ ἄδικος; ἆρα ἀξιοῖ τοῦ δικαίου πλεονεκτεῖν καὶ τῆς δικαίας πράξεως;

Πῶς γὰρ οὔκ; ἔφη, ὅς γε πάντων πλέον ἔχειν ἀξιοῖ;

Οὐκοῦν καὶ ἀδίκου ἀνθρώπου τε καὶ πράξεως ὁ ἄδικος πλεονεκτήσει καὶ ἁμιλλήσεται ὡς ἁπάντων πλεῖστον αὐτὸς λάβηι;

Ἔστι ταῦτα.

Ὧδε δὴ λέγωμεν, ἔφην· ὁ δίκαιος τοῦ μὲν ὁμοίου οὐ πλεονεκτεῖ,
d τοῦ δὲ ἀνομοίου, ὁ δὲ ἄδικος τοῦ τε ὁμοίου καὶ τοῦ ἀνομοίου;

Ἄριστα, ἔφη, εἴρηκας.

Ἔστι δέ γε, ἔφην, φρόνιμός τε καὶ ἀγαθὸς ὁ ἄδικος, ὁ δὲ δίκαιος οὐδέτερα;

Καὶ τοῦτο, ἔφη, εὖ.

Οὐκοῦν, ἦν δὲ ἐγώ, καὶ ἔοικε τῶι φρονίμωι καὶ τῶι ἀγαθῶι ὁ ἄδικος, ὁ δὲ δίκαιος οὐκ ἔοικεν;

Πῶς γὰρ οὐ μέλλει, ἔφη, ὁ τοιοῦτος ὢν καὶ ἐοικέναι τοῖς τοιούτοις, ὁ δὲ μὴ ἐοικέναι;

Καλῶς. τοιοῦτος ἄρα ἐστὶν ἑκάτερος αὐτῶν οἷσπερ ἔοικεν;

Ἀλλὰ τί μέλλει; ἔφη.

e Εἶέν, ὦ Θρασύμαχε· μουσικὸν δέ τινα λέγεις, ἕτερον δὲ ἄμουσον;

Ἔγωγε.

Πότερον φρόνιμον καὶ πότερον ἄφρονα;

Τὸν μὲν μουσικὸν δήπου φρόνιμον, τὸν δὲ ἄμουσον ἄφρονα.

Οὐκοῦν ἅπερ φρόνιμον, ἀγαθόν, ἃ δὲ ἄφρονα, κακόν;

Ναί.

Τί δὲ ἰατρικόν; οὐχ οὕτως;

Οὕτως.

Δοκεῖ ἂν οὖν τίς σοι, ὦ ἄριστε, μουσικὸς ἀνὴρ ἁρμοττόμενος λύραν ἐθέλειν μουσικοῦ ἀνδρὸς ἐν τῆι ἐπιτάσει καὶ ἀνέσει τῶν χορδῶν πλεονεκτεῖν ἢ ἀξιοῦν πλέον ἔχειν;

349b5 πράξεως Richards: δικαίας **ADF** Stob.

Οὐκ ἔμοιγε.

Τί δέ; ἀμούσου;

Ἀνάγκη, ἔφη.

Τί δὲ ἰατρικός; ἐν τῆι ἐδωδῆι ἢ πόσει ἐθέλειν ἄν τι ἰατρικοῦ πλεον- **350**
εκτεῖν ἢ ἀνδρὸς ἢ πράγματος;

Οὐ δῆτα.

Μὴ ἰατρικοῦ δέ;

Ναί.

Περὶ πάσης δὴ ὅρα ἐπιστήμης τε καὶ ἀνεπιστημοσύνης εἴ τίς σοι δοκεῖ ἐπιστήμων ὁστισοῦν πλείω ἂν ἐθέλειν αἱρεῖσθαι ἢ ὅσα ἄλλος ἐπιστήμων ἢ πράττειν ἢ λέγειν, καὶ οὐ τὰ αὐτὰ τῶι ὁμοίωι ἑαυτῶι εἰς τὴν αὐτὴν πρᾶξιν.

Ἀλλὰ ἴσως, ἔφη, ἀνάγκη τοῦτό γε οὕτως ἔχειν.

Τί δὲ ὁ ἀνεπιστήμων; οὐχὶ ὁμοίως μὲν ἐπιστήμονος πλεονεκτή-
σειεν ἄν, ὁμοίως δὲ ἀνεπιστήμονος; **b**

Ἴσως.

Ὁ δὲ ἐπιστήμων σοφός;

Φημί.

Ὁ δὲ σοφὸς ἀγαθός;

Φημί.

Ὁ ἄρα ἀγαθός τε καὶ σοφὸς τοῦ μὲν ὁμοίου οὐκ ἐθελήσει πλεονεκτεῖν, τοῦ δὲ ἀνομοίου τε καὶ ἐναντίου.

Ἔοικεν, ἔφη.

Ὁ δὲ κακός τε καὶ ἀμαθὴς τοῦ τε ὁμοίου καὶ τοῦ ἐναντίου.

Φαίνεται.

Οὐκοῦν, ὦ Θρασύμαχε, ἦν δὲ ἐγώ, ὁ ἄδικος ἡμῖν τοῦ ἀνομοίου τε καὶ ὁμοίου πλεονεκτεῖ; ἢ οὐχ οὕτως ἔλεγες;

Ἔγωγε, ἔφη.

Ὁ δέ γε δίκαιος τοῦ μὲν ὁμοίου οὐ πλεονεκτήσει, τοῦ δὲ ἀνομοίου; **c**

Ναί.

Ἔοικεν ἄρα, ἦν δὲ ἐγώ, ὁ μὲν δίκαιος τῶι σοφῶι καὶ ἀγαθῶι, ὁ δὲ ἄδικος τῶι κακῶι καὶ ἀμαθεῖ.

Κινδυνεύει.

Ἀλλὰ μὴν ὡμολογοῦμεν, ὧι γε ὅμοιος ἑκάτερος εἴη, τοιοῦτον καὶ ἑκάτερον εἶναι.

Ὡμολογοῦμεν γάρ.

350a6 δή **F** Stob.: δὲ **AD**

Ὁ μὲν ἄρα δίκαιος ἡμῖν ἀναπέφανται ὢν ἀγαθός τε καὶ σοφός, ὁ
δὲ ἄδικος ἀμαθής τε καὶ κακός.

Ὁ δὲ Θρασύμαχος ὡμολόγησε μὲν πάντα ταῦτα, οὐχ ὡς ἐγὼ
d νῦν ῥᾳδίως λέγω, ἀλλὰ ἑλκόμενος καὶ μόγις, μετὰ ἱδρῶτος θαυμαστοῦ ὅσου, ἅτε καὶ θέρους ὄντος. τότε καὶ εἶδον ἐγώ, πρότερον δὲ
οὔπω, Θρασύμαχον ἐρυθριῶντα. ἐπειδὴ δὲ οὖν διωμολογησάμεθα
τὴν δικαιοσύνην ἀρετὴν εἶναι καὶ σοφίαν, τὴν δὲ ἀδικίαν κακίαν τε
καὶ ἀμαθίαν, Εἶέν, ἦν δὲ ἐγώ, τοῦτο μὲν ἡμῖν οὕτω κείσθω. ἔφαμεν
δὲ δὴ καὶ ἰσχυρὸν εἶναι τὴν ἀδικίαν· ἢ οὐ μέμνησαι, ὦ Θρασύμαχε;

Μέμνημαι, ἔφη, ἀλλ' ἔμοιγε οὐδὲ ἃ νῦν λέγεις ἀρέσκει, καὶ ἔχω
e περὶ αὐτῶν λέγειν. εἰ οὖν λέγοιμι, εὖ οἶδα ὅτι δημηγορεῖν ἄν με
φαίης. ἢ οὖν ἔα με εἰπεῖν ὅσα βούλομαι, ἤ, εἰ βούλει ἐρωτᾶν, ἐρώτα·
ἐγὼ δέ σοι, ὥσπερ ταῖς γραυσὶ ταῖς τοὺς μύθους λεγούσαις, "Εἶέν"
ἐρῶ καὶ κατανεύσομαι καὶ ἀνανεύσομαι.

Μηδαμῶς, ἦν δὲ ἐγώ, παρά γε τὴν σαυτοῦ δόξαν.

Ὥστε σοί, ἔφη, ἀρέσκειν, ἐπειδήπερ οὐκ ἐᾷς λέγειν. καίτοι τί ἄλλο
βούλει;

Οὐδὲν μὰ Δία, ἦν δὲ ἐγώ, ἀλλ' εἴπερ τοῦτο ποιήσεις, ποίει· ἐγὼ
δὲ ἐρωτήσω.

Ἐρώτα δή.

Τοῦτο τοίνυν ἐρωτῶ, ὅπερ ἄρτι, ἵνα καὶ ἑξῆς διασκεψώμεθα τὸν
351 λόγον, ὁποῖόν τι τυγχάνει ὂν δικαιοσύνη πρὸς ἀδικίαν. ἐλέχθη γάρ
που ὅτι καὶ δυνατώτερον καὶ ἰσχυρότερον εἴη ἀδικία δικαιοσύνης·
νῦν δέ γε, ἔφην, εἴπερ σοφία τε καὶ ἀρετή ἐστι δικαιοσύνη, ῥᾳδίως,
οἶμαι, φανήσεται καὶ ἰσχυρότερον ἀδικίας, ἐπειδήπερ ἐστὶν ἀμαθία
ἡ ἀδικία (οὐδεὶς ἂν ἔτι τοῦτο ἀγνοήσειεν), ἀλλ' οὔ τι οὕτως ἁπλῶς,
ὦ Θρασύμαχε, ἔγωγε ἐπιθυμῶ, ἀλλὰ τῇδέ πῃ, σκέψασθαι· πόλιν
b φαίης ἂν ἄδικον εἶναι καὶ ἄλλας πόλεις ἐπιχειρεῖν δουλοῦσθαι ἀδίκως
καὶ καταδεδουλῶσθαι, πολλὰς δὲ καὶ ὑπὸ ἑαυτῇ ἔχειν δουλωσαμέ-
νην;

Πῶς γὰρ οὔκ; ἔφη. καὶ τοῦτό γε ἡ ἀρίστη μάλιστα ποιήσει καὶ
τελεώτατα, οὖσα ἄδικος.

Μανθάνω, ἔφην, ὅτι σὸς οὗτος ἦν ὁ λόγος. ἀλλὰ τόδε περὶ αὐτοῦ
σκοπῶ· πότερον ἡ κρείττων γιγνομένη πόλις πόλεως ἄνευ δικαιοσύνης τὴν δύναμιν ταύτην ἕξει, ἢ ἀνάγκη αὐτῇ μετὰ δικαιοσύνης;

c Εἰ μέν, ἔφη, ὡς σὺ ἄρτι ἔλεγες, [ἔχει] ἡ δικαιοσύνη σοφία, μετὰ
δικαιοσύνης· εἰ δὲ ὡς ἐγὼ ἔλεγον, μετὰ ἀδικίας.

351c1 ἔχει del. Tucker

Πάνυ ἄγαμαι, ἦν δὲ ἐγώ, ὦ Θρασύμαχε, ὅτι οὐκ ἐπινεύεις μόνον καὶ ἀνανεύεις, ἀλλὰ καὶ ἀποκρίνηι πάνυ καλῶς.

Σοὶ γάρ, ἔφη, χαρίζομαι.

Εὖ γε σὺ ποιῶν· ἀλλὰ δὴ καὶ τόδε μοι χάρισαι καὶ λέγε· δοκεῖς ἂν ἢ πόλιν ἢ στρατόπεδον ἢ λῃστὰς ἢ κλέπτας ἢ ἄλλο τι ἔθνος, ὅσα κοινῆι ἐπί τι ἔρχεται ἀδίκως, πρᾶξαι ἄν τι δύνασθαι, εἰ ἀδικοῖεν ἀλλήλους;

Οὐ δῆτα, ἦ δὲ ὅς. **d**

Τί δὲ εἰ μὴ ἀδικοῖεν; οὐ μᾶλλον;

Πάνυ γε.

Στάσεις γάρ που, ὦ Θρασύμαχε, ἥ γε ἀδικία καὶ μίση καὶ μάχας ἐν ἀλλήλοις παρέχει, ἡ δὲ δικαιοσύνη ὁμόνοιαν καὶ φιλίαν· ἦ γάρ;

Ἔστω, ἦ δὲ ὅς, ἵνα σοι μὴ διαφέρωμαι.

Ἀλλὰ εὖ γε σὺ ποιῶν, ὦ ἄριστε. τόδε δέ μοι λέγε· ἆρα εἰ τοῦτο ἔργον ἀδικίας, μῖσος ἐμποιεῖν ὅπου ἂν ἐνῆι, οὐ καὶ ἐν ἐλευθέροις τε καὶ δούλοις ἐγγιγνομένη μισεῖν ποιήσει ἀλλήλους καὶ στασιάζειν καὶ ἀδυνάτους εἶναι κοινῆι μετὰ ἀλλήλων πράττειν; **e**

Πάνυ γε.

Τί δὲ ἂν ἐν δυοῖν ἐγγένηται; οὐ διοίσονται καὶ μισήσουσι καὶ ἐχθροὶ ἔσονται ἀλλήλοις τε καὶ τοῖς δικαίοις;

Ἔσονται, ἔφη.

Ἐὰν δὲ δή, ὦ θαυμάσιε, ἐν ἑνὶ ἐγγένηται ἀδικία, μῶν μὴ ἀπολεῖ τὴν αὑτῆς δύναμιν; ἢ οὐδὲν ἧττον ἕξει;

Μηδὲν ἧττον ἐχέτω, ἔφη.

Οὐκοῦν τοιάνδε τινὰ φαίνεται ἔχουσα τὴν δύναμιν, οἵαν, ὧι ἂν ἐγγένηται, εἴτε πόλει τινὶ εἴτε γένει εἴτε στρατοπέδωι εἴτε ἄλλωι ὁτωιοῦν, πρῶτον μὲν ἀδύνατον αὐτὸ ποιεῖν πράττειν μετὰ αὑτοῦ **352a** διὰ τὸ στασιάζειν καὶ διαφέρεσθαι, ἔτι δὲ ἐχθρὸν εἶναι ἑαυτῶι τε καὶ τῶι ἐναντίωι παντὶ καὶ τῶι δικαίωι; οὐχ οὕτως;

Πάνυ γε.

Καὶ ἐν ἑνὶ δή, οἶμαι, ἐνοῦσα τὰ αὐτὰ ταῦτα ποιήσει ἅπερ πέφυκεν ἐργάζεσθαι· πρῶτον μὲν ἀδύνατον αὐτὸν πράττειν ποιήσει στασιάζοντα καὶ οὐχ ὁμονοοῦντα αὐτὸν ἑαυτῶι, ἔπειτα ἐχθρὸν καὶ ἑαυτῶι καὶ τοῖς δικαίοις· ἦ γάρ;

Ναί.

Δίκαιοι δέ γε εἰσίν, ὦ φίλε, καὶ οἱ θεοί;

352a1 ποιεῖν **D**: ποιεῖ **AF**

b Ἔστωσαν, ἔφη.

Καὶ θεοῖς ἄρα ἐχθρὸς ἔσται ὁ ἄδικος, ὦ Θρασύμαχε, ὁ δὲ δίκαιος φίλος.

Εὐωχοῦ τοῦ λόγου, ἔφη, θαρρῶν· οὐ γὰρ ἔγωγέ σοι ἐναντιώσομαι, ἵνα μὴ τοῖσδε ἀπέχθωμαι.

Ἴθι δή, ἦν δὲ ἐγώ, καὶ τὰ λοιπά μοι τῆς ἑστιάσεως ἀποπλήρωσον, ἀποκρινόμενος ὥσπερ καὶ νῦν. ὅτι μὲν γὰρ καὶ σοφώτεροι καὶ ἀμείνους καὶ δυνατώτεροι πράττειν οἱ δίκαιοι φαίνονται, οἱ δὲ ἄδικοι
c οὐδὲν πράττειν μετ᾽ ἀλλήλων οἷοί τε, ἀλλὰ δὴ καὶ οὕς φαμεν ἐρρωμένως πώποτέ τι μετ᾽ ἀλλήλων κοινῆι πρᾶξαι ἀδίκους ὄντας, τοῦτο οὐ παντάπασιν ἀληθὲς λέγομεν· οὐ γὰρ ἂν ἀπείχοντο ἀλλήλων κομιδῆι ὄντες ἄδικοι, ἀλλὰ δῆλον ὅτι ἐνῆν τις αὐτοῖς δικαιοσύνη, ἣ αὐτοὺς ἐποίει μή τοι καὶ ἀλλήλους γε καὶ ἐπὶ οὓς ἦισαν ἅμα ἀδικεῖν, διὰ ἣν ἔπραξαν ἃ ἔπραξαν, ὥρμησαν δὲ ἐπὶ τὰ ἄδικα ἀδικίαι ἡμιμόχθηροι ὄντες, ἐπεὶ οἵ γε παμπόνηροι καὶ τελέως ἄδικοι τελέως
d εἰσὶ καὶ πράττειν ἀδύνατοι. ταῦτα μὲν οὖν ὅτι οὕτως ἔχει μανθάνω, ἀλλ᾽ οὐχ ὡς σὺ τὸ πρῶτον ἐτίθεσο· εἰ δὲ καὶ ἄμεινον ζῶσιν οἱ δίκαιοι τῶν ἀδίκων καὶ εὐδαιμονέστεροί εἰσιν, ὅπερ τὸ ὕστερον προυθέμεθα σκέψασθαι, σκεπτέον. φαίνονται μὲν οὖν καὶ νῦν, ὥς γέ μοι δοκεῖ, ἐξ ὧν εἰρήκαμεν· ὅμως δὲ ἔτι βέλτιον σκεπτέον. οὐ γὰρ περὶ τοῦ ἐπιτυχόντος ὁ λόγος, ἀλλὰ περὶ τοῦ ὅντινα τρόπον χρὴ ζῆν.

Σκόπει δή, ἔφη.

Σκοπῶ, ἦν δὲ ἐγώ. καί μοι λέγε· δοκεῖ τί σοι εἶναι ἵππου ἔργον;

e Ἔμοιγε.

Ἆρ᾽ οὖν τοῦτο ἂν θείης καὶ ἵππου καὶ ἄλλου ὁτουοῦν ἔργον, ὃ ἂν ἢ μόνωι ἐκείνωι ποιῆι τις ἢ ἄριστα;

Οὐ μανθάνω, ἔφη.

Ἀλλ᾽ ὧδε· ἔστιν ὅτωι ἂν ἄλλωι ἴδοις ἢ ὀφθαλμοῖς;

Οὐ δῆτα.

Τί δέ; ἀκούσαις ἄλλωι ἢ ὠσίν;

Οὐδαμῶς.

Οὐκοῦν δικαίως [ἂν] ταῦτα τούτων φαμὲν ἔργα εἶναι;

Πάνυ γε.

353 Τί δέ; μαχαίραι ἂν ἀμπέλου κλῆμα ἀποτέμοις καὶ σμίληι καὶ ἄλλοις πολλοῖς;

352b1 ἔστωσαν **ADF** Stob.: ἔστων Hartman: ἔστω Burnet e9 ἂν del. Adam 353a1 ἂν ἀμπέλου **F** Stob.: ἀμπέλου **AD**

Πῶς γὰρ οὔ;

Ἀλλὰ οὐδενί γε ἄν, οἶμαι, οὕτω καλῶς ὡς δρεπάνωι τῶι ἐπὶ τοῦτο ἐργασθέντι.

Ἀληθῆ.

Ἆρα οὖν οὐ τοῦτο τούτου ἔργον θήσομεν;

Θήσομεν μὲν οὖν.

Νῦν δή, οἶμαι, ἄμεινον ἂν μάθοις ὃ ἄρτι ἠρώτων, πυνθανόμενος εἰ οὐ τοῦτο ἑκάστου εἴη ἔργον ὃ ἂν ἢ μόνον τι ἢ κάλλιστα τῶν ἄλλων ἀπεργάζηται.

Ἀλλά, ἔφη, μανθάνω τε καί μοι δοκεῖ τοῦτο ἑκάστου πράγματος b ἔργον εἶναι.

Εἶέν, ἦν δὲ ἐγώ· οὐκοῦν καὶ ἀρετὴ δοκεῖ σοι εἶναι ἑκάστωι ὧιπερ καὶ ἔργον τι προστέτακται; ἴωμεν δὲ ἐπὶ τὰ αὐτὰ πάλιν· ὀφθαλμῶν, φαμέν, ἔστι τι ἔργον;

Ἔστιν.

Ἆρα οὖν καὶ ἀρετὴ ὀφθαλμῶν ἔστιν;

Καὶ ἀρετή.

Τί δέ; ὤτων ἦν τι ἔργον;

Ναί.

Οὐκοῦν καὶ ἀρετή;

Καὶ ἀρετή.

Τί δὲ πάντων πέρι τῶν ἄλλων; οὐχ οὕτω;

Οὕτω.

Ἔχε δή· ἆρα ἄν ποτε ὄμματα τὸ αὑτῶν ἔργον καλῶς ἀπεργάσαιτο μὴ ἔχοντα τὴν αὑτῶν οἰκείαν ἀρετήν, ἀλλὰ ἀντὶ τῆς ἀρετῆς c κακίαν;

Καὶ πῶς ἄν; ἔφη· τυφλότητα γὰρ ἴσως λέγεις ἀντὶ τῆς ὄψεως.

Ἥτις, ἦν δὲ ἐγώ, αὐτῶν ἡ ἀρετή· οὐ γάρ πω τοῦτο ἐρωτῶ, ἀλλὰ εἰ τῆι οἰκείαι μὲν ἀρετῆι τὸ αὑτῶν ἔργον εὖ ἐργάσεται τὰ ἐργαζόμενα, κακίαι δὲ κακῶς.

Ἀληθές, ἔφη, τοῦτό γε λέγεις.

Οὐκοῦν καὶ ὦτα στερόμενα τῆς αὑτῶν ἀρετῆς κακῶς τὸ αὑτῶν ἔργον ἀπεργάσεται;

Πάνυ γε.

353a4 τοῦτο **AD**: τούτω **F** Stob. b15–c1 ἀπεργάσαιτο Heindorf: ἀπεργάσαιντο **ADF** Stob.

d Τίθεμεν οὖν καὶ τὰ ἄλλα πάντα εἰς τὸν αὐτὸν λόγον;

Ἔμοιγε δοκεῖ.

Ἴθι δή, μετὰ ταῦτα τόδε σκέψαι· ψυχῆς ἔστι τι ἔργον ὃ ἄλλωι τῶν ὄντων οὐδὲ ἂν ἑνὶ πράξαις; οἷον τὸ τοιόνδε· τὸ ἐπιμελεῖσθαι καὶ ἄρχειν καὶ βουλεύεσθαι καὶ τὰ τοιαῦτα πάντα, ἔστιν ὅτωι ἄλλωι ἢ ψυχῆι δικαίως ἂν αὐτὰ ἀποδοῖμεν καὶ φαῖμεν ἴδια ἐκείνου εἶναι;

Οὐδενὶ ἄλλωι.

Τί δὲ αὖ τὸ ζῆν; οὐ ψυχῆς φήσομεν ἔργον εἶναι;

Μάλιστά γε, ἔφη.

Οὐκοῦν καὶ ἀρετήν φαμέν τινα ψυχῆς εἶναι;

Φαμέν.

e Ἆρ' οὖν ποτε, ὦ Θρασύμαχε, ψυχὴ τὰ αὑτῆς ἔργα εὖ ἀπεργάσεται στερομένη τῆς οἰκείας ἀρετῆς, ἢ ἀδύνατον;

Ἀδύνατον.

Ἀνάγκη ἄρα κακῆι ψυχῆι κακῶς ἄρχειν καὶ ἐπιμελεῖσθαι, τῆι δὲ ἀγαθῆι πάντα ταῦτα εὖ πράττειν.

Ἀνάγκη.

Οὐκοῦν ἀρετήν γε συνεχωρήσαμεν ψυχῆς εἶναι δικαιοσύνην, κακίαν δὲ ἀδικίαν;

Συνεχωρήσαμεν γάρ.

Ἡ μὲν ἄρα δικαία ψυχὴ καὶ ὁ δίκαιος ἀνὴρ εὖ βιώσεται, κακῶς δὲ ὁ ἄδικος.

Φαίνεται, ἔφη, κατὰ τὸν σὸν λόγον.

354 Ἀλλὰ μὴν ὅ γε εὖ ζῶν μακάριός τε καὶ εὐδαίμων, ὁ δὲ μὴ τὰ ἐναντία.

Πῶς γὰρ οὔ;

Ὁ μὲν δίκαιος ἄρα εὐδαίμων, ὁ δὲ ἄδικος ἄθλιος.

Ἔστωσαν, ἔφη.

Ἀλλὰ μὴν ἄθλιόν γε εἶναι οὐ λυσιτελεῖ, εὐδαίμονα δέ.

Πῶς γὰρ οὔ;

Οὐδέποτε ἄρα, ὦ μακάριε Θρασύμαχε, λυσιτελέστερον ἀδικία δικαιοσύνης.

Ταῦτα δή σοι, ἔφη, ὦ Σώκρατες, εἱστιάσθω ἐν τοῖς Βενδιδίοις.

Ὑπὸ σοῦ γε, ἦν δὲ ἐγώ, ὦ Θρασύμαχε, ἐπειδή μοι πρᾶος ἐγένου
b καὶ χαλεπαίνων ἐπαύσω. οὐ μέντοι καλῶς γε εἱστίαμαι, δι' ἐμαυτὸν ἀλλ' οὐ διὰ σέ· ἀλλ' ὥσπερ οἱ λίχνοι τοῦ ἀεὶ παραφερομένου

353d6 ἐκείνου recentiores: ἐκείνης **ADF** Stob. 354a5 ἔστωσαν **AD** (**F** deficit): ἔστω Stob.: ἔστων Hartman

ἀπογεύονται ἁρπάζοντες, πρὶν τοῦ προτέρου μετρίως ἀπολαῦσαι, καὶ ἐγώ μοι δοκῶ οὕτω, πρὶν ὃ τὸ πρῶτον ἐσκοποῦμεν εὑρεῖν, τὸ δίκαιον ὅτι ποτέ ἐστιν, ἀφέμενος ἐκείνου ὁρμῆσαι ἐπὶ τὸ σκέψασθαι περὶ αὐτοῦ εἴτε κακία ἐστὶ καὶ ἀμαθία, εἴτε σοφία καὶ ἀρετή. καὶ ἐμπεσόντος αὖ ὕστερον λόγου, ὅτι λυσιτελέστερον ἡ ἀδικία τῆς δικαιοσύνης, οὐκ ἀπεσχόμην τὸ μὴ οὐκ ἐπὶ τοῦτο ἐλθεῖν ἀπὸ ἐκείνου·
c ὥστε μοι νυνὶ γέγονεν ἐκ τοῦ διαλόγου μηδὲν εἰδέναι· ὁπότε γὰρ τὸ δίκαιον μὴ οἶδα ὅ ἐστιν, σχολῆι εἴσομαι εἴτε ἀρετή τις οὖσα τυγχάνει εἴτε καὶ οὔ, καὶ πότερον ὁ ἔχων αὐτὸ οὐκ εὐδαίμων ἐστὶν ἢ εὐδαίμων.

354b4 ἐγώ μοι recentiores: ἐγῶιμαι **AF**: ἐγὼ οἶμαι **D**

COMMENTARY

327a1–328b3: *Republic* opens with S., who will be the sole narrator of the dialogue, recounting how he and Glaucon went to the Piraeus to witness the inaugural festival in honor of the Thracian goddess Bendis and to offer prayers to her. While there they encounter, and are detained by, Polemarchus, who insists that they not return immediately to Athens but remain for further festivities and conversation with Glaucon's older brother Adeimantus among others. By having S. serve as narrator, P. steers clear of the dramatic form exhibited by such dialogues as *Crito* and *Euthyphro*, which might have proved awkward in Books Three and Ten, where the mimetic mode is disparaged. *Republic* shares this narrative form with *Charmides* and *Lysis*, which also open with first-person verbs spoken by S. (Ἥκομεν and Ἐπορευόμην). Unlike those dialogues, however, in which S. is headed for one of his regular haunts, a palaestra, here he is found in a less familiar setting, the port of Athens. In this regard *Republic* is comparable to *Phaedrus*, the rural setting of which prompts S.'s companion to observe that he is unaware that S. ventures outside the city walls at all (230c–d); by taking S. out of his normal urban environment, P. prepares us for a S. that we are not accustomed to seeing, a man capable of moving away from his standard practice of questioning others to making lengthy speeches that surpass those of Lysias for rhetorical sophistication. So in *Republic*, we see S. venturing outside the city walls (although not outside the fortifications built to link the city with the coast), and it has apparently been a long time since S. has come this far from the urban center of Athens, except when military service required him to travel outside Attica. By placing S. in this unaccustomed locale, and by presenting the narrative from the point of view of S. himself, P. seems to be asserting the appearance of an altered version of the figure familiar from the earlier dialogues. Traces of that familiar figure are in evidence in Book One, in which S. interrogates others and which ends with S. professing his ignorance regarding the nature of justice. But Glaucon and Adeimantus, the brothers of *Republic*'s author, who have been mostly silent in Book One, are convinced that there is much that S. is hiding, and their challenge at the start of Book Two will conjure this new version of S., who has a great deal to disclose, in his own voice, about justice, the soul, the state and how we should live our lives in such a way that εὖ πράττωμεν (10.621d2–3).

327a1 Κατέβην χθὲς εἰς Πειραιᾶ μετὰ Γλαύκωνος τοῦ Ἀρίστωνος: the opening was famous in antiquity and was the subject of a fictitious anecdote recounted by Dionysius of Halicarnassus: P. was such a perfectionist when it came to the style of his writings that, even as an octogenarian, he kept revising and, after his death, a tablet was found with the order of these opening words variously rearranged (*On literary composition* 25; cf. Quintilian 8.6.64, D.L. 3.37; Swift Riginos 1976: 185–6; also Cicero, *De sen.* 5.13). For the controversy over P.'s alleged production of different versions of *Republic*, see the Introduction, section 1. In any event, the story well illustrates the care P. was believed to have lavished on his writing, especially on the opening of his dialogues (Burnyeat 1997). There is, however, nothing special about the order of the constituents here, which is essentially the same as that of the opening of *Charmides*: Ἥκομεν τῆι προτεραίαι ἑσπέρας ἐκ Ποτειδαίας ἀπὸ τοῦ στρατοπέδου.

Κατέβην: the natural word to use for going from a higher to a lower elevation (328c6); in Book Four a story will be told of Leontius, who walks in the opposite direction (ἀνιὼν ἐκ Πειραιῶς, 439e6). Still, the seemingly casual opening word has been deliberately chosen with programmatic intent; see Vegetti 1998: 93–104, adducing the *katabaseis* of such legendary figures as Odysseus (note *Od.* 23.252 κατέβην δόμον Ἄϊδος εἴσω), Orpheus and Heracles. But unlike his supposed mythical predecessors, S. does not make his descent unaccompanied. He has with him P.'s older brother Glaucon. Nor is he engaged in a journey to the underworld seeking enlightenment or attempting to restore someone to the land of the living. Rather, P.'s language deliberately prefigures the descent of the Callipolitan Guardians, who will be under an obligation to be sent back down into the figurative Cave from which their education has freed them (καταβιβαστέοι ἔσονται ... εἰς τὸ σπήλαιον πάλιν, 7.539e3–4; cf. 520c1–3 where, as Burnyeat 1997: 6 points out, καταβατέον ... θεάσασθαι recalls S.'s purpose in visiting the Piraeus). That the Guardians, like S., do not make their descent solo is implied by the plurals ἕκαστοι (520d8) and ἑκάστους (540b1 and 3). Although S. spends a great deal of time describing in detail the nature of the Guardians' education, it only gradually becomes clear by whom they are to be educated, namely by S., who refers to himself as a διδάσκαλος at 3.392d8, and his interlocutors, including Glaucon, who are together engaged in creating the curriculum (3.398b4, 402c1, 414d5, 4.430a1, 7.521d14, 536b3; cf. 8.546b2). At the end of Book Seven it is made explicit that it is only the Guardians themselves who have the qualifications to train future Guardians (540a–b; White 1979: 99). Thus, with his first word P. prepares us for the "top-down" style of education laid out in subsequent books, in contrast to the elenctic method used by S. in Book One.

χθές: S. gives a firsthand account of the previous day's events, in contrast to, e.g., *Symposium* and *Theaetetus*, which are mediated through the telling of various narrators recounting conversations that took place sometime in the past. According to the scholiast here and Proclus on *Tim.* 17b, the annual festival in honor of Bendis that S. attended "yesterday" took place on 19 Thargelion, corresponding to a day in early June (cf. 350d2).

εἰς Πειραιᾶ: ὁ Πειραιεύς is, like The Bronx, unusual among toponyms in that it is regularly accompanied by the definite article, which, however, is often (but not always: 328c6) omitted in prepositional phrases; see Gildersleeve §557. The contraction, with ε + α > ᾱ rather than η due to the preceding iota, is common in fourth century Attic inscriptions. Not only is the Piraeus at a lower elevation than the city proper, its inhabitants could be looked down upon as socially inferior. Being the port of Athens, it was the embarkation point for the oarsmen of the fleet and served as the landing-place for foreign goods and visitors; it was also the home of many foreigners and metics like Cephalus and Polemarchus (Garland 1987: 58–72). Consequently, as Aristotle notes (*Pol.* 5.1303b11), the inhabitants of the Piraeus are μᾶλλον δημοτικοί than those of the city. During the civil war of 404–403 the Piraeus became the base of operations for the democratic forces that opposed the Thirty, the oligarchic faction that held the city, so that the two sides could be referred to simply as "those from the Piraeus and those from the city (τὸ ἄστυ)," e.g. *Mnx.* 243e4, Lysias 12.92; Garland 1987: 32–7; Munn 2000: 238–44.

a2 προσευξόμενός τε τῆι θεῶι: motivating S.'s descent as he does serves two of P.'s purposes. First, it provides yet another prominent affirmation of S.'s piety (e.g. *Euthd.* 302c, *Phdr.* 242c, 279b–c, *Symp.* 220d), retroactively refuting the allegations raised against him at his trial. Second, by giving an example of behavior that is both willed (βουλόμενος) and prescribed, religious obligation can serve as a model for P.'s subversion of the seemingly strict distinction between compulsion and persuasion, as exemplified by the encounter below between S. and Polemarchus and, more significantly, by the motivation of the Guardians' return to the Cave (Moore 2008). It is surprising that we are not yet told which goddess is the target of S.'s prayers. Only at 354a10 is the festival of the Thracian goddess Bendis named, although the reference just below to "the Thracians," in combination with the location in the Piraeus, would have made it apparent to P.'s Athenian contemporaries. Normally, in an Attic context ἡ θεός means Athena (e.g. *Criti.* 110b5, *Tim.* 21a2), but there would be no reason for S. to leave the city to pray to the patron deity of Athens.

a2–3 τὴν ἑορτὴν … θεάσασθαι τίνα τρόπον "to watch the festival (to see) in what way," prolepsis (*CGCG* §60.37), like 2.376c10–d2 κατιδεῖν … δικαιοσύνην τε καὶ ἀδικίαν τίνα τρόπον ἐν πόλει γίγνεται. For the introduction of Bendis to Athens and the establishment of her cult, see Garland 1992: 111–14; Wijma 2014: 126–55.

a3 νῦν πρῶτον: while there is evidence for the presence of the goddess Bendis in Attica from a somewhat earlier time, the festival to which S.

refers was most likely first held in 429 (Planeaux 2000), approximately the time of the historical Glaucon's birth (Nails 2002: 154–6).

a3–5 καλὴ μὲν οὖν … οὐ μέντοι ἧττον ἐφαίνετο πρέπειν "Well (οὖν), I thought the locals' procession was splendid, but (that of the Thracians) seemed no less impressive." For adversative μέντοι answering a preceding μέν, see e.g. 329e5–6; *GP* 404 ("common in prose"). Here, however, the adversative force is counteracted by the balancing οὐ … ἧττον, which = ὁμοίως.

a5 ἣν … ἔπεμπον: for the expression πομπὴν πέμπειν, "conduct a procession" (e.g. Ar. *Ach.* 248–9, *Birds* 849), see next n. and Chadwick 1996: 239–40, citing further examples.

οἱ Θρᾶικες: there was a large population of Thracian residents in Athens, their presence encouraged by the friendly relations that the Athenians sought, as early as the sixth century, with a region rich in timber and manpower (Wijma 2014: 128–32). That there was a separate procession for Thracians in the Athenian cult of Bendis finds inscriptional confirmation, at least for a later period: *IG* II² 1283.11–12, middle of the third century BC, (πόλεως νόμος) ὅς κελεύει τοὺς Θρᾶικας πέμπειν τὴμ πομπὴν εἰ[ς Π]ε[ι]ραιᾶ, "(the city's law) that directs the Thracians to conduct the procession to the Piraeus."

327b1 θεωρήσαντες: the verb and the related nouns θεωρός and θεωρία are regularly used in connection with traveling to perform some religious function, such as attending the Panhellenic games or consulting an oracle. By the time of P. the words had taken on an additional intellectual connotation in recognition of the supposed broadening effects of travel and contact with natives of different localities; this is especially well captured in Croesus' observation that Solon had traveled widely φιλοσοφέων … θεωρίης εἵνεκεν, Hdt. 1.30.2 (Rutherford 2000; Nightingale 2001). The words' origins in the visual realm – according to Beekes, θεωρός is derived from a combination of two visual elements: *θεᾱ-(ϝ)ορος, "who watches a spectacle" – was congenial to P., who often uses vision as a metaphor for contemplation of the Forms, most prominently in the images of the Sun and the Cave in Books Six and Seven. That he was aware of the etymology is clear from the way in which he uses προσευξάμενοι δὲ καὶ θεωρήσαντες to reprise προσευξόμενος … καὶ ἅμα … βουλόμενος θεάσασθαι.

b3 τὸν παῖδα "his slave"; for this use of the definite article as a possessive pronoun relating to the grammatical subject, see Gildersleeve §534.

περιμεῖναί ἑ κελεῦσαι "to tell (us) to wait for him (ἑ)." This appears to be the only occurrence in Attic prose of the unemphatic (enclitic) third-person singular pronoun in the accusative case, cognate with Latin *se*, used as an indirect reflexive (*CGCG* §29.18). P. is also alone among Attic writers in using orthotone ἕ, which he employs when a contrast is involved (10.617e7, *Symp.* 175a6, c4, 223b8).

b3–4 ὁ παῖς λαβόμενος τοῦ ἱματίου: Book Five opens with a similar diversion of S.'s intention, when Polemarchus interrupts the proceedings by laying hold of Adeimantus' *himation* (λαβόμενος τοῦ ἱματίου, 449b3) to pull him toward him and hinting that they should not let S. continue without explaining his earlier claim that the Guardians must hold everything in common, including wives and children. Polemarchus is a free man, so there is nothing questionable about his laying hands on his companion; it seems impertinent in the extreme for his slave to treat S. in this manner, but the Athenians were notorious for the degree of license that they tolerated in their slaves. According to the "Old Oligarch" ([Xen.] *Ath.* 1.10–12), Athenian slaves behave as though they have the same rights as citizens, and Demosthenes claims that slaves have greater freedom of speech in Athens than citizens in some other poleis (9.3). Later, S. will maintain that the democratic city's devolution into tyranny results from its having reached the extremity of freedom, when its slaves are as free as their masters (8.563b5–8).

b5 αὐτός "himself," i.e. "the master" (*CGL* 4). Callias' doorman similarly uses αὐτός to refer to his master (*Prot.* 314d3), and S. himself is "Himself" to one of the students at the school of which he is the Master (Ar. *Clouds* 219).

b5–6 Οὗτος … προσέρχεται "Here he comes." For this deictic use of οὗτος, cf. Ar. *Clouds* 324 χωροῦσ' αὗται (S. announcing the arrival of the cloud chorus) and Soph. *El.* 1474 αὕτη πέλας σοῦ (Orestes informing Aegisthus of Clytaemestra's whereabouts).

b6 ἀλλὰ … Ἀλλά: for the two uses of the particle, see *GP* 13–15 and 16–20. The first, accompanying an imperative, accentuates the urgency of compliance; the second, "assentient," acknowledges that compliance is the natural, even inevitable, response.

b6–7 ἦ δὲ ὅς: "a fixed colloquial Attic formula" (Biles and Olson on Ar. *Wasps* 795) frequent in P., consisting of the third-person singular of the defective verb ἠμί, "said" (first-person ἦν δὲ ἐγώ is also common in P.; e.g. c6), the particle δέ and the demonstrative pronoun ὅς, "he." Sometimes, as here, a name, always accompanied by the article, is appended to clarify who "he" is. In this expression δέ does not have connective force; see Rijksbaron (2018), who explains P.'s use of ἦ δὲ ὅς/ἦν δὲ ἐγώ, in contrast to ἔφη/ἔφην, as used by the narrator to represent the quoted utterance "either as a closure or to mark a change of speaker and subject matter" (218). This accords with the way ἦ is used in Homer (Hainsworth on *Il.* 9.620–3) and with the culminative force of δή (332d2n.), to which δέ is etymologically related.

327c2 Νικήρατος ὁ Νικίου: as the son of the general Nicias, one of the wealthiest men in Athens, it is not surprising to find Niceratus (Nails

2002: 211–12) in the company of Polemarchus. Like Polemarchus, Niceratus, who is mentioned only here in *Republic*, was murdered by the Thirty in 404 (Munn 2000: 229–31). He was perhaps the same Niceratus who was the target of a disparaging remark by T. (Arist. *Rhet.* 3.1413a7–10), a member of the party he is about to join at Polemarchus' house.

c2–3 ὡς ἀπὸ τῆς πομπῆς: with a prepositional phrase ὡς can have the meaning, "seemingly, to all appearances"; cf. Thuc. 6.61.6 ἀπέπλεον … ἐκ τῆς Σικελίας ὡς ἐς τὰς Ἀθήνας, referring to Alcibiades and those accused with him, who had no intention of returning to Athens to face trial. Here, Polemarchus and his friends are in fact coming from the procession; ὡς serves as one of the many reminders, especially prominent in Book One (Ferrari 2010; Finkelberg 2019: 34–8), that the narrative is presented from the point of view of S.

c5 ὡς ἀπιόντες: here, as often with a future participle (*CGCG* §52.41), ὡς expresses purpose or intention.

c6 Οὐ γὰρ κακῶς δοξάζεις: picking up δοκεῖτε c4 and anticipating the distinction that S. will draw at the end of Book Five between δόξα, based on inference, and γνῶσις or ἐπιστήμη, accessible only to the philosopher and based on direct acquaintance with the Forms.

c7 Ὁρᾶις οὖν ἡμᾶς … ὅσοι ἐσμέν; for the mock-threatening tone, cf. *Phlb.* 16a4–5 Ἆρα, ὦ Σώκρατες, οὐχ ὁρᾶις ἡμῶν τὸ πλῆθος, ὅτι νέοι πάντες ἐσμέν, καὶ οὐ φοβῆι μή …

c9 τοίνυν "Well then," "In that case"; cf. c14, 339e1, 350e11. For this "logical" use of the particle, see *GP* 569–73.

κρείττους γένεσθε ἢ μένετε αὐτοῦ: the playful banter, as often in P., is not unrelated to the more serious issues of the dialogue. The need for the weaker to yield to the interests of the stronger lies at the heart of T.'s definition of justice, and the constraint threatened by Polemarchus will be reinforced by the lure of conversing with young men (328a7–b1). Already we have seen two models for the motivation of the philosopher's return to the Cave: S.'s descent to the Piraeus is driven both by a sense of obligation and by desire (a2n.), and he remains both willingly and in submission to compulsion.

c10 τὸ ἢν πείσωμεν: the neuter definite article can serve to turn any word, phrase or clause into a substantive (Gildersleeve §579), here rendering ἢν … ἀφεῖναι the subject of ἐλλείπεται; cf. 331e3n.

c11 ἀφεῖναι: cf. the beginning of Book Five, where Polemarchus pulls Adeimantus toward him (b3–4n.) and asks if they are going to let S. go (ἀφήσομεν, 449b6; cf. 472a8).

c12 πεῖσαι μὴ ἀκούοντας: the negative is μή because the participle functions as the protasis of a condition.

c14 Ὡς τοίνυν μὴ ἀκουσομένων, οὕτω διανοεῖσθε "Then you must bear this in mind, that we are not going to listen." A genitive absolute may dispense with a substantive if one can be readily supplied from the context (*CGCG* §52.32), here the pronoun ἡμῶν. For οὕτω picking up the ὡς-clause, cf. Xen. *Cyr.* 1.6.11 ὥς γε ἐμοῦ, ἔφη, μηδέποτε ἀμελήσοντος ... οὕτως ἔχε τὴν γνώμην, Aeschin. 3.247 ὡς οὖν μὴ μόνον κρίνοντες ... οὕτω τὴν ψῆφον φέρετε. The negative is μή rather than οὐ under the influence of the governing imperative, as illustrated by the sentences just quoted and by Soph. *Ant.* 1063, Thuc. 7.15.1 and Isocr. 1.17.

328a1 Ἀδείμαντος: Adeimantus (Nails 2002: 2–3) is, like Glaucon (Nails 2002: 154–6), P.'s brother. It is indicative of the differing characters of the two brothers that Adeimantus is enthusiastic about taking part in the further festivities, whereas the younger Glaucon is, like S., not even aware of what is on offer (for the characterization of P.'s brothers, see Blondell 2002: 199–228). The more philosophically gifted Glaucon has come down from the city in the company of S., while Adeimantus is found in the Piraeus associating with the speechwriter Lysias and the teacher of rhetoric T. (b4–6).

Ἆρά γε: it is not merely the case that "γε adds liveliness and emphasis to the question" (*GP* 50). The combination of particles suggests that the speaker already knows the answer to the question and is encouraging the listener to concur; cf. 4.422c2, *Euthd.* 278e3, *Euthphr.* 6a7, *Phdr.* 274c2, *Symp.* 192d5.

οὐδὲ ἴστε "Don't you even know ...?" The implication of οὐδέ is that if S. and Glaucon had so much as known about the torch-race they would surely not be thinking of leaving before they had seen it. As an Athenian, S. would have been familiar with torch-races run on foot through the streets of the city (Ar. *Frogs* 129–33, 1089–98). The starting line for one such race was in the Academy, at an altar of Prometheus (Pausanias 1.30.2), who is celebrated for stealing fire for the benefit of mankind. Some of these were relay races, in which the members of each team passed a lighted torch from one to another; cf. *Laws* 6.776b3–4 καθάπερ λαμπάδα τὸν βίον παραδιδόντας ἄλλοις ἐξ ἄλλων, referring to the succession of human generations. Herodotus (8.98.2) compares the Persian rapid messenger service, in which a relay of mounted messengers pass a written message from one rider to the next, to the torch-races that the Greeks (i.e. the Athenians, among whom such races were uniquely popular: Parke 1977: 171–3; Simon 1983: 53–4) hold in honor of Hephaestus. The novelty of the race at the festival for Bendis is that it is a torch-race conducted not on foot but on horseback. It is not known whether such a race was run in Thrace, notable for breeding horses (Hom. *Il.* 13.4, Hes. *Op.* 507), or was invented for Attic consumption, the horses giving the appearance of an "authentic" Thracian element and the torches appealing to Athenian custom as well as recalling the iconography of Artemis, with whom Bendis was identified (Hdt. 5.7; the sanctuaries of Artemis and Bendis in the Piraeus were not far apart: Garland 1987: 162). Competitive events for individual contestants were frequent features of Greek religious festivals – the Olympic Games and other athletic and equestrian contests were held at the sanctuary of a god, as were the dramatic competitions in Athens – but relay races were unusual in being team events. P. seems to have chosen to open *Republic* with a reference to this race, which depends for victory on the competitors' cooperation with team members, in anticipation of S.'s argument beginning at 351a; there S. gets the intensely competitive T., who thinks almost exclusively in terms of individual success, to acknowledge that collective entities in competition with other such entities can succeed only when their individual members refrain from treating each other unfairly.

a3 λαμπάδια: we need not assume that the torches were small. Rather, P. employs the diminutive as a variant for λαμπάς, which he had just used in a different meaning, "torch-race." The asyndeton is justified by the fact that this question amplifies S.'s earlier question (Ἀπὸ ἵππων;), as at e.g. *Apol.* 25a13.

a4 ἁμιλλώμενοι τοῖς ἵπποις: for the instrumental dative, see *Criti.* 117c6 εἰς ἅμιλλαν τοῖς ἵπποις, *Laws* 8.834a4–5 τόξοις καὶ πέλταις καὶ ἀκοντίοις … ἁμιλλωμένων.

a5 καὶ πρός γε "Yes and, what's more …," with adverbial πρός (LSJ D), a somewhat colloquial expression (Collard 2018: 123); cf. 5.466e4, *Soph.* 234a3, Eur. *Cyc.* 542.

a6 ἄξιον θεάσασθαι: we are repeatedly reminded that we are in the realm of spectacle, appreciated by those for whom P. coined the word φιλοθεάμων (first used by Glaucon at 5.475d2 and found four more times before 479a, but nowhere else in P.), who are distinguished from the philosopher, a voyeur of truth (475e4); Nightingale 2001: 36. A παννυχίς ("all-night celebration") is attested for the cult of Bendis in an inscription found in the Piraeus, dated to 413/12: *IG* I³ 136.27. Such all-night rites were generally celebrated by women; men were not excluded, but their role was normally restricted to that of onlookers (Parker 2005: 166). What seems to be envisioned here is that the men will take advantage of the opportunity to spend the night conversing. As it happens, the torch-race, the dinner and the παννυχίς are lost sight of; the only element that remains is the conversation with young men (d5). Why, then, did P. set up expectations of events that are not to be part of the narrative? Rather than see this as an indication of absentmindedness on P.'s part or as evidence for inadequate revision when the independent dialogue that is now Book One was recast as the proem to *Republic* (see the Introduction, section 1), we should read it as a metaphor for the conversation to come in the later books, which will turn its back on the sights and tastes of the world of the senses and will be directed toward discovering the essence of justice.

328b4–d6: The scene shifts to the house of Polemarchus, where S. finds, among others, Polemarchus' brothers Lysias and Euthydemus and his elderly father Cephalus (for this "two-stage" opening, which *Rep.* shares with *Chrm.* and *Lys.*, see Finkelberg 2019: 27–30). In his speech *Against Eratosthenes,* referring to the aftermath of the murder of Polemarchus in 404, Lysias says that his family had three houses (12.18), in any one of which his brother's funeral could have been held. Each brother, then, had his own house; Polemarchus, being the eldest, had assumed management of his father's estate while Cephalus was still alive, and it is to this residence in the Piraeus that S. and his companions make their way.

328b4 εἰς τοῦ Πολεμάρχου: for the ellipsis, see *Symp.* 174a6 ἐπὶ δεῖπνον εἰς Ἀγάθωνος, "(going) to dinner at Agathon's," with LSJ A.I.4c; also 330d6 ἐν Ἅιδου. The definite article is abnormal in this idiom (Olson on Ar. *Ach.* 1222–3) and should perhaps be deleted here as an intruder from the following line.

b4–5 Λυσίαν τε ... καὶ Εὐθύδημον: for Lysias, whose speech on Eros serves as the point of departure for the discussion in *Phaedrus,* see Nails 2002: 190–4. He is perhaps to be imagined as being responsible for the invitation to T., with whom P. elsewhere associates him (*Phdr.* 266c, 269d). Neither he nor Euthydemus (Nails 2002: 151) contributes to the ensuing conversation.

b6 καὶ δὴ καί: for the use of this combination to call particular attention to what is added to the foregoing, see *GP* 255–7. Here, attention is drawn to the guest of honor, T. (see the Introduction, section 4(d)), a prominent rhetorician and the only person named who is neither an Athenian nor a resident of Athens.

b6–7 Χαρμαντίδην τὸν Παιανιᾶ καὶ Κλειτοφῶντα τὸν Ἀριστωνύμου: in such enumerations of Athenian names, P. likes to vary the designation by alternating between demotic and patronymic; cf. *Gorg.* 487c3–4, *Prot.* 315c2–4. Charmantides and Clitophon have apparently been attracted to the house of Polemarchus by the promise of meeting T.; similarly, S. and Hippocrates go to the house of Callias to meet the visiting sophist in *Protagoras.* It is unclear whether this Charmantides, who plays no further role in the dialogue, is a man known to be roughly contemporary with Cephalus or his grandson of the same name (for details, see Nails 2002: 89–90); the latter would seem a more likely candidate to be paired with Clitophon. Clitophon will be heard from again, when he comes to T.'s defense at 340a; for what is known of him, see Slings 1999: 56–8 and Nails 2002: 102–3.

328c1 διὰ χρόνου γὰρ καὶ ἑωράκη αὐτόν "For it was a long time since I had actually (καί) seen him"; cf. *Euthd.* 273c1 διὰ χρόνου ἑωρακώς, *Phdr.* 247d3 ἰδοῦσα διὰ χρόνου, with LSJ διά A.II.2. The sentence explains (γάρ) S.'s implied surprise at Cephalus' seeming to be quite an old man.

c2 ἐστεφανωμένος: because Cephalus is presiding over a sacrifice (τεθυκὼς γάρ), an activity to which he will return in 331d. Participants in sacrificial ritual are regularly shown wearing crowns on the many vases that depict such scenes; Van Straten 1995: 161–2. Cephalus is sacrificing to Zeus Herkeios, who is "specifically associated with the social ties holding together the close family" (Parker 2005: 17) and whose altar stood in the house's αὐλή, or ἕρκος (*Il.* 24.306 with schol.). His conventional brand of piety will emerge as Cephalus' salient characteristic.

ἐπί τινος προσκεφαλαίου τε καὶ δίφρου: apparently some kind of – S.'s uncertainty is suggested by τινος – improvised seating arrangement for the elderly paterfamilias. A προσκεφάλαιον, "pillow," is literally something on which to rest one's head, appropriate for someone named Cephalus to sit on, but used also for any kind of cushion, like ones brought to the theater (Thphr. *Char.* 2.11). δίφρος is a poetic word, used by P. elsewhere only in Homeric quotations or allusions and in the mythical account in *Critias* (119b1). It is difficult to gauge the tone of this description of Cephalus enthroned in the middle, as we soon learn, of a circle of δίφροι. On the one hand, his advanced age entitles him to respect and deference. On the other, the seeming irrelevance of the details is reminiscent of P.'s elaborate descriptions, replete with Homeric allusions, of the self-important sophists Hippias and Prodicus in *Protagoras* (315b–d).

c2–3 τεθυκὼς γὰρ ἐτύγχανεν: this does not mean that the activities connected with the sacrifice are over; cf. *Lys.* 206e3–4, "we entered to find that the boys had sacrificed (τεθυκότας) and the processing of the victims was by now almost complete (τὰ περὶ τὰ ἱερεῖα σχεδόν τι ἤδη πεποιημένα)." As the officiant, Cephalus still has work to do; see 331d6–7n.

c6 οὐδὲ θαμίζεις: it is very difficult to account for οὐδέ (*GP* 198), which may be corrupt. Ast proposed οὔτι, which would make the expression a quotation from the Homeric line-ending formula πάρος γε μὲν οὔ τι θαμίζεις (*Il.* 18.386, 425, *Od.* 5.88). Regardless, however, of how we explain or emend οὐδέ (perhaps better οὔ τοι), the Homeric allusion is undoubtedly intended. The verb is almost exclusively poetic, appearing in Classical prose only three times in P. (here, *Hp.Ma.* 281b4 and *Laws* 8.843b8) and twice in Xenophon (*Cyr.* 7.3.2 and *Hell.* 5.4.29, in both cases preceded by πρόσθεν, the prose equivalent of πάρος). Further, the two Homeric contexts in which the formula is found can be seen to be particularly appropriate to *Republic* (Gifford 2001: 62 n. 37). In the *Iliad* the expression is used, first by Charis then by Hephaestus, to welcome Thetis into the smith-god's workshop, where she will request that a new shield be made for her son; as it happens, the family business that generated the wealth of Cephalus and his sons was an armory, from which 700 shields were looted by the oligarchs in 404 (Lysias 12.19). In the *Odyssey* the formula is used to greet Hermes, who has flown down from Olympus to visit Calypso in her cave, transmitting Zeus's request that she release her prisoner. In Book Seven S. will use the release of prisoners from a cave as a metaphor for the soul's ascent to the realm of the intelligible, which is how Neoplatonist thinkers, influenced by P., interpreted the Homeric account of Odysseus' release from Calypso's cave (Plotinus 1.6.8, Hermias on *Phdr.* 259a).

c6–7 χρῆν μέντοι "You really ought to have (come more often), you know," referring to S.'s negligence in the past. With χρή (d2) Cephalus urges that S. is still under an obligation. Again (327a1 and 2nn.) we are reminded that S.'s "descent" is a matter of both moral obligation and free choice. The sentiment and much of the vocabulary are notably similar to what the elderly Lysimachus says to S. at *Lach.* 181c1–5: χρῆν … καὶ πρότερόν γε φοιτᾶν … παρὰ ἡμᾶς καὶ οἰκείους ἡγεῖσθαι … νῦν δέ … μὴ ἄλλως ποίει, ἀλλὰ σύνισθι … τούσδε τοὺς νεωτέρους.

328d3 αἱ ἄλλαι αἱ κατὰ τὸ σῶμα ἡδοναί "the other pleasures, (namely) those of the body," other, that is, than those περὶ τοὺς λόγους. In Book Four S. will theorize that the soul comprises three elements, one of which yearns to sate itself on "the so-called pleasures of the body" (τῶν περὶ τὸ σῶμα καλουμένων ἡδονῶν, 442a7–8) and needs to be kept in check by the other two elements, the spirited and the rational. Cephalus thus anticipates this later division, and he seems to recognize the value of engaging in reasoned discussion, but for him this kind of activity is merely a pastime one pursues after the ability to enjoy bodily pleasures has waned. (By contrast, Callicles is convinced that philosophy is a pursuit strictly for the young, which should be abandoned upon attaining adulthood: *Gorg.* 484c.) For S., of course, philosophy is to be pursued throughout one's lifetime, and beyond. In Book Six he will argue that intellectually talented citizens of Callipolis need to be prepared for philosophical pursuits even as young children, otherwise, as is the case now, they will drop out when they encounter the most challenging subject, dialectic (χαλεπώτατον τὸ περὶ τοὺς λόγους, 498a4), and when they reach old age their intellectual capacity will have dimmed in the same way as have Cephalus' sensual appetites.

d5 τοῖσδέ τε τοῖς νεανίαις: referring to his sons, as Lysimachus refers to his son and Melesias' as τούσδε τοὺς νεωτέρους at *Lach.* 181c5 (c6–7n.). Adam considers that the reference is to "Socrates' companions who had come from Athens, as opposed to Cephalus, Polemarchus and the others." But S. was accompanied only by Glaucon.

328d7–329d6: S. was notorious for interrogating others regarding their area of expertise (*Apol.* 21b–22d). Here he questions Cephalus not as a successful businessman (although skill at making money will become a focus of attention later), but as someone who knows what it is like to experience old age. Cephalus responds by saying that, unlike many of his contemporaries, who complain that they are no longer able to enjoy the pleasures that were open to them at a younger age, he shares the opinion of the elderly Sophocles, that youthful passions tyrannize a person and that an old man who is sensible will be relieved to have escaped their oppression. Cephalus' conventional outlook is underlined by his recourse to the authority of a revered poet; later he will quote Pindar and will repeat a bon mot of Themistocles, another figure from an earlier generation.

328d7 Καὶ μήν … χαίρω γε "And I really do enjoy …" (*GP* 353–5). S. is most commonly found conversing with the young, as Cephalus seems to be hinting with his invitation to "get together with these young men." S. flatters Cephalus by suggesting that the elderly, merely by virtue of their age, are able to guide others on life's journey.

328e2 ἴσως δεήσει: not everyone reaches old age. This justifies the use of the adverb, which shows that what is at issue is not "the fated journey" (τὴν εἱμαρμένην πορείαν, *Mnx.* 236d5), about which there is no uncertainty.

e3 τραχεῖα καὶ χαλεπὴ ἢ ῥαιδία: the omission of πότερον in indirect questions is common in P.; e.g. 10.603c2, *Tht.* 151e6, 169d4. All three adjectives are found at Hes. *Op.* 291–2, a passage that P. is fond of quoting or referring to (2.364c–d, *Laws* 4.718e–719a, *Phdr.* 272c, *Prot.* 340d) and which is surely on his mind here. Hesiod describes not the passage through old age but the path leading to ἀρετή: it is steep and craggy at first but, for all its difficulty, it is no trouble once one has reached the pinnacle. (These Hesiodic lines are also the inspiration for Simonides fr. 257 Poltera, a poet whose definition of justice will be subjected to discussion below, at 331d–335e.) The lines seem to have been a favorite of S.'s, for Xenophon represents him as quoting them as an introduction to Prodicus' account of Heracles at the crossroads (*Mem.* 2.1.20–34). Thus, what is on S.'s mind here is not so much the relatively trivial matter of whether old age is difficult or easy, but the question that is central to all the inquiries of P.'s S., how one's life should be lived.

e3–4 εὔπορος: more or less synonymous with ῥαιδία, but chosen here in anticipation of the turn the conversation will take toward the question of resources, specifically financial (Gifford 2001: 64). For εὔπορος meaning "wealthy," see *Symp.* 204b6, where it refers to Eros' prosperous father Poros, who is contrasted with his mother Penia.

e4 καὶ δὴ καὶ σοῦ ἡδέως ἂν πυθοίμην "(I think we should learn from our elders) and I would be particularly happy to learn *your* opinion ..."; for καὶ δὴ καί, see b6n.

e5 ἤδη "marks that a certain stage has been reached" (Burnet on *Euthphr.* 3e2). Here that stage is the point in one's lifetime that Homer and Hesiod call "the threshold (that consists) of old age" (*Il.* 22.60, 24.487, *Od.* 15.348, *Op.* 331). For the genitive with ἐνταῦθα, see 329b6 with LSJ I.3 and II.2, and compare the genitive below with χαλεπόν, "difficult (stage) of life."

ὃ δή: the antecedent is τοῦτο, with which χαλεπόν agrees and to which αὐτό refers. The particle δή is very commonly found in relative clauses containing material familiar to the interlocutor or referring to common usage ("which, as we know, is called ..."), e.g. 5.478d11, 6.501b5 (quoting Homer), 508b1. See Sicking and Van Ophuijsen 1993: 145–6 for this "self-evidential" force of δή.

e7 ἐξαγγέλλεις: the distinction between the compound verb and the simplex corresponds to that between ἐξάγγελος and ἄγγελος: while the latter generally refers to an emissary sent at someone else's behest – hence Herodotus (1.79.2) expresses the speed of Cyrus' arrival at Sardis by saying that he was his own messenger, αὐτὸς ἄγγελος – the former designates an informer who divulges on his own initiative things that would otherwise remain hidden (*Laws* 12.964e6, Thuc. 8.51.1). Thus, at 9.577a–b an intimate associate of the tyrannical man is said to reveal to the world (ἐξαγγέλλειν, b3) what the man is really like, stripped of the theatrical trappings (γυμνὸς ... τῆς τραγικῆς σκευῆς, b1) that disguise his true character. That passage cannot, however, be used to support the view, held by some, that the reference here is to the theatrical ἐξάγγελος (= a character in a drama who reports offstage actions, not personal details about the actor playing Medea), a technical sense of the word not attested before Philostratus.

329a1 νὴ τὸν Δία: a form of oath almost always, in P., spoken by someone other than S., who prefers to omit the definite article when swearing by Zeus, e.g. 345b6, 350e8, 8.554d5. For a comprehensive database of ancient Greek oaths, see https://nottingham.ac.uk/~brzoaths/index.php. The reason Cephalus feels called upon to invoke a divine witness is that he is about to say something that goes against the prevailing sentiment as expressed by his contemporaries and by the composers of sympotiastic verse, e.g. Mimnermus fr. 1 West.

a3 διασῴζοντες τὴν παλαιὰν παροιμίαν: cf. Aesch. fr. 78a col. I 32 *TrGF* (*Theoroi*) εἰ δ' οὖν ἐσῴζου τὴν πάλαι παρο[ιμία]ν, where the context demands "something like 'keep to what you know' (Ar. *Wasps* 1431)," O'Sullivan and Collard 2013: 275. For the proverbial character of the

Aristophanic line (ἔρδοι τις ἣν ἕκαστος εἰδείη τέχνην, which bears a striking resemblance to a principle that will feature prominently in *Rep.*, beginning with 2.370b), see Biles and Olson *ad loc.* The old proverb to which Cephalus refers, however, is the same one alluded to by S. in his first speech in *Phaedrus*, ἧλιξ ἥλικα τέρπει, γέροντα δὲ γέρων (schol. *Phdr.* 240c; *CPG* II 33.10).

a5 ἀναμιμνῃσκόμενοι περί "reminiscing about." The verb seems not to occur elsewhere with περί except once in the active voice in a fragment of a speech by, intriguingly, Cephalus' son Lysias, *Against Hippotherses*, fr. 6 II 5–6 Albini περὶ τῶν αὑτοῦ ἀ[ν]αμιμνήσκων εὐεργ[εσι]ῶν.

a6 ἃ τῶν τοιούτων ἔχεται "that are associated with these sorts of things"; LSJ ἔχω C.I.5.

329b1 εὖ ζῶντες: S.'s view of what constitutes εὖ ζῆν does not correspond with that of Cephalus' associates, or of Cephalus himself. At *Crito* 48b S. and his companion agree that the most important thing is οὐ τὸ ζῆν … ἀλλὰ τὸ εὖ ζῆν and, further, that living εὖ is the same as living δικαίως; cf. *Apol.* 28b. Likewise, at the end of Book One, S. will secure T.'s grudging agreement that the just man will live εὖ (353e10) and that ὁ εὖ ζῶν is μακάριός τε καὶ εὐδαίμων (354a1).

οὐδὲ ζῶντες: compare the Messenger in Sophocles' *Antigone*, who says, of the man who is unable to enjoy life's pleasures, οὐ τίθημ' ἐγὼ | ζῆν τοῦτον (1166–7).

b1–2 τὰς τῶν οἰκείων προπηλακίσεις τοῦ γήρως: when a noun is accompanied by both a subjective and an objective genitive, it is normal for the former to appear in attributive and the latter in predicate position; cf. *Phdr.* 244c5–6 τήν γε τῶν ἐμφρόνων ζήτησιν τοῦ μέλλοντος, Thuc. 1.25.4 τὴν Φαιάκων προενοίκησιν τῆς Κερκύρας. Among the insults to which the elderly could expect to be subjected is being mocked as "tombs" or "corpses" (Collard 2018: 44–5), i.e. as οὐδὲ ζῶντες.

b2 καὶ ἐπὶ τούτωι δή "and on this basis" (LSJ ἐπί B.III.1), the particle suggesting that Cephalus does not regard the occasional verbal abuse from one's relatives as adequate grounds for complaining about the dire effects of old age. Following forms of οὗτος, the particle is "often contemptuous in tone" (*GP* 208).

b3 ὑμνοῦσιν: often used in reference to songs of praise (e.g. 2.372b7), the verb is occasionally found in the deprecatory sense of tediously repeating the same thing (e.g. 8.549d8); cf. LSJ I.2 "descant upon" and II "harp upon."

ἐμοὶ δὲ δοκοῦσιν, ὦ Σώκρατες: vocatives are found not only at the start of an utterance (a1), but also, sometimes repeated, as here, at a later point for the purpose of calling the interlocutor's attention to an especially important or controversial assertion; e.g. *Gorg.* 526a4, c3, *Hp.Mi.* 372d4.

In particular, vocatives are often used in association with the speaker's expression of a personal opinion ("It seems to me …"); *Gorg.* 501c1, 513b3, *Lach.* 182d2, *Meno* 79c4, *Phd.* 85c2. Cephalus begins by giving the impression that his opinion is at variance with that of the majority (cf. 330d3), but he will end up expressing a conventional view, that one's character determines how one responds to adverse circumstances (d3–6, with two more vocatives). In this respect he is like the elderly members of the chorus in Aeschylus' *Agamemnon*, who introduce their assertion, that it is not excessive prosperity that is responsible for bad outcomes but men's evil deeds, by saying δίχα δ' ἄλλων μονόφρων εἰμί, 757–8.

b4 οὐ τὸ αἴτιον αἰτιᾶσθαι "(they seem) not to accuse the (real) cause." P. plays with this *figura etymologica*, rendered by Cicero as *qui mihi non id uidebantur accusare, quod esset accusandum* (*De sen.* 3.7), also at *Phlb.* 22d1–2 αἰτιῴμεθα ἂν ἑκάτερος ὁ μὲν τὸν νοῦν αἴτιον, ὁ δὲ ἡδονήν and *Tim.* 88a7 τὰ ἀναίτια αἰτιᾶσθαι (for the reading, see Taylor 1928: 622–3).

b4–5 καὶ ἂν ἐγὼ τὰ αὐτὰ ταῦτα ἐπεπόνθη "I too would be affected in the same way," the pluperfect tense describing what would have been Cephalus' present state; cf. *Apol.* 31d8, 36a6, *Euthphr.* 14c3.

b6 νῦν δέ: Cephalus demonstrates for S. his ability to engage in rational discussion, invalidating an argument by suggesting counterexamples; if it were the case that old age is itself the cause (αἴτιον) of his acquaintances' sorry condition, all (πάντες) elderly persons would be so affected. Cephalus' participation in the discussion will, however, come to an end when he is compelled to agree that the counterexample to his "definition" of justice adduced by S. is cogent (331c–d).

b7 καὶ ἄλλοις, καὶ δὴ καὶ Σοφοκλεῖ: the first καί is anticipatory ("both others and, in particular, Sophocles"), as at *Lach.* 181a5, *Lys.* 207b4. The impression given by the anecdote recounted by Cephalus, who represents himself as an eyewitness, is that it took place some time ago (ποτε … καὶ τότε … καὶ νῦν), that Cephalus is appreciably younger than Sophocles (c5n.) and, perhaps, that the playwright is no longer alive. But Sophocles, who died in 406 at the age of 90, certainly outlived Cephalus, whose date of birth is not known. According to Lysias (12.4), his father was persuaded by Pericles to come to Athens, where he lived for thirty years. Lysias himself was born in Athens. Regardless, therefore, of whether Lysias' birth is to be dated to 459/8 or, more likely, to the mid-440s (for discussion of the evidence, see Todd 2007: 5–17), Cephalus must have died in the mid-410s at the very latest. If the earlier date is correct, he would even have died when Sophocles was still in his sixties. That does not mean that there is no truth in the story. It may be one of a number of sayings of the elderly Sophocles in circulation (Lefkowitz 2012: 82–3) and P. decided to put it into the mouth of the elderly Cephalus regardless of the chronological incongruity. In any event, the many subsequent retellings of the anecdote all derive ultimately from P. (Cic. *De sen.* 14.47, the source of Val. Max. 4.3.ext.2; Plut. *Mor.* 525a, 788e, 1094e; Athen. 12.510b; Philostr. *Apol.* 1.13.3, 7.31.2); see also the full list of direct quotations of P.'s version in Boter 1989: 292. The anecdote has particular point in view of the reputation of Sophocles in his prime as a connoisseur of attractive boys (Ion of Chios, *FGrHist* 392 F 6 = Athen. 13.603e–604d).

329c1 Πῶς … ἔχεις πρός "How do you feel about …?" a colloquial expression (Collard 2018: 94) occurring also at *Parm.* 131e8, *Prot.* 352b1, *Symp.* 174a9–b1, 176b7.

c2 Εὐφήμει "Hush!" Despite its common use in connection with religious ritual and despite Cicero's rendition, *di meliora!* (*De sen.* 14.47), there is here no necessary religious connotation. Compare *Euthd.* 301a7 (S.'s reaction to Dionysodorus' "proof" that S. is Dionysodorus) and *Meno* 91c1 (Anytus' reaction to S.'s suggestion that Meno take lessons in virtue from a sophist); cf. Xen. *Cyr.* 2.2.12, *Oec.* 10.4.

c3 αὐτό: one might have expected αὐτά (read by a portion of the indirect tradition; see Slings' app. crit.), referring to τὰ ἀφροδίσια. But the plural might have been confusing after the adverb ἀσμενέστατα, and the singular is a better match for the savage master with which "it" is compared. Similar is 4.422b6–7 εἷς πύκτης ὡς οἷόν τε κάλλιστα ἐπὶ τοῦτο παρεσκευασμένος "a single boxer as well trained as possible for this (i.e. boxing)."

c3–4 ὥσπερ λυττῶντά τινα καὶ ἄγριον δεσπότην: cf. 9.586c2 ἔρωτας … λυττῶντας. For the popular notion of Ἔρως τύραννος, see Eur. *Hipp.* 538, fr. 136.1 *TrGF* (*Andromeda*). It is alluded to in Book Nine when S. describes the origin of the "tyrannical man," who is overcome by lust; he suggests that this accounts for Eros' traditional designation as a tyrant (573b6–7). For Sophocles, as for Cephalus, the only escape from the despotism of the bodily desires is to await their abatement in old age. By contrast, S. is committed to the belief that the philosopher is capable of training himself from an early age to divert his desire to indulge in the pleasures of the body and direct that desire toward a love of learning (6.485d); cf. 328d3n.

c5 καὶ νῦν οὐχ ἧττον: i.e. now that I too am an old man (b7n.).

c5–d2 παντάπασι γὰρ … ἀπηλλάχθαι: the text of this sequence is uncertain. There is unmitigated asyndeton either at ἐπειδάν or at the following παντάπασι (depending on whether we take the ἐπειδάν-clause with what follows or what precedes), and there is a further asyndeton at δεσποτῶν. Since temporal clauses introduced by ἐπειδάν more commonly precede the main clause (Rijksbaron 1994: §26.2), it seems on the whole better to take ἐπειδὰν … χαλάσωσιν with what follows than with the preceding clause, which is already defined by a temporal expression (ἐν τῶι γήραι).

The asyndeton in the following line can be eliminated by removing ἐστι with Stallbaum, although it is hard to see how it came to be present in our MSS.

c5–6 τῶν γε τοιούτων: although a genitive of separation is not elsewhere attested with εἰρήνη and only once with ἐλευθερία (*AP* 6.228.4 [Adaeus]), that is how we must understand the construction here; cf. Hdt. 6.135.2 ἡσυχίη τῆς πολιορκίης.

c7 παύσωνται κατατείνουσαι καὶ χαλάσωσιν "stop exerting themselves (intransitive, as at 2.358d5 and 367b3) and loosen their grip."

329d1 τὸ τοῦ Σοφοκλέους: followed by an infinitive spelling out what constitutes "the situation described by Sophocles," as at Ar. *Lys.* 158 τὸ τοῦ Φερεκράτους, κύνα δέρειν δεδαρμένην.

d3–4 οὐ τὸ γῆρας, ὦ Σώκρατες, ἀλλὰ ὁ τρόπος: for the vocative, see b3n. A similar sentiment is expressed in a fragment of Anaxandrides (54.1–3 *PCG*): οὔτοι τὸ γῆράς ἐστιν … | τῶν φορτίων μέγιστον, ἀλλ' ὃς ἂν φέρηι | ἀγνωμόνως αὔθ', οὗτός ἐστιν αἴτιος ("i.e. is responsible for old age being a burden to himself," Millis 2015: 275). Unfortunately, the following line is hopelessly corrupt, but intriguingly it includes the word εὐκόλως. Anaxandrides was active in Athens from the 370s to the 340s; elsewhere he mentions P., referring to someone eating the sacred olives, presumably those of the Academy (Millis 2015: 110), "just like Plato" (fr. 20 *PCG*). There is, however, no reason to believe that Anaxandrides was referring to, or was even familiar with, *Republic.* Rather, like Cephalus, he is expressing a standard sentiment; cf. e.g. Men. *Epitrep.* 1096–8: one's character (τρόπος, 1093) is responsible (αἴτιος) for how one turns out.

d5 εὔκολοι: in Aristophanes' *Frogs,* Dionysus contrasts Sophocles with the disaffected Euripides, saying that the former was εὔκολος during his lifetime and is εὔκολος in Hades (82); that is, he is content with his current status and is therefore less likely to run off with Dionysus to Athens.

329d7–330a8: Cephalus' reasoning has been valid, up to a point. If old age were *eo ipso* responsible for the misery of the elderly, then all old people would be miserable. The contentedness of Cephalus and others of his acquaintance (329b6–7) is sufficient to invalidate the proposition. He has not, however, proved the further point, that one's character determines how well one lives in old age. S. politely challenges Cephalus' appeal to his own case by suggesting that "most people" might consider that it is his wealth that mitigates the discomfort of aging. Implicated in S.'s challenge is a conventional understanding of τὸ εὖ ζῆν, to which Cephalus, but not necessarily S., would subscribe. In response, Cephalus resorts to telling a story about Themistocles.

329d7 Καὶ ἐγὼ ἀγασθεὶς αὐτοῦ εἰπόντος ταῦτα: in Book Two S. similarly introduces his praise of the character (τρόπος, 368b2) of Glaucon and Adeimantus, after he has heard their impressive reformulation of T.'s position (Καὶ ἐγὼ ἀκούσας … ἠγάμην, 367e5–6); this parallel indicates that S.'s complimentary language here is not ironic. The position of αὐτοῦ here shows that it is not part of a genitive absolute but depends on ἀγασθείς (LSJ I.4).

329e1 σου: with ἀποδέχεσθαι, "accept (it) from you"; cf. 337b4, 340c2. For the tendency of enclitic words to appear in second position ("Wackernagel's Law"), see Wackernagel 2009: 15.

e4 φασιν: no such saying is attested, but the alliteration and the gnomic sentiment suggest an original in the form of a trimeter such as παραμύθι' ἐστὶ πολλὰ τοῖσι πλουσίοις.

e5–6 καὶ λέγουσι μέν τι, οὐ μέντοι γε ὅσον οἴονται: cf. *Lach.* 195c5 καὶ γὰρ λέγει γέ τι, οὐ μέντοι ἀληθές γε, spoken by the combative Nicias; Cephalus' response is more conciliatory. For λέγειν τι, "make a valid point," in contrast to οὐδὲν λέγειν, "talk nonsense," see LSJ A.III.6. It is rare for μέντοι and γε to be juxtaposed (*GP* 405; Slings 2005: 1–2); more commonly they are separated by a word, as in the example from *Laches* just quoted. Adam suggests that the usage is justified by Cephalus' non-Attic origin, but the only other time μέντοι γε appears in P. (*Cra.* 424c9, also preceded by οὐ), it is in the mouth of S.

e6 τὸ τοῦ Θεμιστοκλέους: this is a version of a story told by Herodotus (8.125) as part of a suite of anecdotes about Themistocles and his relationship to his native polis: when he returned to Athens after having been given extraordinary honors in Sparta, an envious Athenian repeatedly claimed that his repute was owed to the success of his polis rather than to his personal merit, to which the hero of Salamis replied that his critic was right that he would not have been so honored had he been a citizen of Belbina (the sparsely populated island today called Agios Georgios), but neither would his critic, for all his Athenian status. As a self-contained narrative, Cephalus' version of the saying derives its point from the fact that it is not an Athenian, who by his own account deserves as much honor as Themistocles, but an inhabitant of Seriphos, which had become proverbial for insignificance already in the time of Aristophanes (*Ach.* 542; Constantakopoulou 2007: 103–5), who is now Themistocles' adversary. The definite articles – "the man from Seriphos," "the (well-known) story about Themistocles" – seem to show that this version of the story, like that of Herodotus, was already in circulation in P.'s day. At any rate, this is the version repeated by Cicero (*De sen.* 3.8) and Plutarch (*Them.* 18.5, *Mor.* 185c), who were more familiar with and, as Academics, more sympathetic to the philosopher than to the historian: Frost 1980: 171; Racine 2016: 200–1.

330a3–4 τοῖς δὴ … φέρουσιν: the dative is governed by εὖ ἔχει, "(the same proposition) suits, holds good for," as with other expressions of appropriateness or fitness (KG I 413). For καλῶς ἔχειν = "be appropriate," contrasted with ἀπρεπῶς ἔχειν, see *Phdr.* 274b7.

a4 εὖ ἔχει ὁ αὐτὸς λόγος: the story about Themistocles had implied that both personal accomplishment and membership of a prominent polis are necessary for attaining Themistocles' level of renown. The lesson that Cephalus proceeds to draw from the analogy is that neither good character (ἐπιείκεια) nor wealth is alone sufficient for tolerating the hardships of old age. He seems to have failed to notice that this does not support his earlier assertion that there is a single determinant (μία τις αἰτία, 329d3) of misery in old age, namely one's character (τρόπος). S. tactfully changes the subject.

a6 πλουτήσας: the ingressive aorist betrays Cephalus' (or P.'s?) class prejudice; it is assumed that ὁ μὴ ἐπιεικής, like the potter who experiences a windfall (πλουτήσας χυτρεύς, 4.421d4) cannot have inherited his wealth.

ἐν αὐτῶι: *sc.* τῶι γήραι. The medieval MSS's ἑαυτῶι is superfluous. For MS variation between ἑαυτῶι and ἐν αὐτῶι, see 9.574d2 and *Meno* 92c2.

a8 ἢ ἐπεκτήσω; "or did you acquire it in addition (to what you inherited)?"

330b1–331b7: Though one of the wealthiest men in Athens, Cephalus wishes to represent himself in modest terms (μέσος τις), as neither a spendthrift like his father nor a ruthless tycoon like his grandfather. His answer to S.'s question as to the greatest benefit for the possessor of great wealth revolves around a quotation from Pindar that has nothing to do with wealth. For Cephalus, wealth allows its possessor to have hope (the subject of Pindar's inspiring lines) of leaving this world without any outstanding debts to men or gods. That is, the businessman Cephalus, who thinks in terms of settling accounts (ἀναλογίζεται, 330e4), considers his wealth as an insurance policy against the possibility that the frightful stories about punishment in the afterlife might turn out to be true. As we will learn from the Myth of Er in Book Ten, there is some truth in those stories, but we will also learn that wealth is no insurance against punishment in the afterlife.

330b1 Ὁποῖα ἐπεκτησάμην "With regard to the way I have increased my estate"; γέγονα χρηματιστής virtually = κεχρημάτισμαι. For a relative clause with no syntactic connection to the main clause serving as the "theme" (*CGCG* §60.33), see *Laws* 11.920d1, 933e6, Eur. *Med.* 453, 547, Hdt. 3.81.1, Soph. *OT* 216, Xen. *Mem.* 1.1.17. Most editors retain the MS reading (see app. crit.), punctuating as a question. But when a direct question is introduced by ποῖος it regularly conveys a sense of disbelief, derision, indignation or disdain (Collard 2018: 87–9), none of which is appropriate here. Alternatively, we might read οἷα, with the same meaning as ὁποῖα.

b2–3 πάππος τε καὶ ὁμώνυμος: it is standard for a male child to be named after his paternal grandfather (so, e.g. Pericles' son Xanthippus, Socrates' son Sophroniscus). In the case of Cephalus' son Lysias, his name is a variant of his grandfather's; cf. the hero of Aristophanes' *Clouds*, who is the son of Pheidon (134) and who wished to name his son Pheidonides (65) after him.

b6 τούτοισιν: i.e. his sons. The long form of the dative plural ending disappeared from spoken Attic some time in P.'s youth, if not earlier (Willi 2003: 241). These forms appear, assuming our MSS accurately represent P.'s intention, a handful of times in *Republic* and other works belonging to roughly the same period of P.'s output, with numerous occurrences later in *Laws*.

βραχεῖ γέ τινι πλείω: dative of measure of difference (*CGCG* §§30.54, 32.11). Regardless of the source of wealth, it is incumbent on the head of the *oikos* to preserve and, ideally, increase the value of that wealth – but only modestly, otherwise he will appear to be acquisitive beyond what is felt appropriate to a gentleman. In the case of Cephalus, as it happened, the entire estate was lost due to circumstances beyond the control of his heirs, when it was appropriated by the Thirty.

b6–7 πλείω ἢ παρέλαβον: a compendious comparison, like Xen. *Cyr.* 8.2.21 οὔτε ἐσθίουσι πλείω ἢ δύνανται φέρειν … οὔτε ἀμφιέννυνται πλείω ἢ δύνανται φέρειν, for the expected πλείω ἢ ὅσα παρέλαβον (cf. *Tht.* 210b6–7 πλείω ἢ ὅσα εἶχον … εἴρηκα).

b8 Οὗ τοι ἕνεκα ἠρόμην … ὅτι "The reason I asked (is) because"; cf. *Chrm.* 165a7–8 οὗ δὴ οὖν ἕνεκα λέγω … ταῦτα πάντα, τόδε ἐστίν.

ἔδοξας "you struck me," aorist, referring to Cephalus' response to S.'s previous question.

330c2 διπλῆι ἢ οἱ ἄλλοι: the following sentence explains why the *nouveaux riches* are twice as fond of their wealth, namely because they have two distinct reasons for their attachment to it.

c3 ὥσπερ γὰρ οἱ ποιηταί: for poets and creative persons generally as "begetters" of their intellectual property, see *Phdr.* 275a1, *Symp.* 209d–e, *Tht.* 160e2–3, Ar. *Clouds* 530–2, *Frogs* 96, Arist. *EN* 1120b13–14, 1168a1–3. The metaphor was to prove fruitful: Boyd 2017: 167–75.

c4 ταύτηι τε δὴ καὶ οἱ χρηματισάμενοι "(in the very same way poets …) in that way businessmen also." The usual correlate to ὥσπερ is οὕτω, as at 7.530b6–7 ὥσπερ γεωμετρίαν οὕτω καὶ ἀστρονομίαν μέτιμεν, which also illustrates the common use of καί in such constructions. τε anticipates καί in the following line, marking ταύτηι and κατὰ τὴν χρείαν as the two sources of the businessman's affection for his wealth, with δή highlighting his distinctive source.

c5 ὡς ἔργον ἑαυτῶν, καὶ κατὰ τὴν χρείαν: here and elsewhere P. is trying to work out for the first time a typology for specifying different grounds for classifying things as good (ἀγαθόν) or fine (καλόν). In *Gorgias* (474d–e), S. introduces Polus to the distinction between those things that we judge fine for their usefulness and those for the pleasure they give us (κατὰ τὴν χρείαν … διὰ ἡδονήν). Glaucon in Book Two will make the philosophically important proposal of a threefold division among goods: those that we welcome (ἀσπαζόμενοι, 357b6) for their own sake, those that we embrace (ἀγαπῶμεν, c2) both for their own sake and for their consequences and, third, those that are good only for the profits and other benefits that accrue from them (μισθῶν τε χάριν καὶ τῶν ἄλλων ὅσα γίγνεται ἀπὸ αὐτῶν, d1–2). Here, we are reminded that everyone values wealth for what it can procure, while those who have worked hard to acquire it look upon it in the same way parents look upon their offspring.

c7 ἀλλὰ ἤ: strictly speaking, ἤ is superfluous, since ἀλλά alone in a context like this can = "other than"; cf. *Euthd.* 303d1 οὐδὲν ὑμῖν μέλει, ἀλλὰ τῶν ὁμοίων ὑμῖν μόνον, Soph. *OT* 1331 ἔπαισε δ' αὐτόχειρ νιν οὔτις, ἀλλ' ἐγὼ τλάμων. Similarly, πλὴν ἤ is found = πλήν, LSJ B.II.2. Printed texts and most MSS render ἀλλὰ ἤ as ἀλλ' ἤ, leaving open the possibility of interpreting the combination as ἄλλο ἤ; see KG II 284–5, *GP* 24–7.

330d1 Πάνυ μὲν οὖν: one of the most common response formulas in P., occurring over 300 times. It usually expresses strong agreement with the previous statement or answers in the affirmative a question of the form, "Isn't it the case that …?" (Thesleff 1954: §78; *GP* 477; see, however, *GP* 587 and below, 331d4n.). It seems odd here and uncharacteristic of S. to give such forceful approval of his interlocutor's assent to S.'s own statement.

d3 οὐκ ἂν πολλοὺς πείσαιμι: Cephalus again prefaces his expression of rather conventional sentiments by claiming that few would agree with him (329b3n.).

εὖ γὰρ ἴσθι: Cephalus' confidence regarding what S. can expect when he is "near the point of thinking he is going to die" is ironic given P.'s portrayal, in *Apology*, *Crito* and *Phaedo*, of S.'s behavior when he not only thinks but is quite certain he is going to die.

d5 δέος καὶ φροντίς: a hendiadys, subject of singular verbs, "apprehensive thoughts" or "introspective anxiety." Similar is ὑποψίας … καὶ δείματος e3; cf. 347c1n.

d6–e1 οἵ τε γὰρ λεγόμενοι μῦθοι … καὶ αὐτός: the delayed effect of the stories heard in childhood are now felt in his soul, and he himself, as he approaches death, begins to catch sight of the torments that potentially await him. At the start of Book Three S. will insist that the children of Callipolis should not be exposed to such frightful stories about the afterlife.

d6–7 ἐνθάδε ... ἐκεῖ: standard ways of referring to the land of the living and, euphemistically, the abode of the dead, "*l'au-delà.*"

ἀδικήσαντα ... διδόναι δίκην: these are the first occurrences of words from the root δικ- in *Republic,* as ψυχήν in the next line is the first occurrence of that word. Justice will emerge as the main subject of the dialogue, and the "turning" of the soul toward the truth will appear as the primary metaphor for the education of the philosopher in Book Seven (519b, 526e). It is notable that, at its introduction, justice is spoken of in terms of avoiding ἀδικία and its consequence, the requirement that one "pay the penalty." (In the myth in *Gorgias,* S. says that, of all misfortunes, the worst is to arrive in Hades having a soul brimming with many ἀδικήματα, 522e3–4.) Cephalus thus presents a position against which T. will violently react, arguing that injustice is both praiseworthy and rewarding. Further, justice is initially spoken of in terms of the interaction of one individual with another (τινα, singular, e4). Only when we get to the conversation with T. will the discussion of justice extend beyond the individual to the polis (338d6 with 351c7n.).

330e1 μὴ ἀληθεῖς ὦσιν "(distract his mind with the thought that) perhaps they may be true after all." The subjunctive with μή is found, in both independent and subordinate clauses, in "cautious assertions" (*SMT* §§265–7), often, as here, with the suggestion that what may turn out to be the case is unwelcome.

e2 τῆς τοῦ γήρως ἀσθενείας: it is not clear why the infirmity of old age should make the unpleasantness of death more readily perceptible. The thought seems to be either that the vitality of youth had earlier fortified the now elderly person against the onslaught of terrifying tales about the afterlife, or that the discomfort and debility associated with extreme old age serve as a foretaste of the helplessness and torments threatened by the myths.

e3 δὲ οὖν "at any rate, in any event," indicating that the question of which of the foregoing alternatives is correct is immaterial to the point about to be made; cf. *Apol.* 34e2, *Phdr.* 266b8–c1, *Tim.* 28b4.

e4 ἠδίκησεν: decision between the aorist and perfect (see app. crit.) is difficult. The latter would convey the enduring effect of the injustice, still requiring redress (Slings 2005: 3 compares *Phd.* 113d8, where, however, the same MS variation is found), but the aorist is supported by the final accounting in the Myth of Er, where the penalty must be paid (δίκην δεδωκέναι) by the deceased ὅσα πώποτέ τινα ἠδίκησαν καὶ ὅσους ἕκαστοι (10.615a6–7). According to Lysias, his father ended his life with a clear conscience, at least as far as the Athenian courts were concerned: since he moved to Athens over thirty years previously, neither he nor his sons were subject to prosecution, nor did they bring charges against anyone else (οὐδενὶ πώποτε οὔτε ἡμεῖς οὔτε ἐκεῖνος δίκην οὔτε ἐδικασάμεθα οὔτε ἐφύγομεν, 12.4).

331a2 ὡς καὶ Πίνδαρος λέγει: the implication of καί is that Cephalus imagines Pindar to be agreeing with his characterization of hope as a worthy caretaker in one's old age. The quotation from Pindar (fr. 214 Snell–Maehler) is not known from elsewhere, nor do we know to what genre the poem belongs. The absence of context means that we must rely on Cephalus' claim that the quotation pertains to "the man who has led a just and pious life." But unless P., who was certainly familiar with the context, is deliberately portraying Cephalus as distorting Pindar's intention, which seems unlikely, we should assume that the Hope to which Pindar refers is indeed the reassuring prospect of a blessed afterlife awaiting the virtuous. This is appropriate to its association with the elderly and is consistent with other places where Pindar speaks of glorious rewards for the virtuous after their death: *Ol.* 2.61–77, frr. 129–31 and 133, the last quoted by P. at *Meno* 81b–c.

a5–8 γλυκεῖά οἱ … κυβερνᾷ "a sweet-tempered caretaker of the elderly attends him (οἱ), nurturing his spirit, Hope, the chief pilot of mortals' wayward thoughts."

a6 ἀτάλλοισα = Attic ἀτάλλουσα.

συναορεῖ: from σύν + ἀείρω 2, "to bind together, join" (Beekes); cf. (Attic) συνωρίς, *biga.*

a7–8 πολύστροφον γνώμαν: this Pindaric phrase undoubtedly prompted P.'s expression above, στρέφουσιν αὐτοῦ τὴν ψυχήν.

a9 θαυμαστῶς ὡς σφόδρα "ever so wonderfully," an almost comically exaggerated combination. Nowhere else does θαυμαστῶς ὡς (Thesleff 1954: §§374, 389), a colloquialism (Collard 2018: 47), intensify σφόδρα (§§130–6), which here intensifies εὖ λέγει.

331b1 οὔ τι παντὶ ἀνδρί: as Cephalus had earlier expressed the view that both wealth and good character (ἐπιείκεια) are necessary for putting up with the hardships of old age (330a4n.), so here both are essential as insurance against an unpleasant afterlife.

b2–4 τὸ … ἀπιέναι: serving as the "theme" (330b1n.) of the sentence, picked up by εἰς τοῦτο b4, which is repeated in b6.

b2–3 ἐξαπατῆσαι ἢ ψεύσασθαι: that is, the behavior characteristic of those unable to pay their debts, like Strepsiades, who enrolls in S.'s school in order to learn how to lie and deceive (Ar. *Clouds* 444–51).

b3–4 ὀφείλοντα ἢ θεῶι θυσίας τινὰς ἢ ἀνθρώπωι χρήματα: acquitting oneself of one's obligations to gods and men constitutes, for Cephalus, leading one's life δικαίως καὶ ὁσίως (a3–4). S. had investigated the virtue of ὁσιότης in *Euthyphro*, where it was revealed to be a species of τὸ δίκαιον (12c–d), which will turn out to be the topic of *Republic*. (Sometimes regarded as one of the cardinal virtues, ὁσιότης is excluded below, at 4.427e9–10, presumably because it is subsumed under justice.) Cephalus' attitude, that acting virtuously consists in making payments to men and gods, will be thoroughly discredited in S.'s discussion with Glaucon and Adeimantus. In Book Two the brothers argue that it is in fact the unjust man who, by enriching himself, is best able to influence the gods with sacrifices, appealing to the authority of the poets for the efficacy of this strategy (362c, 364c–365a, 365e). S., however, disallows the poets' claims that good men and gods can be bribed (3.390e–391a) and, indeed, the guardian class in Callipolis, paragons of virtuous behavior, will dispense entirely with ownership of private property (3.416d, 5.464b–465d).

b4 ἔπειτα ἐκεῖσε ἀπιέναι δεδιότα "then (i.e. still in debt) to go off to the next world (330d6–7n.) in a state of fear." For ἔπειτα with a principal verb (here an articular infinitive) following a participle, often conveying some kind of disjunction between the two actions, with that of the principal verb not being the expected outcome of the participle, see LSJ I.3.

b6 ἀλλά γε ἓν ἀντὶ ἑνός "but all things considered (lit. one thing over against one thing)"; cf. *Laws* 4.705b4–5 ἀντὶ ἑνὸς ἕν. Juxtaposed ἀλλά γε is quite rare, in contrast to ἀλλὰ … γε, which is not unusual. Denniston (*GP* 23) notes that there are two occurrences of ἀλλά γε in Gorgias' *Palamedes* (DK 82 B11a = 32 D25.10 and 14 Laks–Most) and, while those instances are not quite comparable to what we have here, Slings (2005: 4) suggests that the Sicilian origin of both Cephalus and Gorgias may indicate that this is a regional usage. We have noted a handful of peculiarities in Cephalus' language, some or all of which may be intended by P. to characterize him, either as an individual or as a non-Athenian; see the notes to 328c6, 329a5, 329c5–d2 and 329e5–6.

οὐκ ἐλάχιστον = μάλιστα, an instance of litotes, a form of understatement that ironically emphasizes a positive by negating its contrary. The regular adverbial form is ἐλάχιστα, but ἐλάχιστον is found as well: 9.587b4 ἐλάχιστον δὲ αἱ βασιλικαί τε καὶ κόσμιαι (*sc.* ἐπιθυμίαι ἐφάνησαν λόγου ἀφεστῶσαι), Thuc. 3.36.2 προσξυνελάβοντο οὐκ ἐλάχιστον τῆς ὁρμῆς αἱ Πελοποννησίων νῆες. For a superlative adverb strengthening a superlative adjective (here χρησιμώτατον), see *Tht.* 186e11–12, *Tim.* 51d2, 92b1–2; KG I 27. The exaggerated emphasis is likely another element in the characterization of Cephalus; cf. a9n.

b7 νοῦν ἔχοντι: i.e. ἐπιεικεῖ; cf. Plut. *Mor.* 1104a τὸ τῶν ἐπιεικῶν καὶ νοῦν ἐχόντων (*sc.* γένος).

χρησιμώτατον: S. had asked τί μέγιστον ... ἀγαθόν (330d1–2). It is characteristic of Cephalus that he thinks of the good in terms of the useful. His view of wealth as, among other things, a means of influencing the gods is reminiscent of the attitude projected in Bacchylides 3, an epinician ode written for another Syracusan, the exceptionally wealthy tyrant Hiero; after mentioning Hiero's many offerings, the poet recounts the story of Croesus on the pyre, who upbraids the gods for their ingratitude after all the sacrifices he has made, whereupon heaven-sent rains extinguish the fire and Croesus is transported to the land of the Hyperboreans on account of his piety (δι' εὐσέβειαν, 61).

331c1–d9: Cephalus had implied that the man who led his life with justice and piety had done so by refraining from lying and defaulting on his debts. That it is just to tell the truth and fulfill one's obligations is uncontroversial. Doing so may even exhibit one's piety if the gods have been invoked as witnesses, as is often the case when testifying in a court of law (δικαστήριον) or when entering into a contract (Dover 1974: 248–50). S. moves the discussion to an entirely different level, however, by showing that telling the truth and repaying one's debts is not, without further qualification, an adequate definition (ὅρος) of justice. Recognizing that he is out of his depth, Cephalus hands over the discussion to Polemarchus and retires to fulfill his religious obligations.

331c1–2 τοῦτο δὲ αὐτό, τὴν δικαιοσύνην "this thing itself, justice." While other words from the same root have appeared (330d6–7n.), this is the first occurrence of the abstract δικαιοσύνη. It is introduced by means of a locution similar to that used elsewhere by S. to focus the attention of his interlocutor on identifying the essential nature of a concept: *Meno* 71a6–7 αὐτὸ ὅτι ποτέ ἐστι τὸ παράπαν ἀρετή, *Prot.* 360e8 τί ποτέ ἐστιν αὐτό, ἡ ἀρετή, *Tht.* 146e9–10 ἐπιστήμην αὐτὸ ὅτι ποτέ ἐστιν. The same language is used in reference to the Forms: *Parm.* 130b4–9, *Phd.* 65c7, d4–5, *Phdr.* 247d6. Adeimantus shows his familiarity with this manner of speaking when he says that fathers tell their sons that one ought to be just, "praising not justice itself (αὐτὸ δικαιοσύνην) but the accolades that ensue from it" (2.363a1–2).

c2 τὴν ἀλήθειαν = τὸ ἀληθεύειν, as is clear from ἀληθῆ λέγειν c8 and d2. This is an uncommon meaning of the noun, but cf. Mimnermus fr. 8 West, from his *Nanno*, ἀληθείη δὲ παρέστω | σοὶ καὶ ἐμοί, πάντων χρῆμα δικαιότατον.

ἁπλῶς οὕτως: a favorite expression of P., suggesting that what has just been expressed or implied ought not to stand without further scrutiny or qualification. It makes little difference whether οὕτως modifies ἁπλῶς ("in so simple a fashion") or vice versa ("simply thus"). Pausanias begins his encomium in *Symposium* by saying that the requirement that the symposiasts "praise Eros *tout court*" (τὸ ἁπλῶς οὕτως παρηγγέλθαι ἐγκωμιάζειν Ἔρωτα, 180c5) is lacking in nuance, since there is more than one variety of love. In *Laws*, the visitor from Athens asks his companions to imagine the confusion that would arise "if someone were simply to establish a competition" (εἴ ποτέ τις οὕτως ἁπλῶς ἀγῶνα θείη, 2.658a6) without further specifying the nature of the competition. Cf. *Gorg.* 468c3, *Phlb.* 12c6–7 and a dozen other occurrences.

c3 ἔστιν "is it possible"; for this accentuation when the word is used in this meaning, see Probert 2003: §282.

c5 εἴ τις λάβοι παρὰ φίλου ... ὅπλα: for the language, compare Xen. *Mem.* 1.7.5 εἴ τις ἀργύριον ἢ σκεῦος παρά του πειθοῖ λαβὼν ἀποστεροίη. Here the specification that the lender is a friend is significant, anticipating Polemarchus' distinction (332a–b) between what is owed to friends and what to enemies. In P., ὅπλον is found only in the plural, except 5.474a2 and *Lach.* 183d6, which are special cases. The word can refer to any sort of tool or piece of equipment, but in the context of S.'s argument, and in a conversation with a manufacturer of armaments, it is to be understood as a weapon. When Cicero translates this passage at *De officiis* 3.95 he renders ὅπλα as *gladium.* The situation hypothesized by S. is staged in Euripides' *Andromache* when the suicidal Hermione demands that her attendant, whom she addresses with ὦ φίλος, return the sword that he took from her hand (841–4).

c6–8 οὔτε δίκαιος ... ὁ ἀποδιδοὺς οὐδὲ αὖ ... πάντα ἐθέλων τὰ ἀληθῆ λέγειν: echoing, and mocking, Cephalus' μηδὲ ἄκοντά τινα ἐξαπατῆσαι ἢ ψεύσασθαι, μηδὲ αὖ ὀφείλοντα, b2–3. Cephalus had proposed that one's wealth makes it possible to act with justice by eliminating the likelihood of telling untruths even under duress (ἄκοντα); in the scenario envisioned by S., the man who refuses to return what he borrowed and who is not willing (ἐθέλων) to tell the whole truth is universally regarded as just. Later (2.382a), a distinction will be drawn between the merely verbal (λόγωι) falsehood, of which this is an example (382c), and the "authentic falsehood" (τὸ ὡς ἀληθῶς ψεῦδος), detested by gods and men alike, that no one willingly propagates (οὐδεὶς ἑκὼν ἐθέλει). Such verbal falsehoods will on occasion be employed even by the Guardians of Callipolis (3.414b–c, 5.459c), who, being philosophers, especially love truth and loathe falsehood (6.485c).

331d4 Πάνυ μὲν οὖν: here the confirmatory (330d1n.) and adversative (*GP* 475) forces of μὲν οὖν are both in evidence: Polemarchus rejects S.'s claim that Cephalus has not provided a definition of justice by asserting that, on the contrary, his definition is indeed valid, at least if (εἴπερ γε) we are to put any credence in what Simonides says. Of course, Cephalus had not thought he was giving a definition of justice but, like the dutiful son he is, Polemarchus comes to his father's defense, with recourse to his father's favorite strategy, appealing to the authority of a poet. There is a hint of irony on the part of P. in the choice of Simonides of Ceos, who lived from the 550s to the 460s. What Simonides was best known for in antiquity, apart from his poetry, was his love of money and his miserliness (Lefkowitz 2012: 57–60; Rawles 2018: 156–93). The only other Platonic character who cites Simonides is Protagoras (see the extended discussion between him and S. at *Prot.* 339a–347a), who had called him a sophist (316d), perhaps on account of his insistence on being paid for his services. When S. criticizes what is apparently another of Simonides' sayings at 6.489b, he does not name him (Rawles 2018: 171–4).

d6 παραδίδωμι ὑμῖν: i.e. to S. and Polemarchus. Cephalus had apparently already handed over management of his estate to his son and heir (κληρονόμος), as Polemarchus immediately points out.

d6–7 δεῖ … τῶν ἱερῶν ἐπιμεληθῆναι: according to Annas (1981: 20), this is a "polite fiction," the sacrifice having already been completed. If so, Cephalus has deceived the narrator S., who describes him as leaving to attend to the rites. Sacrificial ritual was an elaborate affair, involving prayers, preparation of the victim and other preliminaries to the sacrificial act, the act itself, butchering of the victim, consecration of the inedible portions, preparation of the edible portions, distribution of the meat and, finally, the ritual feast (Bowie 1995). Not all this activity required the continual presence of the person responsible for the sacrifice.

d8 Οὐκοῦν, ἔφη, ἐγώ, ὁ Πολέμαρχος: for this pattern, compare, e.g., *Phd.* 70b5 Ἀληθῆ, ἔφη, λέγεις, ὁ Σωκράτης, 71c10, 73b3, 77c1, 78a10, c5, d8. As with ἦ δὲ ὅς (327b6–7n.), the name of the subject of ἔφη, if expressed, is regularly accompanied by the definite article in such "turn-taking scenes" (Rijksbaron 2007: 95–7). Like Latin *inquit*, ἔφη and ἦ δὲ ὅς are postpositive expressions, and there is a tendency to distribute postpositives (*CGCG* §60.11), so that we sometimes find a pattern of alternation involving mobiles (words that can appear anywhere in a sentence or can constitute a complete utterance on their own) and postpositives, including particles, enclitics and, often, vocatives and oaths. An example is Cephalus' earlier utterance, the essence of which is Ἐγώ σοι ἐρῶ οἷόν γέ μοι φαίνεται, with the postpositives underlined. Since the utterance is quoted by S., and since Cephalus amplifies it with an oath and a vocative, the expressions ἔφη, νὴ τὸν Δία and ὦ Σώκρατες are slotted into the sentence as we see it at 329a1–2; cf. 331c1, d3.

331e1–332c3: Polemarchus' correction (Πάνυ μὲν οὖν, d4) of S. is his affirmation that "to tell the truth and to repay what one has received" is indeed a definition of justice, although the support he seeks from

Simonides is not framed in terms of a definition. (Truth-telling is lost sight of in what follows; it is presumably subsumed under the activity of rendering what is due.) Still, S., despite having asked merely what Simonides says περὶ δικαιοσύνης, treats Simonides' saying as if it were a definition of justice (τὸ δίκαιον ὃ εἴη, 332b8–c1), first modifying it and then subjecting it to scrutiny. As this is the only attestation of the saying, we have no independent confirmation of the form it took. We are dealing with an anecdote (= T 86(a) Poltera), like those about Sophocles and Themistocles above, rather than a verse quotation, so there is no metrical check on the wording. We can, however, be fairly confident that Simonides did not intend to provide a definition of justice and that Polemarchus' quotation or paraphrase, "It is just to render to each person what is owed," is reasonably close to what Simonides is supposed to have said. That Simonides used, or was reported as having used, a form of ὀφείλω is implied by S.'s τοῦτο δὲ ὠνόμασεν ὀφειλόμενον (332c2).

331e1 ὁ τοῦ λόγου κληρονόμος: similarly, at *Phdr.* 257b2 S. refers to Lysias as τὸν τοῦ λόγου πατέρα. The metaphor is common (330c3n.): *Phdr.* 275e4, *Symp.* 177d5, *Tht.* 164e2–3.

e3 Ὅτι; for such questions, using the indirect form of the interrogative to repeat the direct form used by the interlocutor before the interlocutor's question is answered, see *Euthphr.* 2c2, *Lach.* 195a4, *Laws* 2.662b1; KG II 517. Only by punctuating as a question can we account for the following τό, which now has the effect of placing τὰ ... ἐστιν in quotation marks (336a1n.; Dickey 2007: 113), like *Phlb.* 48c10 τὸ γνῶθι σαυτὸν λέγεις; "You mean the (familiar) γνῶθι σαυτόν?" Earlier editors, printing a comma after ὅτι, appear to take the article with ἀποδιδόναι. But when an infinitive is the subject of the copula, as below at 335e2, the infinitive normally has no article.

e6 σοφὸς γὰρ καὶ θεῖος ὁ ἀνήρ: cf. *Prot.* 315e7–316a1, where S. says of the sophist Prodicus, πάσσοφος γάρ μοι δοκεῖ ὁ ἀνὴρ εἶναι καὶ θεῖος. In the end (335e2–5), S. will get Polemarchus to agree that whoever said that it is just to render to each person what is owed, if doing so involves harming someone, was not σοφός.

e8–332a1 τό ... ἀποδιδόναι "if someone has handed something over (to you), to return it to him (lit. to anyone) if he is not in his right mind when he asks for it back." Because a counterexample has been acknowledged in the case of a friend and a weapon, a definition that applies to "something" and to "anyone at all" (ὁτῳοῦν, accentuating Simonides' ἑκάστῳ) cannot be accepted. S.'s next question restates the issue in even stronger terms by asking if one should under no circumstances (οὐδὲ ὁπωστιοῦν) return something to someone who is not in his right mind when he asks for it back.

332a5 ἀπαιτοῖ: for the optative in a subordinate clause depending on a primary-tense verb of obligation, see *SMT* §555. P. prefers to use the older Attic endings for the optative of contract verbs (Willi 2003: 245), although there are occasional instances of e.g. συγχωροίη (*Phlb.* 45a3) vs συγχωροῖ (*Tht.* 171b1).

a7 Ἄλλο δή τι ἢ τὸ τοιοῦτον ... λέγει "means (by τὸ ... δίκαιον εἶναι) something other than this sort of thing"; cf. *Gorg.* 489d1–2 πάλαι τοπάζω τοιοῦτόν τί σε λέγειν τὸ κρεῖττον, "I long suspected that by τὸ κρεῖττον you meant something like this."

a9–10 τοῖς γὰρ φίλοις ... μηδέν: the justice of helping one's friends (and harming one's enemies, which Polemarchus will acknowledge presently) was a recognized component of standard Greek ethics; Dover 1974: 180–4; Blundell 1989. Indeed, Meno defines ἀνδρὸς ἀρετή as helping one's friends and harming one's enemies while being active in civic affairs (*Meno* 71e2–4; cf. Xen. *Mem.* 2.6.35). In his reformulation of T.'s argument, Glaucon will point out that one advantage of the unjust man's ill-gotten riches is that they make it all the easier for him to help his friends and harm his enemies (2.362c1).

a11 Μανθάνω ... ὅτι οὐ τὰ ὀφειλόμενα "I understand (the point you are making), because it is not *what is owed*" that one returns to a friend if it is to the friend's detriment. The expression τὰ ὀφειλόμενα is placed in initial position because it is this element of Simonides' definition that Polemarchus wishes to clarify.

a11–b1 ὃς ἂν τωι χρυσίον ἀποδῶι παρακαταθεμένωι "whoever returns gold to someone who has left it (with him) for safekeeping." In Book Four, after he has defined justice, S. will claim that it is now clear *why* the just man is naturally disposed to return gold or silver that has been left with him (442e).

332b2 βλαβερά: it is easier to see how returning a weapon to a friend who is no longer in his right mind might be harmful. Perhaps we are to imagine the friend as asking for his gold back because he intends to squander it on the satisfaction of various deleterious vices, like Timarchus (Aeschin. 1.42, 115) or a young man in New Comedy who has fallen in love with a hetaira. P. seems to have changed the hypothetical situation from borrowing a weapon to being given money for safekeeping in order to prepare for the argument at 333c–d, that justice is useful precisely when the money that has been given for safekeeping is not in use.

b5 Τί δέ; τοῖς ἐχθροῖς: so far, Simonides' "definition" of justice has been applied only to friends. To be valid it will need to extend to everyone. Not everyone, of course, is either one's friend or one's enemy, and S. could invalidate the definition by showing that there is a large number of people who are not covered by it, but he prefers to wait and make the radical argument that harming enemies is not just.

b6–7 ὀφείλεται δέ γε, οἶμαι, ... ὅπερ καὶ προσήκει: the qualification οἶμαι is gently ironic and is not indicative of any hesitancy on the part of Polemarchus; cf. 333a9, *Lach.* 191e6–7 οἱ δέ γε, οἶμαι, δειλίαν [*sc.* κέκτηνται] ἐν τοῖς αὐτοῖς τούτοις, where S. is in no doubt that some people are cowardly under the same circumstances as others are brave. While it is natural to speak of owing a friend a favor, it would be odd to say that one "owed" harm to an enemy, which is why Polemarchus adds a clarification, framing it in the more acceptable terms of appropriateness, "just what he has coming to him." (After ὅσπερ we often find a seemingly superfluous καί; e.g. 353b4, 3.387d5.)

b8–c1 Ἠινίξατο ἄρα ... ποιητικῶς τὸ δίκαιον ὃ εἴη "Simonides defined justice cryptically, then, in the manner typical of poets." S. often playfully suggests that gods, poets and other "wise" individuals express themselves in a riddling idiom that needs to be translated into more intelligible language (*Apol.* 21b3–4, *Chrm.* 162a10–11, *Lys.* 214d3–5, *Phd.* 69c4–6, *Tht.* 152c9–10, 194c8–9). Here P. uses the more "prosaic" τὸ δίκαιον (336a8–9n.) in place of ἡ δικαιοσύνη, which is how "justice" has hitherto been expressed, to underline the point. In what follows S. makes the distinction between what the poet meant (διενοεῖτο) and what he said (ὠνόμασεν), followed by a mock appeal to the poet himself for clarification. P.'s irony is directed especially at the allegorical interpretation of poets of the past, a practice that was common in P.'s day and with which we have become more familiar as a result of the publication of the Derveni Papyrus, whose interpretative strategy frequently uses the language of "riddling"; for this practice, see Struck 2004: 21–76, with discussion of P.'s reactions at 41–59. Presumably there will be no need of such strategies in Callipolis, where the poetry will have been purged of those elements whose meaning is not perfectly straightforward.

332c2 τὸ προσῆκον ἑκάστωι ἀποδιδόναι: in order to avoid the abhorrent collocation τὸ τό (339c7n.; Smyth §1162), which no writer before Aristotle admits, P. uses the article here to do double duty, as at 340c3–4, serving to nominalize both προσῆκον and ἀποδιδόναι.

c3 Ἀλλὰ τί οἴει; cf. *Hp.Ma.* 296a6–7 Ἀλλὰ τί οἴει, ὦ Σώκρατες;

332c4–333d12: S. begins the examination of Simonides' definition, as modified by Polemarchus at the prompting of S., by introducing the craft analogy, familiar from such early dialogues as *Crito, Euthyphro* and *Ion* (see Roochnik 1986). In these and other Platonic works S. operates with a conviction that there is an intimate relationship, sometimes even a relationship of identity, between the virtues and knowledge. That being the case, it seems legitimate to S. to speak of justice in the same way one speaks of viticulture, shipbuilding and other τέχναι, that is, in terms of possessing a specialized knowledge concerning the right way of going about things. There are obvious difficulties with this understanding of virtue: not everyone has the capacity for being trained as an expert surgeon, yet one hopes that everyone has an innate ability to act virtuously; also, the crafts have recognized experts and well-defined areas within which the practitioners exercise their expertise, outside of which they must yield to practitioners of other crafts. Surprisingly, S.'s interlocutors do not object to his use of the craft analogy on these grounds. Rather, their protests have to do with social class: well-bred gentlemen consider it undignified to bring the craft of the blacksmith or the potter into polite conversation about ethical matters (*Gorg.* 490e–491a, *Hp.Ma.* 288d; Xen. *Mem.* 1.2.37, 4.4.5–6). Here, P. seems himself to call into question the applicability of the craft analogy in the case of the virtues, since the argument leads to the conclusion that, if justice is comparable to a τέχνη, there appears to be no well-defined area over which it alone holds sway.

332c4–5 ἡ τίσιν οὖν τί ἀποδιδοῦσα … τέχνη "the art that renders what thing to what recipients." For such double questions, cf. e.g. *Tht.* 208c9 Οἷον τίνα τίνος ἔχεις μοι λόγον εἰπεῖν; "As an example, what account of what thing can you give me?"

c5 ὀφειλόμενον καὶ προσῆκον "owed, that is to say, appropriate." It is a common practice of S. – some would say malpractice – to get his interlocutor to explain a term and then combine, using (τε) καί, the original term with a term from the interlocutor's explanation as though they were synonyms; e.g. 339e1–2, 341b3–4, 342e3, 343c4, 345e1, 349d6, 350b7, c3–4, *Gorg.* 490e1. Here and in c8 S. retains ὀφειλόμενον because it better suits ἀποδιδοῦσα than προσῆκον alone would do. Further, by adhering to Simonides' supposed original wording, S. gives the poet less grounds for claiming that he is being posthumously misrepresented.

τέχνη: S. almost surreptitiously introduces the craft analogy. He begins by asking about the purview of medicine, which everyone would agree is a τέχνη. Next he asks about the art of the chef, which he himself elsewhere contrasts with medicine as being an aptitude rather than a τέχνη (*Gorg.* 500b3–5). When S. finally brings the questioning around to the subject under discussion, the "τέχνη" of justice, Polemarchus is put in the awkward position of either answering the question, which he does only conditionally (Εἰ μέν τι δεῖ …), or asking S. why his question has taken this seemingly misleading form.

332d1 Ἡ τοῖς ὄψοις τὰ ἡδύσματα: the latter are spices and garnishes (e.g. coriander and onions: Ar. *Knights* 676–8) added to the ὄψον, which is "a general word for side-dishes of all sorts intended to add a bit of interest to the starchy staple … that made up the bulk of a meal," Biles and

Olson on *Wasps* 300–2. In Book Three S., relying on Homeric precedent, will recommend a diet that dispenses with ἡδύσματα for the Callipolitan Guardians when they are in training (404c).

d2 δή: it is a familiar pattern in P. for S. to give a couple of examples and then return the interlocutor's attention to the matter at hand using the particle δή; e.g. 333a11, b7, d10, 335c13, d7, 350a6, 353a9, d3, *Alc.1* 126b8, *Euthphr.* 13b4, *Prot.* 311d1. This culminative force of the particle is preserved in the adverb ἤδη (328e5n.), of which δή is an element (see Beekes).

d4–5 ἡ τοῖς φίλοις ... ἀποδιδοῦσα: this is little more than a restatement of what Polemarchus had affirmed at a9–10 and b6–7. The only development in the interim has been that he has tacitly, and unnecessarily, assented to S.'s characterization of justice as a τέχνη. If justice is a τέχνη it will necessarily entail expert knowledge of how to distinguish between friends and enemies, a matter that S. will explore at 334c–335a.

d7 λέγει: *sc.* Simonides.

332e3 πρὸς τί ἔργον "with a view to what outcome," parallel to curing sickness and conferring health in the case of the physician and avoiding peril (and ensuring safety) at sea in the case of the ship's captain; cf. 333a5–11. The assumption here, of course, is that the physician is skilled at curing sickness and the captain skilled in avoiding naval disaster, but a later argument (333e–334b), that the expert who knows best how to prevent harm is also best able to inflict harm, is here foreshadowed.

e5 Ἐν τῶι προσπολεμεῖν καὶ ἐν τῶι συμμαχεῖν: noting that we are not always at war, S. will question whether justice has any relevance in peacetime. A difficulty of a different sort will be raised later. While the distinction between enemies and allies during war is (usually) fairly straightforward, in our personal lives we sometimes make mistakes regarding who is deserving of our friendship and enmity (334c).

333a12 χρήσιμον: it is unclear whether this is intended to be neuter, "a useful thing," as at a1, or feminine, as at c11, d11, *Gorg.* 480b9. P. treats χρήσιμος sometimes as an adjective of two terminations, sometimes three (e.g. *Chrm.* 165c11).

a13 Πρὸς τὰ συμβόλαια: in keeping with his family's commercial background, Polemarchus uses a word that generally refers to formal agreements, often involving contractual arrangements (cf. εἰς ἀργυρίου, b9). There is a special irony in P.'s having Polemarchus give this as his answer. Other, less sympathetic, characters speak as though it is precisely in the realm of formal agreements that the unscrupulous tend to circumvent justice: T., after condescendingly pointing out that S. needs to have his running nose wiped, asserts that, when it comes to συμβόλαια, the unjust man will always succeed in taking advantage of the just man (343d), and in

Gorgias Callicles berates S. for uselessly pursuing philosophy as an adult, saying that the naive people who do so make fools of themselves because they are innocent of the way συμβόλαια are negotiated (484d). Only in Book Four, after justice in the city and in the individual has been defined, will the relationship between justice and the actions of the individual as they relate to money-making and συμβόλαια be clarified (443c–e).

a14 Συμβόλαια δὲ λέγεις κοινωνήματα! S. could have objected, legitimately, that there was no recognized τέχνη, parallel to farming and shoemaking, that governed contracts, but he moves on instead to expand Polemarchus' frame of reference to include interpersonal associations more broadly. Even apart from the fact that this was surely not what Polemarchus intended, the examples that S. gives in two of his next three questions are odd. For it is not clear what kind of "associations" S. has in mind in connection with the game of πεττεία and kithara-playing.

333b1–2 εἰς πεττῶν θέσιν: the game of πεσσεία (Attic πεττεία) resembled the game of Go, involving the strategic placing (θέσις) of stones (πεττοί or ψῆφοι) on a grid in such a way as to block or surround the opponent's pieces (6.487c); Guéniot 2000. Considerable skill was required to master the game; according to Young Socrates, first-rate players make up less than 5 percent of the population (*Pol.* 292e). At *Gorg.* 450d S. himself includes πεττευτική, along with arithmetic and geometry, among those τέχναι that produce little or no ἔργον apart from the thinking and verbal expression that their performance requires.

b4 εἰς πλίνθων καὶ λίθων θέσιν: following εἰς πεττῶν θέσιν it almost seems as though S. is toying with his interlocutor (or P. with his readers). At least housebuilding is often a collaborative undertaking, so that in this instance it is appropriate to speak of a κοινωνός.

b4–5 χρησιμώτερός τε καὶ ἀμείνων: a good illustration of the care P. regularly takes to introduce variation into what might otherwise devolve into a series of formulaic questions and answers. The adjectives from the previous question, now in the comparative, appear in the reverse order, and the connection is τε καί rather than καί. The following question will take yet another form.

b8 εἰς κρουμάτων: *sc.* κοινωνίαν. The kithara was a solo instrument, or was used to accompany the kithara-player's singing (West 1992: 50–70), so it is not easy to see how S. imagines an "associate" in the striking (with a πλῆκτρον < πλήσσω) of the instrument's strings. Perhaps what he has in mind is the giving of instruction or advice; at *Alc. I* 110e S. asks Alcibiades who are the teachers of πεττεία and who are the teachers of justice. In the examples below, the buying and selling of horses and ships, it appears that it is the provision of expert advice that is at issue.

333c2 ὁ ἱππικός: *sc.* ἀμείνων κοινωνός ἐστιν.

c8 Ὅταν παρακαταθέσθαι καὶ σῶν εἶναι "When (there is a need) to hand (it) over for safekeeping and (for it) to be safe." There is a similar change of grammatical subject, from the person who entrusts the money to the money itself, in the following line.

c9 χρῆσθαι ἀλλὰ κεῖσθαι: cf. a11 χρείαν ἢ κτῆσιν. Unlike the gratuitous playing with the sound of words engaged in by Gorgias and his acolytes (pilloried by P. in Agathon's speech in *Symp.* and in Aspasia's speech in *Mnx.*, e.g. κτῆσίν τε καὶ χρῆσιν 238b6), wordplay in P. often has a point. Here the uselessness of acquisitiveness as exhibited by Polemarchus and his family is mocked.

c11 ἐπὶ αὐτῶι: none of the recognized meanings of ἐπί + dative seems appropriate here. Closest, perhaps, is "in the case of" (Herodotean examples in Powell 1938: *s.v.* B.III.6). That adds little to the sense already conveyed by τότε, but that may be the point, to underline the absurdity of justice being of use just then, when its object is not in use.

333d3–4 δρέπανον … ἡ ἀμπελουργική: at 353a, to illustrate his definition of ἔργον, S. will give as an example the pruning hook, the ἔργον of which is the dressing of vines.

d4 καὶ κοινῆι καὶ ἰδίαι: the latter is irrelevant, as it is self-evident that neither justice nor viticulture pertains when an individual is safeguarding his own pruning hook. The "polar expression" (Lloyd 1966: 90–4) allows P. to say, in effect, "in all circumstances," while keeping a word formed on the root κοιν- in the conversation.

d7–8 τὴν ὁπλιτικὴν καὶ τὴν μουσικήν: as with ἀμπελουργική, these are adjectives with which τέχνη is to be supplied, reminding us that, throughout this section of the argument, it is assumed that justice is a τέχνη.

d10–11 ἐν μὲν χρήσει ἄχρηστος, ἐν δὲ ἀχρηστίαι χρήσιμος: cf. 6–7 μηδὲν χρῆσθαι, χρήσιμον. The argument concludes with a flourish worthy of Gorgias, with its paradoxical expression and chiastic arrangement of positive and negative terms, one of which, ἀχρηστία, P. seems to have invented for the occasion. The discussion in *Charmides* similarly ends in aporia when S.'s questioning seems to have revealed that sophrosyne is a thing of no practical value (ἀνωφελές, 175b1, d5).

333e1–334b8: Having shown that, if Polemarchus' definition is valid, justice is useless and, therefore, not a very important thing (τι σπουδαῖον, e1), S. now tries to persuade his interlocutor that it is potentially pernicious. By using examples drawn from those τέχναι whose practitioners are skilled at defending against harm, S. gets Polemarchus to admit that those practitioners are necessarily also best equipped to cause harm, concluding his "proof" with a reference to Homer, a poet whose authority surpasses even that of Polemarchus' Simonides. Polemarchus could have objected by pointing out what is assumed elsewhere in P. (*Chrm.* 165c–d, *Clit.* 409b, *Euthd.* 291e), that the ἔργον of medicine is to bring about health, so that the physician who harms a patient is not, strictly speaking, practicing the ἰατρικὴ τέχνη. Further, there are many τέχναι that are not concerned with protecting or doing damage, like pottery or sculpture, but Polemarchus is not clever enough to point that out. Nor is he as clever (or unscrupulous) as T., who will turn the tables on S. and exalt the perfectly unjust man precisely for his skill at stealing others' property and causing other forms of harm for his own advantage (344a–c).

333e1–2 ἡ δικαιοσύνη … χρήσιμον ὂν τυγχάνει: cf. a1 χρήσιμον … δικαιοσύνη (*sc.* ἐστίν). Here, τυγχάνει + participle virtually = ἐστίν (LSJ A.II.1), with the participle assimilated to the gender of the predicate; cf. 336a8 τοῦτο ἐφάνη ἡ δικαιοσύνη ὄν and, with τυγχάνειν, 351a1 ὁποῖόν τι τυγχάνει ὂν δικαιοσύνη and 354c2 ἀρετή τις οὖσα τυγχάνει (*sc.* τὸ δίκαιον).

e3–4 εἴτε πυκτικῆι εἴτε τινὶ καὶ ἄλληι: S. and his circle, who spent a good deal of time in the palaestra, were familiar with the techniques of boxing and other combat sports, for which see Kyle 2007: 124–6. The importance of defensive skills in these sports is illustrated by Demosthenes, who criticizes his fellow Athenians for employing their military in the same way a barbarian boxes, not knowing or caring about how to hold his guard up or keep an eye on his adversary (4.40).

e6 νόσον ὅστις δεινὸς φυλάξασθαι: while it is true that the physician has the theoretical knowledge that would make him or her particularly skilled at insidiously doing harm – the word φάρμακον can mean "poison" as well as "medicine" – this example is not comparable to boxing or warfare, both of which are designed to cause intentional harm as well as to protect against harm. Polemarchus has already admitted (332e) that the skill of the physician is irrelevant to those who are not ill, and T. will acknowledge that the role of the physician in the true sense of the word is to attend to the sick (341c).

334a1 στρατοπέδου … φύλαξ: the context shows that S. is thinking of the general (for the στρατηγικὴ τέχνη, see e.g. *Euthd.* 290b1) rather than of an individual soldier posted on guard duty, and this is how Polemarchus understands him.

a1–2 ὁ αὐτὸς φύλαξ ἀγαθὸς ὅσπερ καὶ … κλέψαι "the same man (is) a good guardian who (is good) also at stealing"; for the infinitive with ἀγαθός, see LSJ A.I.3. The tactical skill of the general involves stationing sentries (Aeneas Tacticus 6) as well as dispatching spies, as Hector does in the *Iliad* (10.299–312). Xenophon quotes S. as telling one of his young companions that the good general must be, among other things, φυλακτικόν τε καὶ κλέπτην (*Mem.* 3.1.6), and the Spartan general Brasidas, encouraging his troops before launching a surprise attack on the Athenians, says that those stratagems (κλέμματα) that benefit friends by deceiving the enemy are held in the highest regard (Thuc. 5.9.5). P. relies upon the broad range of meanings of κλέπτειν and related words (= not only "steal," but also "cheat, conceal, act stealthily") to arrive at the conclusion that the just man is a common criminal. Here, the verb has as its objects both "the adversaries' plans" and "their doings generally," so that its meaning is something like "covertly frustrating."

a4 Ὅτου τις ἄρα ... φύλαξ, τούτου καὶ φώρ: despite the inferential ἄρα, the logic here is not compelling. (φώρ does not have the same broad range of meaning as κλέπτειν; the skills of boxers or cardiologists do not enable them to "rob" that which they are guarding against.) Still, not wanting to take any chances, P. ensures that the Guardians (φύλακες) in Callipolis have no incentive to steal, since the state will see to their every need and, in any event, they have divine gold in their souls, so there is no reason for them to covet the debased gold hoarded by the class beneath them (3.416d–417a).

a8 Κλέπτης ἄρα τις ὁ δίκαιος ... ἀναπέφανται "Therefore the just man has been exposed as a kind of thief." For this depreciatory sense of τις, cf. b4, *Prot.* 313c4–5 ὁ σοφιστὴς τυγχάνει ὢν ἔμπορός τις ἢ κάπηλος, *Soph.* 231d5.

a8–9 κινδυνεύεις παρὰ Ὁμήρου μεμαθηκέναι: S. implicates both Polemarchus, by using the second person, and Homer in the outrageous conclusion.

334b1 Αὐτόλυκον ἀγαπᾶι: Homer's alleged approval of Odysseus' maternal grandfather Autolycus ("Wolf Incarnate"; see 336d7–e1n. for S.'s comparison of T. to a wolf) is based on nothing more than his use of the adjective ἐσθλός at *Od.* 19.395–6: ἐσθλόν (*sc.* Αὐτόλυκον), ὃς ἀνθρώπους ἐκέκαστο | κλεπτοσύνηι θ' ὅρκωι τε, "worthy Autolycus, first among mortals in the art of thievery and the (devious) use of oaths," arts which, Homer goes on to say, were imparted to him by Hermes himself. Elsewhere, Homer tells us that the helmet worn by Odysseus had been stolen from Amyntor by Autolycus (*Il.* 10.267–71).

b3 καὶ κατὰ Ὅμηρον: nowhere does Homer speak of Autolycus' justice. He does, however, mention his many offerings, which earned the favor of the god (*Od.* 19.397–8).

b4–5 ἐπὶ ὠφελίαι μέντοι ... ἐχθρῶν: acknowledging Polemarchus' contribution to the alleged Homeric–Simonidean doctrine, as well as serving to introduce the next, and more serious, argument.

b6 οὐκέτι οἶδα ἔγωγε ὅτι ἔλεγον: Polemarchus has been reduced to the state of helplessness (ἀπορία) characteristic of those who are subjected to the Socratic elenchus; e.g. *Euthphr.* 11b, *Ion* 532b–c, *Prot.* 312e, *Symp.* 201b. The sensation induced is compared to the numbing effect caused by the sting of the electric ray (νάρκη: *Meno* 80a). Bringing the interlocutor to a state of aporia is characteristic also of the eristic practiced by sophists like Euthydemus and Dionysodorus, whose purpose is to arouse admiration on the part of their hearers (*Euthd.* 276d). The aim of the Socratic method, on the other hand, is to lead the interlocutor, regardless of whether there is an audience present, to the (supposed) status of S. himself, who claims ignorance about the subject under discussion.

b6–7 τοῦτο μέντοι ἔμοιγε δοκεῖ ἔτι: although he has agreed to all the intervening steps in the argument, Polemarchus persists in his original thinking regarding justice. In this he is like some others who are subjected to S.'s questioning (e.g. Hippias, *Hp.Mi.* 369b–c), as well as those who fall victim to eristic display. He also resembles the prisoner in Book Seven who is released from his bondage in the Cave and is compelled to look at the objects casting the shadows that he used to take for reality; when asked to identify those objects he would be at a loss (ἀπορεῖν, 515d6) and would take refuge in what he formerly thought was true.

334c1–335b1: S. next asks Polemarchus if we do not make mistakes in our judgment of friends, sometimes contracting a friendship with a person we think good who is in fact wicked. If so, it will sometimes be just, following Polemarchus' definition, to help the wicked and harm the good. Polemarchus is forced to amend his definition of friends to those who both seem and are good, with enemies being correspondingly redefined. S. ignores the fact that the definition leaves out large swaths of the population – is justice involved, for instance, in one's dealings with a good person mistaken for an enemy? – and moves on to ask if it is ever just to harm someone. The rather inconsequential argument here serves to highlight, again, the difference between Polemarchus and the more astute T. The latter, taking up S.'s underlying assumption that justice is a τέχνη, will argue that the practitioner of a τέχνη, properly so called, does not make mistakes (340d–e). If, therefore, a τέχνη is involved, then the just man qua just man – or, in T.'s view, the perfectly unjust man – cannot err in distinguishing the real from the apparent friend.

334c1 Φίλους δὲ λέγεις εἶναι: this phrase appears before the interrogative, which most commonly occupies initial position, to signal a shift to a new topic (*CGCG* §59.16).

c2 χρηστούς: P. uses this word as a synonym for ἀγαθός (c10) in this discussion of helping friends because of its associations with the idea of usefulness; for the word, see Dover 1974: 296–8, noting that its most common antonym is πονηρός.

c4 Εἰκὸς μέν, ἔφη, οὓς ἄν τις ἡγῆται χρηστοὺς φιλεῖν: on its own what Polemarchus says is quite reasonable (although μέν suggests some recognition that a qualification may be in order; *GP* 382), but by having him ignore the unmistakable hint in ἢ τοὺς ὄντας, P. portrays him as an interlocutor who is easily manipulated. The distinction between those who are good and those who merely seem good will play an important part in Book Two, when Glaucon and Adeimantus ask S. to mount a defense against T.'s position; P.'s brothers want S. to show that the truly just man is better off even if he has a reputation for utmost wickedness (361c–d, 367b–e).

c10 Τούτοις: dative of possessor ("Then they have good men as enemies?").

334d3 οἷοι μὴ ἀδικεῖν "such as not to commit injustice"; in relative clauses of result with οἷος + infinitive (LSJ A.III) the negative is regularly μή (*CGCG* §46.7 and 10).

d5–6 τοὺς μηδὲν ἀδικοῦντας δίκαιον κακῶς ποιεῖν: from "it is just to harm enemies" S. has arrived at "it is just to harm those who have committed no injustice" by getting Polemarchus to agree that we sometimes mistakenly think that a good person, i.e. someone who is not disposed to commit injustice, is an enemy.

d8 Τοὺς ἀδίκους ἄρα: S. infers, correctly, from Polemarchus' vehement objection to the depraved (πονηρός) proposition, "It is just to harm those who have committed no injustice," that he must then believe that it is just to harm the unjust. That the one does not logically follow from the other is lost on Polemarchus.

d11–e1 διημαρτήκασιν τῶν ἀνθρώπων "have completely (δια-) misjudged people"; for the genitive, see *Phdr.* 257c8–d1 τοῦ ἑταίρου συχνὸν διαμαρτάνεις.

334e2 πονηροὶ γὰρ αὐτοῖς εἰσιν "for they have depraved friends"; cf. c10, the difference being that there the article was used with the subject to distinguish it from the predicate.

e3 αὐτὸ τὸ ἐναντίον: not true. "The exact opposite" of what has been attributed to Simonides would be to define justice as harming friends and helping enemies, to which not even T. would subscribe. All S. has shown is that, according to Polemarchus' definition of justice, harming friends in many cases (πολλοῖς, d11) satisfies the requirements. Still, it is rhetorically more effective to claim that your refutation has shown that your interlocutor's statement is the exact opposite of the truth than merely that it is erroneous; cf. 343a2.

335a6 προσθεῖναι τῶι δικαίωι ἤ: because the meaning of the verb, "make an addition to," implies comparison with, and difference from, "how we originally expressed ourselves," comparative ἤ is in order, even in the absence of an explicitly comparative word (LSJ (A)B.1). It is found with such words and expressions as ἴδιον, "peculiar to" (*Gorg.* 481c7), and παρὰ δόξαν, "contrary to expectation" (Hdt. 1.79.2, 8.4.1);

cf. Thuc. 5.20.1 αὐτόδεκα ἐτῶν διελθόντων ... ἢ ὡς τὸ πρῶτον ἡ ἐσβολὴ ... ἐγένετο, "just ten years having passed from the time when the invasion first occurred."

335b2–336a9: Polemarchus is now satisfied that the definition of justice as helping friends and harming enemies is valid as long as we specify that the friends are good and the enemies bad. S. turns the discussion in a radically new direction by asking if the just man harms anyone at all. The argument falls into two parts: (a) Doing harm renders that which is harmed worse with regard to its proper ἀρετή. (b) Justice is a (or the?) human ἀρετή, so that acting justly according to Polemarchus' definition would involve deploying the human ἀρετή justice to render its object unjust, which is as absurd as claiming that it is possible to use the ἀρετή of the musical art to render someone unmusical. S. concludes with the observation that the definition of justice as helping friends and harming enemies must have been propounded not by a revered poet but by some tyrant. Thus does P. set the stage for the intervention of T., who will express unbounded admiration for the tyrant.

335b2 Ἔστιν ... δικαίου ἀνδρὸς βλάπτειν "Is it characteristic of a just man to harm?" With the predicate genitive of quality (*CGCG* §30.26) no specific noun is to be supplied for the genitive to depend on. The conclusion toward which the argument is headed (d11–12) is the more narrowly focused claim that it is not the ἔργον (to be defined at 352e) of the just man to harm anyone, but it is of the unjust man. The doctrine that it is wrong to harm or treat unjustly anyone at all is one of the most notable and admirable features of P.'s portrayal of S. (*Cri.* 49b–c, *Gorg.* 469b), who will assert in Book Two that nothing that is good can be harmful (βλαβερόν, 379b3). But the argument here is not compelling. Stealing someone's money or injuring one's adversary in a boxing match does not make them worse εἰς τὴν ἀνθρωπείαν ἀρετήν, that is, render them less just.

b7 εἰς τὴν τῶν κυνῶν ἀρετήν: the ἀρετή of dogs or horses is assumed to consist in their instrumental value to their human owners. At 2.375a–376c the admirable qualities of a fine hound – keen senses, agility in pursuit, courage, strength – serve as a guide for the selection of Guardians in Callipolis.

335c1 Ἀνθρώπους δέ, ... μὴ οὕτω φῶμεν "And when it comes to humans, are we not to say in the same way that they ...?" Cf. 6.491d10–e1 καὶ τὰς ψυχὰς οὕτω φῶμεν ...; "and when it comes to souls, are we to say in the same way (as we said of plants and animals) that they ...?" For the negative μή, see 337b6, *CGCG* 34.8.

c4 ἡ δικαιοσύνη οὐκ ἀνθρωπεία ἀρετή; ambiguous. S. could be asking whether justice is "a" or "the" human ἀρετή, the absence of the definite article serving to mark ἀρετή as the predicate. For S. the distinction is immaterial, since he adheres to (some version of) the doctrine of the unity of the virtues, according to which each of the virtues can be expressed in terms of knowing what is best (see Rudebusch 2017), but the ambiguity is useful in securing the agreement of Polemarchus, who necessarily regards justice as a human virtue.

c11 ἀφίππους "lacking skill in horsemanship," whereas ἄνιππος = "without a horse or horses." There are a few such pairs, distinguished by whether the negative prefix is ἀπο- or ἀ(ν)-, in which the two words have somewhat different meanings: ἀπόθερμος, ἀπόμουσος, ἀπότιμος.

335e3 τοῦτο δὲ δὴ νοεῖ αὐτῶι "and this is the meaning it has for him, namely ..." In this sense (LSJ A.IV) νοεῖν can have as its subject a word (*Cra.* 397e2, 407e3, 418b5), a phrase (ῥῆμα, *Euthd.* 287e1, 4), a law (Ar. *Clouds* 1186) or an oracle (Ar. *Wealth* 55).

e4–5 οὐκ ἦν σοφός: the implication is either that S. and Polemarchus have misattributed the saying to Simonides or that they have wrongly construed it, for S. earlier called the poet – admittedly ironically – σοφὸς ... καὶ θεῖος (331e6).

e8 Μαχούμεθα ... κοινῆι ἐγώ τε καὶ σύ: the militant tone indicates the intensity of S.'s feeling, which will reappear in Book Seven in connection with the defense of his account of the Form of the Good, ὥσπερ ἐν μάχηι (534c1). The hyperbolic language has a specific point here, for S. will later (351c–d) counter T.'s definition of justice by pointing out that, to be successful, those who fight on the same side in battle must treat each other with justice.

e9 ἢ Βίαντα ἢ Πιττακόν: Bias of Priene and Pittacus of Mytilene, both of whom lived in the sixth century, were two of the Seven Sages whom S. ironically praises, in the course of his interpretation of a poem of Simonides in which a ῥῆμα of Pittacus is criticized (*Prot.* 343a–c), as admirers of Spartan culture and devotees of laconic expression.

e10 σοφῶν τε καὶ μακαρίων: cf. Ar. *Birds* 1271 ὦ μακάρι', ὦ σοφώτατε, the obsequious herald addressing his master Peisetaerus.

336a1 τὸ ῥῆμα, τὸ φάναι "the saying, that is, asserting," with the articular infinitive in apposition to τὸ ῥῆμα; cf. *Alc.1* 110d5–6 τοῦτό σοι οὐκ ὀρθῶς ἀπεκρινάμην, τὸ φάναι ... Elsewhere, P. makes the assertion itself, preceded by the definite article (331e3n.), the apposition: 5.463e5–6 τὸ ῥῆμα, τὸ ὅτι τὸ ἐμὸν εὖ πράττει ἢ ὅτι τὸ ἐμὸν κακῶς, *Euthd.* 287c1–2 τοῦτο τὸ ῥῆμα, τὸ οὐκ ἔχω ὅτι χρήσωμαι τοῖς λόγοις.

a4 Περιάνδρου: Periander was the tyrant of "wealthy Corinth" at the time of its greatest prosperity, the start of the sixth century. He was often included among the Seven Sages (D.L. 1.40–2), but not by P. (335e9n.). According to a story told by Herodotus (5.92.ζ–η), Periander learned from his friend Thrasybulus, the tyrant of Miletus, how to harm his enemies: when Periander sent an emissary to Miletus asking for advice on how to secure his rule over Corinth, Thrasybulus took the emissary to a field of grain and, without a word, cut down all the stalks that stood out above the rest.

Περδίκκου: Perdiccas was the name of the founder of the Macedonian royal family (Hdt. 8.137–9). P. here refers to the second king of that name, who died in 413. During the Peloponnesian War Perdiccas II allied himself sometimes with the Spartans (Thuc. 4.79.2, 4.83, 5.80.2) and sometimes with the Athenians (1.61.3, 4.132.1–2, 7.9). S. would have encountered Perdiccas' Macedonian subjects at the siege of Potidaea in the early years of the war (*Apol.* 28e, *Chrm.* 153a, *Symp.* 219e).

Ξέρξου: in *Gorgias* (483c–e), Callicles gives Xerxes' invasion of Greece as an illustration of his contention that it is natural, even just (δίκαιον), for the strong to exercise power over the weak. Elsewhere, S. says that he is certain that Alcibiades regards Cyrus and Xerxes as the only men who were ever of any consequence, nor does Alcibiades contradict him (*Alc. 1* 105c).

a4–5 Ἰσμηνίου τοῦ Θηβαίου: Ismenias is mentioned once elsewhere in P., as a gratuitous example of someone who became wealthy by means other than intelligence and industry. According to S., Ismenias is the man who just recently (νῦν νεωστί, *Meno* 90a4) came into possession of the wealth of Polycrates. This is a longstanding puzzle (see Bluck *ad loc.*), since Polycrates, the tyrant of Samos, died in the sixth century and it is difficult to imagine how "his" money could have been used as a bribe in the fourth. For Ismenias is noted as having taken bribes at the beginning of the Corinthian War, the money coming from the Persians in 395 BC, after the death of both S. and Meno; for this he was tried before a jury of Spartans and their allies and executed in 382 (Xen. *Hell.* 5.2.35–6). The anachronisms, in both *Meno* and *Republic*, are unmistakable but not unparalleled (Graham 2007); indeed, events related to the Corinthian War and its aftermath are anachronistically referred to also in *Symposium* and *Menexenus* (see the Introduction, section 3; for the cultural significance of the war, see Hanink 2015). Still, the inclusion of Ismenias here is curious, since his wealth cannot have been so great as to justify comparison with kings and tyrants; in 395 Persian money was used to bribe more than half a dozen Greek leaders in addition to Ismenias (Xen. *Hell.* 3.5.1). It may be that what prompted P. to include mention of Ismenias in conversation with Polemarchus was the name of the office he held in Thebes, which was, according to Xenophon (*Hell.* 5.2.25), πολέμαρχος.

a5 ἤ τινος ἄλλου μέγα οἰομένου δύνασθαι: for P., these four wealthy men and others like them only "think" they have great power. In fact, such men lack σωφροσύνη (8.555b–d) and so do not even have the power to control themselves. In *Gorgias*, S. argues at length that politicians and tyrants do not have great power, because they are incapable of doing what is ultimately in their own best interests (466d–468e). There is irony in P.'s choice of these four men as possible authors of the dictum that it is just to help friends and harm enemies. For each of them was conspicuously guilty of harming friends. Periander murdered his wife, imprisoned his father-in-law and was estranged from his son (Hdt. 3.50–3); Perdiccas' changing alliances meant that, for him, the categories of friend and enemy were not even stable; Xerxes had his brother Masistes killed (Hdt. 9.113.2); and the Medism of Ismenias made him, in the eyes of P. and his followers (Dušanić 1985), an enemy of his fellow Greeks, who are by nature his friends (5.470c–d).

a5–6 πλουσίου ἀνδρός: at the very end of this section we are reminded that the discussion began in conversation with a man notable for his wealth and that the definition of justice has been framed in the essentially economic terms of debt and repayment.

a8–9 ἡ δικαιοσύνη ... οὐδὲ τὸ δίκαιον: that the two expressions are regarded as synonyms is clear from αὐτό; both mean "justice" in the abstract, but they have a different "feel." One difference is that, while feminine abstract nouns can be personified and are represented in art and as characters on the stage, the same cannot be said of an expression like τὸ δίκαιον, which would be out of place in the verse of an Archaic poet like Simonides (Aesch. *Suppl.* 79 seems to be the first occurrence of τὸ δίκαιον in an "abstract" sense). The frequent use of neuter adjectives to express abstract concepts is a feature of the fifth-century "enlightenment" (Solmsen 1975: 110–25), and it is notable that they will show up repeatedly in the ensuing discussion between S. and the modish T. That is not to say that δικαιοσύνη will not be found in their conversation – the two expressions will continue to be used more or less synonymously – but P.'s reintroduction of τὸ δίκαιον here (it has only been used once before; see 332b8–c1n.) seems designed to signal that the tone of the conversation is about to change.

336b1–338c1: The suspension of the conversation while S. and Polemarchus ponder their next move provides the opportunity for T. to break into the discussion, which he has been prevented from doing by the other members of the party. The suddenness of T.'s irruption is conveyed by the comparison of him to a predator springing upon his prey and by the profusion of images. The effect is magnified by S.'s role as both narrator (Ferrari 2010; Finkelberg 2019: 34–8) and victim of the onslaught.

Initially, the reason T. gives for his displeasure is the method of S.'s investigation, namely by asking questions and withholding his own view of the matter, but it emerges (as the narrator S. had suspected all along) that T. was eager to put on display his own superior definition of justice.

336b1–2 μὲν … ἔπειτα: for the absence of a connecting particle in the second clause (*GP* 376–7), see 337e5, 352a6–7. The situation here is similar to that in *Charmides* (162c1–4), when S., who is the narrator there as well, says that Critias had long been restraining himself from breaking into the conversation but could no longer contain himself.

καὶ διαλεγομένων ἡμῶν μεταξύ "even in the middle of our conversation"; μεταξύ is frequently associated with a present participle (LSJ A.I.2), here a genitive absolute.

b2 ἀντιλαμβάνεσθαι τοῦ λόγου: the verb can mean "find fault with, criticize," as at *Hp.Ma.* 287a4 and 9. That meaning is active here, but P. has chosen to use it because of its literal meaning, "take hold of," which helps to anticipate διαρπασόμενος, b5–6.

b4 οὐκέτι ἡσυχίαν ἦγεν "he could no longer keep still." Like the English idiom, the Greek is ambiguous. It may refer to motionlessness (e.g. *Tim.* 89a4) or to silence (*Phd.* 117e2). We are thus kept in suspense over the nature of T.'s assault, whether it will be physical or verbal.

b5 συστρέψας ἑαυτὸν ὥσπερ θηρίον "gathering himself (in preparation to pounce) like a wild beast"; cf. Arist. *HA* 9.631a27–8 συστρέψαντες ἑαυτοὺς φέρονται ὥσπερ τόξευμα, of dolphins gathering their strength and leaping out of the water. The image of shooting at a target (itself a frequent metaphor for a verbal utterance) is present in the only other occurrence of the verb in P.: in *Protagoras*, S. speaks approvingly of the capability of a typical Spartan to break his accustomed silence by occasionally pronouncing a pointed, concentrated aphorism, like a skilled marksman, ἐνέβαλε ῥῆμα … βραχὺ καὶ συνεστραμμένον ὥσπερ δεινὸς ἀκοντιστής (342e2–3; cf. 335e9n.). The image is of something under tension – muscles, a bowstring, a customarily reluctant speaker – suddenly being released to great effect. The beast to which T. is compared will later be revealed to be a wolf (d6–7n.). Ironically, T. will later call S. a sycophant, a creature that Xenophon's S. compares to a wolf, against whose predations S. contrives a successful strategy (see 340d2n.).

b5–6 ἧκεν ἐπὶ ἡμᾶς ὡς διαρπασόμενος: διαρπάζειν is a Homeric *hapax* (*Il.* 16.355), used in a simile comparing the Danaans attacking the Trojans to wolves harrying a flock of sheep or goats; cf. *Laws* 10.906d4, also of metaphorical predatory wolves. The sense of ἧκεν is uncertain. Uncompounded ἱέναι is rarely found without a direct object; when used absolutely it normally means "shoot," as with a bow and arrow (LSJ A.I.3b). When P. uses the simple verb with an object expressed, the object is almost always an utterance or a sound, and the one time he uses the verb absolutely (*Tht.* 194a3) it is of perceptions that "miss the mark like an incompetent archer"; cf. previous n. Some scholars have taken the verb here as a form of ἥκειν, which is intransitive, but the tense is wrong and the meaning feeble. Others supply ἑαυτόν from the foregoing, producing a meaning, "he launched himself," that is normally conveyed by the middle, as at *Phdr.* 241b5. In the end, it seems impossible to pin down the exact construction of the verb. But that may have been P.'s intention in expressing himself in just this way. Until T. opens his mouth, we are left in a state of uncertainty whether he is about to launch himself or verbal missiles at S. and Polemarchus.

b6 δείσαντες διεπτοήθημεν "we recoiled in panic." The verb, occurring only here in P., is another Homeric *hapax*, used when the disguised Odysseus threatens Melantho, causing the maids to scatter in terror (*Od.* 18.340); cf. Eur. *Bacch.* 304, the only other occurrence of the verb before P., where Teiresias informs Pentheus of Dionysus' capacity for causing panic in the ranks of an army before an engagement.

336c1 εἰς τὸ μέσον "for everyone to hear." The expression has less to do with the manner of expression than with the attitude of the subject, who confidently regards the utterance as deserving of being exposed to public scrutiny.

c2 εὐηθίζεσθε "act naive," the verb occurring only here in P. Later T. will claim that those who act justly do so merely because they are εὐήθεις (343c6, 348d1, 349b3), and he will address S. scornfully with ὦ εὐηθέστατε Σώκρατες, 343d2.

ὑποκατακλινόμενοι "yielding, submitting," only here and c5 in P. The metaphor is from wrestling or the pankration, referring to a competitor who, out of deference, allows his opponent to prevail (Plut. *Mor.* 58f, 535f). P. thus alludes to T.'s authorship of Ὑπερβάλλοντες, "Overthrowings" (DK 85 B7 = 35 D5 Laks–Most), the title of which echoes and challenges that of Protagoras' Καταβάλλοντες (*sc.* λόγοι). T.'s extremely competitive character will be revealed in the subsequent discussion, from which it is clear that he thinks that everyone naturally strives to be dominant. Therefore he cannot make sense of S.'s behavior, unless it is perhaps based on a devious gambit involving εἰρωνεία (337a4) designed to win arguments (see next n.). P.'s own competitiveness is manifested in S.'s successful charming (2.358b3) or "taming" of T. in the course of Book One (338c7–8n.; Quincey 1981).

c3–6 εἴπερ ὡς ἀληθῶς ... τί φῂς εἶναι τὸ δίκαιον: there are two possibilities. Either (1) P. is portraying T. as so exasperated that he cannot express himself logically, saying that if S. really wants to know what justice is he should say what he thinks it is, or (2) T., hinting that S. is less interested in discovering the nature of justice (for the "skeptical" force of εἴπερ, see *GP* 488 n. 1; Wakker 1994: 325–6) than in tripping up unwary interlocutors, is challenging S. to engage in a debate, in which he expects to get the better of S. The latter seems more likely. That is, in the view of a practiced debater like T. the "Socratic method" is no more than a strategy to display one's superiority in argumentation and humiliate opponents (Beversluis 2000: 223–4).

c4 μηδὲ φιλοτιμοῦ ἐλέγχων: the elenchus (Vlastos 1994) is the characteristic Socratic method of doing philosophy by interrogating an interlocutor, which usually results in bringing to light inconsistencies in the interlocutor's thinking. S. defends himself against criticism of this approach by claiming that he is only seeking to remedy his own near-total ignorance (*Prot.* 360e, *Tht.* 150c; cf. *Apol.* 21b–22a). φιλοτιμία (Dover 1974: 230–3) is the ambitious pursuit of public recognition, often at some personal cost (financial expenditure on civic benefactions, risk of injury in battle) and often at someone else's expense (a political rival's embarrassment, the life of an enemy soldier). It is thus paradoxical to charge S. with seeking glory by seeming to parade his own lack of cleverness.

c6 εἰπὲ τί φῄς εἶναι τὸ δίκαιον: in Xenophon's *Memorabilia* (4.4.9) the sophist Hippias refuses to tell S. what he thinks justice is until S. reveals ὅτι νομίζεις τὸ δίκαιον εἶναι, complaining that S. subjects others to ridicule by questioning and interrogating one and all (ἐρωτῶν … καὶ ἐλέγχων πάντας) while being unwilling to divulge his own view on anything.

c6–d1 καὶ ὅπως μοι μὴ ἐρεῖς "and don't you tell me"; ὅπως μή + future indicative is a peremptory, colloquial form of prohibition or warning (Collard 2018: 72–3), sometimes explained as arising from an ellipsis, "(see to it) that" (*SMT* §§271–7).

336d1–2 δέον … ὠφέλιμον … λυσιτελοῦν … κερδαλέον … συμφέρον: it is not immediately clear what exactly T. is refusing to accept, a response in this *form* (i.e. merely giving a synonym of τὸ δίκαιον) or one that proposes a *meaning* similar to that suggested by these words. With the exception of δέον, all these words unambiguously denote what is advantageous to the agent. That being the case, T. must intend by τὸ δέον not "what is required" but "what is fitting"; cf. *Pol.* 284e6–7 πρὸς τὸ μέτριον καὶ τὸ πρέπον καὶ τὸν καιρὸν καὶ τὸ δέον. In other words, T. is not interested in hearing a definition of justice that makes it out to be a quality that is beneficial for the just person. For him, as we will learn, it is precisely injustice that is worthy of our admiration and envy. In *Clitophon*, the title character gives the same list, omitting τὸ κερδαλέον, of answers to the question, "What is the ἔργον of the just person?," each answer given by a different one of S.'s associates (409c2–3); for that passage, which is clearly derived from ours, see Slings 1999: 180–5.

d3–4 ἐὰν ὕθλους τοιούτους λέγῃς "if you speak such rubbish," rephrased by S. at 337b4 as ἐὰν τοιαῦτα φλυαρῇς, using the verb related to φλυαρία, with which T. had opened his utterance at c1.

d6–7 ἄφωνος ἂν γενέσθαι: this is the earliest reference to the belief that, if a wolf sees you before you see the wolf, you will be struck dumb. That the belief was commonly held is shown by the allusive language used by P. and others (e.g. Virg. *Ecl.* 9.53–4); cf. Pliny, *NH* 8.34.80 and the proverb, quoted at Theocritus 14.22, λύκον εἶδες, "said of those who have suddenly become speechless" (*CPG* II 511.5). Elsewhere as well P. adverts to the unthinkable eventuality of a silent S.: at *Symp.* 198c3–5 S. expresses the fear that Agathon's Gorgianic speech may have rendered him as speechless as a stone statue, and at *Apol.* 37e–38a he dismisses the suggestion that he might avoid the death penalty by keeping quiet. In this way P. tacitly alludes to his own role in keeping S.'s voice alive even after his death.

d7–e1 νῦν δὲ … πρότερος: S. and T. have naturally seen each other before this (328b6). That S. now specifies that he looked at T. before the latter looked at him "at the time when he began to become rabid (ἐξαγριαίνεσθαι)" plays with the idea that T. has suddenly been transformed from a man into a wolf. The evidence that the ancient Greeks were familiar with the notion of lycanthropy includes P. (8.565d–566a, where the transformation of the people's champion into a tyrant is compared to a man becoming a wolf) and Herodotus (4.105.2); see Buxton 2013: 33–52; Ogden 2021.

336e2 χαλεπός: of persons, "harsh, merciless." S. says of the Guardians, just before he compares them with watchdogs, that they should be gentle to friends and aggressive toward the enemy (πράους … χαλεπούς, 2.375c1–2).

e3–4 ἐξαμαρτάνομεν … ἁμαρτάνομεν: it is very common for a compound verb to be followed by the simple verb with little or no difference in meaning; see 340d–e, Renehan 1976: 11–16.

e4 εὖ ἴσθι ὅτι ἄκοντες ἁμαρτάνομεν: cf. *Gorg.* 488a3 εὖ ἴσθι τοῦτο ὅτι οὐχ ἑκὼν ἐξαμαρτάνω (S. addressing Callicles). The error of which S. and Polemarchus are supposedly guilty is intellectual rather than moral, but given that it was committed in the process of defining a moral term, and given that P. denies that moral and intellectual qualities are entirely separate, we should see this as an allusion to the fundamental belief of (the Platonic) S., that no one is willingly unjust or otherwise immoral. For this "Socratic paradox," see e.g. *Prot.* 345d9–e2 οὐδεὶς τῶν σοφῶν ἀνδρῶν ἡγεῖται οὐδένα ἀνθρώπων ἑκόντα ἐξαμαρτάνειν. The challenge posed to S. in Book Two is to disprove the widely held Thrasymachean view, expressed in identical terms by both Glaucon and Adeimantus, οὐδεὶς ἑκὼν δίκαιος (360c6–7 and 366d1).

e5 ἑκόντας εἶναι: the idiomatic addition of the seemingly superfluous infinitive after ἑκών (LSJ A.I.3; Smyth §2012c) is confined, in Attic, to sentences containing an expressed or implied negative.

e7 πολλῶν χρυσίων τιμιώτερον: that intellectual and spiritual matters are more valuable than gold is a common theme in P. (e.g. *Euthd.* 288e–289a, *Symp.* 211d), nowhere more so than in *Republic* (7.521a, 8.547b, 9.589d–e), in which a society is envisioned that is governed by leaders who dispense with earthly gold because they have a never-ending supply of the divine metal in their souls (3.416e).

e9 οἴου γε σύ "you can be sure (that we would make every effort to ensure that it come to light)."

e9–337a2 ἐλεεῖσθαι … χαλεπαίνεσθαι: the sentence elegantly mocks the professional rhetorician by having the last word of the speech return us to the speech's opening with χαλεπός (epanalepsis), by flattering the addressee as among the intellectual elite (οἱ δεινοί) and by capping the a fortiori argument with a sly appeal to likelihood (εἰκός … που), one of the favorite devices of the sophists. The prominent first word of the sentence contains a clear allusion to the title of one of T.'s published works, Ἔλεοι (*sc.* λόγοι), apparently "Speeches designed to arouse compassion," DK 85 B5 = 35 D14 Laks–Most. P. refers to this work also at *Phdr.* 267c7–d1, where again T. is mockingly praised as δεινός; see Quincey 1981: 309–13.

337a3 ἀνεκάκχασέ τε μάλα σαρδάνιον "he burst into a thoroughly derisive laugh." (ἀνα)κακχάζειν (the spelling varies) is an onomatopoetic word derived from the sound of laughter, χὰ χά; cf. Latin *cachinno.* σαρδάνιος (the spelling varies), the origin of English "sardonic," is yet another Homeric *hapax* (336b5–6, b6nn.), and this is its only occurrence in P. After the disguised Odysseus dodged the ox-hoof thrown by Ctesippus, "in his anger he smiled a thoroughly derisive smile," μείδησε δὲ θυμῶι | σαρδάνιον μάλα τοῖον (*Od.* 20.301–2; in both Homer and P., σαρδάνιον is an internal accusative, *CGCG* §30.12). Attempts by ancient critics, as recorded by the Homeric and Platonic scholia, to explain the "sardonic smile" are merely guesses based on this Homeric passage. Most recently, Appendino et al. (2009) propose that it refers to lockjaw caused by ingestion of a poisonous herb common in Sardinia. This does not, however, explain T.'s audible laughter, for which compare *Euthd.* 300d3 μέγα πάνυ ἀνακακχάσας (the only other occurrence of the verb in P.). Later (3.388e–389a), S. will express disapproval of strong laughter as undignified.

a4 Ἡράκλεις: a strong exclamation, registering shock or surprise (e.g. *Symp.* 213b8), often preceding a request for further clarification (e.g. *Lys.* 208e2). Here, however, T. tells us that, so far from being surprised or shocked, he was expecting just this behavior from S.

αὕτη ἐκείνη: a colloquial expression (Collard 2018: 76–7) conveying the speaker's recognition that what has just occurred or just been said conforms to the speaker's experience or expectations; in effect, "Just as I suspected!" Compare Alcibiades' exclamation on being outmaneuvered by S.: Ταῦτα ἐκεῖνα … τὰ εἰωθότα, *Symp.* 223a6.

ἡ εἰωθυῖα εἰρωνεία Σωκράτους: similarly, when S. pleads with Callicles to deal less harshly (πραότερον) with him, the latter accuses him of "putting on a show" or "playing a part" (Εἰρωνεύῃι, ὦ Σώκρατες, *Gorg.* 489e1), a familiar charge brought against S. (*Apol.* 38a1). Indeed, Alcibiades, who tells his fellow symposiasts that S. spends his entire life εἰρωνευόμενος καὶ παίζων (*Symp.* 216e4), identifies irony as S.'s characteristic mode: when he propositioned S. the latter replied μάλα εἰρωνικῶς καὶ σφόδρα ἑαυτοῦ τε καὶ εἰωθότως (218d6–7). S. turns the tables on Callicles, however, mocking him for putting on an act himself when he earlier lectured S. in the guise of the Euripidean Zethus giving advice to Amphion (Μὰ τὸν Ζῆθον … ὧι σὺ χρώμενος πολλὰ νυνδὴ εἰρωνεύου πρός με, *Gorg.* 489e2–3). For P. it is the sophists and their ilk who practice εἰρωνεία (*Euthd.* 302b3, *Laws* 10.908e2). Or, rather, they practice a benighted sort of εἰρωνεία that renders them merely an impersonation of the wise, from whom they (ironically) derive their title (*Soph.* 268a–c). For the distinctive brand of irony cultivated by the Platonic S., see Vlastos 1991: 21–44, 236–42. Those interlocutors who accuse S. of employing irony do so in order to advertise their own discernment, showing that they have seen through the facade that S. has erected; Alcibiades even claims that he alone of those present at Agathon's symposium knows the "real" S. (*Symp.* 216c7–d1).

a5 καὶ τούτοις προύλεγον: suggesting that, as in a lawcourt, he can call upon witnesses to confirm his accurate prediction of S.'s behavior.

a8 Σοφὸς γὰρ εἶ: cf. 331e6n. S. counters T.'s charge of irony with yet more irony, saying essentially, "Clever of you to ask a question and then rule out all possible answers."

a8–b1 εἴ τινα ἔροιο ὁπόσα ἐστὶ τὰ δώδεκα: cf. *Hp.Mi.* 366e3–4 εἴ τίς σε ἔροιτο τὰ τρὶς ἑπτακόσια πόσα ἐστί. Here and in the following line the definite article is used to mark the grammatical subject.

337b2–3 Ὅπως μοι … μὴ ἐρεῖς ὅτι … μηδὲ ὅτι … μηδὲ ὅτι … μηδὲ ὅτι: mocking T.'s tone and fulness of expression in 336c6–d2.

b4 δῆλον, οἶμαι, σοι: enclitics often follow parenthetical expressions such as οἶμαι and vocatives; cf. e4 τις and Barrett on Eur. *Hipp.* 327. The commas that we use to mark off such expressions are visual aids for our convenience in (silent) reading rather than an attempt to represent an assumed pause in oral delivery.

b7 πότερον: disjunctive questions introduced by πότερον usually have an alternative expressed with a following ἤ (*CGCG* §38.10), but here the construction shifts to, "but (instead) should I say something other than the true (answer)?"

μηδὲ εἰ τούτων τι τυγχάνει ὄν "not even if it (the answer) is actually one of these," with τι as the predicate.

337c2 ὡς δή "as if," sarcastic (*GP* 229). Similarly, Polus reacts to S.'s demonstration that the tyrant who harms his enemies is not doing what he wants by saying, "As if (ὡς δή) you wouldn't welcome the opportunity to do what suited your fancy," *Gorg.* 468e6–7.

c3 Οὐδέν γε κωλύει "Very well"; cf. 5.453a10, *Gorg.* 458d5, *Lach.* 181d8, Ar. *Knights* 723, 972. The literal meaning, "there is nothing preventing (the one from being comparable to the other)," is not suitable here, since S. is not seriously claiming that T. has foreclosed all possible answers. Rather, the expression is "a formula of polite concession" (Tucker), equivalent to the rhetorical question τί κωλύει; (e.g. *Pol.* 292a10), granting the legitimacy of T.'s objection, as the following clause does less ambiguously (for εἰ δὲ οὖν, see *GP* 464–6).

c5 ἡμεῖς ἀπαγορεύωμεν: only T. has forbidden certain answers (cf. ἐγὼ ἀπεῖπον in the following line), but S. graciously includes himself. For S., pursuit of the truth is a cooperative enterprise; the word "we" is almost entirely missing from T.'s vocabulary. When he acknowledges that "we say" that the physician has made a mistake (340d–e), it is only to assert that he distances himself from what he considers merely a *façon de parler.*

c6 Ἄλλο τι οὖν ... καὶ σὺ οὕτω ποιήσεις; "I gather, then, that that is what *you* (made emphatic by καί) propose to do?" For ἄλλο τι οὖν introducing a question that expects an affirmative answer, see 342d3, 7.522e1; Riddell 1877: §22.

c8 εἴ μοι σκεψαμένωι οὕτω δόξειεν: for S. the investigation into the nature of justice is ongoing; by contrast, as we learn immediately, T. already knows what justice is.

337d1 ἑτέραν ἀπόκρισιν παρὰ πάσας ταύτας "a response different from all those," i.e. the ones forbidden in 336d. When παρά + accusative expresses comparison it normally implies superiority (LSJ C.I.7). T. adds βελτίω τούτων to make sure the point is not missed; compare S. at *Phdr.* 235c6, in a similarly competitive spirit, but expressing himself less assertively by using litotes: παρὰ ταῦτα ἂν ἔχειν εἰπεῖν ἕτερα μὴ χείρω.

d2 τί ἀξιοῖς παθεῖν; "What penalty do you propose?" Treating the conversation with S. as though it is a forensic contest in which there is a winner and a loser, the rhetorician T. uses language drawn from the lawcourt. In Athens, after the jury has reached a guilty verdict, each party to a legal action is asked to name the penalty (e.g. death, exile, a fine) he thinks appropriate, and the jury must vote for one or the other. At his own trial in 399, after Meletus has proposed the death penalty, S. asks rhetorically what punishment or fine he deserves, τί ἄξιός εἰμι παθεῖν ἢ ἀποτεῖσαι, *Apol.* 36b5; cf. Arist. *Ath.Pol.* 63.3 ὅτι ἂν δοκῆι ἄξιος εἶναι παθεῖν ἢ ἀποτεῖσαι. The same language is used in the death-or-life contest in Aristophanes' *Frogs* (1012), when Aeschylus asks Euripides – as here, before the verdict – τί παθεῖν φήσεις ἄξιος εἶναι;

d4 προσήκει δέ που μαθεῖν: S. uses the rhetorical figure of paronomasia (παθεῖν/μαθεῖν) to mock the rhetorician T. He thinks he deserves something of value, just as, at his trial, he claims that he is owed a reward appropriate to a poor man (ἀνδρὶ πένητι, *Apol.* 36d5) who improves his fellow citizens. There the compensation, free meals at the prytaneion, is intended merely to remedy his alleged financial destitution; here the reward is more substantial, relief from intellectual impoverishment. This accords with the view expressed elsewhere by the Platonic S. that correction of one's failings, whether moral or intellectual (these being indistinguishable; 336e4n.), is to be welcomed; e.g. *Apol.* 25e–26a.

d6 Ἡδὺς γὰρ εἶ "That's because you're naive"; cf. *Gorg.* 491e2 Ὡς ἡδὺς εἶ, Callicles' reaction to S.'s identification of σωφροσύνη with what Callicles regards as simplemindedness. The Platonic lexicon attributed to Timaeus (Dickey 2007: 47) glosses ἡδύς with εὐήθης καὶ ἄφρων. Below, at 348c6, T. will address S. with ὦ ἥδιστε after S. expresses his presumption that T. identifies justice with virtue and injustice with vice.

ἀπότεισον ἀργύριον: the preverb ἀπο-, like Latin *re-*, can convey the idea of recompense or remuneration that is owed in return. T. is not accustomed to providing instruction free of charge. His mercenary disposition, attributed by P. to the sophists in general, seems to be alluded to at *Phdr.* 266c and in a fragment of P.'s contemporary, the comic poet Ephippus (*PCG* 14 = Athen. 11.509c–d), who includes P. himself and the members of his Academy in his allegation of rapaciousness. In contrast to the sophists, S. claims that he does not teach for a fee, citing as the reason his lack of any wisdom to offer for sale (*Apol.* 19d–20c) and pointing to his poverty as evidence that his claim is accurate (31b–c). S.'s "poverty," however, needs to be put in perspective. He was by no means destitute, having served as a hoplite in 424 (*Symp.* 221a1–2). At his trial he says that he could afford to pay a fine of one silver mina (*Apol.* 38b5), and in conversation with Critobulus (Xen. *Oec.* 2.3) he estimates the total value of his estate at five times that amount. (Five minas is equal to 1,000 times the amount paid to an Athenian juror for one day's service, an amount intended to compensate a worker for missing one day of work; see Biles and Olson on Ar. *Wasps* 607–9 for pay for jury duty at 1/2 drachma, with 1 mina = 100 drachmas.) None of the writers of Socratic dialogues portrays S. as plying a trade; rather he is represented as spending his time on familiar terms with the very wealthiest members of society, including metics (Cephalus), visiting sophists (Hippias, Protagoras, Gorgias) and Athenian citizens (Callias, Alcibiades, Nicias; S. estimates the value of Critobulus' estate at more than 100 times that of his own). So, while S. was by no means poor – his allegations of poverty being clearly ironic – his earlier conversation with Cephalus about what it is like to be rich is more a statement about Cephalus' exceptional level of wealth than about S.

d7 Οὐκοῦν ἐπειδάν μοι γένηται "Right, when I get some," implying not that he has no money at all but that the exorbitant fees charged by men like T. are beyond his means. For οὐκοῦν with no verb following it, see Ar. *Peace* 364, where Trygaeus' cheeky reply to Hermes' threatening ἀπόλωλας is οὐκοῦν ἤν λάχω, "Right, if my time is up" (he goes on to ask Hermes to lend him some money to pay for a sacrifice so he can be initiated before he dies).

d8 Ἀλλὰ ἔστιν: *sc.* σοι. Glaucon addresses S. ("Well, you have it.") before turning to T. to assure him that his fee will be paid in full. (The matter of payment is ignored in what follows; after all, T. fails to instruct S.) As at his trial, S.'s wealthy friends are willing to guarantee payment of what he owes: Glaucon's brother P., along with Crito, Critobulus and Apollodorus, offer to increase S.'s proposed fine from 1 to 30 minas (*Apol.* 38b). This reminiscence of the trial is another means whereby P. represents the debate between S. and T. in forensic terms.

337e1 Πάνυ γε οἶμαι ... ἵνα "I strongly suspect (you are doing this) ... so that"; cf. *Cra.* 386c6 καὶ ταῦτά γε ... σοι πάνυ δοκεῖ, *Lys.* 214e1 πάνυ γε ... δοκεῖ. This is preferable to taking οἶμαι as parenthetical, since πάνυ γε on its own normally serves in P. as an affirmative response to a question.

τὸ εἰωθός: cf. a4–7. T. makes sure that the company knows that he is familiar with S.'s tactics and is, therefore, presumably well prepared to thwart them.

e2–3 λαμβάνηι λόγον "require an accounting (of his answer)," the counterpart to λόγον διδόναι, "give an accounting." See LSJ λαμβάνω A.II.1f and Bluck on *Meno* 75d2–3.

e4–5 πρῶτον μὲν ... ἔπειτα: see 336b1–2n. Here the expected parallelism between the two clauses is disrupted by a change of construction, from participles to a finite verb, a form of anacoluthon found elsewhere in clauses connected by μέν and δέ (KG II 100).

e5–6 εἴ τι καὶ οἴεται περὶ τούτων "if he even has some notion about those matters (about which he disclaims knowledge)." This hypothetical τις is, of course, none other than S., who disavows knowledge but who supposes that justice is συμφέρον τι (339b4–5). Some editors punctuate before, rather than after, περὶ τούτων, but it is difficult to justify the prominence the phrase would have if it appeared at the start of its clause, the emphatic element of which is ἀπειρημένον.

e6 ἀπειρημένον αὐτῶι εἴη ὅπως μηδὲν ἐρεῖ "if he is forbidden from saying anything." Although "if" is not explicitly expressed, it is easily understood from the negative μή in the previous line, which marks the participles there as conditional. In any event, the intervening if-clause (εἴ τι καί) would make another "if," if expressed, awkward. The usual construction for verbs of forbidding, preventing and denying is with μή + infinitive (*CGCG* §51.34–5), but S. uses a more expressive construction that virtually quotes T.'s direct prohibition (336c6–d1n.), as he does again at 339a7–8, where ἀποκρινοίμην is future optative in secondary sequence.

338a1 οὐ φαύλου "not insignificant" (litotes), a favorite expression of P.'s, occurring nearly fifty times, often used ironically (e.g. *Symp.* 218d8), as it is here. S. has consistently fed T.'s ego with flattery, calling him δεινός (337a1), σοφός (a8) and ὁ εἰδώς (d4), and will do so again at c1.

a2–3 χαρίζου ... καὶ μὴ φθονήσηις: cf. *Hp.Mi.* 372e6–7 σὺ οὖν χάρισαι καὶ μὴ φθονήσηις, where S., flattering Hippias effusively, begs him to cure him of his ignorance. By using the language of χάρις, S. seeks to remove the exchange of ideas from the commercial realm of the sophists, locating it instead in the venerable practice of gift exchange. S. further includes "Glaucon and the rest" in his request in hopes of appealing to T.'s public-spiritedness and his vanity, and in the expectation that they will support his request, which they do.

a6–7 φανερὸς μὲν ἦν ἐπιθυμῶν εἰπεῖν ἵνα εὐδοκιμήσειεν: compare *Prot.* 317c–d, where S. says that he suspected that Protagoras wanted to show off (ἐνδείξασθαι καὶ καλλωπίσασθαι) for the benefit of Prodicus and Hippias and their followers, so he suggests that they be called in from the other rooms, whereupon Callias, at whose house the gathering is being held, proposes that they arrange a συνέδριον so that they can converse sitting down (as the guests at Cephalus' house have been doing from the start: 328c).

a8 προσεποιεῖτο δὲ φιλονικεῖν πρὸς τὸ ἐμὲ εἶναι τὸν ἀποκρινόμενον "he tried to give the impression that he was eager for me to be the one to give the answers"; cf. *Prot.* 360e3–4 (Protagoras addressing S.) φιλονικεῖν μοι ... δοκεῖς ... τὸ ἐμὲ εἶναι τὸν ἀποκρινόμενον, where the articular infinitive depends directly on the verb. S. is accused of φιλονικία also by Callicles (*Gorg.* 515b5). In P.'s eyes, men like Protagoras, Callicles and T. are convinced that they are engaged in a constant struggle for verbal superiority, and they assume that everyone with whom they interact, including S., is striving for victory (φιλονικεῖν) over them. φιλονικ- is often misspelled φιλονεικ- in our MSS, as if from νεῖκος, which, being an *s*-stem, would give an adjective *φιλονεικής (cf. Πολυνείκης) rather than φιλόνικος (Slings 2003: xviii

n. 16), a word whose derivation from νικᾶν is recognized by P. (9.581b3 with Adam's note, 582e5, 586c9 and Taylor on *Tim.* 70a3).

338b1 Αὕτη δή: for the particle with οὗτος, "often contemptuous in tone," see *GP* 208–9. In the view of T., S.'s "wisdom" is nonexistent; or, rather, it is a devious sort of cleverness that seeks to extract wisdom from others without so much as paying for it.

b2 αὐτόν "he himself." Word order and context show that this is the contrastive use of the pronoun (Powell 1938: A.II.1), most commonly found in the nominative, but here in the accusative as subject of the infinitive, which is in apposition to σοφία (KG II 4).

b3 τούτων: apparently "for those things (which he learned)"; cf. Isocr. 6.73 χάριν ἀποδιδόντες ὧν εὖ πεπόνθασιν.

χάριν ἀποδιδόναι "show appreciation," i.e. pay the fee for tuition. Sophists expect their pupils to give them a large monetary payment and also to be grateful for their willingness to share improving wisdom (*Apol.* 20a2, *Cra.* 391b10, *Gorg.* 519c7). An anecdote told about Simonides (331d4n.) illustrates the value to the recipient of the two forms of recompense: when the man who commissioned a hymn of praise from the mercenary poet thanked him for his work but did not pay him, Simonides said that he had two coffers, one for silver and one for thanks (χαρίτων), only one of which contained anything useful (Stob. 3.10.38).

b5 χάριν ἐκτίνειν: S. substitutes for T.'s verb one that has more explicitly monetary connotations; cf. *Apol.* 37c3–4, where S. says that he has no money with which to pay a fine (οὐ γάρ ἔστι μοι χρήματα ὁπόθεν ἐκτείσω). He thus makes clear that he understands T.'s meaning, but what follows shows that he and T. have completely different notions of appropriate compensation. The coin with which S. enthusiastically repays his "teachers" is praise. This is deeply ironic and is subversive of the ideology of those who teach rhetoric professionally. Traditionally, the merchants of praise are poets, like Simonides (allegedly the first to charge a fee for composing epinician odes: schol. Pind. *Isthm.* 2.9) and Pindar; later the sophists, who saw themselves as inheriting the mantle of wisdom that had earlier adorned poets "such as Homer, Hesiod and Simonides" (*Prot.* 316d7), developed the epideictic genre of the encomium in prose. Thus, by offering praise as payment for instruction S. perverts the roles of producer and consumer. For poets and sophists expected remuneration for displaying their expertise, which included skill in disseminating praise. The anti-sophist S. offers to repay anyone who can teach him with something more valuable than cash, namely truthful praise of his wisdom. For, as S. says in reaction to the poet Agathon's sophistic encomium of Eros, he is of the belief that the encomiast is obligated to tell the truth (*Symp.* 198d3–4). In the case of T., as with all those from whom he hopes to learn, S. will render payment only after his teaching has been subjected to elenctic scrutiny and has proved itself worthy of praise.

338c1 αὐτίκα δὴ μάλα "right away," a vigorous colloquial expression not attested before the fourth century, only here in P., once in Aristophanes (*Plutus* 942) and a score of times in the orators.

338c2–339e7: T. discloses his provocative definition of the just: it is nothing other than that which is advantageous to the superior. This definition is repeated by the Athenian in P.'s *Laws*, saying that some people claim that it represents the natural delimitation of what is just (τὸν φύσει ὅρον τοῦ δικαίου, 4.714c3); Callicles, explaining how the weak attempt to contravene what is natural by making laws for their own advantage (συμφέρον), uses similar language when he says that "nature herself (φύσις αὐτή) makes it clear that it is just (δίκαιόν ἐστιν) for the better to have more than the inferior, and the stronger than the powerless" (*Gorg.* 483c8–d2). T. never uses the language of *physis*, but Glaucon emphatically does so when he elaborates T.'s position in Book Two: he introduces the story of Gyges' ancestor and his magical ring to illustrate the claim that "having more is what every natural creature naturally pursues as a good thing" (πλεονεξίαν, ὃ πᾶσα φύσις διώκειν πέφυκεν ὡς ἀγαθόν, 359c4–5). T. would surely agree that everyone naturally desires to have more, but he never espouses the "social contract" view put forth by Glaucon; rather, the weak act "justly," according to T., because they lack the power to do otherwise. Before S. can commend T. for his wisdom, however, he must first make sure he fully understands the definition. After he satisfies himself that T. is thinking not in terms of brute physical strength, he asks if those who exercise power over others do not sometimes make mistakes regarding what is truly to their own advantage. T.'s affirmative reply involves him in what appears to be a paradox: there will be times when a subject can satisfy T.'s definition of "the just" only by disobeying the ruler.

338c2 Ἄκουε δή: T. uses the same expression to introduce his definition that is used by Phaedrus before he recites the speech of Lysias, the text of which he has been lovingly safeguarding under his *himation* (*Phdr.* 230e5), and by Prometheus to announce the recital of Io's travails that she has been begging to hear ([Aesch.] *PV* 630). S. himself (6.487d9, 10.608d9) and the visitor from Elea (*Pol.* 269c4) express themselves with the more courteous, and less self-important, ἀκούοις ἄν.

τὸ δίκαιον: T. gives a definition of "the just" rather than of "justice," a thing that S. had characterized as more valuable than a great quantity of gold (336e6–7). The two terms can be used interchangeably (336a8–9n.), and T. will occasionally so use them in what follows, but it is to his advantage to define "the just," because it allows him (or, rather, P.) to make use of the ambiguity inherent in τὸ δίκαιον, which can mean "justice" in the abstract, but can also = "the just X," where for X can be substituted "act" or "behavior" (341a3n.). This makes it possible for P. to use locutions in which it is legitimate to omit the definite article, as S. had done at 332c1 and will do immediately below, thereby leaving it ambiguous whether one is giving a definition or is saying "It is just to do Y"; cf. 340a8, b4, 341a3.

c3 τὸ τοῦ κρείττονος συμφέρον: T. will repeat this formulation no fewer than four times in the course of the following discussion, standing by it in the face of S.'s probing critique; cf. 347e1–2n. His use of the comparative κρείττονος is significant, as it raises the implicit question, "Stronger than whom?," the only possible answer being the weaker, whose interactions with the stronger are, as far as T. is concerned, what people are referring to when they use the word "just." T. is thinking in the either/or terms of Realpolitik and the judicial system for which he prepares his pupils. In a court of law, or when engaged in a public debate, one either prevails over one's opponent or is defeated. (This is comically reflected in the agon of Aristophanes' *Clouds*, where, paradoxically, ὁ κρείττων λόγος is decisively defeated by ὁ ἥττων; cf. *Apol.* 18c1.) When the world is viewed in this one-on-one, win-or-lose manner, it follows that everyone is seen as trying to avoid losing and striving to become dominant. The natural reaction of the loser, the one whose property has been appropriated or whose position has been usurped, is to complain, using a form of the word δίκαιον, "That's not fair." Nor would T. dissent. He acknowledges, for instance, that the tyrant acts unjustly (344a). That is not to say that he disapproves of the tyrant's behavior, merely that the tyrant's behavior is the sort of thing we speak of as unjust. The superior, however, cannot admit to acting unfairly or unjustly without seeming to cede control of the discourse to the inferior. Two avenues of response are open. The superior can claim, or even seek to prove, that the behavior conforms to the weaker party's conception of "fair," as Jason outrageously tries to do in Euripides' *Medea* (although that in itself entails an appearance of some degree of weakness); alternatively, the stronger can adopt the more radical approach exhibited by the Athenian envoys at Melos in 416 and simply discount as irrelevant the language of fairness (Thuc. 5.89). What T. is doing here is to explain to S. what S. and people like him "really mean" when they use the Greek word for justice, δικαιοσύνη or its equivalent τὸ δίκαιον. S. never asks T., as he asks others of his interlocutors (10.608d11; Bluck on *Meno* 75e1), whether he thinks the object of their conversation is something (τι), nor does T. ever suggest that he believes in the existence of an entity that might be regarded as the essential nature of justice. For his part, S. is convinced that there is such an entity or "Form," existing independently of the behavior of any human actors, and it is the nature of that entity, conventionally designated "justice," that he is concerned to define. (For the distinction between nominal and "real" definitions, see Cross and Woozley 1964: 6–10.) This gap between the two men is never bridged, or even addressed, so that, quite apart from the fact that their moral outlooks differ radically, the two of them are unable to communicate effectively with each other. For the discussion to continue in a productive manner, it will be necessary for P. to provide S. with new interlocutors, beginning with Book Two (Matthews 2018).

ἀλλὰ τί οὐκ ἐπαινεῖς; we are to imagine that S. is at a momentary loss for words. This silence after the definition, like the long build-up before it (interlocutors in P. generally respond with alacrity to S.'s request for a definition), marks it as particularly significant; it will dominate the discussion for the remainder of Book One. Calling attention to the silence of an interlocutor (*Apol.* 24d7, *Gorg.* 468c7–8, d6, *Hp.Mi.* 363a1, *Prot.* 328d4–6) is a technique borrowed from the drama (e.g. Aesch. *Eum.* 303, Soph. *OC* 1271, *Phil.* 805; Taplin 1972), parodied at Ar. *Frogs* 832, *Thesm.* 144.

c7–8 Πουλυδάμας ... ὁ παγκρατιαστής: for the fantastic accounts of the strength of the Thessalian Polydamas, victor in the pankration at the Olympic Games in 408, see Kyle 2007: 202. His statue at Olympia was alleged to effect a cure for fevers (Lucian, *Deorum concilium* 12). The statue, by the late fourth-century sculptor Lysippus, has not survived, but the badly damaged base has (Archaeological Museum, Olympia, inv. no. Λ 45). The relief on the base illustrates a story told in detail by Pausanias (6.5.7), who saw the statue and its base in the second century AD: the Persian king Darius II, who reigned from 423 to 405 BC, invited Polydamas to his court, where he put on an exhibition of his physical strength by defeating three of the so-called Persian Immortals in single combat (Hyland 2015). By naming Polydamas here, P. is tacitly correcting something T. is supposed to have said in one of his *Proems*. According to Athenaeus (10.416a = DK 85 B4 = 35 D19 Laks–Most; cf. White 1995: 320–1), T. told essentially the same story about the poet Timocreon of Rhodes, saying that he overpowered "countless Persians" with his blows (πληγάς). But the strength of Timocreon is not attested other than in Athenaeus, who is alone in identifying him as a pentathlete in the introduction to this story (415f). Further, "blows" have no place in the pentathlon, while they do in the pankration. P. will have taken particular satisfaction in embarrassing the author of Ὑπερβάλλοντες (336c2n.) by having S. casually bring up the name of the man who was the real subject of T.'s anecdote, a name that means "he who subdues many."

c8 τὰ βόεια κρέα: the definite article implies "the beef diet (that is in vogue for pankratiasts)." Beef was rarely eaten in ancient Greece outside the context of ritual sacrifice, in which case the participants in the sacrifice, with certain honorary exceptions, were given an equal portion of the victim. For this reason the diet of high-level athletes, whose training included consumption of greater amounts (and better cuts) of meat than was available to the ordinary citizen, could be seen as "unfair."

338d1–2 τοῦτο τὸ σιτίον ... δίκαιον: S. occasionally greets an interlocutor's definition with a bathetic example: Charmides' definition of sophrosyne is interpreted as requiring that everyone make their own clothes and shoes (*Chrm.* 161b–e), and S. pretends that, following Callicles' understanding of justice, a physician ought to be given more food in virtue of having higher skills (*Gorg.* 490a–c). Reactions range from Charmides' demurral to Callicles' disparagement to T.'s revulsion.

d3 Βδελυρός: the word appears only here in P., being beneath the dignity of the other speakers in his dialogues (see the Introduction, section 1, with n. 23); elsewhere it is almost completely confined to comedy and the vituperation of the orators. See Theophrastus, *Characters* 11, "The repulsive man," with Diggle's commentary.

d3–4 ταύτηι ... τὸν λόγον "you are giving an interpretation by means of which you can most effectively undermine what I say." For ὑπολαμβάνειν used absolutely, see 3.392c1, 394b9, *Gorg.* 451a1–2; for κακουργεῖν, compare Callicles as quoted in 340d2n. (ἐν τοῖς λόγοις).

d6 Εἶτα "Do you mean to tell me ...?" For this colloquial use of the word to introduce "surprised, indignant or sarcastic questions" (Collard 2018: 104–5), see *Euthd.* 287b2, 302c6, *Hp.Ma.* 290a9, all addressed to S.

τῶν πόλεων: apart from 330a2, this is the first mention of the polis (and just below is the first mention of νόμος) in this work whose title proclaims it to be concerned with the administration of the polis. Both Cephalus and Polemarchus had spoken of justice in terms of one individual's treatment of another, and T. too thinks of justice in binary terms. P.'s introduction of the language of government here serves a number of purposes. By mentioning the three varieties of rule in the polis, the only framework within which an ancient Greek can conceive civilized society, T. can represent his account of justice as universally valid (339a3n.). In addition, it allows P. to take advantage of the language of ruling (κρατεῖν, ἄρχειν) when S. brings into the discussion the analogy of the mastery of a craft (341c). Finally, by using the relationship between the rulers in a polis and its citizens as an example on a large scale of relationships between individuals, P. anticipates the use that will be made in Book Two of the vision of justice in the polis as an aid to understanding justice in the soul of the individual.

d6–7 αἱ μὲν ... ἀριστοκρατοῦνται: the traditional tripartite classification of governments (Pind. *Pyth.* 2.87–8, Hdt. 3.80–3), although the terminology varies according to the speaker's point of view: tyranny (μουναρχίη

Hdt.), democracy (government by ὁ λάβρος στρατός Pind., ἰσονομίη Hdt.), aristocracy (government by οἱ σοφοί Pind., ὀλιγαρχίη Hdt.). A new classification will be presented by S. in Book Eight.

d9 κρατεῖ: spelling out for S. that the ruling power in each polis (δημοκρατοῦνται, ἀριστοκρατοῦνται) is what is meant by τὸ κρεῖττον in T.'s definition. It is irrelevant that Polydamas is physically stronger than the weaker S.; what matters to T. is who exercises authority over whom. In what follows, ἡ ἀρχή and οἱ ἄρχοντες will be used as equivalents of τὸ κρεῖττον.

338e3–4 ἀπέφηναν τοῦτο δίκαιον τοῖς ἀρχομένοις εἶναι: formally ambiguous, either (1) "they proclaim (gnomic aorist: *CGCG* §33.31) that this (τὸ σφίσι συμφέρον) is just for their subjects," or (2) "they proclaim to their subjects that this is just." That is, (2) exactly reproduces T.'s definition while (1) adds a qualification. In view of T.'s repeated claims of consistency, (2) seems more likely. In any event, it is the behavior of the subjects that is defined as just, so long as it conforms to the dictates of the rulers.

e4–5 τὸν τούτου ἐκβαίνοντα ... ἀδικοῦντα: the best commentary on this is provided by P. himself in *Laws* (see 338c2–339e7n.), when the Athenian explains what "some people" mean when they define justice as τὸ τοῦ κρείττονος συμφέρον, saying that the ruling power enacts laws in its own interest and that it will punish anyone who transgresses (παραβαίνηι) its laws "as a wrongdoer, designating those enactments as 'justice,'" ὡς ἀδικοῦντα, δίκαια εἶναι ταῦτα ἐπονομάζων (4.714d6–7). The implication here, surely, is that the application of the words "just" and "unjust" is simply dependent upon the decrees of the rulers: what is done in accordance with the laws that the rulers have enacted in their own interest is called "just," and what violates those laws is "unjust."

339a1 ταὐτόν: this form, with crasis and final -ν, is equivalent to τὸ αὐτό in a3. Both are found frequently in P., and there seems to be no way of telling what determines why one or the other appears in a given place (assuming our printed texts and the MSS on which they rely accurately reflect P.'s intentions). The form with final -ν, like neuter τοιοῦτον and τοσοῦτον, is regular in Old Comedy (Willi 2003: 243–4); Herodotus is inconsistent when it comes to τοιοῦτον and τοσοῦτον (see Powell 1938 for details), but does not add -ν in the case of τὠυτό.

a3 πανταχοῦ εἶναι τὸ αὐτό: with the repetition and with his earlier specification that this holds "in all cities," T. flaunts his awareness that he is expected to give a definition in the form elsewhere approved by S.; e.g. *Euthphr.* 5d1–2 ταὐτόν ... ἐν πάσηι πράξει, *Meno* 72d8 ταὐτὸν πανταχοῦ, 75a7–8 ταὐτὸν ἐπὶ πᾶσιν. Cephalus and Polemarchus had given answers in terms of specific types of actions, but those types did not cover all possible actions to which "just" or "unjust" might be applied (Benson 1990; Beversluis 2000: 224–5). As it happens, however, since the government in each city enacts laws in its own interest, it may be that *the same act* will qualify as just in Athens and unjust in Chalcedon. This disqualifies T.'s account of justice as something S. would regard as a proper definition (338c3n.), but he will defend his account, which we will continue to refer to as a "definition," as coherent within his own frame of reference (Wedgwood 2017). Cross and Woozley (1964: 25) object to certain translators who render T.'s ἀπόκρισιν at 337d1 as "definition," but in this context, as at *Meno* 76d–e, the translation is justified (see also Denyer on *Alc.1* 108b5). After all, S. repeats T.'s ἀπόκρισις first in the form τὸ συμφέρον ... δίκαιον (a6–7) then, with no objection from T., as συμφέρον ... τὸ δίκαιον (b4–5), implying an equivalence between the two.

339b1 δὲ δὴ αὐτόθι "but *there* (in your definition)"; for δή emphasizing that the second element of a μέν/δέ antithesis is the salient one, see *GP* 257, 259.

τὸ τοῦ κρείττονος: the first article serves, in effect, to put τοῦ κρείττονος in quotation marks (331e3n.).

b4–5 καὶ ἐγὼ ὁμολογῶ: by the end of Book Nine it will be clear in what sense S. considers justice συμφέρον τι.

b8 οὐ καὶ πείθεσθαι μέντοι: for μέντοι in questions expecting an affirmative answer, "common in Plato" (*GP* 403), cf. 346a2. The καί further emphasizes the new point introduced by πείθεσθαι, already emphatic by virtue of its position in the sentence: "Surely you maintain that *to obey* the rulers is just?" Cf. *Ion* 537a1 οὐ καὶ περὶ τεχνῶν μέντοι λέγει πολλαχοῦ Ὅμηρος;

339c1 Πότερον δὲ ἀναμάρτητοι: this is the same argument S. used at 334c to call into question Polemarchus' definition of justice as helping friends and harming enemies. In that case it was the knowledge on the part of the agent that was at issue; here it is the ruler's knowledge of what is in the ruler's interest and should, therefore, be decreed as the "just" thing for the agent to do. The essential relationship between knowledge and justice will be explored in the later books of *Republic*.

c1–2 ἐν ταῖς πόλεσιν ἑκάσταις: this addition will allow T. to overcome S.'s objection. He had secured S.'s agreement that different poleis have different forms of government (338d6–8); later he will argue that only the tyrant is κρείττων in the proper sense of the word (344a–c).

c7 Τὸ δὲ ὀρθῶς: *sc.* τιθέναι.

τὰ συμφέροντα: the plural is used to avoid the collocation of two identical forms of the article (332c2n.).

τίθεσθαι: the shift to the middle voice underlines the self-interest involved in the "correctly" enacted laws.

ἑαυτοῖς: with συμφέροντα; cf. 338e4 τὸ σφίσι συμφέρον, 340a4 ἑαυτοῖς κακὰ προστάττειν.

339d3 Τί λέγεις σύ; in Aristophanes' *Clouds*, when Strepsiades welcomes his son after he has learned from S. how to be "refutatious and disputatious" (ἐξαρνητικὸς κἀντιλογικός) and how to "appear to be the victim of unjust behavior while acting unjustly" (δοκεῖν ἀδικοῦντ' ἀδικεῖσθαι), he is delighted to see that his son is radiating τὸ "τί λέγεις σύ;" that he has picked up in the Reflectory (1172–5). This suggests that the expression, which occurs only once elsewhere in P. (*Euthd.* 290e1), was felt to be characteristic of those who engage in eristic confrontations, who include S. in Strepsiades' view.

d4 Ἃ σὺ λέγεις: S.'s manner in pointing out T.'s apparent self-contradiction is abrupt, like his response to the conceited rhapsode at *Ion* 539e7, Οὐ σύ γε φῄς. He is less confrontational with Protagoras, putting into the mouth of "someone" the observation that the statements made earlier by the two of them about the virtues were not self-consistent, at which point (*Prot.* 330e–331a) S. notes that the statements were not his own but Protagoras'.

339e1 Οἴου τοίνυν: S. picks up T.'s "I should think so" with a mocking "Well then you should also think …" For the particle, see *GP* 572–3; Sicking and Van Ophuijsen 1993: 152–64.

e1–2 τοῖς ἄρχουσί τε καὶ κρείττοσι: 332c5n.

e2 ὡμολογῆσθαί σοι: in S.'s previous question no agent was specified for the repeated ὡμολόγηται. Here the spotlight is directed exclusively at T.

e2–4 ὅταν … προσέταξαν: "(You agreed that it is just to do what is disadvantageous to the rulers) whenever (1) the rulers unwittingly issue orders to do what is harmful to themselves, and (2) you say that it is just for the others to follow those orders." The meaning is clear, but S. has not expressed himself according to strict logic, since (2) does not properly depend on "whenever." It should depend on something like "when" in the sense of "given that," which can be expressed by ὅτε (LSJ B.1), but not by ὅταν.

e4–5 ὦ σοφώτατε Θρασύμαχε: sarcastic; cf. *Gorg.* 489c8, addressed to Callicles, who reciprocates at 495d1 with ὦ σοφώτατε σύ. T. is more direct: 343d2.

340a1–d1: Polemarchus breaks into the conversation, triumphantly proclaiming that S. has demonstrated T.'s self-contradiction. Clitophon comes to T.'s defense, offering a way out of the dilemma. What T. meant by the advantage of the superior, according to Clitophon, is whatever the superior thinks is advantageous to itself, and that is what it is just for the inferior to do. S. asks T. if that is indeed what he meant, but he stands by his original definition of justice, saying in effect that "the superior" forfeits its right to be so called in the event that it mistakes what is to its own advantage. This interruption by Polemarchus halfway through Book One is paralleled by his less overt, but more consequential, intervention at the start of Book Five. Interruptions that involve metalepsis, or frame-breaking (Finkelberg 2019: 22–3), are common in those dialogues that combine an implicit and an explicit narrator, that is, intrusions from one narrative level into another (e.g. *Euthd.* 290e, *Phd.* 88c, 102a); the ancestor of this phenomenon is the "intermezzo" in the middle of Odysseus' narration to his Phaeacian hosts (*Od.* 11.333–84). But even in a work like *Republic*, with only one level of narration, P. can employ a comparable technique in order to mark a shift in tone or topic. Here, the interruption allows the option available to T. to be presented by someone else, calling attention to the strength of his commitment to his definition of justice.

340a2 Ἐάν σύ γε … αὐτῶι μαρτυρήσηις: sarcastic, implying that Polemarchus' testimony in support of S. is worthless, given that he is S.'s associate and therefore likely to be biased in his favor. Clitophon's language suggests that, like T., he sees the present discussion in forensic terms, the lawcourt being the context in which witnesses are called; cf. *Gorg.* 471e–472a.

a3 τί … δεῖται μάρτυρος; cf. Eur. *Or.* 532–3 τί μαρτύρων | ἄλλων ἀκούειν δεῖ μ', ἅ γ' εἰσορᾶν πάρα; Dem. 9.41 ὁρᾶτε δήπου καὶ οὐδὲν ἐμοῦ προσδεῖσθε μάρτυρος. Polemarchus, but apparently not T. or Clitophon, recognizes that the argument at 334c, in which he was shown that failure to distinguish real from apparent friends could result in harming friends and helping enemies, is relevant here, for he immediately points out that failure to distinguish real from apparent advantage can result in rulers ordering what is to their own disadvantage, which is damaging to T.'s account of justice. We are thus shown that the elenchus has a more immediate and more positive effect on the person who is subjected to it, in this case Polemarchus, than on bystanders.

a6 γάρ "Yes (it is right for them to follow those orders), because …"

a8 Καὶ γάρ "Yes (he did say that), and he also …" (*GP* 109–10), repeating Clitophon's δίκαιον εἶναι ἔθετο. Like S. and T. (e.g. 339d3–4, d9–e1), Polemarchus and Clitophon engage in verbal sparring using the technique of "capping," for which see Collins 2004.

340c2 οὕτως αὐτοῦ ἀποδεχώμεθα: in contrast to T., who disallowed certain responses (ἐγὼ οὐκ ἀποδέξομαι, 336d3), S. magnanimously permits T. to modify his definition. Even if he were inclined to do so, however, doing so would appear to be at least a partial retreat from a position that he thought was deserving of applause.

c4 ἐάντε συμφέρηι ἐάντε μή: S. phrases the proposed revision of T.'s definition in such a way as to ensure that he not accept it. Having defined justice – and having insistently repeated his definition – as that which is advantageous, he is surely not going to agree to a definition that treats advantageousness as inessential.

c8–d1 ὅτε ... ἐξαμαρτάνειν: recalling the wording of S.'s question at 339c1–2 (with the substitution of T.'s compound verb for S.'s simplex). But the imperfect ὡμολόγεις implies not so much a reference to T.'s affirmative answer, for which one would expect an aorist, but something like, "(I was under the impression that that was what you meant) when you were holding the position that rulers are not infallible." That is, S. subtly hints that T. may no longer be holding the position to which he earlier agreed.

340d2–341c4: T. insults S. and condescendingly throws in his face one of S.'s (and P.'s) favorite examples, that of the physician. We speak loosely of the physician making a mistake on occasion but, T. maintains, the physician, or any other expert in a given field, is incapable of making a mistake in the very field in which he is an expert; at the moment at which the mistake is made, the expertise (ἐπιστήμη, 340e4) that conferred the designation as master (κρείττων) of the field is cast aside. This allows T. to remain consistent, but raises issues that S. will exploit in what follows. T.'s notion of "superiority" is capable of two applications, which he fails to distinguish: it can refer (as he originally intended) to the domination of the weak by the strong, or it can describe the expert's mastery of a field of endeavor. (That P. was conscious of the ambiguity is clear from the way he has Agathon exploit it in his speech at *Symp.* 196c–d.) To be sure, in the only field of endeavor that interests T., the art of ruling, the two applications coincide. The mistake he makes is in adopting the analogy of the physician and other crafts, thereby playing into the hands of S. He could have avoided this mistake if he had been paying closer attention to S.'s conversation with Polemarchus, when S. first introduced the analogy of the physician (332c5). There it was agreed, reasonably, that the craft of the physician is directed at the health and wellbeing of the patient and not, as T.'s use of the analogy requires, at the interests of the physician.

340d2 Συκοφάντης: a term, found mostly in Attic comedy and oratory, used to stigmatize members of the imagined class of those who take advantage of established law to cause harm, or threaten to cause harm, to their "betters" for financial gain (Christ 1998: 48–117). Their targets are wealthy individuals like S.'s friend Crito, who complains to S. that he is beset by sycophants bringing lawsuits against him in hopes that he will be willing to pay them off rather than let the case come to trial; S. devises a strategy that frees Crito from the plague of predatory sycophants, whom he likens to wolves preying upon a flock of sheep, thereby saving him money (Xen. *Mem.* 2.9). In P., the same Crito offers to have S. smuggled out of prison and to pay off, for a surprisingly reasonable fee, any sycophants who threaten to bring charges against him for doing so (*Cri.* 44e–45a). The image of the sycophant, then, is of a profit-seeking man who assails someone of higher social and economic standing by manipulating the law, and the language of the law, in an unscrupulous manner or, as Peisetaerus puts it in driving off a sycophant in Aristophanes' *Birds*, engaging in "justice-perverting mischief-making" (1468). While the sycophant's purpose is to extort money, S.'s alleged sycophancy is aimed at getting the better of T. in private discussion by, as T. sees it, quibbling over words (e2–3). At the same time, the insult carries suggestions of class inferiority (for perceptions of S.'s class status, see 337d4 and 6nn.). As a professional rhetorician, T. is familiar with the strategies likely to be used by his opponents in debate, and he assures S. that he is prepared with a response.

ἐν τοῖς λόγοις: compare Callicles berating S. in *Gorgias*, δοκεῖς νεανιεύεσθαι ἐν τοῖς λόγοις, 482c4, and κακουργεῖς ἐν τοῖς λόγοις, 483a2–3. The force of the definite article is essentially possessive, "in our debate," while "in words" is ἐν λόγοις (e.g. *Cra.* 408a1, *Gorg.* 451a6, *Tht.* 165d6).

ἐπεί: the tone of ἐπεί when introducing a question is confrontational; cf. *Gorg.* 474b7 (Polus addressing S.), Soph. *OT* 390 (Oedipus addressing Teiresias, whom he has just called a deceptive, mercenary charlatan), *OC* 969 (Oedipus addressing Creon). There is an ellipsis involved (LSJ B.4; Collard 2018: 144–5), perhaps arising out of the impatience of the speaker, who hastens to raise a question intended to undermine the addressee's position. Here it is especially difficult to supply the suppressed connection of thought.

d2–3 αὐτίκα "for instance." This meaning (*CGL* 4), which is frequent in P., seems to have emerged from the word's literal meaning, "immediately," by a process suggested by Shorey's translation here, "to take the nearest example."

d4 λογιστικόν "an accountant, auditor." At *Gorg.* 451b–c S. distinguishes between λογιστική (τέχνη) and ἀριθμητική, the latter corresponding to the science of mathematics, the former to skill at performing calculations (see Dodds on 451b3), so that ὁ λογιστικός is someone who is "good with numbers."

d6 λέγομεν τῶι ῥήματι οὕτως, ὅτι "we do express ourselves this way in speaking, (saying) that"; cf. *Gorg.* 450e5 τῶι ῥήματι οὕτως εἶπες, ὅτι … For the distinction drawn here between meaning (λόγος) and verbal expression (ῥῆμα), see *Tht.* 166d7–e2.

d7 τὸ δέ "whereas, but in fact" (LSJ ὁ A.VIII.3), an expression common in P. (examples in Bluck on *Meno* 97c2).

340e2–3 ἐπειδὴ καὶ σὺ ἀκριβολογῆι: καί after a causal conjunction marks the particular appropriateness of the explanation given in the subordinate clause (*GP* 296–7). Here T., "talking down" to S., spells out for him the connection by etymologizing ἀκριβολογῆι < ἀκριβῆ λόγον. P. is being ironic in having T. accuse S. of being overly precise in the use of words; elsewhere S. expresses disdain for verbal precision (*Euthd.* 278b and *Tht.* 184c, where it is stigmatized as low-class), contrasting his own casual approach to language with the practice of the sophists, particularly Prodicus (*Chrm.* 163d, *Euthd.* 277e, *Meno* 75d–e, *Prot.* 339e–340b). Apparently the historical T. was among those inclined toward precision in language (DK 85 A13 = 35 D8 Laks–Most; cf. *Phdr.* 271a4–5) and, indeed, it was T. who first introduced the notion when, in his initial intervention, he demanded that S. declare σαφῶς … καὶ ἀκριβῶς what he thinks justice is (336d2–3).

e4 ἐν ὧι (apparently) "in which case," although the usage is not paralleled. The temporal sense of ἐν ὧι, "while," inappropriate here, is found when the speaker wishes to specify the time during which the action of the main verb takes place (e.g. 6.498b4, *Apol.* 39e2).

e5 δημιουργὸς ἢ σοφὸς ἢ ἄρχων: the middle term is difficult to account for; it is ignored in the next part of the sentence (for the physician as δημιουργός, see *Symp.* 186d). T. may intend it to represent the class to which he himself belongs, namely sophists, a term that, according to Protagoras, members of the class are reluctant to use of themselves (*Prot.* 316d–e). If so, the three terms represent the range, in ascending order, of human skills, from craftsmen like doctors and stonecutters (supposedly the profession of S.'s father: D.L. 2.18) to poets and intellectuals to political leaders. This last is the class to membership of which all men aspire, in the view of T., and it is ὁ ἄρχων that he will use to typify ὁ κρείττων.

e7 τοιοῦτον … ἀποκρίνεσθαι "So naturally such is the way you must understand also my answer to you just now (when I said that rulers sometimes make mistakes)"; for οὖν δή see *GP* 468–9. τοιοῦτος, like οὗτος (*CGCG* §29.33), can be used to refer to what has been said more recently, here the loose way of speaking that "everyone" would use in contrast to ἐκεῖνο, referring to what was said earlier.

e8 τὸ δὲ ἀκριβέστατον ἐκεῖνο τυγχάνει ὄν "but the most accurate (way of putting it) is in fact that (earlier way)," referring to what T. said in e2–6, rephrased in the following τὸν ἄρχοντα … μὴ ἁμαρτάνειν. By using the superlative T. trumps the ἀκρίβεια he had unfairly (see e2–3n.) attributed to S.

341a1 μὴ ἁμαρτάνειν: the negative is μή because the infinitive is in apposition to ἐκεῖνο (Smyth §2718); cf. 6.497b1. The immediately following μή marks the participle as conditional (§2067); cf. b1 μὴ λαθών.

a3 ποιεῖν: this is the one refinement T. has admitted to the definition he has repeatedly given. It is prompted by S.'s questioning that led to the conclusion that, if the ruler errs in laying down a law, it may be seen as just for the ruled *to do* what is not in the ruler's interest (339b8 πείθεσθαι, c10 ποιητέον, e7 ποιεῖν). The addition seems inconsequential, inasmuch as justice, as ordinarily understood, is necessarily manifested in an individual's actions, and the discussion with Polemarchus had assumed that what is at issue is just acts (Wedgwood 2017: 35). It serves P.'s purpose here to focus on actions, since it requires that attention be paid to the identity of the agent. For T., it is only the ruled who are expected or required to act in accordance with the dictates of justice (343c5–d1). For P., on the other hand, justice is a disposition of the soul; cf. 5.449a4 ψυχῆς τρόπου κατασκευήν.

a6 ἐν τοῖς λόγοις: see 340d2n.

κακουργοῦντά σε: earlier, T. had accused S. of attempting to undermine (κακουργήσαις 338d4) the discussion; it is now more personal, with σε as the object of the verb.

a8 Εὖ μὲν οὖν οἶδα "On the contrary, (I don't merely *think* so) I *know* it"; cf. 8.556d5–e3 ἆρα οἴει ...; Εὖ οἶδα μὲν οὖν; *GP* 475–6.

οὐδέν γέ σοι πλέον ἔσται "it won't get you anywhere"; cf. *Symp.* 217c3–4 οὐδὲν γάρ μοι πλέον ἦν, of Alcibiades' unsuccessful attempt to seduce S. by wrestling with him.

341b1 μὴ λαθὼν βιάσασθαι: the antithesis stealth/force is common in a legal context (*Laws* 8.843b4, 846a5) and in speech influenced by the sophists (Thuc. 1.37.4, Critias fr. 19.10–11 *TrGF*). T. is warning S. that he will not be able to get the better of him either by deception (ἐξ ἐπιβουλῆς; cf. 2.380d2), as he has just tried to do, or, his deception having been exposed (μὴ λαθών), by bluster.

b3–4 τὸν ἄρχοντά τε καὶ τὸν κρείττονα: see 332c5n. S. is affirming, and ensuring that T. affirms, that the two terms are, in the strictest sense, synonymous.

b4 τὸν ὡς ἔπος εἰπεῖν "the ruler/stronger in the loose sense of the word."

b7 Τὸν τῶι ἀκριβεστάτωι: see 340e8n. T.'s fondness for superlatives (a1, 343d2, 344a3–5, 348c6, 351b4–5) is one of the means P. uses to characterize his overbearing personality.

πρὸς ταῦτα "in view of that." When preceding an imperative the phrase "expresses defiance" (Burnet on *Apol.* 30b7); e.g. [Aesch.] *PV* 915, 992, Soph. *El.* 820, Eur. *Med.* 1358.

b8 οὐδέν σου παρίεμαι "I'm not asking any favors of you," that is, T. is challenging S. to do his best and not "go easy" on him; cf. *Apol.* 17c7 τοῦτο ὑμῶν δέομαι καὶ παρίεμαι (where the genitive depends on δέομαι), Eur. *Med.* 892–3 παριέμεσθα καί φαμεν κακῶς φρονεῖν | τότ'. The genitive is not elsewhere found with παρίεσθαι, but it is found, once, with παραιτεῖσθαι in a similar meaning: Eur. *Med.* 1154.

341c1 οὐ μὴ οἷός τε ἦις: οὐ μή + subjunctive "expresses an emphatic denial" (*CGCG* §34.9).

c2–3 ξυρεῖν ... λέοντα: earlier, T. was a wolf (336d). Shaving a lion was proverbial for doing something that is either impossible (*CPG* II 758.20) or not in the agent's bests interests (I 274.3). In the strange image at the end of Book Nine, the lion will serve as the emblem of the spirited element of the soul that, in the just person, is tamed by the rational element (588c–589b), as S. will subdue T. (2.358b2–3).

c4 οὐδὲν ὢν καὶ ταῦτα "being a failure (LSJ οὐδείς A.II.2) at that too," i.e. in addition to being unable to define justice.

341c5–342e11: S. proceeds, very gingerly, to shave the lion. He begins by securing T.'s agreement that the expertise of the physician in the strictest sense of the word consists in healing the sick rather than in earning a living (a topic explored in greater detail beginning at 346b). Next, appealing to his interlocutor's authoritarian sensibilities, S. uses the example of the ship's captain, whose skills are agreed to include that of ruling over subordinates. S. then goes back to the example of the physician, whose "sovereignty" is over the bodies of the sick. (He will return to the ship's captain at the end of the section, when it is convenient to reintroduce the language of command in the literal sense.) Just as the physician's craft, like any τέχνη, is in no way deficient, so the practitioner in the strictest sense is in need of nothing extraneous to maintain superiority. Therefore, the interest served by both the practitioner and the craft can only be the interest of that over which the craft has dominion or, in T.'s terminology, of the ruled rather than the ruler. S. as narrator makes it clear that T.'s acceptance of this sequence of reasoning is more grudging the further it progresses.

341c5 Ἄδην ... τῶν τοιούτων: for this manner of moving on to a new topic, cf. *Euthphr.* 11e2 καὶ τούτων μὲν ἅδην and *Pol.* 287a6 καὶ τούτων μὲν ἅλις (the only occurrence in P. of ἅλις, a poeticism: Eur. *Hel.* 143, Soph. *OC* 1016).

c9 ὁ ὀρθῶς κυβερνήτης: a good example of the way P. likes to vary his expressions; ὀρθῶς is synonymous with τῶι ἀκριβεῖ λόγωι (c5–6) and τῶι ὄντι (c7). P. is fond of pairing the ship's captain (for this meaning of κυβερνήτης, see Casson 1971: 300–2) with the physician as examples of practitioners of crafts: 332d–e, *Euthd.* 279e–280a, *Ion* 540b–c, *Pol.* 297e.

c9–10 ναυτῶν ἄρχων ... ἢ ναύτης: this is specious. S. is careful to distinguish the skill of the captain from that of the ordinary sailor, but he fails to make a distinction between the captain's administrative function, which he shares with any professional who has charge of subordinates, such as an architect or a chorus leader, and the proper skill of the captain that differentiates him from the chorus leader and the architect. The expertise of the genuine ship's captain (6.488d4–5 τοῦ ἀληθινοῦ κυβερνήτου, e2–3 τὸν ὡς ἀληθῶς κυβερνητικόν) consists in skill at navigation; the crew that the captain has under his direction is merely instrumental in the exercise of his distinctive skill. T.'s ready assent is understandable in view of the pervasive "ship of state" image in Greek literature (Alcaeus frr. 6 and 208 Voigt, Aesch. *Sept.* 2–3; Brock 2013: 53–67). P. here foreshadows his use of that image in Book Six, where the skillful ship's captain is a metaphor for the ideal ruler, whose expertise combines an understanding of how things should be with an ability to direct his subjects to act in accordance with that understanding (Keyt 2006).

341d4 τὴν τέχνην καὶ τὴν τῶν ναυτῶν ἀρχήν: the expertise consists, as S. and T. have just agreed, in the command of sailors; for this devious use of synonyms by S., see 332c5n. This allows P. unobtrusively to reintroduce the word τέχνη, which has not been spoken since 332c–d, where the "art" referred to was justice. S. is taking advantage of the ambiguity involved in words like κρείττων and ἄρχων. The captain is both master of a τέχνη and commander of his crew; the physician, who acts alone, exercises his "authority" only over the bodies of the sick (342d6 σωμάτων … ἄρχων, *Ion* 540c1 ἄρχων κάμνοντος).

d6 ἑκάστωι τούτων: it is unclear whether this is intended to mean (1) captain and crew, (2) captains and physicians or (3) all of the above; Warren 1985: 7–8. T., whose main concern is with the interest of the superior, may think the reference is only to (2).

d8 Οὐ καὶ ἡ τέχνη: S. moves immediately from the practitioner to the τέχνη itself, counting on T.'s commitment to a consideration of the practitioner "in the strictest sense," thereby identifying the interest of the practitioner with that of the τέχνη. (A similar identification is suggested at *Ion* 537c5–6 and 540a5–6, where "knowledge" is ascribed indifferently to the expert and the craft.) Thus, when S. asks if it is in the nature of a τέχνη to seek out and supply what is advantageous to each, T. understands him to mean something like "that which enables each practitioner to carry out successfully the purpose of the τέχνη."

d12 ὅτι μάλιστα τελέαν: as T.'s reaction shows, he is not sure what it means for each τέχνη to be "as perfect as possible." S.'s explanation will extend to 342b6.

341e4 διὰ ταῦτα καί: "that is precisely (καί) why"; cf. *Prot.* 328b5, *Symp.* 180b4 and *GP* 307–8.

νῦν ηὑρημένη: in P. medicine is a venerable art, invented by Asclepius, the son of Apollo (3.407c–408c), or by Apollo himself (*Symp.* 197a6–7), in contrast to, for example, eristic, the recent development of which was common knowledge: *Euthd.* 285b4 τέχνην ... τὴν νεωστὶ ηὑρημένην. It is not clear, therefore, why S. introduces the notion of novelty, which is, in any event, irrelevant to his argument. We might instead read ἀνηυρημένη; cf. *Phdr.* 273c7 τέχνην ἀνευρεῖν, *Phlb.* 16c2 πάντα ὅσα τέχνης ἐχόμενα ἀνηυρέθη, *Symp.* 197a6–7 ἰατρικὴν καὶ μαντικὴν Ἀπόλλων ἀνηῦρεν.

e5 τοιούτωι: *sc.* πονηρῶι, "deficient."

e5–6 τούτωι ... ἐκπορίζηι τὰ συμφέροντα: by this point, with its repetition of ἐκπορίζειν from d9, it is clear to the reader, and must be assumed to be clear to T., that S. has been talking about the interest of the patient (τούτωι = τῶι σώματι) rather than the agent. But T., having agreed to everything so far, has no grounds for objecting.

342a2–b5 αὐτὴ ἡ ἰατρική ... οὔ τέχνη ἐστίν: the train of thought is, "(1) Is medicine or any other τέχνη deficient (as eyes and ears are deficient and need some τέχνη to supply τὸ συμφέρον), that is, is there a deficiency inherent in a τέχνη itself, which therefore requires another τέχνη to supply τὸ συμφέρον and so on *ad infinitum*, or will a τέχνη itself look to its own interest? (2) Or is it the case that a τέχνη needs neither itself nor another τέχνη to supply τὸ συμφέρον for its deficiency (since no τέχνη is deficient), nor is there anything whose advantage it seeks other than that of which it is a τέχνη?"

a2–3 ἔστιν ὅτι προσδεῖται "has some further need." Just as ἔστιν ὅπηι = πηι (*Prot.* 331d4) and ἔστιν οὕς = τινας (*Prot.* 346e4), so ἔστιν ὅτι = τι (*Gorg.* 504e8, *Tht.* 209b6); cf. Smyth §2515.

a3 ὥσπερ ὀφθαλμοὶ ... ἀκοῆς: the ἀρετή of eyes is vision and of ears hearing, which allows each organ to perform its unique ἔργον, seeing sights and hearing sounds; cf. 353b–c.

a3–5 καὶ διὰ ταῦτα ... ἐκποριούσης "and for this reason (because of their deficiency) they (eyes and ears) have need of some competence over and above them to seek out and provide (cf. ζητεῖν τε καὶ ἐκπορίζειν, 341d9) that which is useful for these purposes (seeing and hearing)"; for συμφέρον εἰς, cf. *Laws* 9.875a3, Xen. *Symp.* 4.59.

a5 ἆρα: a reminder to the reader, after the parenthesis, that this is a question, as at 8.566a2, repeating the ἆρα that began the sentence at 565e3.

a7 σκέψεται, καὶ τῆι σκοπουμένηι: the future of σκοπεῖσθαι is supplied by σκέψεσθαι. If every τέχνη is defective (which is implied by ἑκάστηι τέχνηι, a6), then every τέχνη that sees to the deficiency of another τέχνη will itself be in need of remediation, generating an infinite regress. It would complicate matters unnecessarily to raise, and then have to dispose of, the possibility that some, but not all, τέχναι are defective, positing the existence of one or more non-defective τέχναι whose ἔργον it is to see to the deficiency of others.

τοιαύτης: *sc.* πονηρᾶς; cf. 341e5.

342b1 ἢ αὐτὴ ... σκέψεται; this is introduced only to be immediately dismissed. A τέχνη will have no need to be concerned with its own interest unless it is deficient, which is impossible.

b2 τὸ συμφέρον σκοπεῖν "to look out for its interest." For this "final-consecutive" infinitive, see *CGCG* §51.16.

b5 ὀρθὴ οὖσα: that is, being a τέχνη in the correct sense of the word, explained by what follows: "as long as each τέχνη in the strict sense is entirely just what (ὅλη ἥπερ) it is."

b6 σκόπει ἐκείνωι τῶι ἀκριβεῖ λόγωι "consider (it) according to that 'precision' principle (that you have laid down)"; for the "dative of standard of judgment," see Smyth §1512.

b8 φαίνεται: with his response here and c6, P. shows us T. gradually coming to a recognition of the implications of S.'s argument. With c9 S. begins to record T.'s replies indirectly, making T. the only interlocutor in *Republic* for whom he does this (Ferrari 2010: 23). P. was the first thinker to theorize about the effects of direct vs indirect discourse, which he does in Book Three (392d–394c). T. will regain his voice momentarily at e2 and, in dramatic fashion, at 343a3.

342c5 οὐδὲ γὰρ προσδεῖται "since it has no further need." Being perfect, a τέχνη is not in need of τὸ συμφέρον or anything else. For οὐδὲ γάρ introducing a parenthesis containing an abbreviated a fortiori argument, see *Tim.* 33c7 οὐδὲ γὰρ ἦν, "(the world body needed no organs to interact with what was outside it) since there was nothing."

c7 ἄρχουσι ... καὶ κρατοῦσιν: S. pointedly returns to the language of ruling and domination that had begun this section of the discussion: 341b3–4 τὸν ἄρχοντά τε καὶ τὸν κρείττονα. Since then S. has moved the discussion from the practitioner in the strictest sense to the τέχνη itself.

c10 ἐπιστήμη: only the second time the word has been used in *Republic*, the first being at 340e4, where T. identified it as the *sine qua non* for the craftsman to be called a craftsman. It is introduced here as a synonym of τέχνη, as elsewhere in P. (e.g. *Ion* 532c6, *Prot.* 357b4); see 350a6n. P.'s conception of craft/knowledge is very broad, encompassing such practical activities as weaving as well as more theoretical pursuits, like mathematics (Parry 2020: §2). His use of the two terms interchangeably here is problematic, however. While a case can be made for the physician or the ship's captain as taking charge of and acting in the best interests of patients' bodies and ships' crews, it is hard to see how the stars are "inferior to" or are "ruled by" the astronomer, or how the geometer "looks to the interest" of the right angle. Still, P. wishes to retain the notion of the ruler in order to prepare us for the revelation that the ruler who is truly deserving of the name is a philosopher, whose theoretical knowledge enables him or her to see to the interest of the ruled (5.473c–e) in the same way the physician oversees the health of the patient.

342d3 μάχεσθαι: T. lives up to his name. Contrast Polemarchus, who committed himself to fighting alongside S., not against him (335e11).

d5–6 ὡμολόγηται … ἰατρὸς σωμάτων εἶναι ἄρχων: this had not in fact been agreed to in just these terms. It was agreed that the physician in the true sense of the word is a healer of the sick rather than a money-maker (341c6–8) and that the craft of the physician supplies the body with what is advantageous to it (e5–6). S. is here applying to the physician the language that had been used of the ship's captain, who was agreed to be a ναυτῶν ἄρχων (341d1), as S. immediately reminds T.

342e3 τοιοῦτος: *sc.* ὁ ἀκριβής.

e7 Οὐκοῦν: Denniston (*GP* 433–4) notes that there is "probably always some tinge of interrogation in the tone" of sentences introduced by this particle (for a rare exception, see 337d7n.). Here there is more than a tinge, as is clear from 343a3 ἀντὶ τοῦ ἀποκρίνεσθαι.

e8 κατὰ ὅσον ἄρχων: here and at d4 (κατὰ ὅσον ἰατρός), S. uses the language introduced by T. to assert that the physician qua physician (340e1) and the ruler qua ruler (340e8) are infallible. T. had introduced the ruler and the physician as examples of two different τέχναι, and he would be justified in objecting that S. has illegitimately represented medicine and navigation and all other τέχναι as practiced by a "ruler." Illegitimate or not, that has been the whole basis of S.'s argument in this section, and T. failed to object when he was given the opportunity to do so. It is not clear how S. would reconcile this view with the foundational principle of Callipolis, namely τὸ τὰ αὑτοῦ πράττειν (4.433b4), since the very foundations of the ideal city are threatened when the practitioners of other τέχναι change places with those who practice the τέχνη of governing (4.421a–422a, 434a–c).

e10 ἐκεῖνο … ἐκείνωι: referring to τῶι ἀρχομένωι (neuter, like ἀρχομένου, d1), glossed as ὧι ἂν αὐτὸς δημιουργῆι, "that for the benefit of which the expert (αὐτός) practices his craft," e.g. σώματα in the case of the physician.

343a1–344c7: S. as narrator says that it was evident to everyone that he had turned T.'s definition on its head. In response, T. again resorts to abusing S., this time for his alleged obtuseness and naivete. He launches into a lengthy speech in which he berates S. for not recognizing that the reality is the opposite of what S. thinks is the case. The contrast between the two men's views of the world is conveyed in part by their manner of argumentation, S. confining himself to the method of question and answer while T. is more comfortable with the kind of *epideixis* that is characteristic of the set speeches of the sophists. Using the analogy of the herdsman, who is universally acknowledged to practice his craft ultimately for his own or his master's benefit, T. argues that the ruler in the true sense of the word has his eye on his own wellbeing, which T. assumes to consist in being in a position to have more than the next person. His evidence for this is the tyrant, the exemplar of perfect injustice, who is envied and admired by all because he is supposedly what everyone aspires to be, supremely powerful and, therefore, supremely happy. T. concludes by reiterating his definition of justice, satisfied with having proven that, if one acts justly one is merely playing into the hands of someone more powerful than oneself, while by acting unjustly one is acting in one's own self-interest.

343a2 ὁ τοῦ δικαίου λόγος "his definition of justice"; cf. *Tht.* 208b12 τὸν ἀληθέστατον ἐπιστήμης λόγον.

εἰς τὸ ἐναντίον περιειστήκει "had turned into its opposite"; cf. Thuc. 1.120.5 ἐς τὸ ἐναντίον αἰσχρῶς περιέστη (of overturned expectations). Elsewhere, P. expresses the same thing the other way about, "the opposite is the case": τὸ ἐναντίον περιέστηκεν, *Meno* 70c3–4; cf. Thuc. 6.24.2 τὸ ἐναντίον περιέστη αὐτῶι. Justice had not in fact been mentioned in the course of S.'s argument, which attacked T.'s definition indirectly. S. has been arguing since 341c, on the analogy of the practitioners of other τέχναι, that the ruler in the strict sense acts not in his own interest but in the interest of the ruled. If S. has argued correctly, T.'s definition is shown to be invalid, since no action, just or otherwise, can be in the interest of the ruler, who has been agreed to be, like the τέχνη with which he has been identified, in no way deficient.

a6 κορυζῶντα ... ἀπομύττει: P. characterizes T.'s manner of speaking by giving him vocabulary not used by anyone else in his works; see 338d3n. The first verb means literally to have a runny nose (Ar. fr. 322.9 *PCG*, Hippocr. *Airs* 10), but can be used metaphorically for "talking drivel" (Men. *Sam.* 546). The second implies that S. is so immature that he requires someone else to attend to his basic needs; cf. 345b5n.

a6–7 δεόμενον "when you need (to have your nose wiped)."

a7 αὐτῆι: an unusual "ethical" dative, unusual because this type of dative is not commonly found in the third person (Smyth §1486, citing only this passage). The implication is that his nurse, after all her efforts, has given up looking after S. since he (for this force of ὅς γε, see *GP* 141–2) is ineducable and cannot even (οὐδέ) identify "for her" the difference between sheep and shepherd.

πρόβατα ... ποιμένα: the comparison of the political leader to a herdsman is commonplace in Greek thinking, attested frequently in Homer and, before him, in Near Eastern texts (Brock 2013: 43–52). The analogy, however, is not straightforward. The Homeric king, exemplified by Agamemnon, takes very seriously his responsibility for the security of his "flock," but he also uses his position to acquire as much as he can.

Agamemnon's concern for the safety of his men is seen at the beginning of Book Ten of the *Iliad* when he, described by the formula ποιμένα λαῶν, lies awake at night (cf. b6 below), moaning and tearing his hair. At the same time, his status entitles him to expect, even demand, that his authority be tangibly recognized, in the form both of revenues derived from the land he controls and the pick of the booty in war. That is, depending on one's view of what constitutes the ruler in the strictest sense, one can use the analogy of the shepherd to portray the ruler either as benefactor (*Criti.* 109b–c, *Pol.* 275a–b; Xen. *Cyr.* 8.2.14, *Mem.* 3.2.1) or, with T., as unbridled self-aggrandizer (*Tht.* 174d). Surprisingly, despite all S. says in Book One, he makes very little use of the analogy in connection with the philosopher-ruler later in *Republic.* When he does liken the population of Callipolis to a flock that needs protection from predators, he is more concerned to compare the city's Guardians to watchdogs (3.416a, 5.451d), making only passing mention of the fact that they are in service to the shepherds who rule the city (4.440d).

343b3 τῶν δεσποτῶν: unlike metaphorical shepherds, who are rulers in their own right, literal herdsmen often themselves work for the benefit of a king or landowner, like Eumaeus in the *Odyssey*. T., as his application (καὶ δὴ καί) of the analogy shows, is not concerned with the likes of "the worthy swineherd who took the best care of Odysseus' property" (*Od.* 14.3–4).

b4 τοὺς ἐν ταῖς πόλεσιν ἄρχοντας: those who rule in the cities are the true rulers, according to T. (cf. 345e2–3), not ship's captains or physicians, who are themselves ruled by those who hold political power. S. had gotten T. to agree that expert practitioners of any τέχνη are in a sense rulers, but T. returns the discussion to literal rulers since, if the discussion is about the nature of justice, the relationship between, e.g., the cobbler and his shoes is of no relevance.

b5 διανοεῖσθαι πρός "are disposed toward"; for the construction, cf. *Laws* 1.626d1–2, 635c4.

343c1 τοῦτο ὅθεν αὐτοὶ ὠφελήσονται "that from which they themselves will derive benefit," a relative clause (cf. *Gorg.* 517b6–7) rather than an indirect question ("this, namely from where …"). They know whence come their profits.

οὕτω πόρρω: either ironic, "so advanced, so far along," or "so aberrant, so far gone (in your thinking)." No convincing parallel has been adduced in favor of either interpretation; T.'s blunt pretense of treating S. as a simpleton makes the latter seem slightly more likely.

c1–2 περί τε τοῦ δικαίου: for the word order, which is not uncommon (*GP* 518–19), cf. 345e1, 6.485b7–8 περί τε τῶν φιλοτίμων καὶ ἐρωτικῶν. Like other postpositives, τε tends to appear in second position (*CGCG* §60.7).

c3–4 ἀλλότριον ἀγαθὸν τῶι ὄντι: cf. Arist. *EN* 5.1134b5–6 ἀλλότριον εἶναί φασιν ἀγαθὸν τὴν δικαιοσύνην, also 5.1130a3–4. S. had argued that the ruler only does what he does and says what he says for the benefit of another; T. turns this around and says that acting justly is indeed (for the force of τῶι ὄντι here, see Boter 1986: 276) for the benefit of someone else, namely one's superior (and, he adds, it is done at one's own expense). That is, T. is reacting to S. when he says that justice is someone else's advantage, so that it is unlikely that P. wishes to represent this as T.'s true position, as some have held (Kerferd 1947 and 1964, Nicholson 1974). Rather, this is P.'s method of moving the discussion to the question that will only be fully answered in the course of the next nine books, whether justice is conducive to the happiness or the wretchedness of the agent. The claim here that the just is someone else's good has aroused considerable debate among critics, some of whom regard this as another definition of justice, one that is difficult to reconcile with T.'s earlier definition, while some think that P. is portraying T. as someone who has no clear conception of justice and is merely spouting provocative statements with no reasoned justification behind them; for a survey of views, see Boter 1986, with more recent bibliography in Barney 2017. What T. is trying to explain, and what S. simply cannot accept, is that just actions all have in common that they are performed for the benefit of someone more powerful than the agent; that they are performed for someone else's good is therefore a corollary of his original definition, which he will repeat once again at the end of his speech; see also 347e1–2n.

c4 κρείττονός τε καὶ ἄρχοντος: the two terms are used synonymously (332c5n.), as are, in the following clause, πειθομένου τε καὶ ὑπηρετοῦντος (it is perhaps relevant that the literal meaning of the latter has to do with rowing, given the earlier metaphor of the ship's captain as ruler). That is, T. is not focused exclusively on the political ruler, but wishes his definition to be applicable in all interpersonal relationships, as will be clear from his examples below.

c5 ἡ δὲ ἀδικία τὸ ἐναντίον: the sense in which injustice is the opposite, or rather the converse, of justice is spelled out in what follows and, more economically, in Adeimantus' summary of T.'s position in Book Two: "the just is what is good for someone else, advantageous for the stronger, while the unjust is advantageous and profitable for oneself, but disadvantageous for the weaker" (367c3–5).

c6 ἄρχει: the literal subject is injustice. As earlier a τέχνη and its practitioner had been identified (341d8n.), so here injustice and the person who engages in unjust acts (= ἐκεῖνος in the next line) are spoken of indifferently as the master of "the truly naive, i.e., the just." Similarly, tyranny will be spoken of as carrying out the actions of the man who masters the tyrant's craft (344a5–6).

c6–d1 ποιοῦσιν … ποιοῦσιν: see 341a3n.

c7 εὐδαίμονα: T. clearly thinks that one's wellbeing consists in little more than πλέον ἔχειν (d5) and having power over the weaker, whose subservience conduces to one's happiness. P. seems to have this passage in mind when in *Theaetetus* he has S. describe the naivete of the philosopher who, when he hears an encomium of a tyrant or king, thinks a herdsman is being glorified (εὐδαιμονιζόμενον, 174d6) for his success in exploiting his livestock. The view of S., as reflected in Xenophon (*Cyr.* 8.2.14, *Mem.* 3.2.1) as well as in P., is that it is the wellbeing of the flock that is the prime concern of both the metaphorical and the literal herdsman. It is thus with pointed irony that P. chooses to make T. the person who first introduces εὐδαιμονία here in *Republic*, a concept that is fundamental to Platonic and Socratic ethics. Book One ends with S. saying that he must first find out what justice is before he can know whether the just person is εὐδαίμων or not, and at the conclusion of Book Ten he recounts the Myth of Er, which will show that by choosing the just life one becomes εὐδαιμονέστατος (619b1).

343d2 εὐηθέστατε: T. intends this as a term of abuse (to be contrasted with S.'s more subtle method of expressing superiority: 339e4). But, given his identification of εὐήθεια with justice (348d1, 349b3), he is unknowingly confirming the characterization of S. conveyed in the last word of *Phaedo* as the most just person of his time.

d3–5 πανταχοῦ … οὐδαμοῦ: emphatically reaffirming the universality of his definition (339a3n.).

d3–4 ἐν τοῖς πρὸς ἀλλήλους συμβολαίοις: like Polemarchus (333a13), T. gives commercial contracts (4.425c10–11) as an example of the arena in which an individual's propensity to act justly may be observed, or exploited. Similarly, Callicles mentions business contracts as the kind of interaction in which the philosopher's lack of practical experience can expose him to being taken advantage of (*Gorg.* 484d–e).

d6 ἐν τοῖς πρὸς τὴν πόλιν: that is, in civic affairs (no specific noun is to be supplied with τοῖς) as opposed to the private dealings that he has just mentioned. For the restriction of the word συμβόλαιον to private obligations, see Knopf 2005: 103–4.

d7 εἰσφοραί: the *eisphora* was an ad hoc levy by the Athenian state to finance occasional, as opposed to regularly recurring, expenditures, often for the military. Only the relatively wealthy were subject to this form of taxation, the amount of the assessment being based on the value of an individual's assets. If one were unscrupulous and lacked civic-mindedness one might be tempted to find ways of concealing or minimizing the value of those assets; see Christ 1990. In this way the unjust citizen could, and according to T. always would, pay less in taxes than the just citizen on the basis of equal levels of wealth (ἀπὸ τῶν ἴσων).

343e1 λήψεις: just as modern governments use private contractors to provide certain public services, so the Athenian state let contracts to private citizens for such purposes as tax farming and supplying slaves to work the silver mines at Laurium (Xen. *Vect.* 4.14; Fawcett 2016: 174–6). As is the case today, one could become rich by doing business with the government, but the just man merely breaks even (οὐδὲν κερδαίνει = "makes no profit"). Not only citizens, but metics like Cephalus and Polemarchus could act as government contractors (Xen. *Vect.* 4.12), and presumably the state of Athens was a major customer for the armor that their factory mass-produced (Lysias 12.8, 19).

καί "also" or "even" (*GP* 108; *Phdr.* 231d2, *Symp.* 188b3). Holding public office in Athens carried with it no remuneration beyond a modest daily allowance, but it was seen as an opportunity for misappropriating funds from the treasury (ἐκ τοῦ δημοσίου) that were entrusted to certain higher-level magistrates, who therefore were required to submit to an accounting at the end of their term of office. According to Diodorus Siculus (*Bibl.* 12.38.3–4), Alcibiades advised Pericles on how to find a way of avoiding giving an accounting of the funds to which he had access.

e2 ὅταν ἀρχήν τινα ἄρχηι ἑκάτερος "whenever each holds some public office" (LSJ ἀρχή A.II.3). T. is not here referring to "ruling" the state. In the *Apology*, S. says that he never held any office in the state other than serving as one of the 500 members of the Boule: ἄλλην μὲν ἀρχὴν οὐδεμίαν πώποτε ἦρξα ἐν τῆι πόλει, ἐβούλευσα δέ (32a9–b1).

ὑπάρχει: there is a shift of construction, the verb first having as its subject ζημία (and possibly τὰ οἰκεῖα) then being used impersonally with ὠφελεῖσθαι. A similar shift happens at 7.530b1 (ἄτοπον; see Adam *ad loc.*) and *Chrm.* 153b9 (ἤγγελται).

e3 ζημία: magistrates could be prosecuted for taking bribes, for embezzlement or even for actions that might be construed as minor inadvertencies (Dem. 19.293).

τά γε οἰκεῖα: it is unclear whether this is to be taken as subject of ἔχειν, in which case a new subject must be supplied for ὠφελεῖσθαι and ἀπεχθέσθαι, or as an accusative of respect (*CGCG* §30.14), with the just man as subject. At any rate, the word order and the "limitative" particle (*GP* 140–1) emphasize the damage the just man does to his personal affairs, even if his public service does not put him in jeopardy. In *Laches,* Lysimachus, the son of Aristeides the Just, laments that his father and the father of his companion Melesias neglected their upbringing because they devoted so much of their time and effort to public service (179c–d). T., however, like

Cephalus (330b), seems more concerned about efforts directed at making money than about the education of one's sons.

μοχθηροτέρως: this ending for the comparative is regular when the adverb is used with ἔχειν = "be in a certain condition"; e.g. 7.527d2, *Clit.* 406a12, *Euthd.* 285a2, *Phdr.* 278d5, Thuc. 4.71.2.

e4 μηδέν: the usual negative with the infinitive following ὑπάρχει: 9.587a4, *Ion* 542b3–4, Soph. *El.* 1340.

δίκαιον: masculine, agreeing with the subject of ὠφελεῖσθαι.

e5 πρὸς δὲ τούτοις ἀπεχθέσθαι: not only does the just man fail to enrich himself, he incurs in addition (πρὸς τούτοις) the animosity of his friends and family for failing to enrich them. Callicles, after reproving S. for his naivete (see 337d6n.), derides justice as a pitiful thing, since it cannot enable a man in power to do more for his friends than for his enemies (*Gorg.* 492c) which, as we have seen (332a9–10n.), is what was expected of any self-respecting Greek. Themistocles, the rival of Aristeides the Just, is supposed to have aspired never to hold a position of power unless it enabled him to do more for his friends than for others (Plut. *Arist.* 2.5).

e7 ὅνπερ νυνδὴ ἔλεγον: the ruler in the truest sense of the word (343b4; cf. 340e8, 341b7), soon to be identified with the tyrant, the supreme example of "the superior" whose advantage is served by those who act justly.

344a1 τὸν μεγάλα δυνάμενον πλεονεκτεῖν "the man capable of exercising tremendous superiority," a striking expression, with μεγάλα (adverbial accusative with πλεονεκτεῖν; *CGCG* §30.18) calling attention to itself both by its dislocation and its plural number. Word order makes it appear that it is attributive to δυνάμενον, but "the very powerful man" is regularly expressed with μέγα (many examples in S.'s discussions with Polus and Callicles, *Gorg.* 466e–470a and 510d–513b) and does not govern an infinitive.

a2 τὸ δίκαιον "justice," the definition of which (as τὸ τοῦ κρείττονος συμφέρον) T. has been defending since 338c2. If P. had intended us to understand εἶναι, "to be just," he would have written τὸ ἄδικον (as conjectured by Bremi *apud* Fäsi 1819: 287) in the previous clause.

a3 τὴν τελεωτάτην ἀδικίαν: this expression will be repeated in Book Two (361a6) when Glaucon insists that S. must assume the perfectly unjust person to be capable of perfect injustice. Glaucon goes beyond T., however, in allowing that person the greatest reputation for justice; for his part, T. is content to call the behavior of the perfectly unjust person perfectly unjust.

a4 εὐδαιμονέστατον: if being unjust conduces to one's wellbeing (343c7), it is reasonable to assume that perfect injustice conduces to perfect wellbeing.

a5 ἀδικῆσαι οὐκ ἂν ἐθέλοντας: T. is remarkably reticent about the motives of those who "would be unwilling to act unjustly." Unlike Callicles, who has a theory to account for the behavior of the weak vis-à-vis the strong (*Gorg.* 483b–c), T. seems uninterested in the reason some people choose to act justly, merely dismissing them as simpleminded (343c6).

a5–6 τυραννίς: for the traditional association between the tyrant, who alone is free to do as he pleases, and εὐδαιμονία, see Pind. *Pyth.* 3.84–6, Soph. *Ant.* 506–7, Eur. *Alc.* 653–4 and in particular *Phoen.* 549 τὴν τυραννίδ', ἀδικίαν εὐδαίμονα. The assumption that the tyrant's limitless power leads to happiness, and that no one would decline an opportunity to secure such power, lies behind the myth Glaucon tells in Book Two about the ring of Gyges' ancestor. The universal appeal, illustrated by these passages and others extolling the happiness of the Persian king (Dodds on *Gorg.* 470e4), made the threat of tyranny a perceived danger in democratic Athens, and curses were pronounced at meetings of the Boule directed at anyone conspiring to introduce tyranny into the city (see Austin and Olson on Ar. *Thesm.* 335–9). A very different picture of the tyrannical man emerges from S.'s account at the beginning of Book Nine and in the Myth of Er in Book Ten. T. introduces the tyrant here, as he had introduced the various forms of governmental authority at 338d, as an example – indeed the most compelling example – of what he means by ὁ κρείττων. His earlier examples dealt with private transactions and small-scale interactions with the state to illustrate the universality of his definition of justice; to open the eyes of S., who seems to be having difficulty understanding that definition, T. presents him with a vision of pure, unadulterated injustice.

a6 καὶ λάθραι καὶ βίαι: compare the hypothetical master of injustice described by Glaucon (a3n.), who is to escape detection for his crimes (λανθανέτω, 2.361a3) but, when necessary, will resort to using violence (βιάσασθαι, 361b4). Earlier, at 341a8–b1, T. had declared himself impervious to any stealth or coercion on the part of S.

344b1 καὶ ἱερὰ καὶ ὅσια: an almost formulaic expression (e.g. Antiphon 5.62, Isaeus 9.13, Isocr. 7.66, Thuc. 2.52.3), used to refer to the totality of what the citizens of the democratic polis regard as "theirs," and thus marking their communal identity, embracing the (often overlapping) realms of the sacred, τὰ ἱερά, and the civic, τὰ ὅσια (LSJ A.I.2); see Connor 1988.

καὶ ἴδια καὶ δημόσια: also formulaic (e.g. Andoc. 1.9, Isaeus 7.30, Isocr. 17.54, Thuc. 1.90.3). Such "polar expressions" (333d4n.) are rhetorically impressive ways of saying "everything," or of amplifying "everything": *Apol.* 30b4 ἅπαντα καὶ ἰδίαι καὶ δημοσίαι.

b1–5 ὧν ἐπὶ ἑκάστωι μέρει ... καλοῦνται: the meaning is clear – those who are caught committing injustice piecemeal are reviled and punished for doing so – but we must wait for clarification of the construction of the prepositional phrase, which is placed early to mark the contrast with συλλήβδην; it should be construed with ζημιοῦταί τε καὶ ὀνείδη ἔχει: "(he is punished and reviled) for each category (?) of these (infractions)"; cf. Xen. *Mem.* 2.2.3 αἱ πόλεις ἐπὶ τοῖς μεγίστοις ἀδικήμασι ζημίαν θάνατον πεποιήκασιν and Arist. *Rhet.* 1.1374a21–2 τὰ … ἀρετῆς καὶ κακίας, ἐπὶ οἷς ὀνείδη καὶ ἔπαινοι καὶ ἀτιμίαι. T. sees the tyrant as having mastered the entire field of injustice (τὴν ὅλην ἀδικίαν, c2), whereas petty criminals are specialists in only isolated departments, not to mention the fact that they are by definition subject to being made miserable by someone more unjust (i.e. κρείττων) than themselves.

b3–4 ἱερόσυλοι … κλέπται: similar lists of crimes or wrongdoers are found at 9.575b7–8, *Gorg.* 508d6–e4, Ar. *Thesm.* 817–18. The absence of articles with the nouns marks them as predicative (*CGCG* §28.9).

b3 ἀνδραποδισταί "kidnappers" or "traffickers in living human beings"; ἀνδράποδα are persons taken into slavery by violence at the hands (literally "feet") of ἄνδρες (Gaca 2011), to be sold as chattel or redeemed for ransom. As a boy, S.'s companion Phaedo was taken in the defeat of his native Elis and sold into prostitution, eventually to be ransomed by members of S.'s circle (D.L. 2.105).

b4–5 τῶν τοιούτων κακουργημάτων: the genitive is usually construed as depending on μέρη, following the scholiast, who says that the normal word order would be κατὰ μέρη τῶν τ. κ. ἀδικοῦντες (for this meaning of the scholiast's τὸ ἑξῆς οὕτως, see Dickey 2007: 120). But κατὰ μέρη is adverbial and the genitive is likely partitive, with ἀδικοῦντες; compare 4.445d10–e1 κινήσειεν ἂν τῶν ἀξίων λόγου νόμων. If so, the meaning is something like "(those who act unjustly piecemeal by committing) some offenses of this nature"; cf. *Gorg.* 514a6 πράξοντες τῶν πολιτικῶν πραγμάτων.

b5–6 πρὸς τοῖς τῶν πολιτῶν χρήμασιν "in addition to (appropriating) the property of the citizens."

b6 καὶ αὐτοὺς ἀνδραποδισάμενος δουλώσηται: trafficking in slaves or abducting citizens of one city to be sold in another was considered to be the occupation of disreputable individuals; enslaving one's own fellow citizens was the mark of a tyrant or the king of Persia, whom Polus regards as the standard by which εὐδαιμονία is to be judged (*Gorg.* 470e4–5).

344c2–3 οὐ γὰρ … τὴν ἀδικίαν: one of the rare occasions on which T. ascribes a motive to those who act justly. He does not, however, tell us what motivates their just actions, only what prompts their spoken disapproval of others' unjust actions. Throughout this passage, T. has been focused on the language conventionally used to describe people and their actions (ὀνείδη, καλοῦνται, ὀνομάτων, κέκληνται, ὀνειδίζουσιν). He seems more concerned to explain why people say what they say than why they do what they do (a5n.), perhaps because he thinks people's motives for what they do are self-evident.

c4 ἐλευθεριώτερον: in Book Eight S. will attribute the rise of tyranny to the insatiable thirst for freedom found in the democratic polis (562b–c).

c6–7 τὸ δὲ ἄδικον ἑαυτῶι λυσιτελοῦν τε καὶ συμφέρον: T. is giving a description of injustice, not defining it, for which we would expect <τὸ> ἑαυτῶι (proposed by Van Herwerden 1883: 334), but the MS reading is confirmed by Adeimantus' restatement in Book Two, quoted in 343c5n. On its surface, this last statement by T. appears paradoxical and even self-contradictory, since both justice and its opposite are described as profitable and advantageous. But paradox and seeming paradox are among the devices cultivated by the sophists (Gagarin 2002: 16–18) and, in any event, T. has been careful to specify that he is describing complete injustice (ἱκανῶς γιγνομένη), which can only be practiced by the perfectly unjust man. Therefore, those actions to which we commonly attach the label "just" are performed by the weaker for the benefit of the stronger (ὁ κρείττων), and those stigmatized as "unjust" are in fact the actions of the stronger, carried out to his own (ἑαυτῶι) advantage and profit.

344d1–347a5: The disagreement between S. and T. is not over which actions are "just" and which "unjust." Both men would agree that the word "just" is regularly used to refer to those actions that Cephalus and Polemarchus spoke of as just, namely telling the truth and returning what one has borrowed. The fundamental difference between the two is in their view of what actions one *ought* to engage in. T. has not once spoken in deontological terms (White 1995: 321–2), confining himself to explaining what (he thinks) we mean when we speak of "the just" and "the unjust," whereas for S. the question most urgently in need of an answer is how one should one live one's life (352d6–7, *Apol.* 38a1–6, *Cri.* 48b5, *Gorg.* 500c1–4). He fastens upon T.'s last statement, that injustice is profitable (λυσιτελοῦν) for the unjust person, and seeks to convince him, as he had tried to do earlier, that profit to the agent comes from the practice of a separate τέχνη, that of money-making, not from the arts of ruling or healing or making shoes, all of which are practiced for the benefit of someone or something other than the agent. He adds that, this being the case, the ruler in the strict sense must be induced to rule either by the lure of payment or the threat of suffering harm.

344d1 ἐν νῶι εἶχεν ἀπιέναι: having made a sensational entry into the conversation, T. hopes to make an equally dramatic exit. But P. sees to it that he simply fades from view in the subsequent books.

d1–2 ὥσπερ βαλανεὺς ἡμῶν καταντλήσας: comparing verbiage to rushing water is among the most common of metaphors (e.g. *Tim.* 75e3–4 τὸ δὲ λόγων νᾶμα ἔξω ῥέον). Usually, however, the force of the metaphor lies in the unremitting character of the stream of words, as at Aesch. *Sept.* 557 (of Parthenopaeus) and Ar. *Peace* 757 = *Wasps* 1034 (both of Cleon). Here, T. is said to exhaust his supply all at once, like a bath attendant emptying a bucket of water over the head of a kneeling customer (for the posture, see the various copies of the statue of the crouching Aphrodite attributed to Doidalsas, or the athlete on the red-figure kylix attributed to the Codrus Painter in the British Museum, inv. no. 1869,0205.3). The terminology is not intended to be flattering to T. βαλανεύς, a word occurring only here in P., names a worker in a rather disreputable profession: bath attendants are paired with prostitutes as those with whom the humiliated Paphlagon (i.e. Cleon) is condemned to engage in screaming-matches (Ar. *Knights* 1403; Diggle on Theophr. *Char.* 9.7). P. elsewhere uses καταντλεῖν of pouring scorn on something (7.536b6) and in disparaging reference to the besotted Hippothales' recitations of atrocious poems and encomia in honor of Lysis (*Lys.* 204d5; cf. Ar. *Wasps* 483).

d2 ἀθρόον καὶ πολύν "all at once and in profusion." For the quasi-adverbial force of adjectives like ἀθρόος and πολύς when they appear in predicate position (*CGCG* §28.12), see KG I 275. S. elsewhere contrasts the philosopher's leisurely conversational style with the frenzied urgency of the pleader in the lawcourt who has one eye on the device that limited his time to speak (*Tht.* 172 d–e). The device used in Athenian courtrooms was the *klepsydra*, a timer consisting of a bowl of water pierced at the bottom to allow its contents to flow out at a given rate (Biles and Olson on Ar. *Wasps* 92–3).

d3 οὐ μὴν εἴασάν γε: as earlier the assembled company prevented T. from breaking into the conversation (336b), so here they will not allow him to depart. In *Protagoras* it is S. who announces his intention to abandon the discussion, but Callias restrains him and insists that he remain (335d2).

d4 τῶν εἰρημένων λόγον "a discussion of what has been said," object of both ὑπομεῖναι ("put up with," *CGL* 11) and παρασχεῖν. Virtually all translators treat λόγον παρασχεῖν as a synonym of λόγον δοῦναι, "give an account," for which there are no parallels; at Ar. *Peace* 148 the phrase means "supply the story line" for a tragedy, and at Thuc. 2.101.4 "provide a topic of conversation." Rather, the two verbs here express the give-and-take of the conversation that, it is hoped, will ensue, as καὶ λέγειν καὶ ἀκούειν does at *Symp.* 173b8.

d4–5 καὶ δὴ ἔγωγε καὶ αὐτός: the combination καὶ δὴ καί, "and in particular" (nearly 200 times in P.; *GP* 255–7), is only very rarely interrupted (*Apol.* 21a4 ποτε, *Soph.* 251c5 τι); the intrusion here of ἐγώ, itself emphasized through the addition of γε and accompanied by αὐτός, marks the unusual eagerness on the part of S. that the discussion continue.

d5 Ὦ δαιμόνιε Θρασύμαχε: the vocative δαιμόνιε is frequent in P. and is often used with little difference in meaning from that of other "friendship terms" (Dickey 1996: 141–2, 280). But when it accompanies the addressee's name it seems to signal a particularly urgent appeal to a person behaving unreasonably in the opinion of the speaker, as when Crito begs S. to escape from prison and save his life (*Cri.* 44b6).

d6 ἐμβαλών: given the use of this verb at *Prot.* 342e2 (see 336b5n.) and *Tht.* 165d7, it seems that P. intends us to understand this as a metaphor from the discharge of a missile, a common image used for speech (Garvie on Aesch. *Choe.* 1033). Elsewhere, expressions referring to what would later be called a "Parthian shot," derived from the practice of those who could shoot arrows from horseback while retreating (Xen. *Anab.* 3.3.10), use the uncompounded βαλών: *Symp.* 189b8, Eur. *Alc.* 680, Plut. *Mor.* 548b, *Suda* β 87.

πρὶν διδάξαι ἱκανῶς ἢ μαθεῖν: earlier, T. had criticized S. for going around learning from others and refusing to teach (338b1–3); here S. chides T. for going off without doing either.

344e1–2 ἢ σμικρὸν οἴει ... ἀλλὰ οὐ: cf. *Lach.* 185a3–4, where S. asks Melesias whether he and Lysimachus think they are running a risk over some trivial matter (ἢ περὶ σμικροῦ οἴεσθε) and not (ἀλλὰ οὐ; *GP* 1–2) about what is of greatest importance, the education of their sons.

e1 σμικρόν: in modern texts of P. forms with this spelling outnumber those in μικρ- 20:1. (In tragedy, where the spelling can in some cases be confirmed by the meter, the ratio is 3:1; in Aristophanes, by contrast, μικρ- is more than twice as frequent as σμικρ-.) The spelling in σμικρ- is original, with μικρ- perhaps arising in colloquial speech under the influence of its antonyms μακρός and μέγας; similarly, in popular American English "covert" has come to rhyme with "overt" and in late Latin *greuis* (for *grauis*) was influenced by the sound of *leuis.*

e1–2 διορίζεσθαι "determine." Aristotle opens Book Seven of *Politics* by saying that, before a decision can be reached regarding the best form of government, "it is necessary first to determine (διορίσασθαι) what way of life is most worthy of being chosen," 1323a15–16.

e3 λυσιτελεστάτην: T. had earlier forbidden S. to define justice as τὸ λυσιτελοῦν (336d1–2). We have since learned that, for T., it is precisely injustice that λυσιτελεῖ. S., however, will not be satisfied until he has proven that justice is beneficial and profitable for the agent (354b–c), which he will finally accomplish to his own satisfaction and that of Glaucon and Adeimantus only at the end of Book Nine.

e4 Ἐγὼ γὰρ ... ἄλλως ἔχειν; T. answers S.'s question with a γάρ-question conveying his astonishment (*GP* 78–9) that S. might consider the possibility that he thinks otherwise, *sc.* than that this is a matter of utmost importance. At the same time, his ἄλλως ἔχειν echoes ἄλλως ἔχει e1, suggesting that what he has been saying all along is both consistent and sincere.

e5 Ἔοικας ... ἤτοι "You seem (to think otherwise), or else." This meaning of ἤτοι is uncommon (*GP* 553), but is seen also at 3.400c4 and 4.433a3. The force of τοι ("you know") is to bring home to T. the shame that he ought to feel if the latter is the case, namely that he does not care whether withholding the fruits of his wisdom will affect his companions' quality of life.

345a1 ἐνδείξασθαι: S. appeals to T.'s ego by presenting this as an opportunity for him to show off his superior intelligence. Similarly, he suggests that Prodicus and Hippias be brought into his conversation with Protagoras, because he supposed that the great sophist wished to give a display and flatter himself (ἐνδείξασθαι καὶ καλλωπίσασθαι, *Prot.* 317c7) that S. and Hippocrates had come to see him rather than the others.

a1–2 οὔ τοι κακῶς σοι κείσεται ... εὐεργετήσῃς: the language is that of the conferral of benefits among aristocrats and the consequent inventory of gratitude that is expected to be maintained. Compare the letter of Xerxes to Pausanias quoted at Thuc. 1.129.3, κείσεταί σοι εὐεργεσία ἐν τῶι ἡμετέρωι οἴκωι ἐς αἰεὶ ἀνάγραπτος; cf. also *Gorg.* 506c2–3 εὐεργέτης παρὰ ἐμοὶ ἀναγεγράψηι, Hdt. 8.85.3 εὐεργέτης βασιλέος ἀνεγράφη, Soph. *OC* 1519 κείσεται, Thuc. 1.128.4 εὐεργεσίαν ... ἐς βασιλέα κατέθετο. Here the gratitude is multiplied by the number (τοσούσδε) of beneficiaries. S.'s appeal is ironic in the extreme, since he is calling upon T. to benefit his audience by explaining to them why he thinks benefiting others is something done only by simpletons.

a3 τό γε ἐμόν: word order, and the fact that ἐγώ has already been prominently expressed, suggests that this is the object of λέγω, "I am expressing my own view, namely that ..." (with γε conveying, "regardless of what others may think": *GP* 140–1), rather than adverbial, "for my part," for which cf. e.g. *Prot.* 338c5–6 ἐπεὶ τό γε ἐμὸν οὐδέν μοι διαφέρει.

a4–5 πράττειν ἃ βούλεται: governed by both ἐᾶι and μὴ διακωλύηι. The literal subject is ἀδικία, but the identification of abstractions with their human representatives has been seen before; see 341d8, 343c6nn.

a5 ἔστω μὲν ἄδικος "let there be an unjust man."

a6 ἢ τῶι λανθάνειν ἢ τῶι διαμάχεσθαι: cf. 344a6 καὶ λάθραι καὶ βίαι, in T.'s description of the perfectly unjust tyrant.

πείθεις: the principal MSS read πείθει, the subject of which must be ἀδικία or τις or the hypothetical unjust man. But apart from the difficulty of choosing among those confusing options, no one but T. is currently engaged – the verb is present indicative – in trying to persuade S.

345b1 κερδαλεώτερον "a more profitable thing," predicative to ἀδικίαν as at a4.

b4–5 πείσω … ποιήσω: deliberative subjunctives (*CGCG* §34.8), like ἐνθῶ.

b5 φέρων "just like that," a colloquialism (Collard 2018: 125); cf. *Hp.Ma.* 282e5.

ἐνθῶ: the image is of masticating food and putting it in a baby's mouth; cf. the Sausage-Seller in Ar. *Knights* (716–18) accusing Paphlagon of cheating the people, the way nurses (τίτθαι) do, putting only a small amount in (ὀλίγον ἐντιθεῖς) Demos' mouth while swallowing three times as much himself. (For the corresponding noun ἔνθεσις, "mouthful," see Ar. *Knights* 404, Antiphanes fr. 202.12 *PCG*; LSJ A.II.1.) T. had earlier asked S. if he has a nurse (343a3); here he continues his condescending treatment of S. with the suggestion that he has to "spoon-feed" his dull-witted pupil. In Book Seven (518b–c) S. contrasts the proper method of education with that professed by some – undoubtedly intended as a reference to the sophists – which consists in inserting (ἐντιθέναι) understanding into the souls of those who lack it. For the mature P. all education is re-education, a notion that is fully developed in *Meno*, *Phaedo* and *Phaedrus* in terms of "recollection," that is, the soul's reacquaintance with the Forms, to which the immortal soul had been previously exposed (Ferejohn 2006).

b6 πρῶτον μέν: there is nothing in what follows with which this marks a contrast, giving it almost the force of "above all," with the implication that if T. does not observe the first requirement, namely that he maintain a consistent position, further discussion is fruitless. By charging T. with inconsistency, and even suggesting that he has engaged in deception to conceal his sophistry, S. is attacking him at what T. considers to be his strong point, since he has consistently maintained that his definition of justice is unchanged (341a2–3, 344c5).

b7 μὴ ἐξαπάτα: the force of the present imperative, as opposed to the aorist subjunctive, is to request the cessation of an ongoing action, as opposed to making a preemptive prohibition (e.g. 338a3; *CGCG* §38.30).

345c1 τὰ ἔμπροσθεν: S. reminds T. that he had earlier agreed that the physician in the strict sense pursues the craft of healing the sick rather than that of enriching himself (341c, 342d), and this led to the generalization that the practitioners in the strict sense of all crafts are concerned not with what is advantageous to themselves but with what is good for the product of their craft (342e). S. now accuses T. of abandoning that principle in the case of the shepherd, whom T. himself had introduced as the analogue of the political ruler, who cares for his flock only for the ulterior purpose of benefiting himself or his master.

c2–3 τὸν ὡς ἀληθῶς ἰατρὸν … ἀκριβῶς φυλάξαι "when you were defining the genuine physician at the beginning, you thought that you were under no further obligation to adhere strictly to the genuine shepherd later on." This sentence explains the deception that S. thinks T. is trying to carry out. The tense of ὁριζόμενος, making it contemporaneous with ᾤου, shows that S. is claiming that even at the time when T. was insisting on precision in the case of the physician he felt no need to maintain consistency when it came to the herdsman. But the precision that T. had insisted on (and which he unfairly attributed to S.: 340e2–3) had to do with defining the genuine craftsman strictly as someone who practices the craft flawlessly. As T. explained to S., the craft of the genuine ruler entails seeing unerringly to what is in the best interest of the ruler (340e8–341a2).

c3 οὐκέτι: for the non-temporal meaning that the word bears here (despite the presence of πρῶτον and ὕστερον), see Wilson 1987.

πιαίνειν: see the app. crit. The rarity of the verb, which occurs only here and *Laws* 7.807a5 in P., caused it to be corrupted in one MS and replaced by a gloss (349b5n.) in another.

c4–5 οὐ πρὸς τὸ … ἀλλά: S. may be forgiven for presenting this as an either/or situation. He is responding to T.'s overstated assertion (343b1–3) that it is naive to think that herdsmen care for and fatten their flocks "with a view to anything other than (πρὸς ἄλλο τι βλέποντας ἤ) their own or their masters' benefit." But there is a reason people care for and fatten pigs and sheep rather than, say, mice (which would involve protecting them from owls, ferrets and domestic cats and feeding them the grain that has been harvested). It is precisely that reason – the obvious fact that pigs and sheep can be exploited to benefit their human keepers – that caused the Muses to address Hesiod and his fellow shepherds as "simply bellies" (*Theog.* 26) and was behind T.'s use of the herdsman to illustrate what he believes to be the motivation of the political ruler, who chooses to govern men rather than mice.

345d1 χρηματιστὴν ἀλλὰ οὐ ποιμένα: S.'s argument is that, qua herdsman (κατὰ ὅσον ποιμήν ἐστιν), the shepherd does not care for his flock in the manner of someone invited to dinner and anticipating a fine feast or of a merchant intending to sell his livestock for cash. But the shepherd's craft does not involve doing something distinct from what earns him his living (Garland 1976: 12–13). Keeping the flock safe from predators and providing abundant pasturage are the very activities that earn money for the herdsman (or lose money if they fail to be carried out or are carried out negligently).

d2 ἐπὶ ᾧι τέτακται: the "antecedent" of the relative pronoun is τούτωι in the following clause. The position of the prepositional phrase is determined by the desire to emphasize the contrast between "that over which the herdsman's art is set" (the flock) and the art itself, as embodied in the practitioner (the herdsman).

d3–4 ἐκπεπόρισται: middle, in contrast to active ἐκποριεῖ; the herdsman's art "has adequately provided for itself" that which is peculiarly its own (τὰ αὑτῆς, placed initially to maximize the contrast with the good of that ἐπὶ ὧι τέτακται) so as to be the best. S. is reminding T. that he had agreed (342a–b) that every τέχνη, as long as it is entirely that which it is, is concerned solely with providing what is advantageous to the object of the τέχνη. S.'s argument, however, has repeatedly relied on his identification, when it was convenient, of the art and its practitioner, but while the art "has adequately provided for itself" simply by being that which it is, the same cannot be said of the practitioner, who is of necessity a human being and not an abstraction.

d5 ὤιμην ἔγωγε νυνδή: at 342e7–11.

345e1 τῶι ἀρχομένωι τε καὶ θεραπευομένωι: by treating the two words as synonyms (332c5n.), S. is assuming that he has been successful in proving that the object of every τέχνη is, like the physician's patient who was T.'s initial example (340d), the sole beneficiary of the ministrations of the τέχνη, seen as a form of "rule" over its object (342c7–8). Suspecting that T. has not yet been thoroughly convinced, and perhaps himself not entirely confident of the rigor of his argument, S. approaches the question from a new direction, making the further argument that the practitioners of every form of rule (that is, of every τέχνη) require payment over and above what is involved in the practice of the τέχνη.

e2–3 τοὺς ὡς ἀληθῶς ἄρχοντας: echoing T.'s claim (343b4) that those who rule in the cities are the genuine rulers, as opposed to physicians and ships' captains, who are merely rulers in an extended sense.

e3–4 οἴει . . . ἀλλὰ εὖ οἶδα: cf. 341a6–8. T.'s self-confidence is undiminished.

e5 τὰς ἄλλας ἀρχάς: i.e. the other τέχναι. S. is relying on T.'s reluctant agreement to the proposition that the τέχναι "rule" that of which they are τέχναι (342c). The accusative is a "cognate" accusative (*CGCG* §30.12) with ἄρχειν; cf. 343e2n. The phrase appears initially, in "topic" position (*CGCG* §60.25–30).

e6 οὐδεὶς ἐθέλει . . . ἑκών: P. uses this seemingly redundant expression in situations where what is embraced "willingly" (or, more commonly, is not embraced) is something unpleasant, like the lie in the soul (2.382a8), a hangover (*Symp.* 176d2) or death (*Phd.* 68a5). Thus S. portrays rule, which T. thinks is the object of everyone's desires, as something undertaken only under duress.

e6–346a1 ὡς οὐχὶ αὐτοῖσιν ὠφελίαν ἐσομένην: the accusative absolute construction is commonly found with impersonal verbs (*CGCG* §52.33) but, when it is introduced by ὡς, "on the grounds that," other verbs can be used as well (*SMT* §853). Here, ὠφελίαν ἐσομένην is equivalent in meaning to an impersonal λυσιτελῆσον. For the form of αὐτοῖσιν, see 330b6n.

346a2–3 τούτωι ἑτέραν εἶναι, τῶι ἑτέραν τὴν δύναμιν ἔχειν "(each of the τέχναι) is distinct in this respect (Smyth §1516), namely that the capability that it has is distinct (see *CGCG* §28.12 for the force of the predicate position)." S. defines δύναμις in Book Five (477c–d) in terms both of what it does and on what it operates, ἐπὶ ὧι τε ἔστι καὶ ὃ ἀπεργάζεται.

a3–4 μὴ παρὰ δόξαν ἀποκρίνου: the following clause implies that the continuation of the discussion depends on T.'s giving an answer that is not contrary to his genuine belief; cf. 349a4–5, 350e5, *Cri.* 49c11–d2, *Gorg.* 500b5–7, *Prot.* 331c4–d1. It is not clear why this "sincere assent requirement" (for which, see Beversluis 2000: 37–58) is invoked on some occasions and waived on others (e.g. 349a8–b1, *Prot.* 333c5–7). In any event, T. will later admit (351c5) that he is responding as he does to humor S., and in Book Two Glaucon and Adeimantus will try to make the best possible case in support of T.'s position, which they explicitly reject.

346b1 μισθωτική: the word, and the synonymous μισθαρνητική, b9 (for both, see Ammann 1953: 128–9), which are almost certainly coinages of P.'s, are not attested prior to their appearance here, presumably because no one other than P. thought to recognize the existence of a distinct craft of procuring wages (Beversluis 2000: 234–5). S. is careful to distinguish the δύναμις and ὠφελία of each of the τέχναι, so that the physician is practicing ἰατρική, and only ἰατρική, when curing patients, but practicing μισθαρνητική when collecting payment for services rendered. But S. is forgetting, or hoping that T. has forgotten, that they have just agreed that the benefit of every τέχνη accrues not to the practitioner of the τέχνη but to its object. This can only mean, in the case of μισθαρνητική, that the benefit accruing to the wages procured is that they be as large as possible. Significantly, S. does not stop to wait for an answer. It is hard to believe that P. takes this argument seriously.

αὕτη: *sc.* τὸ μισθὸν παρέχεσθαι, agreeing in gender with δύναμις (*CGCG* §27.9).

b3 ὥσπερ ὑπέθου: at 341c–d, where T. agreed that the crafts of the genuine physician and the genuine ship's captain are distinct and strictly limited to tending to the sick and commanding sailors, respectively.

b7 Οὐδέ γε, οἶμαι, τὴν μισθωτικήν: *sc.* καλεῖς ἰατρικήν.

b9 ἐὰν ἰώμενός τις μισθαρνῆι: this is specious. Someone becoming healthy, like the ship's captain, simultaneously with earning wages is not comparable, despite the parallel construction, to someone earning wages simultaneously with *and in compensation for* providing treatment aimed at producing health.

346c1 Οὔκ, ἔφη: whether this or Οὐκ ἔφη more accurately represents P.'s intention cannot be determined. It seems, however, that S. changes from direct quotation of T.'s responses to indirect only at c11, where the change is marked by S.'s editorial μόγις; cf. 342b8n.

c5–7 Ἥντινα ἄρα ὠφελίαν . . . ὠφελοῦνται "Then whatever common benefit all workers enjoy obviously derives from the common employment of some additional (προσ-) thing, (which is) the same (in all cases)," with ἀπὸ ἐκείνου referring back to τινι. The language (προσχρώμενοι) implies the use of some further *means* of securing the benefit, a means that S. wishes to characterize as a distinct τέχνη. But this is not obviously true. In the case of a subsistence farmer the benefit is precisely the product of the craft of farming; in the case of a thief the benefit consists of the very stolen goods that the thief's craft has procured; in the case of a tyrant, T. might argue, the benefit is whatever the tyrant desires. None of these qualifies as a δημιουργός, but S. is using the physician and the ship's captain merely as examples of practitioners of a τέχνη that entails rule (ἀρχή) over someone or some thing distinct from the practitioner.

c9 τὸ μισθὸν ἀρνυμένους ὠφελεῖσθαι τοὺς δημιουργούς: subject of γίγνεσθαι. P. uses the poetic verb ἄρνυσθαι with μισθόν as its object (also at *Laws* 7.813e4, *Prot.* 349a4) to etymologize μισθαρνεῖν and μισθαρνητική. Elsewhere in his work it appears only with ζωήν and the poetic κλέος as objects (*Laws* 12.944c6, 969a7).

346d4 αὐτῆι ἑπομένη "accompanying it (*sc.* τῆι οἰκοδομικῆι τέχνηι)." While ἑπόμενα had not yet become the technical term in logic (*consequens* vs *antecedens*) that it was shortly to become in Aristotle, P. was not unfamiliar with its use in that sense (*Pol.* 271e3). S. is hoping that T. – and P. is hoping that his readers – will not notice the fragility of the argument. For it is not the case that the relationship between building houses and earning wages is one of mere accompaniment; without house-building (or the practice of medicine or the making of shoes) there is no wage-earning.

d6 ἐὰν δὲ μὴ μισθὸς αὐτῆι προσγίγνηται: S. has painted himself into a corner. By arguing that the practitioner of every τέχνη is willing to practice that τέχνη only if compensated *and* by positing the existence of an independent wage-earning τέχνη, he leaves himself open to the objection that no one would willingly practice the wage-earning τέχνη without being additionally compensated for doing so. Since T. does not raise this obvious objection, P. is either portraying him as enchanted by S.'s sophistry, as Glaucon claims at 2.358b2–3, or asking us to imagine that T. is now merely humoring S. with his responses. The other possibility, that P. is not himself aware of the difficulty, seems much less likely. Rather, he is willing to tolerate it because he is already committed to the proposition toward which this argument has been leading, namely that the ruler in the strict sense requires an incentive to practice a τέχνη that he or she would not otherwise willingly practice.

346e1 Ἆρα ... προῖκα ἐργάζηται; the point of this question is to secure T.'s agreement that there is still a benefit even when the craft is practiced without the practitioner receiving a wage, the benefit accruing, according to S., to the object of the craft, which S. regards as the only beneficiary of any craft.

e3 ἤδη "by this point"; 328e5n.

e3–4 οὐδεμία τέχνη οὐδὲ ἀρχή: in keeping with the claim that every τέχνη is a form of rule, S. feels free to use the two words essentially as synonyms (332c5n.). Still, he alludes to the distinction between them by using the verbs παρασκευάζει καὶ ἐπιτάττει below.

e7 ἄρτι ἔλεγον μηδένα ἐθέλειν: at 345e6. After ἔλεγον we would expect a ὅτι-clause and the negative to be οὐ, but there are occasions when an infinitive with μή is found following other verbs of speaking or thinking (*SMT* §685), sometimes, as here, where a categorical denial is made.

e8 τὰ ἀλλότρια κακὰ μεταχειρίζεσθαι ἀνορθοῦντα: essentially defining ἄρχειν as "taking in hand and rectifying deficiencies that are not one's own," with ἀλλότρια κακά recalling and recontextualizing T.'s description of justice (343c3–4) as ἀλλότριον ἀγαθόν and advantageous to the ruler. S. has in mind primarily (his own understanding of) political rule, but ἄρχειν here must stand for the practice of any τέχνη. In the case of medicine, the deficiencies that are remedied are obvious, but we must assume that poets and sculptors are imagined as fulfilling a demand for statues and poems, not normally thought of as a κακόν requiring remediation.

347a2–3 κατὰ τὴν τέχνην ἐπιτάττων: that is, as long as the orders are given in accordance with the genuine practitioner's adherence to the criteria of the τέχνη.

a3 δεῖν: *sc.* ἔλεγον, at 345e6.

347a6–348b6: Glaucon is puzzled by S.'s reference to a penalty for not ruling, something that T. would immediately understand in terms of the humiliation associated with being among the ruled rather than acting as ruler. Clearly this is not what S. has in mind, and P. has a mystified Glaucon break in to satisfy himself (and the reader) that S. is not saying something that aligns him with T.'s thinking. The penalty for not ruling is explained briefly here, but we have to wait until Book Seven for the more detailed account of the philosopher-rulers and their reluctant return to the Cave (Kahn 1993: 138). Later still, in Book Nine, S. will describe the three types of soul, each actuated by the pleasures and desires that hold sway over one of the soul's three elements (580d–581e). That division is anticipated here, where the motivation of "the best people," those ruled by the love of learning, is distinguished from the lower desires that drive the rest of the population, namely the pursuit of either wealth or honor. Also anticipated in this interlude is the role that Glaucon, along with his brother, will play in the remaining books. Unlike T., Glaucon shares S.'s moral outlook, and this is marked by S.'s frequent use of value terms on whose application S. and Glaucon can agree (βελτίστων, ἐπιεικέστατοι, ὄνειδος, οἱ ἀγαθοί, αἰσχρόν, πονηροτέρου, βελτίοσιν).

347a7–8 τὴν δὲ ζημίαν ... οὐ συνῆκα "but as far as the penalty is concerned, I do not understand what it is you are referring to and have assigned to the category (LSJ μέρος A.IV.3) of reward"; cf. *Tht.* 155e6 οὐκ ἀποδεχόμενοι ὡς ἐν οὐσίας μέρει, Arist. *Magn. Mor.* 1204a34 οὐκ οἴονται δεῖν τὴν ἡδονὴν ὡς ἐν ἀγαθοῦ μέρει λαμβάνειν.

347b2 ὅταν ἐθέλωσιν ἄρχειν "when they consent to rule." According to S., the "best people" do not *wish* to rule but, under certain circumstances, may be *willing* to do so; for this distinction between ἐθέλειν and βούλεσθαι, see 4.437b8–c5, with Adam *ad loc.*

b2–3 τὸ φιλότιμόν τε καὶ φιλάργυρον: despite the shared article (Gildersleeve §§603–5) and the coupling by means of τε καί, the two words do not refer to qualities that are comparably valued. The latter, "avarice, covetousness," is unambiguously a term of reproach (*Gorg.* 515e6, Soph. *Ant.* 1055, Xen. *Mem.* 3.13.4). But φιλοτιμία, like English "ambition," is more complicated (Dover 1974: 229–33). P. uses it as a term of abuse (e.g. *Apol.* 23e1) and associates it with love of money also at *Phd.* 68c2 (φιλοχρήματος καὶ φιλότιμος; cf. Thuc. 2.65.7, 3.82.8). It is the δεινὸν κακόν (Eur. *IA* 527) that helps make Odysseus the most complicated of Greek heroes (Stanford 1963: 115–17) and that is finally overcome by that hero in P.'s Myth of Er (10.620c5). It is also, according to Diotima, what motivated Alcestis, Achilles and Codrus to carry out their most admirable accomplishments (*Symp.* 208c–d), and it is what characterizes the man whose soul is dominated by the "spirited" element, which occupies the middle station, between the money-loving and the philosophical elements of the soul (9.581a–b).

b3 ὄνειδος λέγεταί τε καὶ ἔστιν: while everyone welcomes honor (τιμή), it is thought tasteless to seek it out; cf. c3 αἰσχρὸν νενομίσθαι and Arist. *EN* 4.1125b8–10 τόν ... φιλότιμον ψέγομεν ὡς μᾶλλον ἢ δεῖ καὶ ὅθεν οὐ δεῖ τῆς τιμῆς ἐφιέμενον. When Mika opens her speech in *Thesmophoriazusae* with an oath to the effect that her decision to speak publicly is not motivated by φιλοτιμία (383), Aristophanes is parodying a courtroom *topos*; see Austin and Olson *ad loc.*, citing Lysias 19.56. What we might approvingly regard as public-spiritedness the Greeks, more cynically and perhaps more accurately, would class as φιλοτιμία.

b7 μισθωτοὶ … κεκλῆσθαι: no gentleman would wish to be known as a "hireling" (2.371e4, 4.420a1, *Lys.* 208a6, *Pol.* 290a4), someone who exacts a fee (μισθὸν πράττεται) for providing services. Among those who openly required payment for their services were professional sophists (*Meno* 90d3, e3, 91b5, *Prot.* 328b4, *Soph.* 222e7), from whom S. distinguishes himself by never charging a fee (*Apol.* 31c1, Xen. *Mem.* 1.2.60).

b8 αὐτοί "on their own initiative" ("*sua sponte*," KG I 653), as opposed to receiving a wage, to which they are entitled; cf. 349c8 αὐτὸς λάβηι.

347c1 αὐτοῖς: its position marks it for contrast. They (οἱ ἀγαθοί), unlike members of the lesser classes, need to be compelled to rule.

ἀνάγκην … καὶ ζημίαν: a hendiadys; the penalty, or the threat of a penalty, is the constraint. Here the penalty is the unacceptable fate of being ruled by one's inferiors; for this as the motivation for the rulers in Callipolis, see Sedley 2007b.

c2–3 ὅθεν κινδυνεύει … νενομίσθαι "that is probably why (LSJ κινδυνεύω A.4.b) it is generally thought to be shameful to seek political power on one's own initiative and not (*GP* 1–2) to wait to be compelled."

c3–4 τῆς δὲ ζημίας μεγίστη: for the assimilation of the adjective into the gender of the dependent genitive, cf. 3.416b6 τὴν μεγίστην τῆς εὐλαβείας, *Cra.* 391b9 ὀρθοτάτη … τῆς σκέψεως, *Symp.* 209a6 καλλίστη τῆς φρονήσεως; KG I 279–80.

c4 πονηροτέρου: essentially "lower-class" (LSJ A.III.3), although the moral connotation, "more depraved," is inevitably also felt. For the contrast πονηρός/ἐπιεικής, see Isocr. 7.72, 15.164.

c6–7 οὐχ ὡς ἐπὶ ἀγαθόν τι … ἀλλὰ ὡς ἐπὶ ἀναγκαῖον: in Book Two Glaucon will undertake to resuscitate T.'s argument and show that those who practice justice do so unwillingly, ὡς ἀναγκαῖον ἀλλὰ οὐχ ὡς ἀγαθόν (358c3–4).

c7 ἐν αὐτῶι: *sc.* ἐν τῶι ἄρχειν, "in power" or "in office," normally expressed with ἐν τῆι ἀρχῆι (Thuc. 6.55.3, Xen. *Ages.* 1.6, *Cyr.* 8.2.16).

347d1 οὐδὲ ὁμοίοις: a puzzling addition to the sentence, seemingly contradicted by what is said next. While it is understandable that οἱ ἐπιεικεῖς would not want to be governed by an inferior, they ought to welcome their equals as rulers. And indeed, in the hypothetical πόλις ἀνδρῶν ἀγαθῶν everyone seeks to avoid ruling, presumably because they are content to be ruled by other ἀγαθοί. The addition of these words seems designed to appeal to T., for whom the ideal ruler is the tyrant, who has no peers.

d1–2 πόλις ἀνδρῶν ἀγαθῶν εἰ γένοιτο: that P. is here anticipating the construction of the ideal polis later in *Republic,* which has sometimes been denied, is strongly supported by two related considerations: (1) the uncertainty S. expresses as to the feasibility of such an endeavor is echoed at 6.502c6 (εἰ γένοιτο), where the endeavor is immediately declared to be "difficult but not impossible"; (2) S. uses the existence of such a hypothetical city *as the grounds for believing* that it is manifest (καταφανές) that a genuine ruler is naturally concerned with the welfare of the ruled.

d2–3 περιμάχητον ... τὸ ἄρχειν: in Book Seven S. and Glaucon agree that it is just for them to compel the philosopher-rulers of Callipolis to take turns descending into the Cave, this being the only way the city will be well governed (520a–521b), for when control of the government becomes the object of contention (περιμάχητον γὰρ τὸ ἄρχειν γιγνόμενον, 521a6–7) the resulting civil war spells the ruin of the city and its inhabitants.

d5–6 ὥστε πᾶς ... πράγματα ἔχειν: an extraordinary statement, expressed in such a way as to be acceptable to T., indeed to any ancient Greek, for who would not rather be benefited than take the trouble of benefiting someone else? But S. has just argued that the genuine ruler, like the genuine practitioner of any craft, benefits that on which the craft operates, which, in the case of the craft of ruling, is the ruler's human subjects. Thus this statement, while it supports S.'s claim that the ruler requires compensation for taking the trouble to govern, also suggests that every sensible person would rather receive the benefit of being ruled than be bothered to rule others, a sentiment that T., indeed any ancient Greek, would vehemently reject.

d5 πᾶς ... ὁ γιγνώσκων "every person of discernment" (Tucker). This absolute use of the verb is difficult to parallel. P. may, however, be parodying a mannerism of T.'s if Blass' conjecture (1887: 257 n. 2) at DK 85 B1 = 35 D16 Laks–Most is correct: τί δῆτα μέλλοι τις ἂν γιγνώσκων [γιγνώσκειν MSS] εἰπεῖν; "Why then would any person of discernment hesitate to speak out?"

τὸ ὠφελεῖσθαι: Richards (1911: 87) proposed deleting the article, since αἱρεῖσθαι is elsewhere construed with the simple infinitive. P. does occasionally use an articular infinitive in constructions that ordinarily take the infinitive alone; cf. *Tht.* 166d4–5, KG II 45. But in view of the two anomalies in this line we may consider the possibility that τό is a corruption of what P. intended as the object of γιγνώσκων, e.g. αὐτό, "everyone who recognizes it (τὸ τῶι ἀρχομένωι συμφέρον, i.e. what is in the best interests of the person being ruled, namely to be ruled by an ἀνὴρ ἀγαθός)."

347e1–2 τὸ δίκαιόν ἐστι τὸ τοῦ κρείττονος συμφέρον: by repeating exactly T.'s original formulation (338c2–3), P. allows us to understand that T. has been consistent in his definition throughout.

e2 εἰς αὖθις σκεψόμεθα: S. does not in fact take up this precise issue subsequently. P. on occasion ends a dialogue with the expectation that a topic will be investigated further on a later occasion (*Cra.*, *Prot.*), so this promise should not be used as evidence of careless revision (see the

Introduction, section 1) or forgetfulness on the part of P. The direction in which S. turns the discussion here will render irrelevant the question whether justice is advantageous for the superior person, and will avoid an awkward, and potentially fruitless, discussion between S. and T. regarding the identity of "the superior person."

e3 ὃ νῦν λέγει Θρασύμαχος: referring to 344c4, where T. said that injustice is ἰσχυρότερον καὶ ἐλευθεριώτερον καὶ δεσποτικώτερον than justice, which S. interprets at 344e to mean that T. is describing what he considers the most rewarding (λυσιτελεστάτην) course of life. By the end of Book One S. will have concluded that injustice is never more rewarding than justice, although he still does not know what exactly justice is. The remainder of *Republic* will be devoted to discovering what justice is, so that, by the end of Book Nine, S. and Glaucon will understand why justice is more rewarding than injustice.

e5 πότερον: neuter, i.e. ὃ νῦν λέγει Θ. or the converse. Glaucon replies by saying, "I for my part (think the more correct proposition is) that the life of the just person is more rewarding."

348a1–2 τῶι τοῦ ἀδίκου: *sc.* βίωι, the dative going with ὅσα ἀγαθά, "how many advantages to the life of the unjust person T. listed."

a7–b2 Ἂν μὲν ... ἂν δέ: S. lays out for Glaucon two potential methods of persuasion, one in which alternating speeches present the arguments in support of each position, the other by a process of mutual accommodation in which, S. claims, they have just been engaging. The first is the procedure preferred by the sophists; it is familiar from the lawcourts and is found in the *agones* of fifth-century tragedy, in the debate on types of government in Herodotus (3.80–2), in the paired speeches in Thucydides and in the "tetralogies" of Antiphon. The second is the customary practice of S., involving question and answer, which he cannot help but use even in the lawcourt (*Apol.* 24c–28a) and even after agreeing to deliver an encomium (*Symp.* 199b–201c, 201e–207a). Elsewhere as well, P. calls attention to the distinction between these two styles of discourse: 350d–e, *Gorg.* 449b, 461d–462a, *Prot.* 334c–d. To this point in *Republic* S.'s questioning has been used as in the elenchus (336c4n.), for the purpose of arriving at the truth. Here, however, S. explicitly applies the technique in an attempt to persuade T. of something that S. is already convinced is true, that the life of the just person is more rewarding than that of the unjust. At the end of Book One it will be clear that he has not succeeded in persuading T., nor will he have discovered the essence of justice. P. may by now have "lost interest in the Socratic method" (Matthews 2018) as a means of finding the truth, but the format of philosophical inquiry by a process of question and answer was too firmly rooted in P.'s compositional style to be abandoned, at least until his very last works.

a7 ἀντικατατείναντες almost = "engaging in a (verbal) tug-of-war," lit. "straining in opposition (to one another)." The verb is used in the Hippocratic Corpus (see LSJ) in connection with reducing dislocated joints by means of traction. For similar expressions of the intense effort invested in debate, see 2.358d5 κατατείνας ἐρῶ τὸν ἄδικον βίον ἐπαινῶν, 367b2–3 ὡς δύναμαι μάλιστα κατατείνας λέγω.

a8 λόγον παρὰ λόγον: at *Hp.Mi.* 369c6 the sophist Hippias invites S. to deliver a speech in opposition (ἀντιπαράβαλλε λόγον παρὰ λόγον) to the speech he proposes to give on the subject of Achilles' superiority to Odysseus. S. declines, preferring the method of question and answer.

a9 ἀριθμεῖν δεήσει τὰ ἀγαθά: for S., it is not a legitimate method of determining the truth merely to enumerate examples (*Cra.* 437d) or to compare the numbers of those who support a particular position (*Gorg.* 471e–472a, *Lach.* 184d–e, *Tht.* 171a).

348b1 ἐν ἑκατέρωι: *sc.* λόγωι.

ἤδη "presently," the meaning the adverb has when found with a future tense, usually as here with a first-person verb; cf. *Mnx.* 248c4, Lysias 31.16.

b1–2 δικαστῶν τινων τῶν διακρινούντων "some judges to make the decision." The article regularly accompanies a future participle with indefinite reference expressing purpose, obligation or intent (*SMT* §826), and is sometimes, as here, found with indefinite τις; e.g. 342a4–5 δεῖ τινος τέχνης τῆς ... σκεψομένης, Dem. 18.71 φανῆναί τινα ... τὸν ταῦτα κωλύσοντα ... ἐχρῆν.

b3 δικασταὶ καὶ ῥήτορες ἐσόμεθα: the language of the lawcourt; e.g. *Apol.* 18a5–6 δικαστοῦ μὲν γὰρ αὕτη ἀρετή (*sc.* τὸ σκοπεῖν εἰ δίκαια λέγω ἢ μή), ῥήτορος δὲ τὰ ἀληθῆ λέγειν. One would think that consolidating the roles of pleader and judge would not be a recipe for arriving at an unbiased result. But for P. the conventions of Athenian legal practice, contaminated as they were by the malign influence of contemporary rhetorical practice and discredited by the conviction of S. in 399, were anything but a model of rectitude. Much fairer and more productive, supposedly, is the Socratic method of using question and answer to arrive by stages at a mutually agreeable solution to a disputed issue.

b6 Οὗτως "the latter" (*CGCG* §29.33).

348b7–349a9: S. resumes his questioning of T., who has unambiguously indicated his positive valuation of injustice and his negative valuation of justice. S. tries to involve T. in a contradiction, as he had done with Polus in *Gorgias* (474c–475d), by seeing if he can get him to associate injustice with some value term that is indicative of universal disapproval. When he is unable to do so, he admits that he cannot persuade T. along lines in keeping with the way people in general think (κατὰ τὰ νομιζόμενα, 348e8), so he resolves to try a different approach.

348b7 Ἴθι δή … ἀπόκριναι ἡμῖν ἐξ ἀρχῆς: cf. *Prot.* 333d3 Ἴθι δή … ἐξ ἀρχῆς μοι ἀπόκριναι, *Meno* 79e5 Ἀπόκριναι τοίνυν πάλιν ἐξ ἀρχῆς. In both cases S. has brought his interlocutor to a state of embarrassment over his contradictory answers to S.'s questions about ἀρετή and its "parts," Meno even comparing the effect of S.'s interrogation to the numbness caused by the sting of an electric ray. Here it is S. who is nonplussed by T.'s negative valuation of what S. and Glaucon consider to be a component of ἀρετή.

b7–8 τὴν τελέαν … φῄς εἶναι: summing up what T. had said at 344a–c, that τελεωτάτη ἀδικία is rewarding (λυσιτελοῦν) and is mightier, more independent and more dominant than justice; the addition of "perfect" justice is S.'s contribution, irrelevant here but destined to return in Book Two, when Glaucon stipulates that S. must weigh the happiness of the perfectly unjust person against that of the perfectly just (360e).

348c2–3 ἀρετὴν … κακίαν: S. intends these to be understood in terms of what we would regard as "moral" values, but T. is free to understand them as meaning, respectively, "superiority, capability" and "weakness, deficiency," and S. will come to recognize that he does so understand them (e8–9).

c6 Εἰκός γε "Right, that's a likelihood," spoken sarcastically.

ἥδιστε: the only occurrence of this vocative in the Classical period (Dickey 1996: 282). At 337d6 T. had called S. ἡδύς, "naive"; for T.'s fondness for superlatives, see 341b7n.

c8 Ἀλλὰ τί μήν; "Well, what then?"; cf. *Symp.* 206e4; *GP* 332.

348d1 γενναίαν εὐήθειαν "genteel ingenuousness." The noun, literally "having a good character," can be used as a term of approval for the "simple" nature of people of an earlier time not yet corrupted by modern sophistication (*Phdr.* 275b8), but more often is used by modern sophisticates to disparage a lack of worldly experience (*Phdr.* 275c7). T. had addressed S. as εὐηθέστατε at 343d2, and in his initial outburst he expressed his impatience with S. and Glaucon's excessive politeness (εὐηθίζεσθε, 336c2) and deference to each other, which was preventing them from grasping the truth about human nature.

d2 κακοήθειαν: S. playfully proposes this as the "opposite" of εὐήθειαν. That they were not considered opposites, and that P. did not so consider them, is clear from what he has S. say at 3.400d–401a. The one is an unfortunate, but pardonable, lack of sophistication; the other is a deplorable nastiness of character.

d3 εὐβουλίαν "good sense, prudence." T. counters S.'s κακο- with a compound in εὐ-, using the word with which P.'s Protagoras specifies the skill that he teaches his pupils whereby they are best able to manage their own affairs and those of the city (*Prot.* 318e5). In Book Four S. and Glaucon will agree that Callipolis will be εὔβουλος by virtue of the wisdom of its ruling class (428b–d). In conversation with S. Alcibiades comes to identify εὐβουλία (*Alc.1* 125e6) as the quality, introduced at 124e3 as ἀρετή, needed for the ruler to administer successfully and preserve the city.

d4 φρόνιμοι ... καὶ ἀγαθοί: S. intends these to mean "wise and virtuous"; T. understands them as "sensible and capable," which makes it possible for him to give a positive, albeit qualified, response to S.'s incredulous question.

d6 πόλεις τε καὶ ἔθνη: effectively, Greeks and barbarians; cf. Hdt. 7.8.γ3, 8.108.3, Xen. *Symp.* 4.47. T.'s ideal, like Polus' (344b6n.), is the Great King, who does not have to suffer the indignity of being ruled by someone else and is therefore supremely happy.

d7–8 βαλλάντια: small pouches closed with a drawstring (*Symp.* 190e7–8) in which coins were carried, a tempting target for cutpurses, βαλλαντιοτόμοι (8.552d6); see Olson on Ar. *Ach.* 130–1.

348e1–2 ἐθαύμασα "I was taken aback," an ingressive aorist (*CGCG* §33.29) expressing the onset of the feeling of surprise, which persists at the time of utterance; cf. the opening words of Isocrates' *Panegyricus* and of Xenophon's *Memorabilia* (Πολλάκις ἐθαύμασα), and of the spurious preface to Theophrastus' *Characters* (Ἤδη μὲν καὶ πρότερον πολλάκις ... ἐθαύμασα, ἴσως δὲ οὐδὲ παύσομαι θαυμάζων).

e2 ἐν ἀρετῆς καὶ σοφίας ... μέρει: cf. 347a7–8n. The nouns correspond, chiastically, to the adjectives φρόνιμοι ... καὶ ἀγαθοί above.

e5 ἤδη στερεώτερον ... καὶ οὐκέτι ῥάιδιον: the two adverbs are complementary, the first indicating that a conceptual boundary has now been reached (346e3n.), the second that, while progress up to that boundary may have been relatively easy, that is no longer the case (see Wilson 1987: 197, citing *Laws* 6.757b6 οὐκέτι ῥάιδιον). Similarly, in Book Two S. says that the expansion of the hypothetical city has now, ἤδη, reached a point at which further categories of citizen need to be introduced, since the blueprint for the healthy city is no longer, οὐκέτι, satisfactory (373b2).

e6 ὅτι τις εἴπηι: the deliberative subjunctive, ὅτι εἴπω (345b4–5n.), expressed as a universalized dilemma by being put in the indefinite third person (KG I 222); cf. *Prot.* 348d4–5 περιιὼν ζητεῖ ὅτωι ἐπιδείξηται καὶ μετὰ ὅτου βεβαιώσηται.

e7 ὥσπερ ἄλλοι τινές: for example Polus, who acknowledges that acting unjustly is αἴσχιον than suffering injustice (*Gorg.* 474c7–8). T. would never describe (perfect) injustice as αἰσχρόν, which for him is merely a word people use to denigrate small-scale criminal activity that is not worth serious attention (344b7).

e8 δῆλος εἶ ὅτι φήσεις "it is clear that you will say"; for the personal construction, see *Cri.* 46d3, Thuc. 1.93.2, Xen. *Mem.* 4.2.21.

e9 καὶ καλὸν καὶ ἰσχυρόν "both admirable and powerful," opposed chiastically to κακίαν … ἢ αἰσχρόν, "a weakness or a thing to be ashamed of." S. is expressing his recognition that, while he and T. speak the same language, T. will respond to S.'s vocabulary of moral disapproval with terms that can be construed in a purely descriptive or instrumental sense.

349a1 ἃ ἡμεῖς τῶι δικαίωι προσετίθεμεν "which we have been ascribing to the just," an instance of the very widespread practice of using the first-person plural to mean "I" (Wackernagel 2009: 134–6); the expression of ἡμεῖς, along with its position, marks an emphatic contrast with the subject of προσθήσεις. That S. is referring to himself alone, both here and at 348e7–8, and is not including Glaucon and such other guests as may be assumed to agree with him, is shown by the singular σκοπούμενον, a5.

a1–2 ἐν ἀρετῆι … καὶ σοφίαι = ἐν ἀρετῆς καὶ σοφίας … μέρει, 348e2.

a4 τῶι λόγωι ἐπεξελθεῖν: the image, reinforced by οὐκ ἀποκνητέον, is from the military, of venturing out (ἐξ-) against (ἐπι-) an adversary (e.g. Thuc. 2.23.1, 6.97.5). The adversary here is the dangerous argument deployed by T.; cf. *Gorg.* 492d1 Οὐκ ἀγεννῶς γε … ἐπεξέρχηι τῶι λόγωι, *Prot.* 345d1–2 ἐπεξέρχεται τῶι τοῦ Πιττακοῦ ῥήματι.

a8–9 ἀλλὰ οὐ τὸν λόγον ἐλέγχεις; as earlier (346a3–4), S. seemed to suggest that he is concerned to refute only T.'s sincerely held beliefs. But S. abruptly agrees with T. that it makes no difference whether T. is committed to the truth of the *logos* and what matters is whether the *logos* can be successfully refuted or defended; for S.'s inconsistency in this regard, see Beversluis 2000: 56–8. We may compare *Chrm.* 161c, where S. agrees with Charmides that the identity of the author of a particular doctrine is irrelevant and that it is the doctrine itself that needs to be examined. Later (3.394d8–9) S. will espouse the principle, applauded by Adeimantus, that, like sailors at the mercy of the winds, they must allow the *logos* to plot their course for them. It should be remembered that T. entered the conversation in the first place because of his frustration at S.'s refusal to declare a thesis of his own which, presumably, T. hoped to refute. Moore (2015: 331) considers that T. was on that occasion (336c) insisting, inconsistently, on the principle that S. must express his sincerely held belief, but there is nothing in the text that requires that view. In an intellectual milieu dominated by the sophists, who pride themselves on an ability to argue both sides of a case with equal effectiveness, it no longer matters what one's adversary believes; arguments can only overthrow other arguments, while beliefs may remain unchanged, if indeed they were even stable to begin with. What is at stake for T. is the position he initially, and forcefully, espoused, which he must defend successfully or face professional humiliation.

349b1–350e10: The following argument has been called "almost embarrassingly bad" (Cross and Woozley 1964: 52), "weak and unconvincing to an amazing degree" (Annas 1981: 50) and "grossly fallacious" (Reeve 1988: 20). The argument relies on S.'s use of the verb πλεονεκτεῖν, "get the better of, surpass," which he uses interchangeably with πλέον ἔχειν, "have more (than)." It is clear that T. regards the unjust person, whom he admires, as someone who seeks to surpass, and to have more than, everyone else. S. begins by securing his agreement that the just person seeks to surpass only unjust persons, not other just persons. Thus the just seek to surpass only those who are unlike themselves, whereas the unjust are indiscriminate in seeking to surpass those who are like them (other unjust persons) as well as those whom they do not resemble (just persons). According to T., the unjust are, and resemble, the intelligent and good; the just are, and resemble, neither. Experts, such as musicians and physicians, are, qua experts, intelligent and good; non-experts are neither. The experts seek to surpass only the non-experts, whereas the latter, being ignorant, seek to surpass all indiscriminately. The experts, who are intelligent and good, do not seek to surpass what they resemble, but only what is different and opposite, whereas the non-experts, who are ignorant and deficient, seek to surpass both what they resemble and what they do not. Therefore the unjust, who seek to surpass both what they resemble and what they do not, are like the ignorant non-experts, whereas the just, who seek to surpass only what they do not resemble, are like the experts, who are intelligent and good.

It is not clear that P. is justified in asking us to believe that the T. he has thus far portrayed would be likely to give the answers he gives here. For one thing, the class of expert to which T. belonged – sophists are not mentioned in Book One – would have provided T. with an easy counterexample of an expert who seeks to surpass everyone. For another, the only sense in which he might agree that the just person seeks to "surpass" the unjust is in being just or in acting justly, which is a peculiar application of πλεονεκτεῖν or πλέον ἔχειν, to put it mildly, nor would we expect the T. we have met in these pages to understand those terms as conveying anything other than naked self-aggrandizement. Those who have defended the coherence of the argument, such as Joseph (1935: 31–6), Warren (1985) and Lycos (1987: 121–36), have done so by concentrating on notions like limit, measure and harmony (see 349e9n.) and by appealing to passages elsewhere in *Republic*. This may allow us to infer that the argument satisfied P., who had already formulated the theories that S. will expound in subsequent books, but it does not sit well in the context of the discussion with T., and it may be an indication of P.'s gradual abandonment of the

Socratic elenchus – which was designed with the intention of effecting a transformation in the soul of a live interlocutor – in preference for a less tentative method of doing philosophy (Matthews 2018).

349b2 πλέον ἔχειν: here and below used as a synonym for πλεονεκτεῖν, which for S. means something like "surpass, outdo, excel." T., however, understands these expressions to refer more concretely to "having more (power or material goods)"; see 343d5, 344a1, where it is clear that he thinks primarily in binary terms, of the unjust having more than the just, with the supremely unjust person having more than anyone. For πλεονεξία in general, see Balot 2001.

b3 ἀστεῖος ... καὶ εὐήθης: the latter relates to the characterization that T. has just given of justice as γενναία εὐήθεια (348d1); the former, as its etymology indicates, stands in implicit contrast to ἄγροικος, "rustic, uncouth, ill-mannered" (Dover 1974: 112–14). S. uses ἀστεῖος to describe the kindly, sensitive deputy of the Eleven who dutifully brings him the hemlock and sheds honest tears, γενναίως ἀποδακρύει, when he does so (*Phd.* 116d5), and Ctesippus refers to Hippothales' blushing as ἀστεῖον (*Lys.* 204c4), when the latter modestly declines to name the boy who is the object of his affections. The hard-nosed, unsentimental T., however, regards these terms, and the behavior they describe, with contempt, and in his mouth they characterize disparagingly the kind of well-bred, polite souls who are destined to be taken advantage of by the unscrupulous people whom T. admires.

ὥσπερ νῦν "as is the case," with counterfactuals also at 6.507a2, 10.610d3, *Symp.* 189c7. But there is also a suggestion that the situation in which T. and S. now find themselves is illustrative of his point. T. initially burst into the conversation because of his impatience with the behavior of S. and Polemarchus, who, he thinks, know perfectly well how to define justice but keep deferring to one another and mounting a pretense of naivete (εὐηθίζεσθε, 336c2), for fear of giving offense.

b5 Οὐδὲ τῆς πράξεως: S. asked first about surpassing the just person, then about surpassing the just act, apparently meaning "acting more justly"; cf. c4–5 τοῦ δικαίου (*sc.* ἀνδρός) πλεονεκτεῖν καὶ τῆς δικαίας πράξεως, 350a1–2 πλεονεκτεῖν ἢ ἀνδρὸς ἢ πράγματος. Having replied that the just person would not be inclined to surpass the just person, T. now says, "And not the act, either," with "just" easily understood from the context. For a gloss replacing the true reading (see app. crit.), cf. 339a2 καθεστηκυίας **AF**: οἰκείας **D**, 2.360b7 τολμήσειεν **AD**: θέλοι **F**, 4.440a6 τὴν ὀργήν **ADF**: τὸν θυμόν Laur. 80.19, and see 345c3n.

b8 ἀλλὰ οὐκ ἂν δύναιτο: this is quickly brushed aside as irrelevant by S. (Ἀλλὰ οὐ τοῦτο ... ἐρωτῶ; cf. 353c4n.), but it is not clear why P. makes T. say this, for it calls attention to an incoherence in the argument. In what sense might the just person think it right (δίκαιον) to surpass the unjust but be unable to do so? Perhaps we are to imagine T. thinking that the just person, out of a sense of righteous indignation, feels that it is right to have more (recognition? prosperity?) than the unjust, which is out of reach of the just person, for reasons that T. has explained earlier (344a–c). But this ignores the addition of the language of acting justly, which is repeated throughout the argument (see previous n.). The just person can easily surpass the unjust in acting justly. What the just person cannot do is surpass the unjust in acting unjustly. And yet, if this is what is at issue, T. has just asserted that this is what the just person thinks it right to do.

349c8 ἁμιλλήσεται ὡς ... λάβηι: verbs expressive of effort or striving are sometimes followed by ὡς or ὡς ἄν with the subjunctive (Smyth §2217), but the construction is rare and is not found elsewhere in P. (Slings 2005: 14–15).

ἁπάντων: masculine. S. is asking T. to confirm and make explicit that, when he says "everyone" (c6), he means that the unjust person will surpass also (καί) the unjust (i.e. in addition to the just), and will strive to have (not only more than but) the most of anyone, whether just or unjust. The superlative is very often intensified with πάντων (Thesleff 1954: §207), itself here further intensified with the prefix ἁ-.

c10 Ὧδε δὴ λέγωμεν: summing up, with culminative δή (332d2n.), what S. and T. have agreed to, but now introducing the language of resemblance, in preparation for the next stage of the argument.

349d3 φρόνιμός τε καὶ ἀγαθός: T. had agreed that the perfectly unjust person is sensible and capable at 348d6.

d9 ὁ δὲ μὴ ἐοικέναι; "And the other (i.e. the person who is neither sensible nor capable) would not resemble (those who are sensible and capable)." For this use of ὁ δέ without a preceding ὁ μέν, see Gildersleeve §517.

d11 Ἀλλὰ τί μέλλει; the same response is given at *Hp.Mi.* 373d5 to a question whose expected answer is, "Why, of course." The thought seems to be, "What is likely (to be the case, if not what you have said)?"

349e5 ἅπερ φρόνιμον, ἀγαθόν: this is a crucial step in the argument. By securing T.'s agreement that it is by virtue of being intelligent – S. will presently substitute σοφός for φρόνιμος – that the expert is good (i.e. at accomplishing the objectives of the craft), S. establishes that intelligence is an essential, and not a merely accidental, quality of the expert. Without this S. would not be justified in making the argument that he proceeds to make based on the "resemblance" between the just and the musician, the physician and the expert in general (Joseph 1935: 32–3; Lycos 1987: 125–6). For T. has maintained that it is by virtue of intelligence that the unjust are successful in their pursuit of injustice (and by virtue of ignorance that the just are unsuccessful).

e9 ἁρμοττόμενος λύραν: for the middle voice, see Ar. *Knights* 989–90 τὴν Δωριστὶ μόνην ἂν ἁρ-|μόττεσθαι θαμὰ τὴν λύραν. P. has chosen to use the example of the musician "tuning his lyre" (for which, see West 1992: 61–2) for two reasons. At the end of Book Nine the just person, who has now been fully defined, will be compared to a musician, in that he or she is constantly tuning (ἁρμοττόμενος, 591d1–2) the body's condition to bring it into harmony with that of the soul (cf. also Simmias' comparison of the soul to the attunement of the lyre, *Phd.* 85e–86a). More immediately, however, the example of the lyre provides S. with an incontestable instance where perfection is, to the extent that it is humanly possible, attainable. For all expert musicians will agree that no amount of tightening or loosening can improve the tuning of a string that is properly tuned; cf. *Phd.* 93a14–b3, d2–4. (Whether it is realistic to suppose that a non-musician can be found who will claim to do a better job is another matter.) In everyday experience, of course, expert musicians constantly strive to surpass other expert musicians in singing or playing, and they are awarded prizes at the games for doing so. The same spirit is in evidence among physicians (the Hippocratic Corpus is filled with criticisms of other doctors and other doctrines) and potters (see the dipinto on the amphora, Munich 2307, in which Euthymides taunts his rival Euphronius; Stewart 2008: 38–9, with fig. 8; cf. Hes. *Op.* 25 κεραμεὺς κεραμεῖ κοτέει καὶ τέκτονι τέκτων). But T. had ill-advisedly relinquished his right to appeal to everyday experience when he introduced the practitioner in the strict sense (340d–e), leaving it open to S. to argue that, if two practitioners claim that their performance of their craft is better than, and therefore different from, their rival's, at least one of them is not a practitioner in the strictest sense, since the performance of the two would be identical if they were.

350a1 ἐν τῆι ἐδωδῆι ἢ πόσει: i.e. in prescribing food or drink. For the importance of diet in maintaining health, see *On ancient medicine* 3–4 and *Regimen in health*, two works in the Hippocratic Corpus generally dated to the end of the fifth century.

a2 ἢ ἀνδρὸς ἢ πράγματος: cf. 349c7 ἀνθρώπου τε καὶ πράξεως. P. likes to avoid repeating himself exactly.

a6 Περὶ πάσης δὴ … ἐπιστήμης "With regard to every (form of) expertise," as ἐπιστήμη … οὐδεμία (342c10) = "no (form of) expertise"; cf. 7.522c7–8 πᾶσα τέχνη τε καὶ ἐπιστήμη, *Euthd.* 292c7–9 πᾶσαν ἐπιστήμην, σκυτοτομικήν τε καὶ τεκτονικὴν καὶ τὰς ἄλλας ἁπάσας. To this point the discussion has been mostly in terms of τέχνη (332c–d, 341d–342c, 346a–347a). But S. is justified in substituting a synonym, and he is justified in generalizing (using culminative δή) from only two instances. For T. had earlier asserted that it was precisely the absence of ἐπιστήμη (340e3–4) that disqualifies a person from claiming the status of expert in medicine or accounting or any field, saying explicitly that this disqualification extends even to the ruler in the strictest sense (340e8–341a1).

a8 ἢ πράττειν ἢ λέγειν: depending on ἐθέλειν αἱρεῖσθαι, "deliberately choose," and governing πλείω, meaning, in effect, "to surpass another expert in speech or act."

τὰ αὐτὰ τῶι ὁμοίωι ἑαυτῶι "the same as the person who is like him or her" (*CGCG* §32.14), reintroducing the language of resemblance and subtly reminding T. that he had earlier agreed that the just person, in contrast to the unjust, does not seek to surpass the person who is like him or her (349c10–d2).

a9 εἰς τὴν αὐτὴν πρᾶξιν "(do and say the same) with regard to the same activity," LSJ εἰς A.IV.2. Two expert cobblers may have differing views on how best to treat influenza, but when it comes to making shoes their practice (πράττειν) will be the same. Likewise, two expert physicians will prescribe (λέγειν) the same treatment under identical circumstances.

a10 ἴσως ... ἀνάγκη: the unusual collocation conveys the awkward position T. now finds himself in, reluctantly acknowledging the compelling nature of S.'s argument. Contrast S.'s response to Callicles' one-word answer, Ἴσως, at *Gorg.* 515d8: Οὐκ ἴσως δή, ὦ βέλτιστε, ἀλλὰ ἀνάγκη ἐκ τῶν ὡμολογημένων.

a11–b1 ὁμοίως μὲν ἐπιστήμονος ... ὁμοίως δὲ ἀνεπιστήμονος: cf. *Symp.* 181b7–8 ὁμοίως μὲν ἀγαθόν, ὁμοίως δὲ τὸ ἐναντίον.

350b10 τοῦ τε ὁμοίου καὶ τοῦ ἐναντίου: the article appears twice because two different entities are named; contrast τοῦ δὲ ἀνομοίου τε καὶ ἐναντίου just above, where the common article unites two descriptions of the same entity (Gildersleeve §603). This principle, however, is often violated, and it is violated immediately below, with τοῦ ἀνομοίου τε καὶ ὁμοίου, verbally exemplifying the unjust person's indiscriminate behavior.

b12 ἡμῖν: an "ethical" dative (343a7n.; *CGCG* §30.53), conveying "our" intimate concern with describing the behavior of the unjust person.

350c3 Ἔοικεν: the resemblance is not superficial (349e5n.); S.'s "therefore" (ἄρα) is justified.

c4 κακῶι καὶ ἀμαθεῖ: mirroring σοφῶι καὶ ἀγαθῶι in chiastic order.

c6 ὡμολογοῦμεν: this is not in fact what was agreed to, nor is it a valid statement. At 349d T. agreed that the perfectly unjust person *is* sensible and capable, while the just person is neither. In response to S.'s question whether the unjust person also *resembles* the sensible and capable, while the unjust resembles neither, T. said that, of course, whatever something is it also resembles. It does not follow, as S. is suggesting here (and T.

unaccountably agrees to), that whatever the just and unjust resemble they also are. We would not reasonably expect a person described as "child-like" to be a child.

c9 ἡμῖν ἀναπέφανται "has been revealed to us"; cf. *Soph.* 233c11, 250d2. Similarly, at 334a8 S. and Polemarchus were alarmed to discover that the just person turned out (ἀναπέφανται) to be a kind of thief. There too the middle-passive form was used, seeming to absolve S. of any agency in the matter, as though the argument had arrived at this conclusion on its own. In each case the conclusion comes as an unwelcome surprise to S.'s interlocutor.

c11 ὡμολόγησε μέν: the implication of the particle is, "(Well, he agreed to all this) but there is more to the story." The "more" is supplied in what follows by a somewhat more elaborate structure than the usual δέ-clause that we see at, e.g., 342d2–3 Συνωμολόγησε μὲν ... ἐπεχείρει δὲ περὶ αὐτὰ μάχεσθαι. Here, as there, the combative character of T. is accentuated, as is the role of S. as narrator (Ferrari 2010).

c11–d1 οὐχ ὡς ἐγὼ νῦν ῥαιδίως λέγω "not in the casual manner in which I am now reporting," with the "antecedent" of ὡς incorporated into the relative clause. This is not uncommon with substantive antecedents (*CGCG* §50.15), but is exceptional in the case of an adverb. The effect is to contrast the fluent character of S.'s (i.e. P.'s) narrative with the discomfort of T. that it depicts, ῥαιδίως being as easily construed with λέγω as (οὐ) ῥαιδίως is with ὡμολόγησε.

350d1–2 θαυμαστοῦ ὅσου "ever so much," a colloquialism (Collard 2018: 47); cf. 331a9 θαυμαστῶς ὡς, *Lach.* 184c2 θαυμαστὸν ὅσον.

d2 ἅτε καὶ θέρους ὄντος "since it was, after all, summer"; for ἅτε καί, see *Meno* 70c1 with Bluck *ad loc.* and *GP* 321–3. We are reminded that the conversation took place "yesterday," at the festival in honor of Bendis in June (327a1n.).

d2–3 τότε καὶ εἶδον ἐγώ, πρότερον δὲ οὔπω, Θρασύμαχον ἐρυθριῶντα "then I even saw (what I had seen) on no previous occasion, T. blushing." The asyndeton (Denniston 1952: 112–23), the profuse sweating just mentioned and the content of the words prepare us for a momentous occurrence. His blush is obviously a sign of T.'s profound humiliation, but what is the source of his embarrassment? Has he come to recognize, like so many of the victims of Socratic elenchus, that one of his fundamental beliefs cannot withstand scrutiny, or has he simply been outdone in a kind of verbal contest of which he considered himself to be a master? What we can say with certainty is that no other character in P. blushes on account of the aporia brought on by the elenchus. Apart from T., the other characters who blush are young, well-brought-up Athenians whose embarrassment is occasioned by an awkward social situation (*Chrm.* 158c,

Euthd. 275d, *Lys.* 204b–d, 213d, *Prot.* 312a; Lateiner 1998: 171–2) – with one instructive exception. The sophist Dionysodorus of Chios is an experienced teacher of both the martial and the verbal arts (Hawtrey 1981: 13–14; Nails 2002: 136–7) and, like T., he is a mature non-Athenian whose professional success depends on being seen using his skill with words to win arguments. Dionysodorus blushes (*Euthd.* 297a), and then quickly changes the subject when his younger brother Euthydemus scolds him for his untimely interruption that spoils Euthydemus' demonstration. This parallel strongly suggests that what P. wishes to convey with T.'s blush is not so much an awareness that one of his sincerely held beliefs has been shown to be faulty but embarrassment at having been bested in a verbal duel over justice by someone who professes not even to know what justice is. Like Dionysodorus and his brother, T. is characterized by uncompromising competitiveness. But it is not only that his manner is so characterized; this is his very identity (Blondell 2002: 180–3; Moore 2015). Further, the thesis that he is defending represents ruthless *pleonexia* as the sure path to happiness and success. He has now been outdone, humbled by S.'s demonstration, using techniques familiar from the playbook of sophists and practitioners of eristics, that the win-at-all-costs approach is counterproductive when it comes to serious intellectual discussions, which are more fruitfully pursued in a spirit of cooperation, a message that will be driven home in S.'s next argument, conducted without recourse to any devious methods, and in the following nine books.

d3 διωμολογησάμεθα: T.'s reaction, however, shows that he and S. are not necessarily in complete agreement regarding the nature of justice and injustice. S. is taking advantage of T.'s momentary discomfiture and pretends that the matter is now settled, as far as they are concerned (ἡμῖν … κείσθω).

d5 ἔφαμεν: it was T., not "we," who said that injustice is a potent thing (344c4, 348e9). This is an instance of the "speaker-exclusive" first-person plural, a widespread phenomenon in which the speaker's "we" does not include "I," serving a variety of discourse strategies, ranging from deferential politeness to patronizing condescension (Wackernagel 2009: 61–3; Santulli 2020). The latter is the effect here.

d7 ἔμοιγε "as far as *I'm* concerned"; i.e. whatever *you* might say or think (*GP* 119, 121–3).

d7–e1 ἔχω περὶ αὐτῶν λέγειν "I am capable of speaking on the subject." But, as translators generally recognize, what is needed is something like, "I have something to say about it" (Emlyn-Jones). ἔχειν λέγειν, without an object expressed, is most commonly negated; e.g. 3.400a5, c4. An object is easily supplied here, and its disappearance from our MSS before περί easily explained, if we assume that P. wrote ἔχω τι; cf. Eur. *Med.* 1132–3 ἔχω τι κἀγὼ τοῖσι σοῖς ἐναντίον | λόγοισιν εἰπεῖν.

350e2 εἰπεῖν ὅσα βούλομαι "to speak at such length as I choose" (cf. Polus at *Gorg.* 461d8–9 οὐκ ἐξέσται μοι λέγειν ὁπόσα ἂν βούλωμαι;), which T. knows will be dismissed by S. as haranguing (δημηγορεῖν, lit. "addressing the δῆμος"; cf. Biles and Olson on Ar. *Wasps* 34–6). At 348a–b S. and Glaucon had set the rules for the ensuing discussion, which excluded a courtroom-style debate, λόγος παρὰ λόγον. S. makes clear his preference for διαλέγεσθαι over δημηγορεῖν at *Prot.* 336b, when he threatens to break off his conversation with Protagoras unless the sophist agrees to engage in the former rather than the latter. Not that S. is incapable of the latter; he ends a lengthy speech of his own at *Gorg.* 519d by claiming that Callicles' refusal to answer has compelled him δημηγορεῖν.

e3 γραυσὶ ταῖς τοὺς μύθους λεγούσαις: for the scornful dismissal of such tales as old women tell, cf. *Gorg.* 527a, *Lys.* 205d, *Tht.* 176b.

e4 καὶ κατανεύσομαι καὶ ἀνανεύσομαι: similarly, Lucius answers questions by either nodding or shaking his head (Luc. *Asin.* 48) after he has been transformed into an ass.

e6 Ὥστε σοί ... ἀρέσκειν: the only way of "pleasing" S. would be for T. to comply with S.'s strongly worded (Μηδαμῶς) request that he at least (γε) not respond contrary to his sincerely felt beliefs. T.'s words here have been interpreted to mean that he will assent or dissent in whatever way is pleasing to S., in other words, that he will *not* express his own beliefs (Beversluis 2000: 239–40 with refs. in n. 40). But S. had recently noted with some alarm that T. has up to now been expressing what he genuinely thinks to be the case (τὰ δοκοῦντα, 349a6–7), and T.'s answers to S.'s next questions clearly reflect his own opinions, even earning S.'s surprised approval of T. for not merely nodding and shaking his head (351c3–4). After that, however, T.'s responses become less fulsome, as he begins to recognize that his grudging acceptance of the ground rules laid down by S. allows his opponent to mount an effective assault on his stated position, and his only face-saving device will be the claim that he is answering as he does out of politeness (351d6, 352b4–5).

οὐκ ἐᾷς λέγειν: *sc.* ὅσα βούλομαι; cf. e2.

350e11–352b5: Having demonstrated, to his own satisfaction at least, that the just person is good and wise, S. turns the discussion in a new direction, attempting to secure T.'s agreement that the unjust person has less power (δύναμις) than the just. His point of departure is a proposition that T. is likely to approve, that corporate entities such as cities and bands of thieves, no less than individuals, can be unjust and can act unjustly. Indeed, it was T. who had first introduced the political element (338d6n.). The argument proceeds as follows: unjust cities overpower other cities using injustice (351b–c); but to be effective unjust groups require their individual members to refrain from unjust behavior toward one another (c), because injustice breeds strife, whereas justice brings about concord (d); so, since it is the ἔργον of injustice to implant strife, its presence will prevent individuals from cooperating on a common venture (d–e); even in an individual, the presence of injustice will do ἅπερ πέφυκεν ἐργάζεσθαι, namely implant strife, rendering the individual powerless to act (352a). This section, therefore, foreshadows the analogy drawn between the individual and the state that will be fundamental to the argument in subsequent books of *Republic*: as in Book Two, where S. begins the search for justice on the larger scale of the city to facilitate the inquiry into the nature of justice in the individual (368c–e), so here the divisive effects of injustice in the city and other groups serve as a model for the disarray that allegedly afflicts the unjust person's soul (Kahn 1993: 138–9).

350e11 Τοῦτο: explained by the ὁποῖον-clause ("namely, what sort of thing ..."), with ὅπερ ἄρτι in apposition. S. has "just now" (350d5–6) referred back to T.'s claim (344c4–5) that injustice is ἰσχυρότερον than justice.

351a1–2 ἐλέχθη γάρ που "A proposal, I believe, was made to the effect that," again avoiding assigning responsibility specifically to T. (350d5n.).

a2 δυνατώτερον: S. introduces this word – not used by T. but surely intended to appeal to his political sensibilities – because he will speak below of the capability (δύναμις) of injustice which, S. will argue, renders states and individuals incapable of concerted action.

a3–5 δικαιοσύνη ... ἡ ἀδικία: as is often the case with abstract nouns, it is not clear why the article appears with one but not the other.

a5 ἔτι "still"; i.e. after hearing our discussion of the matter.

οὕτως ἁπλῶς "in such a simple, straightforward manner," as at 331c2 (a colloquialism; Collard 2018: 56). S. is toying with T., suggesting that he could easily refute T.'s position, "just like that," merely by showing that, inasmuch as justice has now been identified with knowledge and superiority (which, of course, T. denies), injustice must be identified with their opposites, inferiority and ignorance. In Book Two Adeimantus will implore S. to prove not merely that justice is superior (κρεῖττον, 367b and e) to injustice but that the just person is better off than the unjust.

a6–b1 πόλιν φαίης ἂν ἄδικον εἶναι καὶ ἄλλας πόλεις ἐπιχειρεῖν δουλοῦσθαι ἀδίκως "Would you say of a *city* that it is unjust and that it unjustly undertakes to enslave other cities?" The conversation to this point has concerned itself with the (completely unjust) person; now S. extends to the city and its actions the language of injustice that has thus far been applied only to individuals, the position of πόλιν at the start of the sentence signaling the introduction of a new topic (*CGCG* §60.27–9). Talk of a city that unjustly enslaves other cities is topical in the Athens where the conversation between S. and T. is set (White 1995: 323), the city whose representatives notoriously dismissed as irrelevant any talk of "justice" in the debate with their unfortunate Melian counterparts (Thuc. 5.89–90). Thus, current events seem to support T.'s contention that injustice is more powerful than justice, which is what S. is determined to disprove. In *Republic*'s sequels, *Timaeus* and *Critias*, an account of the legendary city of Atlantis will be given which assumes that S. has proven his case. The inhabitants of Atlantis were filled with ruthless acquisitiveness and power (πλεονεξίας ἀδίκου καὶ δυνάμεως ἐμπιμπλάμενοι, *Criti.* 121b6–7), and they attempted to enslave (ἐπεχείρησεν ... δουλοῦσθαι, *Tim.* 25b4–5) other cities; the virtuous citizens of antediluvian Athens, who are explicitly identified with the inhabitants of the ideal city of *Republic* (*Tim.* 26c–d), single-handedly overpowered the might of Atlantis and magnanimously liberated those who had been enslaved (25c).

351b2 καὶ καταδεδουλῶσθαι: the middle term in a progression. S. asks if T. thinks the unjust city endeavors (ἐπιχειρεῖν) without justification to bring about the enslavement of other cities, does so successfully (note the perfect tense and the intensifying force of the preverb κατα-; LSJ E.v) and even continues to hold *many* (πολλὰς δὲ καί) cities in its power after having enslaved them.

b4 ἀρίστη "best" in T.'s estimation, as is clear from S.'s response and from T.'s explanatory addition, οὖσα ἄδικος. The unjust city, corresponding to T.'s supremely unjust man (348d6–7), will be most effective and most thorough in imposing its will on others.

b4–5 μάλιστα ... καὶ τελεώτατα: cf. *Pol.* 270c1–2 μεγίστην καὶ τελεωτάτην τροπήν. For T.'s fondness for superlatives, see 341b7n.

b6 ὅτι "because," as at 332a11. S. understands why T. answered as he did, namely because he still adheres to his stated position (λόγος), even in the face of S.'s proof that injustice is to be identified with frailty and ignorance.

περὶ αὐτοῦ: *sc.* τοῦ σοῦ λόγου.

b8 ἡ ἀνάγκη αὐτῆι: *sc.* τῆι πόλει (τὴν δύναμιν ταύτην ἕξειν).

351c1–2 Εἰ μέν, ... εἰ δέ: the ruthless imposition of power over others requires what T. calls σοφία, or the successful application of intelligence in pursuit of the agent's own interest. The word has a different meaning for S. (and P.); cf. 4.442c, where S. ascribes σοφία to the ruling element of the individual's soul, corresponding to the ruling element in the polis, which possesses an understanding of what is advantageous (συμφέρον) for itself, for each of the other elements individually and for the whole as a collective.

c1 [ἔχει]: the intrusive word perhaps arose as a marginal variant to ἕξει in the previous line and found its way into the text in the wrong place.

c2 μετὰ ἀδικίας: because T. assigns injustice to the category of excellence and intelligence (348e2–4). T. is treating the prepositional phrase, which occurs only here in P. (and rarely elsewhere), as a synonym of ἀδίκως in the sentence at a6–b3, not anticipating the argument that follows, in which T. will be led to acknowledge that the individual citizens of the unjust city will need to treat each other μετὰ δικαιοσύνης in order to succeed.

c5 Σοὶ γάρ ... χαρίζομαι: cf. *Gorg.* 516b4 ἵνα σοι χαρίσωμαι and *Prot.* 360e4 χαριοῦμαι οὖν σοι, where Callicles and the sophist Protagoras cover their embarrassment by magnanimously declaring that they are answering as they do to humor S., in the latter case after S. has just been accused of φιλονικία.

c7 ἢ πόλιν ... ἢ ἄλλο τι ἔθνος: when T. introduced the polis into the conversation (338d6), he represented the ruling element in each city, regardless of its type of government, as a unified entity acting effectively in furtherance of its own interest. S. cleverly takes advantage of T.'s concern with political power to point out that the polis is, like any corporate entity, a collection of individuals, each of whom is, on T.'s view, engaged in the unjust pursuit of personal interest. T. could argue that the best polis, i.e. the perfectly unjust one, is ruled by a tyrant, in which case the interest of the polis is identified with that of its ruler (Annas 1981: 52–3); apart, however, from the awkwardness of making such an argument in the context of fifth-century Athens, he has foreclosed that option with his earlier reference to "all poleis," democracies, tyrannies and aristocracies alike, at 338e–339a. Alternatively, it might be argued that a collective can be made to cooperate out of fear or other motives (Cross and Woozley 1964: 55–6; Lycos 1987: 139), but to address this would unnecessarily complicate S.'s argument.

ἔθνος: for the use of this word, sometimes disparagingly, to refer to any group or class of individuals, see *Pol.* 290b1 τὸ κηρυκικὸν ἔθνος, *Tim.* 19d6 τὸ μιμητικὸν ἔθνος.

ὅσα: plural because referring to several antecedents but agreeing in gender with ἔθνος. S.'s concern at this point is exclusively with cities and other groups of people, who are the subjects and objects of ἀδικοῖεν below. The effects of injustice in the individual will be introduced only later (352a5n.).

c8 ἀδίκως: the question is equally valid with and without the adverb, but its inclusion is rhetorically effective. Can a group succeed collectively (κοινῆι) in achieving its dishonorable goals if its own members treat each other dishonorably?

351d1–3 Οὐ δῆτα ... Πάνυ γε: T. can answer as he does without entirely abandoning his stated position. The unjust city achieves success in dominating other cities by treating them unjustly but, as T. earlier explained (343c–e), the ruling power within each city attains its dominance thanks in part to the simple-minded deference to authority on the part of the weak, which he calls "justice." It is only with S.'s next set of questions that T. parts company with him, although out of a sham spirit of cooperation he declines to dissent. In any event, at this point T. is merely admitting that refraining (temporarily?) from acting unjustly – which is not the same as acting justly – is more conducive to the success of the collective. Thus S. still has more work to do in order to show that justice is ἰσχυρότερον than injustice. It will be the aim of the remaining nine books to prove that justice is κρεῖττον, in every sense of the word, than injustice, in response to the challenge posed by Glaucon and Adeimantus (2.367b4, e2).

d4–5 Στάσεις ... ὁμόνοιαν καὶ φιλίαν: cf. Lysias 18.17, where ὁμόνοια is said to be the greatest good for a city, and στάσις the cause of all its ills. That justice produces concord and amity (cf. *Pol.* 311b9 ὁμονοίαι καὶ φιλίαι) does not follow from the claim that injustice produces their opposites, strife and hatred. It is merely stated without proof, relying on T.'s current inclination to answer S.'s questions with polite condescension. Still, P. was likely aware that the historical T. professed, in a speech addressed to the Athenians, to approve ὁμόνοια: in the only substantial fragment of T.'s work to survive, he at one point decries the fact that ὁμόνοια has been replaced by hatred and political disorder (ἔχθραν καὶ ταραχάς, DK 85 B1 = 35 D16 Laks–Most). In Book Four ὁμόνοια will be identified with σωφροσύνη (432a7), the virtue that enables the disparate elements of the individual and the polis to function harmoniously. The concept of ὁμόνοια seems to have come to prominence in intellectual circles – the physician Eryximachus claims that the skill of the doctor and the musician consists in the creation of ἔρως καὶ ὁμόνοια (*Symp.* 186e1–2, 187c3–4) – in the late fifth and early fourth centuries, particularly among those who adhered to a moderate political outlook (Romilly 1972). The concept is briefly the subject of some inconclusive scrutiny in *Clitophon* (409e–410a) and *Alcibiades 1* (126c–127d), likely influenced by *Republic*; see Slings 1999: 185–93.

d6 ἵνα σοι μὴ διαφέρωμαι: the verb will be used shortly (352a2) in reference to political strife. There is, thus, considerable irony, undoubtedly intended by P., in the choice of this word. Just as individual citizens need to refrain from acting unjustly toward one another in order for their city to function successfully, so participants in a philosophical discussion about the nature of justice must cooperate (336e) to arrive at the truth. The irony, however, is complex. T.'s cooperation is merely feigned, and the discussion in Book One is ultimately inconclusive; it will require less combative and more unselfish interlocutors to make progress toward a definition of justice.

d8 ἔργον "product" or "outcome," as at 330c5, 332e3. Presently (352e2–3), ἔργον will be given a more narrow definition ("specific function"), hinted at already in ἅπερ πέφυκεν ἐργάζεσθαι (352a5–6). But that definition does not suit the present passage, since it is not the case that injustice is the only thing or the thing that best enables enmity to be produced, nor would T. agree to its application here.

d8–9 ἐλευθέροις τε καὶ δούλοις: various explanations have been given for the seemingly irrelevant inclusion of slaves, e.g. that this is merely an instance of polar expression (for which, see 333d4n.). But S. began this line of inquiry by asking about cities that enslave other cities, so that we seem to be encouraged to think in terms of a city acting in concert with its "allies," that is, other cities that it has enslaved. S. and T. could easily supply a contemporary example (Thuc. 1.98.4 notes that Naxos was the first city to be subjugated, ἐδουλώθη, setting the precedent for the treatment of other cities that revolted from the Athenian alliance).

351e3 ἐν δυοῖν: two cities or other groups, the (human) members of which are the subjects of the plural verbs that follow.

e4 ἀλλήλοις τε καὶ τοῖς δικαίοις: the two are ex hypothesi unjust, injustice having been implanted in them. Each of them, therefore, will attempt to surpass both the other and the just (349d1), who will shortly be said to include the gods.

e6 μῶν μή "surely ... not," a strengthened form of μῶν, itself derived from μή + οὖν. The combination is attested only in P.

e9 τοιάνδε τινά: the article with δύναμιν shows that these words are predicative ("the power that injustice has is something like this"); cf. 346a3 ἑτέραν τὴν δύναμιν ἔχειν.

e9–352a1 οἵαν ... ἀδύνατον αὐτὸ ποιεῖν πράττειν: the infinitive with οἷος conveys the notion of "ability, fitness, or sufficiency" (*SMT* §759). Here S. is having fun with the conceit that the conspicuous δύναμις of injustice is of the sort to make its possessor ἀδύνατον πράττειν.

ὧι ... ἄλλωι ὁτωιοῦν: neuter, as is shown by the following αὐτό. S. is still concerned with groups infected by injustice; he will begin to ask about injustice in individuals only at 352a5.

352a3 τῶι ἐναντίωι παντί "everything that is its opposite." For this use of πᾶς in predicate position "with a generic singular," see Gildersleeve §648.

a5 Καὶ ἐν ἑνὶ δή, οἶμαι: this is the first unambiguous reference to injustice in a single individual; compare ἀδύνατον αὐτὸν πράττειν ποιήσει (a6) with ἀδύνατον αὐτὸ ποιεῖν πράττειν (a1). S. has by no means demonstrated that the unjust person, like the unjust collective, will be unable to accomplish anything or that elements within the person are necessarily in conflict with one another, hence the hesitant οἶμαι. Later, in Book Four (440b, 444a–b; cf. 9.586e), the claim will be made, based on the analogy with the city, that injustice in the individual is a sort of factional strife among the elements within the soul. For now, S. is relying on the questionable claim that the ἔργον of injustice is to implant hatred wherever it is found (351d8 with n.), allowing him to say here that injustice will have the very same effects in the individual that it is by nature disposed to produce. P. tries to give the impression that the parallelism is exact by using strikingly similar language to ask about injustice in the city and other groups (351e6–352a3) and in the individual (352a5–8).

a8 τοῖς δικαίοις: masculine; contrast τῶι δικαίωι neuter (a3).

a10 Δίκαιοι ... καὶ οἱ θεοί; this is the ace S. has been holding until now. He could have played it earlier, at 349c, securing T.'s agreement that, since the unjust person attempts to get the better of the just and the unjust alike, he or she would attempt to get the better of the gods. By saving it for now S. can embarrass T. into an admission that the unjust person is the *enemy* of the gods, an especially embarrassing admission given the religious celebration during which the dialogue is set. T.'s refusal to give a negative answer to this and S.'s next question, "in order not to antagonize the present company," is, however, susceptible of more than one interpretation. On the surface, T. appears to be politely acquiescing in the popular view of the gods as upholders of justice in the traditional sense of the word, for which see Dover 1974: 257–61. But T. had defined justice as genteel ingenuousness (348d1) and had argued that the just are regularly taken advantage of by the unjust, who are experts in self-aggrandizement (343c–e). In Adeimantus' expansion of T.'s argument (2.365d–e), he will invoke the possibility that either the gods do not exist or they do not concern themselves with human affairs and, even if they do, they can be bribed with sacrifices and offerings (compare Cephalus at 331b3), with which the supremely unjust person is best supplied as a result of unjust behavior. So it is conceivable that T.'s response, in full, might have taken the form, "Yes, the gods are just, but in my sense of the word; that is, they can be easily fobbed off with gifts to ignore the actions of the supremely unjust person." The matter is further complicated, however, by a fragment from one of T.'s own writings preserved in Hermeias' comment on *Phdr.* 267c (= DK 85 B8 = 35 D17 Laks–Most), illustrating the intensity of T.'s rhetoric: "The gods do not pay attention to human affairs, since (if they did) they would not have overlooked the most important of the good things among humans, namely justice (τὴν δικαιοσύνην), which we see being neglected by mortals." This assumes that the gods are just in the conventional sense, since their failure to enforce justice among humans (generally? in a specific case being argued?) is attributed not to their own debased character but to their alleged indifference to the human condition (the original of Adeimantus' εἰ ... μηδὲν αὐτοῖς τῶν ἀνθρωπίνων μέλει, 365d8–9?). Without knowing the context, or the nature of the work that Hermeias is paraphrasing – he introduces the fragment by saying that T. ἔγραψεν ἐν λόγωι ἑαυτοῦ τοιοῦτόν τι – we do not know whether T. is expressing his own view or a view that he expects his audience (or his client?) to share.

352b1 Ἔστωσαν: this form of the third-person plural imperative appears in the MSS at 354a5, *Meno* 92d2 and *Soph.* 231a9, as well as over a dozen times in *Laws* (alongside two occurrences of ἔστων). Slings adopts Burnet's ἔστω, which is correctly transmitted over 200 times in P., often as a response formula; it is unclear why it should have been subject to corruption just here and 354a5.

b2–3 θεοῖς ἄρα ἐχθρὸς ἔσται ὁ ἄδικος ... ὁ δὲ δίκαιος φίλος: similarly, in *Gorgias* (507d–e), S. explains to Callicles that the person who lacks justice and temperance, living the life of a brigand (λῃστής; cf. 351c7), will not be προσφιλής either to mortals or gods, since that person will be unable to enter into associations. Glaucon in Book Two, however, professes not to be persuaded. In his reframing of T.'s position he claims that the perfectly unjust person, because of wealth and a reputation for justice, will turn out to be θεοφιλέστερος than the just person (2.362c). It will not be until the end of Book Ten that he will be satisfied that, indeed, the just person is θεοφιλής (612e5, 621c6–7).

b4 Εὐωχοῦ τοῦ λόγου ... θαρρῶν "Go ahead and gorge yourself on the conversation!" For the defiant tone of θαρρῶν with an imperative (usually expressing support and encouragement), cf. Aesch. *Ag.* 1671, *PV* 916; for the genitive, as with other expressions referring to the enjoyment of food and drink, see KG I 355. The "feast of words" (e.g. 5.458a1, 9.571d9) is a frequent metaphor in P., sometimes applied ironically to a sophistic or rhetorical display (*Gorg.* 447a, 521d–522a, *Phdr.* 227b), but also used by S. to introduce Timaeus' exposition (*Tim.* 27b). In reference to conversation, we find it at *Lysis* 211c–d, where Ctesippus complains that S. and Lysis are keeping their discussion to themselves and not sharing their repast with him. In *Republic* the metaphor has a thematic significance. At the start of Book One we were led to expect dinner and postprandial conversation at a παννυχίς (328a6–7), but in the end it will emerge that the conversation was the main course (354a–b), with Book One providing the hors d'oeuvre.

352b6–354c3: In the closing pages of the book S. makes two claims, one merely asserted on the basis of the previous argument and the other argued for at some length. Although they appear unrelated, they are in fact closely intertwined. The first, invalidating T.'s admiring portrait of the tyrant as perfectly unjust, is that there can be no such thing as perfect, unadulterated injustice, since it would render groups incapable of performing any actions at all. The extension of this notion to the individual, suggested at 352a5–7, is developed in Book Four (see 352a5n.), but the reasoning behind it is grounded in the argument that closes Book One. S. begins by establishing the definition of X's ἔργον as "that which one can do only, or most efficiently, by means of X." Every X has a specific ἀρετή which enables it to perform its ἔργον well. Among the ἔργα of the soul is living. The soul's ἀρετή is justice, and its κακία is injustice. Therefore, the just soul and the just person will live well and the unjust badly. Living well leads to happiness, which is universally desired, so that being just is more rewarding than being unjust. QED. Specific issues raised by this argument will be dealt with below, but here it is appropriate to explain the connection between this latter argument and S.'s earlier dismissal of the possibility of perfect injustice. Throughout, S. is careful to speak in terms of X's ἀρετή as enabling it to perform its ἔργον *well*, not wishing to entertain the possibility that X might be entirely deprived of its ἀρετή and therefore be incapable of performing its ἔργον *at all.* (T. notes this possibility at 353c3, when he suggests that eyes cannot see when bereft of their singular ἀρετή, but S. brushes off T.'s comment and moves on.) When it comes to the soul, which is immortal (10.609b–611a), it is impossible that it should be prevented from performing its ἔργον, even by its specific κακία. Therefore (although the connection is not made explicit) no soul can entirely lack ἀρετή.

352b7 ὥσπερ καὶ νῦν: that is, in the accommodating manner of T.'s recent responses.

b7–d1 ὅτι μὲν γὰρ ... πράττειν ἀδύνατοι: the sentence begins as though it is going to continue with something like, "(That the just are wiser etc.) we have demonstrated," but our hopes of encountering a main verb are disappointed. Instead, S. seems to have changed his mind about what he was going to say, and the sentence goes off in another direction, with the next sentence beginning ταῦτα μὲν οὖν ... μανθάνω (d1), "Well, this is how I (now) understand the matter." P. often uses anacoluthon (Slings 1997: 192–214) to enhance the impression of spontaneity in his carefully crafted dialogues. The train of thought here is: "(We have shown that) the unjust are incapable of acting effectively in concert, since their injustice renders them unable to cooperate, or rather (since the unjust are not completely incapacitated) there must be some modicum of justice in them that enables them to achieve whatever success they enjoy."

352c1–2 καὶ οὓς φαμεν ... ἀδίκους ὄντας "even those of whom we say that they have ever effectively accomplished something in partnership with one another while being unjust." Here too there is a slight anacoluthon, since the (unexpressed) antecedent of οὕς has no construction, τοῦτο in the following line meaning, in effect, "this statement about them."

c4 κομιδῆι ὄντες ἄδικοι "if they were *completely* unjust," the position of the adverb giving it the emphasis.

c5 μή τοι καὶ ἀλλήλους γε "at least not each other, too (in addition to their victims)." For the forceful μή τοι ... γε, see 3.388b8–c2, where it occurs twice ("not *the gods* ..., but if the gods, at the very least not *the greatest* of the gods!"); *GP* 546–7.

c6–7 ἀδικίαι ἡμιμόχθηροι ὄντες "being (only) semi-degenerate (an adjective invented by P. for use here) by reason of injustice," the position of ἀδικίαι being dictated by a desire to juxtapose it with ἄδικα.

352d2 οὐχ ὡς σὺ τὸ πρῶτον ἐτίθεσο: at 344c4–5, taking as his model the tyrant, who practices "the most perfect injustice" and is therefore supremely happy (344a3–6), T. concluded that injustice is mightier than justice. S. has now completely reversed that, having shown that those who are completely wicked and perfectly unjust are essentially powerless and require a minimal amount of justice to accomplish anything at all.

d2–3 ἄμεινον ζῶσιν ... καὶ εὐδαιμονέστεροί εἰσιν: the two are equivalent. Everyone would agree that the better life consists of being εὐδαιμονέστερον. S. and T., however, are still as far apart as ever about what constitutes εὐδαιμονία.

d3–4 ὅπερ τὸ ὕστερον προυθέμεθα σκέψασθαι "which we subsequently set as a task for ourselves (*CGL* προτίθημι 10) to investigate." The task that "we" (i.e. S. and Glaucon) set was to persuade T. that the life of the just person is better and more rewarding than that of the unjust (347e–348b). At the end of Book One S. will claim to have demonstrated that there are no circumstances in which injustice is λυσιτελέστερον than justice (354a8).

d5–6 περὶ τοῦ ἐπιτυχόντος: literally, "about that which one happens upon" (LSJ A.II.4), i.e. some random issue; cf. *Apol.* 17c2–3 εἰκῆι λεγόμενα τοῖς ἐπιτυχοῦσιν ὀνόμασιν, "spoken in a disorganized way, using whatever words come to mind."

d6 περὶ τοῦ ὅντινα τρόπον χρὴ ζῆν: unlike English, which can make an indirect question the object of a preposition (e.g. "about what constitutes εὐδαιμονία"), Greek uses the (neuter) definite article to make the question into a noun, in the same way it can substantivize any word or group of words (Smyth §1153g). For S., the question of how best to live one's life is of fundamental importance: 344e2–3, 9.578c6–7, 10.608b4–5, *Gorg.* 472c6–d1, 492d3–5, 500c3–4, *Lach.* 187e6–188a2.

d8 δοκεῖ τί σοι εἶναι ἵππου ἔργον; the accent on enclitic τι is owed to the following σοι: Probert 2003: §297. Presumably, the "function" of a horse is to be exploited by humans for work, war and sport.

352e2–3 ὃ ἂν ... ἄριστα: T.'s reaction calls attention to the novelty of S.'s definition. The significance of the definition will become clear in Book Two, when S. and Adeimantus agree that the city they are imagining will function most efficiently only when each citizen performs that ἔργον (cognate with English "work") for which he or she is by nature best suited: 369e–370b (see Santas 2006b: 132–41). S.'s definition presupposes that, for every X, there is an intelligence responsible either for creating X to perform its specific function or for adapting it to serve that function. Horses and pruning hooks are examples of Xs that were either manufactured or customized by humans to perform the function for which they are best suited. Eyes and ears were created by the gods (*Tim.* 45b, 47c) for the functions which only they can carry out; that is, S. and P. were proponents of what today would be called "intelligent design" (Sedley 2007a: 75–132).

e7 ἀκούσαις: ἄν is understood from the previous question, as at 2.382d11; see *SMT* §226.

e9 δικαίως ... φαμέν: cf. *Phd.* 73c10 δικαίως λέγομεν. The intrusive ἄν has come from two lines below (where see app. crit.).

353a1 μαχαίραι ... καὶ σμίληι "a butcher's knife ... and a leather-cutting tool"; for the latter, see Austin and Olson on Ar. *Thesm.* 778–80.

a10 τι is not essential, since the subject of ἀπεργάζηται is easily supplied from ἑκάστου.

κάλλιστα τῶν ἄλλων: this locution, strictly illogical, is not uncommon (*CGCG* §32.8). It results from a conflation of the partitive genitive ("most efficiently of all") and the genitive of comparison ("more efficiently than the rest"); cf. 5.456d12–13 τῶν ἄλλων πολιτῶν ... ἄριστοι; KG I 23–4.

353b3 οὐκοῦν καὶ ἀρετή: as will become clear, by ἀρετή is meant that good quality that enables anything to perform its given function well and, correspondingly, its κακία is the deficiency that hinders the optimal performance of its function. Thus, sharpness is the ἀρετή of a pruning hook and dullness its κακία. This understanding of ἀρετή was assumed earlier, when S. and Polemarchus agreed that dogs, horses and humans, when their particular ἀρετή is impaired, are rendered inferior specimens of their species (335b–c). The question of what the specific human ἀρετή is serves as the point of departure of *Meno*, the title character of which, however, proposes that each class of person (man, woman, free, slave) has a specific ἀρετή (and a corresponding κακία) πρὸς ἕκαστον ἔργον, 72a3. For this he is mocked by S., who is looking for the one differentia of ἀρετή.

b4 ἔργον τι προστέτακται: the verb is often found with ἔργον as object, in the sense of assigning a task; e.g. *Parm.* 136d1 and 6, Hdt. 1.114.2, Xen. *Cyr.* 4.5.25. Its use here assumes an agent, either human or divine (352e2–3n.), responsible for making the assignment.

b9 ὤτων ἦν τι ἔργον; the imperfect in effect turns the question into, "Didn't we agree (at 352e7–10) that there is a function that ears have?"

b15 Ἔχε δή "Hold on," an expression confined in P. to S. and the visitor from Athens in *Laws*; see Dodds on *Gorg.* 460a5 and Rijksbaron on *Ion* 535b1. The effect is to acknowledge the interlocutor's acquiescence in what has been agreed to so far, before moving on either to a new point or to an examination of the implications of the foregoing.

353c1–2 ἀντὶ τῆς ἀρετῆς κακίαν: S. creates difficulties for himself by presenting this as an either/or situation. For how well the eyes perform their function is not a matter of their having *either* ἀρετή *or* κακία, but of the degree to which one outweighs the other. T.'s response calls attention to the inadequacy of the eyes and ears, which can be entirely deprived of their ἀρετή, as analogues of the immortal soul, the ἀρετή of which is living.

c3 τυφλότητα … ἀντὶ τῆς ὄψεως: vision, ὄψις, was identified as the ἀρετή of the eye at 342a3 (cf. *Alc.1* 133b4–5), but S. does not want to admit blindness, the absence of vision, as the eye's κακία (352b6–354c3n.). In Book Ten S. will identify as the affliction that damages and destroys the eye ὀφθαλμία (609a1), which can refer to blindness (e.g. Ar. *Wealth* 115) but need not.

c4 Ἥτις … αὐτῶν ἡ ἀρετή "Whatever their ἀρετή is (is not pertinent)," with the omission clarified by the following sentence; cf. (without ellipsis) *Prot.* 357b5–6 Ἥτις μὲν τοίνυν τέχνη καὶ ἐπιστήμη ἐστὶν αὕτη, εἰς αὖθις σκεψόμεθα. For comparable ellipseis (with ὅπως ἄν, "However …") in stichomythia, see Eur. *Med.* 331, *Tro.* 1052. S. professes not now to be interested in this (τοῦτο), namely whether ὄψις is the eye's ἀρετή, ignoring T.'s identification of the eye's κακία. At 349c1–2 S. had similarly dismissed as irrelevant that portion of T.'s answer that went beyond what the question strictly demanded. There, as here, P.'s motive in having T. say more than S. wants him to say is unclear. This practice, of requiring the interlocutor to limit answers strictly to what was asked, is characteristic of eristic: *Euthd.* 296a–c, 300c.

c5–6 τὰ ἐργαζόμενα "the things that perform the function," i.e. the eyes, subject of ἐργάσεται ("will perform"), the object of which is ἔργον ("function," i.e. seeing).

c8 στερόμενα τῆς αὑτῶν ἀρετῆς κακῶς: deprived of their own ἀρετή the ears will not perform their function badly; they will not perform it at all.

353d1 τὸν αὐτὸν λόγον: in effect, "the same logical pattern."

d3 Ἴθι δή ... ψυχῆς ἔστι τι ἔργον: culminative δή (332d2n.) marks the arrival at the end point of the discussion. The soul is, for S. and P., both the beginning and the end, indeed the whole, of the philosopher's concern. In *Apology* S. explains his mission as exhorting his fellow Athenians to care for nothing so much as their souls (29e–30b). In *Republic* the soul will serve as an analogue of the whole of human society (4.434d–435c) and, later, *Timaeus* will end with a plea for the care (θεραπεία, 90c6) of the human soul, itself created using the same ingredients that went into the creation of the soul of the cosmos (41d).

d6 ἐκείνου: since this refers to that hypothetical other thing that is contrasted with the soul, as is clear from T.'s answer, it cannot be feminine (see app. crit.). Among the late MSS that read ἐκείνου in place of ἐκείνης is one, Parisinus 1810, whose correctors elsewhere differ from the primary MSS in occasionally preserving what appear to be true readings; see Boter 1989: 239.

d8 Τί δὲ αὖ τὸ ζῆν; in *Cratylus* (399d–e) S. says that those who gave ψυχή its name did so because it is responsible for life, (correctly) connecting the word etymologically with the breath that enables life and whose departure accompanies the body's death.

d10 καὶ ἀρετήν φαμέν τινα ψυχῆς: agreement to this is obligatory after it was agreed (353b6) that everything that has an ἔργον also has a corresponding ἀρετή. Despite what is said below, a consensus was not reached regarding what exactly that ἀρετή is; at 350d3–5 S. claimed that he and T. concluded that justice was (an) ἀρετή and injustice (a) κακία, presumably of nothing other than the soul (cf. *Gorg.* 477c3–4).

353e1 τὰ αὐτῆς ἔργα: unlike the eye and the pruning hook, the soul has several ἔργα, in addition to living, some of which were enumerated above (d4–5) and are repeated just below.

e5 εὖ πράττειν: the last words of *Republic* are εὖ πράττωμεν. The expression, however, has more than one application, and P. plays upon the ambiguity. In the sphere of ruling and management, it refers to performing well a defined function; in the case of living, it is synonymous with εὐδαιμονεῖν, acknowledged to be the *summum bonum* (Adkins 1960: 252). If, therefore, one has a defective soul, one will do a substandard job of ruling countries or chairing academic departments; more importantly, one will live a miserable existence, deprived of human happiness.

e12 κατὰ τὸν σὸν λόγον: cf. 339d1, where S. has argued T. into a position where, he says, it is just to do both X and the opposite of X, "according to your argument." Here, T. uses the same words to indicate that he is not convinced by S.'s demonstration.

354a1 μακάριός τε καὶ εὐδαίμων: earlier, T. had said that those who behave with perfect injustice are universally admired and are called by everyone εὐδαίμονες καὶ μακάριοι (344b7).

a5 Ἔστωσαν: see 352b1n.

a8 μακάριε: Dickey finds no significant difference between this vocative and others in P., such as φίλε or ἀγαθέ (1996: 140, with occurrences listed at 278–9). Given the context, however, particularly the appearance of μακάριος at a1, here it must be intended sarcastically.

a10 Ταῦτα δή σοι ... εἱστιάσθω "Well, let this serve as your entertainment," the perfect tense conveying T.'s conviction that the festivities have come to an end (Smyth §712), a sentiment that S. initially shares. Book Two, however, begins with S. saying that, while he thought the discussion had ended, as it happened it proved to be only the προοίμιον.

ἐν τοῖς Βενδιδίοις "at the festival in honor of Bendis." The names of festivals are regularly plural, like τὰ Παναθήναια (*sc.* ἱερά) or Διονύσια. Only now can we appreciate why P. has chosen to set *Republic* at the feast for Bendis (327a2n.), and why he has T. remind us of the fact at the point at which, as S. says, T. has become πρᾶος (a11). We have learned more about the iconography of the Thracian goddess, whom the Greeks identified with Artemis, as a result of the discovery of the "Rogozen treasure," a hoard of Thracian silver vessels dating to the fifth and fourth centuries BC. Among them are representations of the goddess, in one case mounted on a lion and in another holding two wolves by the forepaws, one in each hand (Fol et al. 1989: catalogue nos. 155 and 158, identifying the latter, however, as domestic dogs). Wolves and lions are the two creatures to which T. was compared (336d, 341c), and he has now been rendered docile by the enchanting power of S.'s conversational skills. (Glaucon will later liken the taming of T. to the charming of another wild animal, a snake: 2.358b2–3.) We learn from *Charmides* that S. owes his knowledge of charms that treat the soul (τοὺς λόγους τοὺς καλούς) to his period of military service in northern Greece, which ended in 429 BC, where he received instruction from a Thracian physician in the service of the divine king of Thrace, Zalmoxis (156d–157c).

a11 Ὑπὸ σοῦ γε "(Provided) by *you*!" S. toys with T. to the end, first pretending to ignore the fact that T. had disavowed the λόγος as his own (353e12), then suggesting that his enjoyment of the festivities coincides with the time since T. became docile (ἐπειδή μοι πρᾶος ἐγένου) and, finally, seeming to blame himself (διὰ ἐμαυτόν) for not having done a more thorough job of refuting T. S.'s serious point is that he has been repeatedly distracted from the original question, explored in conversation first with Cephalus then with Polemarchus, What is justice (331c)? T.'s interruption has diverted the discussion into considerations of whether injustice is stronger than justice, which of the two more closely resembles a skill and which is more beneficial to the agent. It is a common theme in P.'s dialogues that it is impossible to know what qualities a thing possesses without knowing exactly what that thing is: *Chrm.* 175b–176a (σωφροσύνη), *Euthphr.* 11a–b (τὸ ὅσιον), *Lach.* 190b–c (ἀρετή), *Meno* 71b (ἀρετή), *Prot.* 361c–d (ἀρετή).

354b1 χαλεπαίνων ἐπαύσω: the first words S. addressed to T., which he was able to speak only because he had seen the wolf before the wolf saw him, were μὴ χαλεπὸς ἡμῖν ἴσθι, 336e2–3.

b2–3 ὥσπερ οἱ λίχνοι τοῦ ἀεὶ παραφερομένου ἀπογεύονται ἁρπάζοντες "the way gourmands grab a taste of whatever course is being served." For the culinary metaphor, see 352b4n., *Tht.* 157d1. This passage is imitated by Polybius (3.57.7–8), Lucian (*Demosth. encom.* 18), Themistius (*Or.* 18.220b) and the emperor Julian (*Or.* 2.69c). In the case of Lucian, the banquet is specified as "Syracusan," the proverbial lavishness of which is noted elsewhere by P. (3.404d1, *Epist.* 7.326b7–8; cf. *CPG* I 158.11). Either, therefore, Lucian is displaying his learning by alluding to the Sicilian origin of S.'s host, or P. is himself discreetly referring to a familiar saying or anecdote that was already connected with a Syracusan context.

b8 οὐκ ἀπεσχόμην τὸ μὴ οὐκ "I couldn't restrain myself from"; cf. Xen. *Cyr.* 1.6.32 οὐκ ἀπείχοντο … τὸ μὴ οὐ πλεονεκτεῖν αὐτῶν πειρᾶσθαι, *SMT* §811. S. portrays himself as at the mercy of the λόγος, which has waylaid him; cf. *Laws* 7.799d5 ἐμπεπτωκότος λόγου, *Prot.* 314c4–5 λόγου … ὃς ἡμῖν … ἐνέπεσεν. In P. the argument is often spoken of as existing independently of the interlocutors, who either pursue it or are driven by its force; e.g. 2.365d1–2, 3.394d8–9, Burnet on *Phd.* 88d9.

354c1 ἐκ τοῦ διαλόγου "as a result of our discussion." Given that P.'s literary output consists almost entirely of "dialogues," the noun is surprisingly uncommon in his works, appearing fewer than a dozen times, in contrast to the hundreds of occurrences of the verb διαλέγεσθαι. It generally occurs, in the plural, in reference to the conditions required for discussion to continue (*Alc.1* 110a3, *Lach.* 200e3, *Prot.* 335d3, 336b1, 338a2, c7); in *Sophist*, the visitor from Elea uses it, in the singular, in the context of his explanation of διάνοια as silent conversation with oneself (263e4, 264b1; cf. *Tht.* 189e–190a).

μηδὲν εἰδέναι: S.'s profession of ignorance is among the most consistent features of his portrayal (Forster 2007), beginning with *Apology*, where he describes his attempt to disprove the claim of the oracle at Delphi that no one is wiser than him, concluding that his (limited) wisdom consists merely in acknowledging "that I do not even think I know that which I do not know" (ὅτι ἃ μὴ οἶδα οὐδὲ οἴομαι εἰδέναι, 21d7–8).

c1–2 ὁπότε γὰρ ... μὴ οἶδα ..., σχολῆι εἴσομαι: cf. *Phd.* 84d10–e2 χαλεπῶς ἂν τοὺς ἄλλους ἀνθρώπους πείσαιμι ... ὅτε γε μηδὲ ὑμᾶς δύναμαι πείθειν. The negative is μή in both instances because of the conditional force of the temporal clauses; *SMT* §520.

c2–3 εἴτε ἀρετή τις οὖσα τυγχάνει εἴτε καὶ οὔ: somewhat disingenuous, given that S. and Polemarchus had expressed the firm conviction that justice is ἀρετή τις, namely ἀνθρωπεία ἀρετή (335c4–5). By the time we get to Book Four we will learn that, so far from being unsure whether justice is an ἀρετή or not, S. is quite certain that it occupies precisely that segment of ἀρετή not held by wisdom, courage and sophrosyne (427d–428a).

c3 οὐκ εὐδαίμων ἐστὶν ἢ εὐδαίμων: the chiastic arrangement with εἴτε ἀρετή ... εἴτε καὶ οὔ places the positive values both first and last. It will come as no surprise to the reader who perseveres through Book Nine that S. and Glaucon – there identified as "the son of Ariston" – arrive at the conclusion that the best and most just person is the most well-off, while the worst and most unjust is the most wretched (τὸν ἄριστόν [punning on the name of Glaucon's, and P.'s, father] τε καὶ δικαιότατον εὐδαιμονέστατον ... τὸν δὲ κάκιστόν τε καὶ ἀδικώτατον ἀθλιώτατον, 580c1–4).

WORKS CITED

There is an excellent bibliography, arranged by topic, in Ferrari 2007: 474–510. An annual bibliography of work on Plato, beginning with 2000, is available online at https://platosociety.org/plato-bibliography.

Adam, J. 1902. *The Republic of Plato*, Cambridge.

Adkins, A. W. H. 1960. *Merit and responsibility*, Oxford.

Ammann, A. N. 1953. -ικος *bei Platon*, Freiburg.

Annas, J. 1981. *An introduction to Plato's Republic*, Oxford.

Appendino, G., F. Pollastro, L. Verotta, M. Ballero, A. Romano, P. Wyrembek, K. Szczuraszek, J. W. Mozrzymas and O. Taglialatela-Scafati 2009. "Polyacetylenes from Sardinian *Oenanthe fistulosa*: a molecular clue to *risus sardonicus*," *Journal of Natural Products* 72: 962–5.

Arnaoutoglou, I. 2015. "Cult associations and politics: worshipping Bendis in Classical and Hellenistic Athens," in V. Gabrielsen and C. A. Thomsen (eds.), *Private associations and the public sphere*, Copenhagen: 25–56.

Austin, C. and S. D. Olson 2004. *Aristophanes: Thesmophoriazusae*, Oxford.

Balot, R. K. 2001. *Greed and injustice in Classical Athens*, Princeton.

Baltzly, D., J. F. Finamore and G. Miles (eds. and transl.) 2018. *Proclus: Commentary on Plato's Republic*, vol. 1, Cambridge.

Bambrough, R. (ed.) 1967. *Plato, Popper and politics: some contributions to a modern controversy*, Cambridge.

Barney, R. 2006. "Socrates' refutation of Thrasymachus," in Santas 2006a: 44–62.

2017. "Callicles and Thrasymachus," *Stanford encyclopedia of philosophy*, https://plato.stanford.edu/entries/callicles-thrasymachus.

Barrett, W. S. 1964. *Euripides: Hippolytos*, Oxford.

Benson, H. H. 1990. "Misunderstanding the 'What is F-ness?' question," *Archiv für Geschichte der Philosophie* 72: 125–42.

Beversluis, J. 2000. *Cross-examining Socrates*, Cambridge.

Biles, Z. P. and S. D. Olson 2015. *Aristophanes: Wasps*, Oxford.

Blair, E. D. 2012. *Plato's dialectic on woman*, New York.

Blass, F. 1887. *Die attische Beredsamkeit*[2], vol. 1, Leipzig.

Blondell, R. (formerly M. W. Blundell) 2002. *The play of character in Plato's dialogues*, Cambridge.

Bluck, R. S. 1961. *Plato's Meno*, Cambridge.

Blundell, M. W. 1989. *Helping friends and harming enemies*, Cambridge.

Boter, G. J. 1986. "Thrasymachus and πλεονεξία," *Mnemosyne* 39: 261–81.

1989. *The textual tradition of Plato's Republic*, Leiden.
Bowie, A. M. 1995. "Greek sacrifice: forms and functions," in A. Powell (ed.), *The Greek world*, London: 463–82.
Boyd, B. W. 2017. *Ovid's Homer: authority, repetition, reception*, Oxford.
Brandwood, L. 1990. *The chronology of Plato's dialogues*, Cambridge.
1992. "Stylometry and chronology," in Kraut 1992: 90–120.
Brock, R. 1990. "Plato and comedy," in E. Craik (ed.), *"Owls to Athens,"* Oxford: 39–49.
2013. *Greek political imagery from Homer to Aristotle*, London.
Brown, L. 2018. "*Aporia* in Plato's *Theaetetus* and *Sophist*," in G. Karamanolis and V. Politis (eds.), *The aporetic tradition in ancient philosophy*, Cambridge: 91–111.
Burnet, J. 1911. *Plato's Phaedo*, Oxford.
1924. *Plato's Euthyphro, Apology of Socrates and Crito*, Oxford.
Burnyeat, M. F. 1997. "First words: a valedictory lecture," *Proceedings of the Cambridge Philological Society* 43: 1–20.
Buxton, R. 2013. *Myths and tragedies in their ancient Greek contexts*, Oxford.
Casson, L. 1971. *Ships and seamanship in the ancient world*, Princeton.
Chadwick, J. 1996. *Lexicographica Graeca*, Oxford.
Chambry, É. 1932. *Platon: Oeuvres complètes*, vol. 6: *La République, livres I–III*, Paris.
Christ, M. R. 1990. "Liturgy avoidance and *antidosis* in Classical Athens," *Transactions of the American Philological Association* 120: 147–69.
1998. *The litigious Athenian*, Baltimore.
Cobet, C. G. 1873. *Variae lectiones quibus continentur observationes criticae in scriptores graecos*[2], Leiden.
Collard, C. 2018. *Colloquial expressions in Greek tragedy*, Stuttgart.
Collins, D. 2004. *Master of the game: competition and performance in Greek poetry*, Washington, DC.
Connor, W. R. 1988. "'Sacred' and 'secular': ἱερὰ καὶ ὅσια and the Classical Athenian concept of the state," *Ancient Society* 19: 161–88.
Constantakopoulou, C. 2007. *The dance of the islands: insularity, networks, the Athenian empire, and the Aegean world*, Oxford.
Cross, R. C. and A. D. Woozley 1964. *Plato's Republic: a philosophical commentary*, London.
Cufalo, D. 2011. *Scholia Graeca in Platonem: Scholia ad Clitophontem et Reipublicae libros I–V continens*, diss. Pisa.
Denniston, J. D. 1952. *Greek prose style*, Oxford.
Denyer, N. 2001. *Plato: Alcibiades*, Cambridge.
2019. *Plato and Xenophon: Apologies of Socrates*, Cambridge.
Dickey, E. 1996. *Greek forms of address from Herodotus to Lucian*, Oxford.
2007. *Ancient Greek scholarship*, Oxford.

Diggle, J. 2004. *Theophrastus: Characters*, Cambridge.
Dodds, E. R. 1951. *The Greeks and the irrational*, Berkeley.
1959. *Plato: Gorgias*, Oxford.
Dover, K. J. 1974. *Greek popular morality in the time of Plato and Aristotle*, Oxford.
Dušanić, S. 1985. "Le médisme d'Isménias et les relations gréco-perses dans la politique de l'Académie platonicienne (383–378 av. J.-C.)," in *La Béotie antique*, Paris: 227–35.
Emlyn-Jones, C. 2007. *Plato: Republic 1–2.368c4*, Oxford.
Fäsi, J. U. 1819. "Einige Bemerkungen und Vorschläge über das erste Buch der Platonische Republik," *Philologische Beyträge aus der Schweiz* 1: 277–91.
Fawcett, P. 2016. "'When I squeeze you with *eisphorai*': taxes and tax policy in Classical Athens," *Hesperia* 85: 153–99.
Ferejohn, M. T. 2006. "Knowledge, recollection, and the Forms in *Republic* VII," in Santas 2006a: 214–33.
Ferrari, G. R. F. (ed.) 2007. *The Cambridge companion to Plato's Republic*, Cambridge.
2010. "Socrates in the *Republic*," in M. L. McPherran (ed.), *Plato's Republic: a critical guide*, Cambridge: 11–31.
Finkelberg, M. 2019. *The gatekeeper: narrative voice in Plato's dialogues*, Leiden.
Fol, A. (ed.) 1989. *The Rogozen treasure*, Sofia.
Forster, M. N. 2007. "Socrates' profession of ignorance," *Oxford Studies in Ancient Philosophy* 32: 1–35.
Friedländer, P. 1964. *Plato*, vol. 2: *The dialogues, first period*, Engl. transl., New York.
Frost, F. J. 1980. *Plutarch's Themistocles: a historical commentary*, Princeton.
Gaca, K. L. 2011. "Manhandled and 'kicked around': reinterpreting the etymology and symbolism of ἀνδράποδα," *Indogermanische Forschungen* 116: 110–46.
Gagarin, M. 2002. *Antiphon the Athenian*, Austin, TX.
Garland, R. 1987. *The Piraeus from the fifth to the first century B.C.*, Ithaca, NY.
1992. *Introducing new gods: the politics of Athenian religion*, Ithaca, NY.
Garland, W. J. 1976. "Notes on two Socratic arguments in *Republic* I," *Apeiron* 10.2: 11–13.
Garvie, A. F. 1986. *Aeschylus: Choephori*, Oxford.
Giannopoulou, Z. 2013. *Plato's Theaetetus as a second Apology*, Oxford.
Gifford, M. 2001. "Dramatic dialectic in *Republic* Book I," *Oxford Studies in Ancient Philosophy* 20: 35–106.

Graham, J. 2007. "Plato's anachronisms," in N. Sekunda (ed.), *Corolla Cosmo Rodewald*, Gdańsk: 67–74.
Guéniot, P. G. 2000. "Un jeu clef: la petteia," *Revue de philosophie ancienne* 18.2: 33–64.
Hainsworth, B. 1993. *The Iliad: a commentary*, vol. 3: *Books 9–12*, Cambridge.
Hanink, J. 2015. "'Why 386 BC?' Lost empire, old tragedy and reperformance in the era of the Corinthian War," *Trends in Classics* 7.2: 277–96.
Hartman, J. L. V. 1896. *Notae criticae ad Platonis de Republica libros*, The Hague.
Hawtrey, R. S. W. 1981. *Commentary on Plato's Euthydemus*, Philadelphia.
Herwerden, H. van 1883. "Ad Platonis libros De re publica," *Mnemosyne* 11: 332–6.
Hyland, J. O. 2015. "The prince and the pancratiast: Persian–Thessalian relations in the late fifth century B.C.," *Greek, Roman, and Byzantine Studies* 55: 315–28.
Jonkers, G. 2017. *The textual tradition of Plato's Timaeus and Critias*, Leiden.
Joseph, H. W. B. 1935. *Essays in ancient and modern philosophy*, Oxford.
Kahn, C. H. 1993. "Proleptic composition in the *Republic*, or why Book 1 was never a separate dialogue," *Classical Quarterly* 43: 131–42.
1996. *Plato and the Socratic dialogue*, Cambridge.
Kaklamanou, E., M. Pavlou and A. Tsakmakis (eds.) 2021. *Framing the Dialogues: how to read openings and closures in Plato*, Leiden.
Kerferd, G. B. 1947. "The doctrine of Thrasymachus in Plato's 'Republic,'" *Durham University Journal* 40: 19–27.
1964. "Thrasymachus and justice: a reply," *Phronesis* 9: 12–16.
Keyt, D. 2006. "Plato and the ship of state," in Santas 2006a: 189–213.
Knopf, E. 2005. *Contracts in Athenian law*, diss. City University of New York.
Kraut, R. (ed.) 1992. *The Cambridge companion to Plato*, Cambridge.
Kyle, D. G. 2007. *Sport and spectacle in the ancient world*, Malden, MA.
Lateiner, D. 1998. "Blushes and pallor in ancient fictions," *Helios* 25: 163–89.
Ledger, G. R. 1989. *Re-counting Plato: a computer analysis of Plato's style*, Oxford.
Lefkowitz, M. R. 2012. *The lives of the Greek poets*[2], Baltimore.
Leigh, M. 2013. *From polypragmon to curiosus*, Oxford.
Levinson, R. B. 1953. *In defense of Plato*, Cambridge, MA.
Lloyd, G. E. R. 1966. *Polarity and analogy*, Cambridge.
Lycos, K. 1987. *Plato on justice and power: reading Book 1 of Plato's Republic*, Albany, NY.
Lygouri-Tolia, E. 2020. "The gymnasium of the Academy and the school of Plato," in P. Kalligas, C. Balla, E. Baziotopoulou-Valavani

and V. Karasmanis (eds.), *Plato's Academy: its workings and its history*, Cambridge: 46–64.
Matthews, G. 2018. "Why Plato lost interest in the Socratic method," *Oxford Studies in Ancient Philosophy* 54: 27–49.
Millis, B. 2015. *Anaxandrides: introduction, translation, commentary*, Heidelberg.
Moore, C. 2008. "Persuasion and force in Plato's *Republic*," *Society for Ancient Greek Philosophy Newsletter* 350, https://orb.binghamton.edu/sagp/350.
Moore, H. 2015. "Why does Thrasymachus blush? Ethical consistency in Socrates' refutation of Thrasymachus," *Polis* 32: 321–43.
Morosi, F. 2020. "Staging philosophy: poverty in the agon of Aristophanes' *Wealth*," *Classical Philology* 115: 402–23.
Munn, M. 2000. *The school of history: Athens in the age of Socrates*, Berkeley.
Nails, D. 1995. *Agora, Academy, and the conduct of philosophy*, Dordrecht.
1998. "The dramatic date of Plato's *Republic*," *Classical Journal* 93: 383–96.
2002. *The people of Plato: a prosopography of Plato and other Socratics*, Indianapolis.
Narcy, M. 2016. "Thrasymaque de Chalcédoine," in R. Goulet (ed.), *Dictionnaire des philosophes antiques*, vol. 6, Paris: 1172–7.
Nicholson, P. P. 1974. "Unravelling Thrasymachus' arguments in 'The Republic,'" *Phronesis* 19: 210–32.
Nightingale, A. W. 2001. "On wandering and wondering: *theôria* in Greek philosophy and culture," *Arion* 9.2: 23–58.
Ogden, D. 2021. *The werewolf in the ancient world*, Oxford.
Olson, S. D. 2002. *Aristophanes: Acharnians*, Oxford.
O'Sullivan, P. and C. Collard 2013. *Euripides: Cyclops and major fragments of Greek satyric drama*, Oxford.
Pache, C. O. 2001. "Barbarian bond: Thracian Bendis among the Athenians," in S. R. Asirvatham, C. O. Pache and J. Watrous (eds.), *Between magic and religion: interdisciplinary studies in ancient Mediterranean religion and society*, Lanham, MD: 3–11.
Parke, H. W. 1977. *Festivals of the Athenians*, Ithaca, NY.
Parker, R. 2005. *Polytheism and society at Athens*, Oxford.
Parry, R. 2020. "*Episteme* and *techne*," *Stanford encyclopedia of philosophy*, https://plato.stanford.edu/entries/episteme-techne.
Planeaux, C. 2000. "The date of Bendis' entry into Attica," *Classical Journal* 96: 165–92.
Poltera, O. 2008. *Simonides lyricus: Testimonia und Fragmente*, Basel.
Popper, K. R. 1945. *The open society and its enemies*, vol 1: *The spell of Plato*, London.

Powell, J. E. 1938. *A lexicon to Herodotus*, Cambridge.

Probert, P. 2003. *A new short guide to the accentuation of ancient Greek*, London.

Quincey, J. H. 1981. "Another purpose for Plato 'Republic' I," *Hermes* 109: 300–15.

Racine, F. 2016. "Herodotus' reputation in Latin literature from Cicero to the 12th century," in J. Priestley and V. Zali (eds.), *Brill's companion to the reception of Herodotus in antiquity and beyond*, Leiden: 193–212.

Rawles, R. 2018. *Simonides the poet*, Cambridge.

Reeve, C. D. C. 1988. *Philosopher-Kings: the argument of Plato's Republic*, Princeton.

Renehan, R. 1976. *Studies in Greek texts*, Göttingen.

Richards, H. 1911. *Platonica*, London.

Riddell, J. 1877. "A digest of Platonic idioms," in *The Apology of Plato*, London: 118–252.

Rijksbaron, A. 1994. *The syntax and semantics of the verb in Classical Greek*², Amsterdam.

2007. *Plato: Ion, or: on the Iliad*, Leiden.

2018. "On the syntax and pragmatics of *inquit* formulae in Plato's narrated dialogues," in *Form and function in Greek grammar*, Leiden: 210–22 [originally 2015].

Romilly, J. de 1972. "Les différents aspects de la concorde dans l'œuvre de Platon," *Revue de philologie* 46: 7–20.

Roochnik, D. L. 1986. "Socrates's use of the techne-analogy," *Journal of the History of Philosophy* 24: 295–310.

Rowe, C. J. 1998. *Plato: Symposium*, Oxford.

Rudebusch, G. 2017. "The unity of virtue, ambiguity, and Socrates' higher purpose," *Ancient Philosophy* 37: 333–46.

Rutherford, I. 2000. "*Theoria* and *darśan*: pilgrimage and vision in Greece and India," *Classical Quarterly* 50: 133–46.

Santas, G. (ed.) 2006a. *The Blackwell guide to Plato's Republic*, Malden, MA.

2006b. "Methods of reasoning about justice in Plato's *Republic*," in Santas 2006a: 125–45.

Santulli, F. 2020. "*We shall fight*: speaker-exclusive *we* as a grammatical metaphor," *International Journal of Linguistics* 12.4: 43–64.

Schneider, C. E. C. 1830. *Platonis Civitas I–IV*, Leipzig.

Sedley, D. 2007a. *Creationism and its critics in antiquity*, Berkeley.

2007b. "Philosophy, the Forms, and the art of ruling," in Ferrari 2007: 256–83.

2013. "Socratic intellectualism in the *Republic*'s central digression," in G. Boys-Stones, D. El Murr and C. Gill (eds.), *The Platonic art of philosophy*, Cambridge: 70–89.

2017. "Divinization," in P. Destrée and Z. Giannopoulou (eds.), *Plato's Symposium: a critical guide*, Cambridge: 88–107.

Shorey, P. 1930. *Plato: The Republic, Books I–V*, Cambridge, MA.

Sicking, C. M. J. and J. M. van Ophuijsen 1993. *Two studies in Attic particle usage*, Leiden.

Simon, E. 1983. *Festivals of Attica: an archaeological commentary*, Madison.

Slings, S. R. 1997. "Figures of speech and their lookalikes: two further exercises in the pragmatics of the Greek sentence," in E. J. Bakker (ed.), *Grammar as interpretation*, Leiden: 169–214.

1998. review of E. A. Duke, W. F. Hicken, W. S. M. Nicoll, D. B. Robinson and J. C. G. Strachan (eds.), *Platonis opera*, vol. 1, *Mnemosyne* 51: 93–102.

1999. *Plato: Clitophon*, Cambridge.

2003. *Platonis Respublica*, Oxford.

2005. *Critical notes on Plato's Politeia*, Leiden.

Solmsen, F. 1975. *Intellectual experiments of the Greek Enlightenment*, Princeton.

Stanford, W. B. 1963. *The Ulysses theme*, Oxford.

Stewart, A. 2008. *Classical Greece and the birth of Western art*, Cambridge.

Storey, I. C. 1988. "Thrasymachos at Athens: Aristophanes fr. 205 (*Daitales*)," *Phoenix* 42: 212–18.

Struck, P. T. 2004. *Birth of the symbol*, Princeton.

Swift Riginos, A. 1976. *Platonica: the anecdotes concerning the life and writings of Plato*, Leiden.

Taplin, O. 1972. "Aeschylean silences and silences in Aeschylus," *Harvard Studies in Classical Philology* 76: 57–97.

Tarrant, H., D. A. Layne, D. Baltzly and F. Renaud (eds.) 2018. *Brill's companion to the reception of Plato in antiquity*, Leiden.

Taylor, A. E. 1928. *A commentary on Plato's Timaeus*, Oxford.

Thesleff, H. 1954. *Studies on intensification in early and Classical Greek*, Helsinki.

1982. *Studies in Platonic chronology*, Helsinki [repr. in Thesleff 2009: 143–382].

1997. "The early version of Plato's Republic," *Arctos: Acta philologica Fennica* 31: 149–74 [repr. in Thesleff 2009: 519–39].

2009. *Platonic patterns*, Las Vegas.

Todd, S. C. 2007. *A commentary on Lysias, Speeches 1–11*, Oxford.

Tucker, T. G. 1900. *The proem to the ideal commonwealth of Plato*, London.

Untersteiner, M. 1954. *Sofisti: testimonianze e frammenti*, vol. 3, Florence.

Van Straten, F. T. 1995. *Hierà kalá: images of animal sacrifice in Archaic and Classical Greece*, Leiden.

Vegetti, M. 1998. *Platone: La Repubblica, Libro I*, Naples.

Vlastos, G. 1991. *Socrates, ironist and moral philosopher*, Ithaca, NY.
1994. "The Socratic elenchus: method is all," in *Socratic studies*, Cambridge: 1–37 [originally 1983].
Wackernagel, J. 2009. *Lectures on syntax, with special reference to Greek, Latin, and Germanic*, Engl. transl., Oxford [originally Basel 1920–4].
Wakker, G. 1994. *Conditions and conditionals*, Amsterdam.
Warren, E. 1985. "Plato's refutation of Thrasymachus: the craft argument," *Society for Ancient Greek Philosophy Newsletter* 124, https://orb.binghamton.edu/sagp/124.
Wedgwood, R. 2017. "The coherence of Thrasymachus," *Oxford Studies in Ancient Philosophy* 53: 33–63.
West, M. L. 1992. *Ancient Greek music*, Oxford.
White, N. P. 1979. *A companion to Plato's Republic*, Indianapolis.
White, S. A. 1995. "Thrasymachus the diplomat," *Classical Philology* 90: 307–27.
Wijma, S. M. 2014. *Embracing the immigrant*, Stuttgart.
Willi, A. 2003. *The languages of Aristophanes: aspects of linguistic variation in Classical Attic Greek*, Oxford.
Wilson, J. R. 1987. "Non-temporal οὐκέτι/μηκέτι," *Glotta* 65: 194–8.
Yunis, H. 1997. "Thrasymachus B1: discord, not diplomacy," *Classical Philology* 92: 58–66.

INDEXES

References in the form "3" or "4(e)" are to the numbered sections of the Introduction; those in the form "28a1" are to notes in the commentary, omitting the first digit of the Stephanus page number.

GENERAL INDEX

Academy, 5, 28a1, 29d3–4, 37d6
accusative
  absolute, 45e6–46a1
  adverbial, 44a1
  cognate, 45e5
Adeimantus, 3, 4(e), 27b3–4, 28a1, 31c1–2, 51a5, 52a10
anacoluthon, 37e4–5, 52b7–d1, c1–2
analogy, argument from, 4(d), 43a2
aorist, 30b8, e4
  gnomic, 38e3–4
  ingressive, 30a6, 48e1–2
Aristophanes
  references to *Rep.* 1
  reference to Thrasymachus? 4(d)
Aristotle, 1
asyndeton, 28a3, 29c5–d2, 50d2–3
Athena, 27a2

Bendis, 2, 3, 27a1–28b3, 27a2, 50d2, 54a10

Cave, 3, 27a1, c9, 34b6–7, 47d2–3
Cephalus, 2, 4(b), 4(c), 28c2, 29b7, 31b6
Clitophon, 28b6–7, 40a1–d1
colloquialisms, 27b6–7, 29c1, 31a9, 36c6–d1, 37a4, 38c1, d6, 45b5, 50d1–2, 51a5
courage, 2
courtroom practice, 37a5, d2, d8, 38c3, 40a2, 44d2, 48a7–b2, b3, 50e2
craft analogy, 32c4–33d12, 32c5
crowns, 28c2

dative, 30a3–4, b6, 42b6
  "ethical," 43a7, 50b12
definite article, 27b3, c10, 28b4, 29a1, e6, 31d8, e3, 32c2, 36a1, 37a8–b1, 38c2, c8, 39b1, c7, 40d2, 44b3–4, 47d5, 48b1–2, 50b10, 51e9, 52d6

elenchus, 4(d), 34b6, 36c4, 40a3, 48a7–b2, 50d2–3
ellipsis, 28b4, 40d2, 53c4
epanalepsis, 36e9–37a2
euphemism, 30d6–7

figura etymologica, 29b4
Forms, 27b1, 31c1–2, 38c3, 45b5
function, *see* ἔργον

genitive, 29b1–2, c5–6, 35b2, 41b8, 44b4–5, 52b4, 53a10
  absolute, 27c14, 36b1–2
Glaucon, 3, 4(a), 4(e), 27a1, 28a1, 30c5, 32a9–10, 37d8, 38c2–39e7, 44a3, a5–6, 47a6–48b6
Guardians, 27a1, 31b3–4, c6–8, 32d1, 34a4, 36e2, 43a7

hendiadys, 30d5, 47c1
Hesiod, 28e3
Homer, 28c6, 34b1

imperfect tense, 40c8–d1
irony, *see* εἰρωνεία

justice
  ἔργον of, 2
  relationship to other virtues, 2, 4(d), 35c4, 54c2–3

litotes, 31b6, 37d1, 38a1
Lysias, 4(b), 4(c), 4(d), 28b4–5

money-making, 4(b), 33a13, 38b3, 43e3, 44d1–47a5, 45d1, 46b1, d4, d6, 47b7

narrative vs dramatic form of dialogues, 1

oaths, 29a1, 31d8
optative, 32a5

perfect tense, 30e4, 54a10
piety, 2, 27a2, 31b3–4, b7
Pindar, 31a2, 38b5
Piraeus, 3, 27a1–28b3, 27a1
pluperfect, 29b4–5
poetic vocabulary, 28c2, c6, 46c9
polar expression, 33d4, 44b1, 51d8–9
Polemarchus, 4(b), 4(c), 27b3–4, c2, 31d4, 40a1–d1
prolepsis, 27a2–3
pronouns, personal, 27b3
proverbs, 29a3, 36d6–7, 41c2–3

response formulae, 1, 30d1
Republic
book divisions, 1n.5
Book One, relationship to rest of *Rep.*, 1, 2, 4(a), 4(d), 38c3, 47d1–2, 50e11–52b5, 51d1–3, 52a5, 52b6–54c3
date of composition, 1
setting and dramatic date, 1n.6, 3
title, *see* πολιτεία
transmission and MSS, 5, 29c5–d2, 30a6, b6, c7, 38a8, 39a1, 45c3, 49b5, 50d7–e1, 52b1, 53d6

sacrifice, 28c2, c2–3, 31d6–7
scriptio plena, 5, 30c7
Simonides, 28e3, 31d4, 35e4–5, e9, 38b3, b5
"sincere assent requirement," 4(d), 46a3–4, 49a8–9, 50e6
slaves, 27b3–4
Socrates, 4(a)
poverty of, 37d6
"Socratic paradox," 36e4
sophists, 4(d), 34b6, 36e9–37a2, 37d6, 38b5, 48a7–b2
Sophocles, 29b7, d5
sophrosyne, 2
soul, parts of, 28d3
style
as indicative of date of composition, 1
of individual interlocutors, 1
subjunctive, 30e1, 49c8
deliberative, 45b4–5, 48e6
sycophants, 40d2

Themistocles, 29e6
the Thirty, 4(b), 4(c), 27a1, c2, 30b6
Thrace and Thracians, 3, 27a5, 28a1, 54a10
Thrasyllus, 1, 5
Thrasymachus, 4(a), 4(c), 4(d), 36c2, 36e9–37a2, 38c7–8
characterization of, 1, 36b5, c3–6, 37d6, 38d3, 40e2–3, 41b7, 43a1–44c7, 43a6, 45e3–4, 47d5, 48c6, 49b3, 50c11, d2–3
torch-races, 28a1
tyranny, 44a5–6

virtue, 2
vocative, 29b3, d3–4, 44d5, 48c6, 54a8
vowel contraction, 27a1

wolves, 34b1, 36d6–7, d7–e1, 40d2
word order, 29b1–2, d7, e1, 31d8, 32a11, 34c1, 37e5–6, 38b2, 43c1–2, e3, 44a1, 45d2, e5, 47c1, 49a1, 51a6–b1, 52c4, c6–7

INDEX OF GREEK WORDS

ἀλλά, 27b6
ἀλλά γε, 31b6
ἀλλὰ ἤ, 30c7
ἄλλο τι οὖν, 37c6
ἀστεῖος, 49b3
αὐτός = "the master," 27b5

γε, 28a1, 29e5–6, 31b6, d4, 43e3, 50d7

δέ, 27b6–7
δὲ οὖν, 30e3
δή, 28e5, 29b2, 30c4, 37c2, 38b1, 39b1, 53b15
culminative, 27b6–7, 32d2, 49c10, 50a6, 53d3
δίκη, δικαιοσύνη, τὸ δίκαιον, 30d6–7, 31c1–2, 32b8–c1, 36a8–9, 38c2
δύναμις, 46a2–3, b1, 51a2

εἰρωνεία, 4(a), 32b8–c1, 36c2, 37a4
ἐξαγγέλλειν, 28e6–7
ἐπί, 33c11

ἐπιστήμη, 42c10, 50a6
ἔργον, 2, 30c5, 32e3, 33d3–4, 33e1–34b8, 35b2, 42a3, 50e11–52b5, 51d8, 52a5, 52b6–54c3, 52e2–3
εὐδαιμονία, 43c7, 44a4, a5–6, b6, 52d2–3, 53e5
εὐήθεια, 36c2, 43d2, 48d1, 49b3

ἤ, comparative, 35a6
ἦ δὲ ὅς, 27b6–7
ἤδη, 28e5, 32d2, 46e3, 48b1, e5
ἡδύς "naive," 37d6, 48c6

θεωρία, 27b1, 28a6

καὶ δὴ καί, 28b6, e4, 29b7, 44d4–5
κλέπτειν, 34a1–2
κρείττων/ἥττων, 38c3, d9

μέν *solitarium*, 34c4, 45b6, 50c11
μὲν … ἔπειτα, 36b1–2, 37e4–5
μὲν οὖν, 31d4
μέντοι, 29e5–6, 39b8
answering a preceding μέν, 27a3–5

μή, 27c12, c14, 34d3, 37e6, 41a1, 43e4, 46e7, 51e6, 54c1–2
with subjunctive, 30e1, 35c1

οὐδέ, 28a1, c6
οὐκοῦν, interrogative, 42e7
οὗτος, deictic, 27b5–6

πεττεία, 33b1–2
πολιτεία, 1, 38d6

σαρδάνιος, 37a3
συμφέρον, 38c2–39e7

(τε) καί, joining synonyms, 32c5, 39e1–2, 45e1
τοίνυν, 27c9
τρόπος, 2, 4(b), 29d3–4, d7

φιλονικεῖν, 38a8
φιλοτιμία, 36c4, 47b2–3
φύσις, 38c2–39e7

ψυχή, 30d6–7

ὡς, 27c2–3, c5

Printed in the USA
CPSIA information can be obtained
at www.ICGtesting.com
LVHW010127290624
784240LV00001B/82

9 781108 970471